Theatre for
Working-Class
Audiences
in the
United States,
1830-1980

Recent Titles in
Contributions in Drama and Theatre Studies
Series Editor: Joseph Donohue

American Popular Entertainment: Papers and Proceedings of the Conference
on the History of American Popular Entertainment
Myron Matlaw, editor

George Frederick Cooke: Machiavel of the Stage
Don B. Wilmeth

Greek Theatre Practice
J. Michael Walton

Gordon Craig's Moscow *Hamlet:* A Reconstruction
Laurence Senelick

Theatrical Touring and Founding in North America
L. W. Conolly, editor

Bernhardt and the Theatre of Her Time
Eric Salmon, editor

Revolution in the Theatre: French Romantic Theories of Drama
Barry V. Daniels

Serf Actor: The Life and Career of Mikhail Shchepkin
Laurence Senelick

Musical Theatre in America: Papers and Proceedings of the Conference on the Musical
Theatre in America
Glenn Loney, editor
The American Society for Theatre Research, The Sonneck Society, and the Theatre Library
Association, joint sponsors

Garrick Claims the Stage: Acting as Social Emblem in Eighteenth-Century England
Leigh Woods

A Whirlwind in Dublin: *The Plough and the Stars* Riots
Robert G. Lowery, editor

German Actors of the Eighteenth and Nineteenth Centuries:
Idealism, Romanticism, and Realism
Simon Williams

William Archer on Ibsen: The Major Essays, 1889-1919
Thomas Postlewait, editor

Theatre for Working-Class Audiences in the United States, 1830-1980

EDITED BY
Bruce A. McConachie
AND
Daniel Friedman

CONTRIBUTIONS IN DRAMA AND
THEATRE STUDIES, NUMBER 14

Greenwood Press
Westport, Connecticut • London, England

Library of Congress Cataloging in Publication Data

Main entry under title:

Theatre for working-class audiences in the United States,
  1830-1980.

  (Contributions in drama and theatre studies,
ISSN 0163-3821 ; no. 14)
    Bibliography: p.
    Includes index.
    1. Workers' theater—United States—History—
Addresses, essays, lectures.   2. Theater and society—
United States—Addresses, essays, lectures.   3. Theater—
Political aspects—Addresses, essays, lectures.
I. McConachie, Bruce A.   II. Friedman, Daniel.
III. Series.
PN3307.U6T43   1985   792'.022   84-19773
ISBN 0-313-24629-7 (lib. bdg.)

Copyright © 1985 by Bruce A. McConachie and Daniel Friedman

Library of Congress Catalog Card Number: 84-19773
ISBN: 0-313-24629-7
ISSN: 0163-3821

First published in 1985

Greenwood Press
A division of Congressional Information Service, Inc.
88 Post Road West
Westport, Connecticut 06881

Printed in the United States of America

10 9 8 7 6 5 4 3 2 1

3-11-86

Contents

Illustrations

Theatre for
Working-Class
Audiences
in the
United States,
1830-1980

Introduction

Bruce A. McConachie and Daniel Friedman

I

Theatre for working-class audiences has a long history in the United States, a history that has been largely ignored by cultural historians in general and by theatre historians in particular. We hope that this collection of pioneering essays on the topic will end the neglect of this rich vein of our cultural heritage.

As with any new area of investigation, it is incumbent upon those doing the research to define the limits of their work and to justify those boundaries as a distinct field of study. Specifically, given the controversies raging in the areas of performance study, sociology, and political science, we must define what we mean by the terms *theatre* and *working class* and the relationship between them.

First, our approach to understanding these terms is historical; that is, we consider both theatre and the working class not as static, unchanging categories, but as social phenomena in history. They have evolved within the crucible of social interaction, and as such they have changed and are changing as human history continues. The apocalyptic melodramas of the 1830s and 1840s were quite different from the agitprop skits of the 1930s or the passionate political romances of the New York Street Theatre Caravan in the 1980s. In like manner, the Bowery "b'hoys" who packed the theatres along that famous street to applaud such shows as *Nick of the Woods* were different in significant ways from the primarily immigrant radicals who cheered for the *Prolet-Buehne*'s *15 Minute Red Revue* in the early 1930s and from the office workers who laughed at the portrayals of their bosses in *The Union Is Us*, performed in the hallways of Columbia University by Workers' Stage in 1982. Our understanding, then, proceeds from history to denotation, not the other way around.

In defining theatre and working class we have, of course, judged each category to have enough in common to distinguish it from other categories related to it. Thus, despite vast differences in content, dramatic structure, and performance style, all of the cultural production discussed in these pages consists of performances by live actors enacting a conflict between individuals or social groups. These common characteristics distinguish theatre not only from movies, radio, and television—all of which have been immensely popular with workers in the twentieth century—but also from live popular entertainment that lacks sustained dramatic conflict, such as minstrel shows, vaudeville, and the circus.

In like manner, our understanding of working class proceeds from characteristics that have continued for over 150 years to distinguish a particular social stratum in the United States from other, related social strata. We consider the working class to include all those whose primary means of making a living is through the sale of their labor power for wages or salaries and who, as a consequence, exert little or no control over the institutions in which they work. This definition is broad enough to include the mechanics of the early nineteenth century who were forced out of a journeymen-master relationship into the ever-larger mills and factories of the industrial revolution, to the unskilled textile workers who performed *The Pageant of the Paterson Strike* in 1913, to the clerical workers and computer operatives who make up much of the audience of contemporary workers' theatre in New York and Boston.

Ours is a definition based on social relationships, not static categories of income, living standard, or type of work. As a group of people who do not own any means of making money other than their own physical and mental labor, which they exchange for wages in the marketplace, workers stand in a particular social relationship to that group of people who, because of their ownership of the means of production or control of service institutions, buy their labor power. In this regard, income alone is not a determining characteristic. It is possible, for example, that a skilled union worker will have a yearly income that is higher than that of the owner of a small business. The distinguishing feature is that the worker's income derives from the sale of his or her labor power, while the small business person's income derives from his or her business. Nor is type of work, in our understanding, a distinguishing characteristic of this social group. While we obviously include blue-collar factory, transportation, and farm workers, our definition also encompasses white-collar clerical, service, and educational employees as working class becuse they live by the sale of their labor and have little or no control over the institutions to which they sell their skills. This is not to say that poverty, lack of formal education, and low social status have not been, and continue to be, widespread problems for working people in the 150 years under consideration. Rather, these ills are an outgrowth of particular social-historical relationships and are not defining characteristics in themselves.

It is the relationship between this particular cultural expression and this particular social grouping that concerns us here. That relationship may be understood, in Frederick Jameson's words, as an "aesthetic contract" between the cultural producer and the class. The worker-audience, by regularly attending, and the producer, by presenting characters, points of view, and emotional conflicts that specifically relate to this audience, together create theatrical conventions from working-class realities and perceptions. Over a period of time such a contract creates "its own validation and specificity," as Jameson notes.[1] Thus our focus is on the ongoing relationship between theatre people and American workers, a give-and-take involving the development and change of large-scale dramatic and theatrical conventions as well as the articulation of various ideological themes.

Consequently, there are important differences between theatre for working-class audiences and theatrical forms of mass entertainment. From touring shows at the turn of the century to Broadway musicals today, the theatre of mass entertainment has always attracted working-class spectators. With rare exceptions, however, no "aesthetic contract," to use Jameson's term, has cemented an ongoing relationship between the producers of mass entertainment and the working-class portion of their audience. Rather, producers of vaudeville shows and television sit-coms—two examples of mass entertainment that are more pervasive than their theatrical counterparts—have generally sought to appeal to the widest possible audience, regardless of class. Because of this, forms of mass entertainment have not developed conventions that could, in any way, be considered specific to working-class expectations. The producers of such entertainment have not looked to working-class audiences for financial or aesthetic validation of their efforts. Nor have most workers validated their own experiences and perceptions in forms of mass entertainment.

Further, there is an important distinction between political theatre, as such, and theatre for working-class audiences. If we understand political theatre to mean theatre that self-consciously includes political content, that aims to propagate certain ideological concepts, or that agitates for political action, then much, but not all, of the theatre for working-class audiences in the United States has been political. However, much political theatre in this country has not been performed for the working class. Particularly in the 1960s and 1970s, students and a political left dominated by the middle class created lots of theatre with radical political content for themselves. This is not to say that we do not recognize the significance of such middle-class political theatre. It is simply that the class character of its audience renders it fundamentally different from the theatrical phenomena we are concerned with here.

Our approach to the study of theatre in this collection is, therefore, sociological. Theatre is examined as part of the process of social relations, organization, perception, and change. Put more directly, working-class theatre depends on involving and affecting its audience. We are not primarily concerned with the performance style, dramatic structure, aesthetic assumptions, or political content of the theatre. All of those factors are, to be sure, carefully analyzed in the pages that follow, but they are analyzed as they relate to the working-class audience for whom they were performed.

The audience, however basic, is but one side of the theatrical dynamic. Further distinctions may be drawn regarding the social class of the producers. Thus theatre for working-class audiences may be divided into theatre organized and performed by middle-class, or even ruling-class producers, and theatre created by working people for themselves. The motivation for the first type has either been financial, as in the case of nineteenth-century melodramatic theatre and the various immigrant professional theatres that catered to workers early in this century, or ideological, as with the industrial theatre movement in the 1920s when corporations organized pageants and other theatricals to propagate their own views among their employees. This is not to imply that theatre organized by others has simply been imposed on working-class audiences. In the commercial ventures under study in the following pages, the theatre makers clearly developed the content, form, and style of their performances in a dynamic interaction with their working-class audiences. After all, they had to sell tickets.

Theatre created by working people for themselves has been of two types. The first type we call "imitative" because it consisted of amateur imitations of professional and "art" theatres, drawing its dramatic repertory and production values from established conventions. While this type of theatre rarely flourished among native-born workers or the earliest immigrants, by the last decades of the nineteenth century, workers from Europe were bringing with them a social-democratic cultural tradition that encouraged worker productions of the classics. Such imitative theatrical performances were widespread in the early twentieth century among Finns, Jews, Russians, Italians, and many other immigrant groups. Preserving the national culture often motivated this theatrical activity, along with the idea that workers should not be denied the advantages of "high" culture. Because of its essentially imitative nature, such theatre is not examined in detail in this collection.[2]

The second type of theatre that workers have performed in the United States is more indigenous because the plays were written or created by the workers themselves, using styles and contents meant to reflect the specific needs and interests of the worker-actors and their audiences. The motivation for the creation of this theatre was basically political, usually Marxist, anarcho-syndicalist, or trade unionist. Its basic assumption was that workers as a social group had economic and political interests distinct from, and in conflict with, the interest of other classes, particularly those of the owners of the means of production. These distinct interests demanded the creation of a working-class theatre creatively and financially controlled by the workers themselves. The investigation of this type of theatre, which has been a dominant trend among theatre for working-class audiences in the United States in the twentieth century, concerns about half of the chapters gathered here.

In focusing our attention on the audience rather than spotlighting the on-stage presentation, we realize that this anthology departs in significant ways from the norms of scholarship in theatre history as practiced today. To begin with, we make no claim that the plays discussed in the present volume are aesthetically "good" in any ahistorical, universal sense. Indeed, the issue of good theatre, as it is usually understood, must be discarded in favor of the question, "Good for whom?" Many theatre critics, reviewers, and historians have ignored or scoffed at the plays discussed in the following essays. Working-class audiences, on the other hand, employing different standards and values, found these plays aesthetically pleasing. Nor should "different" be understood as "lower." Aesthetic values, like political views and other ways of perceiving the world, are historically evolved and socially organized. Our concern here is not primarily with why the middle-class critic did not like the performance, but with why the working-class theatregoer did.

Our second departure from the usual canons of theatre history is that we do not examine theatre as part of a particular national culture. Despite the limitation of our study to performances that have taken place within the boundaries of a specific nation-state, the evolution of working-class theatre in this country is more closely related to class as a social unit than it is to national citizenship. Throughout the 150 years under examination, the development and change of the dramatic and theatrical conventions and the articulation of various ideological themes in theatre for working-class audiences in the United States has had closer parallels with theatre for workers in other industrializing countries than with the evolution of the mainstream American stage. The melodramas that raised passions along the Bowery were often the same plays performed for London workers in the mid-nineteenth century. The tableaux and festival plays of the German-American workers of the 1870s and 1880s drew directly from the working-class dramatic literature emerging in their homeland. The agitprop skits of American workers in the 1930s differed very little in performance style and ideological content from the skits of workers' theatre groups active in the 1920s and 1930s in the Soviet Union, Germany, France, England, China, and Japan. Contemporary theatres for working-class audiences in the United States have far more in common with their equivalents in Central and South America, the British Isles, and continental Europe than they do with contemporary Broadway, off-Broadway, and mainstream regional shows. Thus the generalizations usually made about the history of the American theatre since 1850—in particular that it has gradually evolved from melodrama to realism—cannot be applied with any consistency to theatre for working-class audiences in the United States. The theatre investigated here is more successfully understood in relation to a modern, transnational class, the working class, than to American theatre as such.

Finally, we depart from positivist historical assumptions in locating the phenomenon of theatre not on the stage but in the dialectic between the spectators and the actors. Many theatre historians focus their investigations on theatre buildings, scenery, costumes, performance style, and so on—the seemingly objective facts of the theatrical experience. It is our working assumption, however, that the detailing of such facts, while a necessary component of the study of the history of theatre, does not constitute its essence. The institutional parts do not add up to a whole known as theatre. Theatre happens when actors and audiences communicate with each other through mutually shared conventions. This process occurs in history, the study of which, in our view, ought to be the main concern of theatre historians.

II

From its inception, theatre for American workers took its performance conventions from the crucible of its audience's lives. As Bruce McConachie's essay "The Theatre of the Mob: Apocalyptic Melodrama and Pre-Industrial Riots in Antebellum New York" points out, a certain kind of melodrama, acting style, and scenic illustration spoke directly to the hopes and fears of workers in the 1830s and 1840s. Performances of such plays as *The Carpenter of Rouen* legitimated their heartfelt need to strike back against their "aristocratic" oppressors through riots which closely paralleled the inherent structure of the melodramas they were applauding.

Pittsburgh ironworkers enjoyed a similar Bowery-like theatre during the 1870s and 1880s. Francis Couvares, in his "The Plebeian Moment: Theatre and Working-Class Life in Late Nineteenth-Century Pittsburgh," outlines the contours of working-class culture in the Iron City and traces its gradual decline under the impact of changing industrial relations and the emergence of competing forms of entertainment. During its moment on the historical stage, working-class theatre in Pittsburgh drew applause for plays like *The Lower Million*, which praised the skilled craftsman as the moral center of early industrial life.

The waves of immigrants drawn to American shores by the hope of employment and the despair of poverty and oppression in numerous old countries added immensely to the sheer variety of theatre for working-class audiences. In her "German-American Socialist Workers' Theatre, 1877–1900," for instance, Carol Poore demonstrates that theatre for working-class immigrants sometimes took an avowedly political turn. Fleeing Bismarck's antisocialist laws, these German immigrants brought with them their tradition of presenting socialist plays in German-language clubs before mainly sympathetic audiences. Unlike the previous theatres for working-class audiences in America, these German-American productions featured workers performing consciously political theatre for their fellow workers. In the 1880s especially, German socialists reached wide audiences in New York, Chicago, Milwaukee, St. Louis, and elsewhere, performing short plays, didactic tableaux, and festival pieces like *The Nihilists*, which commemorated the Paris Commune.

More typical of first-generation immigrant theatre for working-class audiences were commercial productions adapted to immigrant needs and performed in their native language. As described by Mel Gordon in "The Yiddish Theatre in New York: 1900" and by A. Richard Sogliuzzo in his "Shakespeare, Sardou, and Pulcinella: Italian-American Working-Class Theatre in New York, 1880–1940," both groups of immigrant theatre artists sought to validate the continuity of their cultural traditions amid the threatening surroundings of the new world. Despite attempts to preserve the trappings of elite culture from their old countries, both Yiddish- and Italian-American actors and managers shifted their performance conventions to accomodate the social and psychological needs of workers, their biggest audience. If this resulted in such anomalies as *The Yiddish Medea* and an Italian *Othello* punctuated by the strong smell of fried onions, it also led to the tragic power of Jacob Adler and the comic brilliance of Eduardo Migliaccio, in whose Fanfariello Italian-Americans found their own theatrical version of Charlie Chaplin. For both immigrant groups, going to the theatre reassured them that life was more than sweatshops and social discrimination. Indeed, in such productions as *The Jewish Heart* and *Executed Man*, both theatres celebrated visions of traditional solidarity over the excesses of American capitalism and individualism.

In general, working-class theatre from the 1830s through 1910 showed its audience attempting to maintain old traditions in the face of new and ever-changing realities. By World War I, however, American capitalism had reached maturity, thus rendering hopes for a return to traditional ways among immigrant and native-born workers even more dubious than before. Moving pictures, gradually replacing the theatre as the chief form of working-class and mass entertainment, proved a primary means of increasing the grip and reach of capitalist hegemony. In the decade before World War I, Hollywood was fast bankrupting and transforming into movie houses commercial theatres in all the major industrial centers which had catered to the needs of working-class spectators. These changes made it obvious that if theatre primarily linked to working-class audiences was to survive at all, it would have to adopt different means.

Believing that workers could increase their ability to organize and to seize power by creating their own cultural events, the Industrial Workers of the World (IWW) encouraged its members to write songs, hold debates, and stage plays. The song "Solidarity Forever" and *The Paterson Strike Pageant* of 1913, discussed by Linda Nochlin, were significant artistic efforts of the IWW. As Nochlin points out, the IWW's show took the pageant conventions of civic ritual that were common throughout America and turned them from conservative to radical ends. Instead of trumpeting the virtues of hard work, individualism, and American nationalism, *The Paterson Strike Pageant* reenacted an actual strike of mostly immigrant silk workers against the silk manufacturers of Paterson, New Jersey, to dramatize what the IWW termed the class war. The Paterson pageant continued the tradition of the German-American socialists, using workers themselves to dramatize their political goals through spectacle and rhetoric in a noncommercial theatrical venture.

In " 'Let Them Be Amused': The Industrial Drama Movement, 1910–1929,'' Hiroko Tsuchiya reports on a phenomenon of theatre for working-class audiences at the opposite end of the political spectrum from the Paterson pageant. The industrial drama movement involved corporate executives organizing in-house pageants, minstrel shows, and melodramatic entertainments for their employees, who were expected to ingest company ideology while they applauded their fellow workers. Theatre writers and directors hired by these corporations also designed company theatricals to propagate Americanism (i.e., servility, assimilation, and hard work) among largely immigrant work forces. Capitalists frightened by the red scare of the early 1920s used the industrial drama movement as one of several means to stop the plague of Bolshevism from infecting their employees.

The 1930s was a decade of special significance in regard to indigenous working-class theatre in the United States; it was the only period when theatre by workers assumed the dimensions of a movement. In the first half of the decade, amateur workers' theatres sprang up all over the country. By 1935 there were 400 such theatres in twenty-eight cities associated with the League of Workers' Theatres and publishing their own monthly, *Workers' Theatre*. Politically, most of these troupes were influenced by Marxism and understood their theatre work as part of an ongoing class struggle with the owners of the means of production. They performed at council meetings for the unemployed, at evictions, on hunger marches, at rallies, wherever whey felt a performance might lift spirits or educate people politically. They also developed a performance style based on their poverty, need for mobility, production conditions, and political aims—a performance style deliberately at odds with the dominant aesthetic trends toward realism in the theatrical mainstream. Daniel Friedman provides an overview of this era in "A Brief Description of the Workers' Theatre Movement of the Thirties." Douglas McDermott examines the aesthetics and influence of the leading theatre in this movement in his essay "The Workers' Laboratory Theatre: Archetype and Example."

The organizing drives of the Congress of Industrial Organizations (CIO) later in the decade also generated indigenous workers' theatre. Paul Sporn examines this trade-union phenomenon in "Working-Class Theatre on the Auto Picket Line." Sporn traces the history of performance created during or inspired by the long struggle to unionize the automobile industry which climaxed in the Flint Sit-Down Strike, considered by many historians to be the turning point not only in the organization of the automobile, but of most basic industry. In particular, he examines the creation and performance of *The Strike Marches On* which was rehearsed by auto workers in Flint during the strike and performed for a jubilant audience the night that General Motors gave in to their demands.

John O'Connor's article, "The Federal Theatre Project's Search for an Audience," discusses a unique experiment in American theatre history: the direct intervention of the federal government in theatrical production, an intervention that not only put unemployed theatre professionals to work, but also employed activists from the indigenous workers' theatres. The Federal Theatre Project successfully brought theatre to working-class audiences on a scale unprecedented in America since before World War I.

Theodore Shank's "El Teatro Campesino: The Farmworkers' Theatre" carries the study of trade-union-related theatre into the 1960s and 1970s. Agricultural workers organized El Teatro Campesino during their struggle to win recognition for the United Farm Workers. The relationship of contemporary theatres for working-class audiences, such as the New York Street Theatre Caravan, the Little Flags Theatre Collective, and the Mass Transit Street Theatre, to trade unions is discussed by Daniel Friedman in the final chapter, "Contemporary Theatre for Working-Class Audiences in the United States." This study examines the resurgence of theatre for workers as a cultural phenomenon since the late 1960s. Using information gathered from the theatres themselves, Friedman describes their histories and analyzes their creative processes, performance styles, and politics, providing an on-the-spot report of a living theatrical tradition.

Despite the wide scope of the articles collected here, tremendous gaps remain in our investigation. Most striking is the absence of a discussion of theatre for black workers. Such theatre has, of course, existed and flourished in the Harlem of the 1920s, in black agitprop troupes of the 1930s, in the Free Southern Theatre, and in other black theatre groups of the 1960s, 1970s, and 1980s. Obviously no history of theatre for the working class in the United States can be complete without an understanding of black theatre. Among our other omissions is the Finnish-American workers' theatre, probably the most prolific of any of the indigenous theatres for immigrant workers. The Red Dust Players, who performed for tenant farmers and oil-rig roughnecks in the late 1930s, are not mentioned. The Japanese-American working-class community also had an array of workers' theatres during the depression. From the nineteenth century, the "ten-twent-thirt" melodramatic theatre of the 1890s which flourished in most industrial centers is a major omission. We could go on for pages listing what is *not* included, but we will stop here.

This partial list, we hope, is not simply an exercise in self-criticism; it is an invitation to further research. Most of these topics are not included because no one, to our knowledge, has done the necessary research. As further work is done in the area of theatre for working-class audiences in the United States, the shortcomings of this initial effort will, undoubtedly, become all the more glaring. This, of course, is as it should be.

III

In retrospect, the theatres for working-class audiences discussed in this collection share several similarities. While there are notable differences as well— differences often due to the vagaries of historical circumstance—the continuities among these theatres over a span of 150 years suggest, at the very least, that the tradition of theatre for workers has unique qualities that distinguish it from other theatrical traditions in the United States. This is not to say that theatre workers and audiences within this tradition consciously built upon the dramatic and theatrical conventions of those who preceded them. Indeed, there is much evidence to the contrary, evidence suggesting that the roots of working-class theatrical appeal had to be constantly rediscovered, at least during most of the twentieth century. Many theatre troupes in comparative ignorance of the history of theatre for working-class spectators, for instance, increased their audience of workers in the 1970s. What follows, then, is less an attempt to define the main characteristics of a sustained, self-consciously vital tradition and more a way to trace the common threads of dramatic and theatrical conventions which have tended to recur in this kind of theatre, whether or not the producers and audiences involved were aware of the historical roots of their shared experience.

The tendency for plays to draw their contents and forms from folk and popular traditions is one of these common threads, woven into the woof and warp of theatre popular with workers during the last 150 years. Nineteenth-century melo-dramas, for example, borrowed heavily from religious beliefs, folk tales, and novels that were popular with American workers. Each ethnic theatre, of course, married its own folk traditions to images of new experiences in the United States to create plays that its working-class spectators enjoyed. The results were as varied as the traditions of German socialism and the Italian commedia dell'arte. In the twentieth century, the conventions of popular culture have tended to replace the folk tradition as a significant basis for working-class plays, though several contemporary theatres, including the Roadside Theater and the Dakota Theatre Caravan, continue to fashion their vehicles by drawing on such age-old traditions as story telling and oral history. More frequently, though, contemporary theatres for working-class audiences take much of their material from the mass media, often parodying popular tunes and television commercials. This tendency to refashion the clichés of mass entertainment for political purposes probably began in the late 1920s with the *Prolet-Buehne*'s use of vaudeville comedy routines in their agitprop shows.

Another common source for popular theatrical vehicles among workers has been the audience's own experience of social and economic reality. Conse-quently, most working-class shows of the last 150 years have had strong ties to a specific local or regional historical situation. For nineteenth-century steel work-ers in Pittsburgh or Jewish immigrant workers in New York, the realities of their lives in the steel mills and neighborhoods of Pittsburgh or in the sweatshops and streets of the Lower East Side generated the laugh lines and the melodramatic victories of their theatrical experiences. Many twentieth-century theatres for workers continued this tradition. The plays of the auto workers in the late 1930s or the farmworkers in the 1960s drew directly from the organizing experiences of their audiences. The Everyday Theatre in Washington, D.C., presents plays based on local situations such as rent strikes and neighborhood politics. Even though some working-class plays have reached toward a universal meaning—as did apocalyptic melodramas of the 1830s and some political allegories of the 1930s—the main characters and conflicts of these dramas were firmly rooted in the local experiences of its spectators. Not in the universal but in the particular and historical lies the source of truth and action in most of these plays.

In line with this characteristic, most plays popular with working-class spec-tators have stressed themes of social morality rather than psychological insight. Although this is obvious enough in the politically motivated vehicles of twentieth-century troupes from the *Paterson Strike Pageant* players to *El Teatro Cam-pesino*, it is also true of most of the melodramas popular among native-born and immigrant workers before World War I. The social morality of *The Carpenter of Rouen*, *The Lower Million*, or *Executed Man* may not have been very politically sophisticated, but it usually understood that the solidarity and victory of a class or ethnic group was more important than the temporary psychological problems of one of its good characters. Melodrama, in fact, continued to provide a compelling dramatic framework for fingering villains and celebrating heroes for many twentieth-century groups and their audiences, from the Living Newspaper productions of the Federal Theatre Project in the 1930s to *The Victim*, presented by El Teatro de la Esperanza in 1976. Even the corporate manipulators behind the industrial drama movement of the 1920s relied on melodramatic conventions to push their ideology. On the other hand, most contemporary theatres tend toward comedy and satire, rather than melodrama, to shape their themes of social protest.

The German-American socialists of the 1870s and 1880s were probably the first group of American workers to use theatre as one of several vehicles in the struggle for working-class hegemony in the United States. Since then, troupes as diverse as the Workers' Laboratory Stage and the Little Flags Theatre Collective have continued to view their theatrical productions as significant means for transforming American society to give working people more political power and cultural influence. Several of the following chapters demonstrate that many dramas popular with workers before World War I served a similar purpose, though in most cases these visions of hegemony applauded by working-class audiences were milder and less politically explicit than after 1920. Apocalyptic melodramas, for instance, rumbled darkly of an imminent Day of Judgment against capitalist "aristocrats," suggesting that all would be well if workers were allowed their traditional liberties to practice their trades in peace. Likewise, Migliaccio's comic skits lifted his Italian-American audiences out of their ghettos in New York City, allowing them to envision a time in the future not unlike the happier moments of their collective past when the Italian-American worker would stand as the equal of any American boss, gangster, or judge.

Regarding theatrical style as distinct from dramatic form and content, working-class theatre since 1830 has been and continues to be predominantly presentational. Instead of attempting to represent a "slice of life" on the stage, its scenic and costuming conventions have projected bold, simplified images; its acting style has bulked larger than life; and its general staging conventions have favored stylized movement, unrealistic explosions of music and sound effects, and direct address to the audience. These, of course, were the conventions of the nineteenth-century melodramatic stage, and they remain current among theatres for working-class audiences for many of the same reasons that melodramatic forms such as pageant pieces, agitprop shows, and *actos* retain their popularity. While the specifics of style have varied from the bravura performance of the nineteenth-century actor to the choreographed movement and mass recitation of the agitprop troupes of the 1930s, most theatres for workers over the last century and a half have stood squarely in the realm of the presentational, using undisguised means to make theatre. This approach continues today. The San Francisco Mime Troupe draws on a variety of presentational styles from vaudeville and minstrelsy to circus techniques and commedia dell'arte.

Yet another historical attribute of theatre for working-class audiences was, and remains, their emphasis on strong emotional effects. Rather than sadness or polite laughter, this kind of theatre tends to generate sobs of despair, horselaughs of joy, and occasional silent shocks of rage. In the nineteenth-century theatres for native-born and immigrant workers, the local star actor was the chief means of reaching such emotional climaxes. Together with well-aimed musical and scenic effects, stars like J. R. Scott and Jacob Adler worked up their audiences through thunderous rhetoric, well-timed comedy, and sheer emotional energy. Since the 1920s, the close coordination of ensemble playing has been the primary means of effecting a similar catharsis in the audience. The *Prolet-Buehne*, the Workers' Laboratory Theatre, and other workers' theatre troupes of the early 1930s used percussion instruments, rhythmic chants, and dancelike movement to energize their audiences. Similar devices were used by auto workers in *The Strike Marches On* to demonstrate the company's speedup of production. When workers decided to strike in this play, the actors turned to the audience and asked, "Auto workers are you with us?" The crowd responded with "Cadillac here! Chrysler here! Dodge is ready!" Today the New York Street Theatre Caravan joins bold makeup and exaggerated costumes with forceful acting to create moving images of poverty and discrimination. This flow of emotional electricity bonds actors to audiences and continues to be the most important convention in theatre for working-class spectators.

This electrical current, in turn, gives rise to enthusiastic exchanges between audiences and actors. Whether in Pittsburgh in 1885, in a New York Yiddish theatre in 1907, in a Federal Theatre Project production in Chicago in 1938, or in a Workers' Stage performance in Newark in 1982, working-class spectators interrupt the show to trade comments with the actors. The actors, trained to expect and even to enjoy such outbursts, might incorporate the remarks into the play, ignore them, or occasionally stop the forward movement of the show and continue their performance on another level entirely—by talking with the spectators. The mutual feelings of commitment and relationship generated in these encounters are often related to the immediacy of the theatrical effect. After all, if the audience member experienced the conflicts being acted out or if the actor lives and works in the same neighborhood, why not give voice to your emotional response or talk to the actor, your neighbor or co-worker, when he or she is on stage? In theatres for working-class audiences, such exchanges are not bad manners; they are part of the rules of the game. This last convention, perhaps more than any other, has separated working-class theatre from performances meant for middle-class and ruling-class playgoers.

The characteristics discussed above, while individually not unique to theatre for workers, together combine to provide working-class theatre with its own distinctiveness. We began this discussion by defining our area of study as the relationship between workers and theatre producers; we end with generalizations about the type of theatre that has emerged from that ongoing relationship. This distinctiveness of theatre for working-class audiences may be more clearly understood when contrasted briefly with the development of American theatre for other audiences in the same period. Since the Civil War, most mainstream American plays have drawn their content from the conflicts within middle-class families or from matters of national or supposedly universal concern, focusing on the psychological complexity of their main characters and implicitly upholding the legitimacy of the dominant social order. Theatrical conventions for non-working-class Americans since at least 1900 have tended toward representational realism, with the consequence that restraint and decorum have dominated the social habits of these playgoers. Our intention is not to argue that one line of theatrical development is better than the other. Indeed, as pointed out earlier, such aesthetic judgments have little meaning outside a class-specific context. The study of theatre for workers points to a different conclusion: different historical experiences create quite different theatre.

NOTES

1. "Reification and Utopia in Mass Culture," *Social Text*, 1 (Winter 1979), 136.

2. For extensive information on "imitative" theatre among immigrant groups, see *Ethnic Theatre in the United States*, ed. Maxine S. Seller (Westport, Connecticut, 1983).

1

"The Theatre of the Mob": Apocalyptic Melodrama and Preindustrial Riots in Antebellum New York

Bruce A. McConachie

I

Following the bloody Astor Place riot of 1849, Horace Greeley's *New York Tribune* demanded, "When will the stage, that vaunted school of Morality, that fulsome adulator and corruptor of Popular Liberty, begin to teach its votaries clearer and truer ideas of Freedom?" A few years earlier, a bank clerk compared an antiabolitionist riot in Cincinnati to a "Saturnalia," the Roman festival celebrated on the stage and in the streets with theatrical costumes and props. "Great cities have ever been and probably ever will be . . . the theatre of the mob," concluded another antebellum writer.[1] In the thirty years before the Civil War, many Americans vaguely perceived a link between the riots that were wracking their cities with greater frequency than at any time before (or since) and theatrical performances and conventions. Was there a genuine relationship, or were Americans falsely blaming the dominant artistic medium of the period for societal ills that had nothing to do with the theatre?

This question cannot be answered without a discussion of the general relationship between communication media and society. If theatrical performances and other media merely reflect social roles, behavior, and values—the traditional theoretical position of Marxists and Aristoteleans—antebellum theatrical practitioners cannot be blamed for helping to cause the riots that some Americans wanted to pin on them. But perhaps the relationship between theatrical and social perceptions and conventions is dialectical and dynamic. Rather than passively mirroring social reality, theatrical performances—especially immensely popular ones—may help to legitimate certain forms of social interaction which, in turn, may have their own impact on initiating, reinforcing, and ultimately altering theatrical events. Given an ongoing seesaw of tension and interpenetration between actions on the stage and in the streets, the question of causation becomes a chicken-egg problem. Instead of searching for a mechanical "cause" which may have precipitated the plays and the riots, the dialectically-minded historian looks for significant conflicts or similarities among the roles, actions, and beliefs embodied in urban riots and in certain kinds of play performances. Further, the historian must pay particular attention to the participants in one and the audience for the other. Only if the same people or at least the same *kind* of people were involved in both can we say that mutual influence has occurred; only then might the metaphor "the theatre of the mob" hold substantial historical reality.

The dramatistic theory of reality advanced by Kenneth Burke and viewed in the context of Peter L. Berger's and Thomas Luckmann's *Social Construction of Reality* lends credence to the notion of a dialectical-historical relationship between theatre and society. "Ritual drama," according to Burke, lies at the "hub" of all social systems, from the center of which radiate spokes imitating and expressing derivative meanings concretized in art forms and various symbolic rituals. Hence, the ritual drama at the center of a society organizes and legitimates truth and reality for the culture, embodying "the social structures of meanings by which the individual forms himself." Moreover, this hub of collective truths and its derivative imitations change over time as historical events, social cere-monies, role playing and other phenomena from "real" life come into conflict with the roles, actions, and definitions of the ritual drama itself. In this way, the fundamental ritual and its spin-offs in the theatre and other symbolic-ex-pressive activities continue to legitimate social reality. With their culture's ritual drama as a foundation, all societies use symbolic forms to construct an ever-changing "symbolic universe," Berger and Luckmann's term for the partly conscious body of tradition, religion, and other orientational notions that "in-tegrate different provinces of meaning" and encompass the social order "in a symbolic totality." From the point of view of an individual within the culture, the symbolic universe "puts everything in its right place."[2]

Anthropologist James Peacock uses this theoretical framework in his *Rites of Modernization* to discern the tensions and continuities between contemporary (1968) Javanese theatre and social realities resulting from the gradual modern-ization of Indonesia. According to Peacock, *ludruk*, the Javanese name for performances of their indigenous melodramas, helps its audience identify the heroes, heroines, and villains of their lives, "seduces [them] into empathy with modes of social action," and involves them "in aesthetic forms that structure their most general thoughts and feelings." "Unless we deny that such basic psychological processes as stimulus-generalization and response-generalization occur among the Javanese," he concludes, their melodramatic theatre "affects the behavior" of its audience by legitimating certain thoughts and actions. In reference to the theories of Burke and Berger and Luckmann, *ludruk* may be said to have imitated aspects of the underlying ritual drama of Javanese culture and hence to have played a significant role in shaping the symbolic universe of *ludruk* spectators.[3]

Similarly, apocalyptic melodramas flourishing on the stages of working-class theatres in New York between 1835 and 1850 helped to legitimate many of the preindustrial riots in the city involving working-class mobs during the same period. Melodrama in all its forms and meanings constituted much of the symbolic universe of antebellum Americans, drawing its strength from traditions deeply embedded in the ritual drama of the culture. More specifically, apocalyptic melodrama spoke to the social and psychic needs of many American workers, providing not only a justification but also a ritual form through which they might legitimately act out their frustrations. Hence, the confluence between the kinds of plays many workers watched and the mob violence they performed and enjoyed was not accidental: one helped to legitimate and, quite literally, to inform the other.

This is not to say that working-class antebellum riots and apocalyptic melodrama imitated each other with precision. Since social behavior is neither scripted nor rehearsed in any formal way, life will always be messier than theatre. Although the relationship between the roles and actions in the riots and the melodramas is analogous and generally congruent, it could not be equivalent. Nor did these working-class plays and their counterparts in the streets directly cause each other. Social historians have discerned a variety of political, ethnic, and economic causes for antebellum riots involving workers. Theatre historians, likewise, have pointed to the escapist entertainment value of working-class melodrama to explain its popularity. These historians are not wrong, but their often implicit assumption that isolating a cause provides a full explanation of the phenomenon is only a partial explanation.[4] Though it may be that the plays and the riots indirectly helped to cause each other, such a conclusion could never be demonstrated. Rather, what concerns us here is the striking similarity in roles, actions, and perceptions that points to a shared symbolic universe between working-class melodrama and mob violence and hence underlines their effect of mutual legitimation. We are looking, then, for what Kenneth Burke would term a fundamental ''grammar'' for understanding part of the structure of preindustrial working-class behavior and belief.

II

When Thomas S. Hamblin took over the Bowery Theatre in 1830, he departed from managerial precedent by ignoring the tastes of the fashionable elite and choosing plays and actors designed to appeal to the carpenters, blacksmiths, carriers, and other skilled and unskilled workers in New York City. To attract these artisans and others to his theatre, Hamblin gradually increased his offering of melodramatic and equestrian spectacles and invested his profits in publicity, scenery, costumes, and animal feed. That there were considerable profits is confirmed by the fact that even when the Bowery burned down three times between 1835 and 1850, twice leaving Hamblin with a total loss, the intrepid manager was able to secure financing for the construction of new theatres and to rebuild his stocks of theatrical finery.[5] Hamblin's success also led to competition for working-class patronage. The Chatham Theatre, opened in 1839 with the initial expectation of attracting the elite of the city, soon fell into the practices of its near neighbor as the various managers of this struggling playhouse borrowed Hamblin's tactics (and sometimes his actors and plays) during the 1840s to attract the workers of the area. Other theatres in the Bowery district, such as the Chambers Street and Olympic, concentrated on comic entertainment for working-class spectators. The managers of these playhouses used blackface acts, stage Yankees, and burlesques of Shakespeare—programs occasionally seen at the Bowery and Chatham as well—to rival the success of Hamblin's melodramatic spectacles. As theatre historian Mary C. Henderson concludes, "During the third and fourth decades of the nineteenth century, the Bowery began to develop an independent theatrical life of its own. The theatres built along it appealed mainly to the residents of the area and never constituted a strong threat to the fashionable theatres that were beginning to appear along Broadway at the same time.[6]

Though some elite and middle-class playgoers occasionally ventured into the Bowery theatre district, there is little doubt that most of the patrons of its playhouses were workers. In an 1847 article comparing audiences at the opera and at the Bowery Theatre, a journalist for *The Spirit of the Times* depicted a fictitious, though only slightly exaggerated, visit of "Yankee Doodle" to the Bowery. His guide, "Bill Skiver," introduces him to his friends at the bar: "Firemen, butcher-boys, cab and omnibus drivers, fancy men, and b'hoys, generally." From their chairs in the boxes, Bill Skiver and Yankee Doodle observe in the pit below

a vast sea of upturned faces and red flannel shirts, extending its roaring and turbid waves close up to the footlights on either side, clipping in the orchestra and dashing furiously against the boxes—while a row of luckier and stronger-shouldered amateurs have pushed, pulled and trampled their way far in advance of the rest, and actually stand with their chins resting on the lampboard [of the footlights], chanking peanuts and squirting tobacco juice upon the stage.

Walt Whitman, in his capacity as play reviewer for the *Brooklyn Eagle*, praised the sturdy democracy of Bowery audiences in the 1830s, recalling "well-dress'd, full-blooded young and middle-aged men, the best average of American born mechanics . . . bursting forth in one of those long-kept-up tempests of hand-clapping, peculiar to the Bowery—no dainty kidglove business, but electric force and muscle from perhaps 2,000 full sinew'd men." Partly because of its working-class audience and their boisterous behavior, the Bowery Theatre was frequently snubbed by newspapers and journals wishing to prove their respectability. "The house was full, but what an audience. However, it was what we had been led to expect and induced us to make our visit as short as possible," sniffed *Brother Jonathan*. The Chatham Theatre fared even worse at the hands of contemporary commentators, who generally agreed that its patronage was below that of the Bowery. "It has been useful as a kind of sewer for the drainage of other establishments," stated one writer. "There must be some place for a certain class of people to effervesce in their excitements of pleasure."[7]

While the class bias of the above reports (Whitman excepted) no doubt undercuts their reliability as historical sources, these and similar accounts of working-class behavior in the theatre and elsewhere underline the loss of social status many workers experienced in the 1830s and 1840s. Before that period, skilled artisans had occupied the middle rungs of the social ladder, above unskilled laborers and servants and below the merchant elite. Community leaders had praised them for their sacrifices in American wars and for their hearty civic virtue. Craftsmen had been encouraged to think of themselves, in words used by the Butcher's Guild of Philadelphia, as "a fraternity of men essential and indispensable to the body politic."[8] Now, complained a labor newspaper in 1842, "the capitalists have taken to bossing all the mechanical trades, while the practical mechanic [i.e., the master craftsman] has become a journeyman, subject to be discharged at every pretended 'miff' of his purse-proud employer." Especially galling to the artisan was the wide gulf that had opened between his status and that of the new middle class. Instead of enjoying the fruits of early industrialization—larger homes, indoor plumbing, and public education for his children—the mechanic saw himself sinking to the position of an English factory worker, becoming a permanent member of a dependent, proletarian class. An 1845 editorial in *The Voice of Industry* noted that mechanics yearned to be "reinstated into the bonds of nature's brotherhood."[9]

What had happened? In brief, the rapid growth of trade and cities in the 1820s forced a greater demand for handicraft products than the traditional craft organizations could produce. Entrepreneurs, either outside capitalists or well-to-do master craftsmen, gathered together the isolated shops of a specific craft into a unified "putting out" system geared to quantity production. This economic rationalization reduced other master craftsmen and almost all journeymen and apprentices to piecework and then to working for wages. The traditional web of obligations and loyalties binding together workers in the same trade—a system which had already begun to unravel in the late eighteenth century—further deteriorated, exacerbated by economic rivalry between master and journeymen and by the emerging ethos of commercialism. With the pressure for quantity production came the introduction of simple machinery, increasing the pace of work and occasionally making obsolete crafts which had flourished for centuries. Working-class fears of economic exploitation and lower social status increased during the depression years of the late 1830s and early 1840s and remained high throughout the decade because of the perception of competition from Irish and German immigrants. Ethnic tensions were aggravated by the crowded living conditions in New York. As land values soared, modest homes were torn down and native-American workers crowded their families into tenements, often paying high rent for a bare room or two. By 1850, the traditional ladder up, on which the ambitious and skillful apprentice had risen to become a master craftsman, gaining a measure of economic independence and social prestige along the way, had been flattened by the forces of the early industrial revolution.[10]

Some workers responded to the decline of their economic and social standing by joining political parties, utopian ventures, and labor unions. Reformers and radicals, many of them not workers themselves, established a Working Men's party in New York in 1829 to demand the ten-hour day, free public education, and an end to the monopoly power of the rich. Strikes for better pay and shorter hours—over 160 of them in New York City between 1833 and 1837—led to the formation of a citywide union embracing all the trades. By the late 1830s, working-class political and union activity had forced modest gains in public education, working conditions, and hours of employment for skilled mechanics. With few exceptions, these achievements were obliterated by the panic of 1837 and the depression that followed. Consumer cooperatives, Fourierist societies, land reform groups, and other vaguely utopian schemes flourished in the 1840s— testaments, primarily, to the bewilderment felt by many workers. Although the labor movement and these utopian associations continued to press for humanitarian reforms, their activities did little to alter the fearful circumstances of the laborer's daily life.[11]

Many found direct release from their frustrations in violent sports and entertainment and in occasional outbreaks of mob violence. Watching cockfights, bullbaiting, and boxing matches were popular pastimes among Bowery workers. Many Bowery teenagers and young men sought boisterous fun in the volunteer fire companies—a social, ethnic, and political institution for many antebellum New Yorkers whose least important function, it often seemed, was putting out fires. Different companies competed in fire-engine races and street brawls, and most had close ties to neighborhood gangs and local Democratic political organizations.[12] Between 1833 and 1838, American workers participated in most of the fifty-two riots that rocked New York, the worst outbreak of antebellum mob violence in the city in a five-year period. The bloodiest of these, the Five-Points riot in 1835, dragged on for three days between native-born workers and Irish immigrants in a slum not far from City Hall, leaving scores of injured and several dead. Mob violence slackened during the depression years but revived again in the mid-1840s, culminating in the Astor Place riot of 1849, a disturbance costing twenty-three lives. Michael Chevalier, a French visitor to the United States in the 1830s, noted that in one antiabolitionist riot "the destruction of the churches and schoolhouses of the blacks in New York was looked upon as a show . . . ; the fall of [one] building was greeted with large cheers."[13] When workers went to the Bowery theatres, they expected a similar display of violence and destruction.

Not all workers patronized the theatre, however. Some simply could not afford it. In an 1851 *New York Tribune* editorial, Horace Greeley estimated that a Philadelphia carpenter earned $10.50 per week, barely enough to afford the minimal necessities for a family of five. "Where," he asked, "is the money to pay for amusements, for ice-creams, his puddings, his trips on Sundays . . . to pay the doctor or apothecary, to pay for pew rent in the church, to purchase books, musical instruments?" Where, indeed, was the money for his New York counterpart to pay for a bench seat in the pit or gallery of a Bowery theatre, despite the fact that Hamblin and other managers kept prices low to attract working-class patronage? Although other skilled craftsmen made more than carpenters, most were subject to periods of temporary unemployment, especially during the winter months when artisan poverty was often severe. Unskilled workers, who were paid considerably less than artisans, may have attended the theatre even less frequently than craftsmen.[14] On the other hand, young, unmarried workers, even unskilled or semiskilled ones, probably had enough money to go to the theatre occasionally. Contemporary accounts, condescending and vague though they are, give the impression that young men made up the bulk of the audience.[15] Bowery theatre, then, attracted predominantly young male workers—journeymen and semiskilled laborers—together with some master craftsmen and a sprinkling of men from other classes.

Among young New York workers, however, were some who considered the theatre an immoral and wasteful pastime. The transition from a handicraft to the beginnings of a factory system of production wrenched artisan values and work habits, dividing workers between those who favored traditional ways and those who were influenced by the new industrial morality. The "traditionalists," as labor historian Paul Faler terms them, continued the work habits of preindustrial times: coming to work when it suited them, taking frequent breaks for horseplay and alcoholic refreshment, and, in general, working at their own pace regardless of the clock or the customers. Most traditionalists voted Democratic and remained uninvolved in radical union activity and utopian schemes, though they might join a volunteer fire company or a traditional labor society. Many traditionalists in the 1830s and 1840s had emigrated to New York from American or foreign farms and small communities. Irish-Catholic workers, especially, stuck to traditional work habits, socialized with their own kind, and often looked on the changes wrought by early industrialization with fatalistic eyes. The emergent working-class culture, on the other hand, "made a sharp distinction between work and leisure and regarded preindustrial culture as wasteful, frivolous and, above all, sinful," according to labor historian Bruce Laurie. These new men might be either "loyalists" who "combined the new morality with deference toward their employers" or "rebels," workers "who had accepted a code of morality which they shared with their employers but used in their own class interest." In general, loyalists and rebels, combining eighteenth-century notions of frugality and industry with the newer values of temperance and success, eschewed strong drink, mob violence, and the theatre.[16]

These were the rough divisions in antebellum working-class values and behavior, so it is likely that the traditionalists were the primary patrons of the Bowery theatres. There were more of them than there were loyalists and rebels combined in the period from 1835 to 1850, especially since traditionalist ranks were constantly being reinforced from abroad. But the withering fire from nontraditional artisans and their middle-class allies or opponents no doubt cut into the percentage of native-American workers among traditionalists. Ethnic conflict between native-Americans and Irish and German immigrants, especially virulent in the 1840s, further divided theatregoing traditionalists among themselves. Indeed, the changing nature of the traditionalist audience in Bowery theatres gradually eroded the base of support for the popularity of apocalyptic melodramas. By the mid-1840s, new kinds of plays were already gaining popularity by appealing to the specific needs of native-, Irish-, or even German-American audiences. After 1850, the foundation for apocalyptic melodrama, written to appeal primarily to native-American workers, gradually collapsed.

Until then, however, performances of apocalyptic melodrama helped to shape and to reinforce the symbolic universe of many a young tradition-oriented worker, assuaging his nagging fears about status and exploitation through plays containing potent metaphors of the evil he perceived, the vengeance he longed to express, and the final justice he hoped to witness. Like other melodramas of the Jacksonian period, these plays structured reality in a circular pattern beginning with a vision of peaceful bliss, followed by an expulsion from this earthly paradise caused by a villain and ending with the banishment of evil and the restoration and transcendental elevation of the initial vision. Characterization was at the level of moral, elemental types with dialogue generic and hyperbolic, lending vivid expression to the quasi-religious clash of opposites that drove the action. The formula for apocalyptic melodrama was unique, however, in its focus on the righteous quest of an Avenger, its depiction of good and evil ritual activities, and especially in its climactic scene of a catastrophic final judgment. These structural and thematic features, rather than any limitation of subject matter, distinguished apocalyptic melodrama from other types of plays. Indeed, the wild West, piracy on the high seas, and the Protestant Reformation in France were among numerous subjects dealt with in these melodramas of catastrophe. A final distinguishing characteristic of the plays—and perhaps the most significant one considering their popularity among Bowery audiences—was their reliance on extravagant scenic spectacle.

In these days before copyright laws, Bowery theatre managers followed conventional practice by hiring their own playwrights or pirating melodramas from rival houses. Most apocalyptic melodramas in New York originated at the Bowery Theatre and were later stolen or readapted for performance at the Chatham and elsewhere. Hamblin's most prolific playwright in the 1830s was Louisa Medina who turned out over thirty plays in five years—most of them melodramas of catastrophe—before her early death in 1838. Primarily an adapter of contemporary novels, Medina gained a considerable reputation in the popular press. "Her power of composition is said to be astonishingly rapid," marveled *The New-York Mirror*. "She is partial to startling and terrible catastrophes. Her knowledge of stage effect is very great and there is an impassioned ardour in her poetry, which enhances the thrilling interest of her pieces. It has been objected to them that their story departs from that of the novels on which some of them are based; and this objection, as we think, redounds to her favor." Similar praise in the *Mirror* and elsewhere is suspect, however. According to one detractor, Medina paid printers generously "for inserting the puffs she [wrote] on her own plays.''[17] Among Medina's more popular adaptations were *The Last Days of Pompeii* and *Ernest Maltravers*, from novels by Edward Bulwer-Lytton, and *Nick of the Woods*, from the novel by the American author Robert Montgomery Bird.[18]

In 1841, Hamblin hired playwright J. S. Jones away from a rival Boston manager, William Pelby. An actor, stage manager, and writer who later became a medical doctor, Jones had already achieved success with several of his apocalyptic melodramas among the working-class audiences of Pelby's National Theatre. Hamblin capitalized on Jones's renown by producing three of his most popular plays, *The Carpenter of Rouen*, *The Surgeon of Paris*, and *Captain Kyd*, soon after Jones's arrival in New York.[19] Though working independently from Medina and other earlier Bowery playwrights, Jones developed essentially the same formula as theirs for his melodramas of catastrophe. This is all the more surprising since his *Carpenter* and *Surgeon* plays, though not *Captain Kyd*, were written from scratch, without a novel to steal from. The similarity of these plays to Medina's, as well as the apparent similarity of both to other apocalyptic melodramas, suggests that the formula of these plays was more indebted to popular demand than to the individual concerns of different playwrights.[20] These six plays, then, are representative of the hundreds of apocalyptic melodramas that flourished on the Bowery stage, saturating their eager audiences of young workers most completely between 1835 and 1850.

The circular pattern of these plays conventionally begins with a scene set in a pastoral Arcadia or a humble village shop. ''Forest Glade and Log Hut, Cattle grazing; trees lying about; Sunset'' opens *Nick of the Woods*, for instance. The heroine soon assures us concerning the settlers in this part of the American frontier that ''a kinder or more hospitable people exist not on the earth'' (p. 4). *The Carpenter of Rouen* locates its opening Eden in the tidy carpenter's shop of its hero, Marteau. Other apocalyptic plays, notably *Ernest Maltravers* and *The Surgeon of Paris*, delay the presentation of their potential paradise but eventually allow the audience to see Ernest and his wife living in a pleasant country cottage and ''Michael, the artisan'' in *Surgeon* working in his shop. A vision of potential utopia later violated by villainy is fundamental to apocalyptic melodrama, as it is to other melodramas of the period. The tensions, conflicts, and divisions normally associated with everyday experience ought to be, indeed *can* be, eliminated, these plays insist, if only the villains are banished and man follows his natural impulses of charity, brotherhood, and moral order. Avenging the wrongs of villainy to restore this lost vision is the essential action of these melodramas, which accounts for the overall circularity of their architecture.

The eventual triumph of virtue, however, seems almost impossible in these plays, given the pervasiveness and power of evil. While a few of the villains are merely greedy and lusty materialists, most have demonic, superhuman powers and seek absolute control over their victims. Standing astride the decadent sins of Pompeii in Medina's melodrama is Arbaces, a colossus of villainy, who consorts with witches and Egyptian gods and whose ''empire is the mind'' of man (p. 13). Elpsey, a witch in *Captain Kyd*, performs a hellish ritual to control her pirate son and gain his bloodstained riches, calling down fire, thunder, and lightning in chanting reminiscent of the witches' scenes in *Macbeth*. Most of these plays, in fact, contain primal scenes of incantation and ritual which mesmerize their heroes, rendering them passive and limp in confrontations with evil. Ernest Maltravers is duped into believing his fiancée is a "wanton," and Roland in *Nick of the Woods* stands idly by while ravaging savages carry off the heroine.

The urge to do evil is pervasive in these plays and infects the activities of many minor characters whose deeds might otherwise be good or at least morally neutral given the dictates of the plot. *The Surgeon of Paris* features a striking example of immorality among secondary characters. Following the Massacre of St. Bartholomew—a savage attack on a stage full of defenseless Huguenots ordered by the Catholic Queen of France (in effect, a Protestant version of the biblical massacre of the innocents)—soldiers pick among the dead for money and jewelry. "Here is a diamond in this woman's ear. I can't loosen it," says a Catholic soldier. "Tear it out," retorts his greedy captain (p. 39). Eric Bentley has remarked that melodramatic vision is paranoid: "We are being persecuted and we hold that all things, living and dead, are combining to persecute us."[21] Bentley's insight is particularly appropriate for apocalyptic melodrama, where evil powers in the phenomenal and noumenal world conspire against and almost overwhelm virtue.

The conventions of villainy in melodramas of apocalypse accord quite closely with what historian Richard Hofstadter terms "the paranoid style in American politics":

The central image is that of a vast and sinister conspiracy, a gigantic and yet subtle machinery of influence set in motion to undermine and destroy a way of life.... The paranoid spokesman sees the fate of this conspiracy in apocalyptic terms—he traffics in the birth and death of whole worlds, whole political orders, whole systems of human value. He is always manning the barricades of civilization.... The enemy is clearly delineated: he is a perfect model of malice, a kind of amoral superman: sinister, ubiquitous, powerful, cruel, sensual, luxury-loving. Unlike the rest of us, the enemy is not caught in the toils of the vast mechanism of history, himself a victim of his past, his desires, his limitations. He is a free, active, demonic, agent.[22]

While the vision of villainy defined by Hofstadter is indeed paranoid from the point of view of the "real" world, such a view is completely realistic in the nightmarish realm of apocalyptic melodrama. So completely has the formula captured "the paranoid style" in its sequence of actions that characters who lack this vision are dismissed by others as foolish or simpleminded.

As in the paranoid style of political belief, good actions often mirror evil ones in melodramas of catastrophe: the flames of wickedness must be fought with the purging fire of virtue. To counteract the rituals of the villainous Catholic nobleman De Saubigne, Marteau and his fellow mechanics (an antebellum synonym for artisan) spend an entire act of *The Carpenter of Rouen* in the ritual initiation

of a young apprentice into the Confrierie, a secret association of French mechanics. This primal scene climaxes in a tableau elevating banners depicting the
tools of the carpenters' trade: "R[ight] H[and], One Banner, Arms of France—
'Bare Arm and Banner.' L[eft] H[and], One Banner, Arms of Rouen—'Hammer
and Saw.' L[eft] C[enter], One Banner, Cross of Rome—'Plumb-line and
Chisel' "(p. 20). These ritual props not only contravene the power of Catholic
censors, crosses, and relics seen later in the play, they also serve as rallying
points in the mechanics' attack on De Saubigne's palace. (Interestingly, the anti-
Catholic bias found in the initial promptscript of *Carpenter* was softened in later
printed editions of the play—probably in response to increasing Irish-American
attendance at the Bowery theatres.) In a similar, though less obvious way, the
flowers given away by the blind flower girl Nydia in *The Last Days of Pompeii*
offer ritual protection against the diabolism of Arbaces. As in other melodramas
of the period, good and evil activities are frequently mirror images of each
other—the rituals and signs of one delineating and defining the nature of the
opposite one.

The progression of activities in apocalyptic melodrama plunges the spectator
from heady hope to bleak despair with increasingly dreamlike suddenness. The
purpose of this pattern is not merely to entrance the spectator with a rollercoaster
ride of thrills and chills (though this is certainly part of the effect), but to stretch
the patina of reality so thinly that the transcendental realm within and beyond
it may begin to glow through, preparing the way for the blinding light of divine
revelation at the climax of the play. Thus the action of many scenes, and of
most scenes at the ends of each act, builds to a climax in which the truth of a
heretofore unresolved mystery is revealed, followed by a tableau which allows
the moment of revelation to establish its transcendental significance. At the end
of act 2 of *Ernest Maltravers*, for instance, part of the secret of Ernest's mysterious parentage is unveiled when the protagonist learns from Richard Darvil
that his wife is also his half-sister. The moment is frozen in a tableau and held
until the curtain falls. Given the position of this revelation at a climactic point
and the conventions of apocalyptic melodrama, the audience *knows* there is some
truth in this allegation, despite their knowledge that Darvil is an Avenger who
might be lying. Sure enough, at the end of the play the spectators learn that
Ernest and Alice are indeed related but that Darvil could not have known earlier
that they were only cousins.

A similar partial revelation concerning the truth about the heroine's past in a
scene in *Nick of the Woods* is followed quickly by an Indian raid and by a
surprising rescue by a mysterious Avenger. Just as the hero and heroine are
about to cross a raging river below a waterfall to escape the savages, "the
Jibbenainosay is precipitated down the cataract in a canoe of fire; the Indians
all utter a yell of horror and fall on their faces." The scene closes in a "tableau
of astonishment" from the others (p. 22). The pattern of increasing tension in
these plays, then, capped by scenes which partly lift the veil of mystery surrounding man's innermost desires, prepares for the apocalypse of fire and blood

at the end when the veil is burned away completely, revealing God's judgment in all its vengeful finality.[23]

Indeed, the revelation of final judgment provides the climactic scene in all melodramas of apocalypse. Typically, this involves a pitched battle between armies or ships, a revolution of the poor against the rich, or a natural disaster such as an avalanche or flood. Pirates and Dutchmen fight a naval battle, fully rigged ships and all, with the Dutch hero defeating the pirate villain in *Captain Kyd*. At the climax of *The Last Days of Pompeii*, Arbaces is accused of murder and strides to the center of a gladiatorial arena to glory in his crimes, taunting the crowd to punish him. He is answered with an apocalypse of flames and destruction: "The fire breaks forth from the mountain and the walls of the arena fall. Everybody cries, 'The earthquake—the earthquake!' Curtain falls on a grand tableau" (p. 31). Arbaces's revelations are followed by Revelation itself as an avenging God rains down fire from the mountaintop.

Although the conclusion of *Pompeii* is more pessimistic than usual for apocalyptic melodrama, the devastation wrought by divine intervention is entirely typical. Dead bodies of good and evil characters litter the stage in *Nick of the Woods* and *Ernest Maltravers* as well. This conventional ending is a long way from any notion of poetic justice, a conclusion often identified with other types of nineteenth-century melodrama. The desire for complete and total vengeance, it seems, is more fundamental to these plays than a traditionally defined happy ending.

In *The Surgeon of Paris* and *The Carpenter of Rouen*, the apocalypse takes the form of a successful revolution of the people against aristocratic oppression— a happier, though still by no means a poetic, conclusion. Marteau's assault on De Saubigne's palace of privilege culminates in stage fire and the crashing of scenery. Like all scenes of mob violence in these plays, the climax of *Carpenter* suggests a reenactment of the French Revolution. It is probably no accident that the two plays by J. S. Jones climaxing in rebellion are set in France, convenient both for its revolutionary heritage and its supposedly idle and lascivious aristocracy. The apocalyptic scenes in these melodramas are similar to their counterparts in the Parisian boulevard pantomimes—the predecessors of nineteenth-century melodrama—performed in the 1790s in which, time and again, the Bastille or its metaphorical equivalent was attacked and destroyed. In the plays as in the early pantomimes, climactic events are realized primarily in action and in scenic displays with dialogue playing a distinctly subsidiary role.[24] A popular apocalyptic melodrama on the Bowery in the late 1840s, in fact, was titled *The Destruction of the Bastille*.

The pattern of these plays comes full circle in their final tableau. The potential utopia suggested earlier in the action—Ernest's and Alice's cottage of love, Michael-the-artisan's freedom, the frontier Arcadia in *Nick of the Woods*—is typically embodied center stage in a static pose of the virtuous characters. Although these plays are given historical settings, they press toward this final moment when history vanishes and an ideal vision without conflict or change takes its place. As cultural historian Wylie Sypher states concerning nineteenth-century melodrama in general, "[It] cannot admit exceptions for they would immediately involve action too deeply within the context of actuality and trammel the gesture. The [character] types must behave with a decorum of extremes; the resolution must be vividly schematic. The tensions must concentrate toward a last overwhelming tableau, a final stasis beyond which one must not think."[25] Apocalyptic melodrama works within this schematic idealization, but, as previously noted, its static tableau is far from utopian. After all, Darvil's corpse lies beside the picture of the two lovers in *Ernest Maltravers*, and "burning wigwams" (p. 30) mar the pastoral bliss of *Nick of the Woods*. Revenge similarly disfigures the utopian finale typical of most other apocalyptic melodramas.

The centrality of vengeance in apocalyptic melodrama is also apparent in its conventions of characterization. As in other antebellum melodramas, characters in these plays are essentially variations on the archetypes of mother, father, and child.[26] In addition to the frequent use of children on the stage in performances of melodramas of catastrophe (one parody of Hamblin's plays advertised for "750 Infants, to aid in the getting-out of the new piece"[27]), childlike characters, usually stage comics, were common as well. Rosignol in *The Surgeon of Paris* runs after squealing young girls in a manner similar to Harpo Marx's pursuit of lithe beauties in *Duck Soup*. Roaring Ralph Stackpole, a fun-loving Davy-Crockett type in *Nick of the Woods*, has more of a social conscience but is just as full of himself. Most heroines in these plays are young mothers, such as Madelon in *The Carpenter of Rouen* who, with her child, is lured into the palace by the wicked De Saubigne. For the most part, however, apocalyptic melodramas center on men: virtuous fathers like Marteau, villainous fallen-fathers such as Arbaces, and heroic fathers-to-be like Ernest. Male deeds are paramount: persecuting heroines, unveiling virtue, and striking back to avenge a history of wrongs.

Just as ritual scenes of virtuous incantation mirror the rites of the wicked, so too are Avengers in the cause of justice similar to their villainous counterparts. In *Captain Kyd* the villain and the true Avenger were exchanged in the cradle, and a dominant thread of the play's action involves untangling their identities— not an easy task, since both are proud, quick to anger, and unforgiving of past wrongs. The Avenger's identity and his reason for vengeance are often masked in these melodramas, leaving the spectator in some doubt as to whether the Avenger will ultimately come down on the side of right. Only at the conclusion of *Nick of the Woods*, for example, does the audience learn that the tortured, half-crazed wanderer Bloody Nathan is also the avenging scourge of the Indians, the Jibbenainosay—as well as Reginald Ashburn, the Spirit of the Waters, and Nick of the Woods, other mysterious figures in the drama. The reason for these five identities is revealed at the end of the play: Indians tortured and killed the wife and child of Reginald Ashburn—"That was my name ere hell hounds seared my brain and turned my blood to fire" (p. 30), he says—turning mild-mannered father into superhuman Avenger. The result is a power for good that is just as secretive, vengeful, and doomed as the villains of the piece. A conspiracy of wickedness begets a conspiracy for virtue, and both perish in the final catastrophe.

In performance of apocalyptic melodramas, leading actors were regularly cast in the roles of Avenger and villain. J. R. Scott, a minor star in the antebellum period known for his booming voice and magnetic stage presence, usually played Jibbenainosay, Marteau, and other Avengers at the Bowery Theatre. Scott's success with Bowery audiences was widely enough known to be celebrated in a verse of the popular song, "The Boys of the Bowery Pit":

> But presently the Actors are seen looking at the wings,
> As if they were watching for Somebody or Something,
> The Gallus Boys are Wide-Awake, they know what's coming now—
> For J. R. Scott is coming, and then there's such a row.

At the Chatham Theatre during the 1840s, J. Hudson Kirby often performed the Avenger roles. Celebrated especially for his tempestuous stage deaths, Kirby was in the habit of walking through the early scenes of a play to save his energy for his upcoming agonizing expiration. "Wake me up when Kirby dies" was a standing jest for years among Bowery spectators, signifying, in a wry way, the importance of the apocalyptic conclusion.[28]

Hamblin himself, well known in the Bowery for his Shakespearean roles despite an asthmatic condition that hindered his vocal projection, often took the villainous roles in these melodramas of catastrophe. His Arbaces in *The Last Days of Pompeii*, for instance, was a frequent crowd pleaser. Significantly, *The New-York Mirror*, in its initial review of the play, noted, "It is evident that Arbaces (like Milton's devil) is the real, although Glaucus is the poetic hero of the piece." Occasionally, big-name touring stars played villains in these plays, as when J. B. Booth, father of Edwin and John Wilkes, performed Robert Lester in *Captain Kyd*. Some actors made a name for themselves in the comic roles of these melodramas (a seven-and-a-half-foot giant gained popularity as Roaring Ralph Stackpole in *Nick of the Woods*), but Bowery audiences came to the theatres primarily to applaud actors playing villains and Avengers.[29]

The "clap-trap" language spoken by Avengers certainly provided many opportunities for applause. "A mechanic, sir, is one of God's noblemen," thundered J. R. Scott as Marteau. "What have they not done under his Fatherly providence! Who opens the secret chambers of the deep and makes the tractless ocean a highway for nations? The mechanic! Who holds the elements of fire and water in subjection and at his command makes sea and air the playthings of his power? The mechanic sir! At his bidding mountains are torn asunder and all things in nature changed to do his command! The Supreme Ruler of the Universe is Himself the Great Mechanic" (p. 9). Here was hyperbole enough to heighten the hopes of any apprentice or journeyman in the house! Other set speeches drummed up applause by damning villainy. "What scenes of intrigue, riot, pollution and murder are acted in these walls by villains clad in ermine and in silks,'' proclaimed J. Hudson Kirby as the Mask in *The Surgeon of Paris*, adding, ''Monuments of infamy shrouded in velvet and costly jewels, while the poor deluded people, charmed with the blaze of royalty, feel not the foot that is on their necks, but bow them down in slaves' devotion to the tread of the proud despot'' (p. 12). When not haranguing the crowd on stage (and in the audience) with speeches set in antithetical phrases and propounding axiomatic truths, the Avengers uttered slogans to urge them on to action. ''Blood for blood,'' stated in *Surgeon* (p. 41), echoes through the other plays as well, typifying the lust for revenge embedded in the structure of these dramas.

Interestingly, the generality of the rhetoric matches the vagueness of the political goals in the revolutions occurring in *Surgeon* and *Carpenter*. Although the Mask wins a victory for freedom, the precise nature of this freedom is never specified. Presumably, Michael-the-artisan and his fellows are now free to practice Protestantism and to pursue their trade, but this goal is never articulated. Likewise, the return of traditional artisan freedoms is only hinted at in *Carpenter*. More significant in the final tableau is the picture of the wicked duke hanging on a gibbet constructed by Marteau himself. To involve the action and language of these plays too deeply in a specific historical struggle, it seems, would detract from their transcendental purpose. Further, general rhetoric of revenge allowed the artisan in the audience greater imaginative liberty for substituting his own villain and Avenger and also in defining his own vision of freedom. The vague, idealized language in the dialogue of apocalyptic melodrama was intended to set the spectators dreaming of a primal revenge beyond any man's realistic hopes.[30]

Extravagant scenic spectacle was the chief theatrical means of putting across climactic scenes of vengeful catastrophe. Stage directions for scenic effects in the scripts of these plays are frequently complex and often more important than the dialogue. For Elpsey's incantation scene in *Captain Kyd*, the script demands:

Half dark. Interior of the Witch's Hut, composed of rocks, trees, old boots, etc. on R[ight] H[and] flat. An invisible transparency of the pirates boarding the Ger Falcon on the L[eft] H[and] flat. Another transparency of a pirate hanging on a gibbet, both to be lighted up at the end of the act. In the C[enter] a cauldron. Two seats on stage. A skull with a thigh bone fastened to it for a ladle. Skeletons and skulls around the stage. Cotton batting, wet with fluid to light for incantation. The trap to be masked with a crocodile; a serpent to twist around Elipsey's waist; another for her head, and two others for her arms. (p. 25).

As is evident from this description, revelation was effected visually whenever possible, with scenic transparencies paralleling the transparent primal characters indicated in the script. Blue or red fire, property destruction, bloated corpses, and noise and confusion were the normal ingredients of most final effects. To the printed instructions in the scripts of the final scene of *The Carpenter of*

Rouen, one stage manager penned the note: "Shouts. Alarm bell. Red fire. Wood crashes. Stamping and running about. Confused noises."[31] These theatrical effects were an integral part of the performance of apocalyptic melodramas serving as legitimate extensions of the dramatic motive to purge demonic power by calling in unseen soldiers from the spiritual realm immediately offstage. At Bowery theatres, the stage manager played God, fighting fire with the flames of soaked cotton batting.

Hamblin, as usual, was in the forefront among Bowery managers in the profitable building and use of scenery. Reinforcing his stage manager with several stage machinists and more than the usual number of scene painters, Hamblin also purchased a small factory to build the practical waterfalls, disappearing rooms, and fully rigged ships needed for his shows. Besides a variety of trap doors on stage and complicated rigging in the fly space above, Hamblin installed an enormous door connecting the backstage area to an alleyway behind the theatre so that the cavalry and artillery used in the final scenes of *Ernest Maltravers*, *Nick of the Woods*, and other plays could make an exciting entrance. So effective were many of Hamblin's costumes, sets, and machinery that he was able to rent them out to other theatre managers after the initial close of his own show. Probably Hamblin's scenic spectacles did not always go off as planned—stage managers at other theatres reported volcanoes that fizzled and waterfalls that burned up—but they must have succeeded most of the time because his audience kept coming back for more. Nevertheless, he paid an ironic price for his profitable adventure into the machinery of apocalypse. Two of the three fires that burned the Bowery to the ground were related to the staging or manufacture of special effects: the first when a spark from some flaming cotton batting lodged in a rolled-up scenic drop and the second in which a fire in the carpentry shop later spread into the theatre.

The advertising campaigns mounted by Hamblin and his fellow Bowery managers underscore the importance of spectacle in attracting crowds to performances of apocalyptic melodrama. Bowery programs, which often doubled as handbills and posters, regularly allowed more space to announce the various scenic effects than to display the names of the characters and actors. A program for *Ernest Maltravers*, for instance, printed in banner headlines: "*Tableau of Courage, Tableau of Female Heroism, Tableau of Horror, Tableau of Revenge and Disappointment,*" and so forth, ending with a final proclamation in even bolder type, "*TABLEAU! DEATH OF DARVILL [sic] AND SUBJUGATION OF THE BRIGANDS.*" Program space was also allotted to praise forthcoming productions. An 1837 Bowery Theatre program carried the following typical announcement: "*The Bronze Horse*, or *The Spell of the Cloud King*, or *The Enchanted Flying Steed*, which has been four months in preparation, at the enormous expense of $5,000 and the manager has every confidence that it will be pronounced the most gorgeous spectacle ever produced."

Parodies of such program puffery in the popular press and even in other theatres were common in the antebellum period. One particularly well-aimed satire announced a "Grand Domestic, Cosmic, Tragic, Melo-Dramatic, Operatic, Systematic, Democratic and Emblematic Piece entitled *The Pirate Husband or The Ensanguined Shirt*," further noting that "this piece has been got up without regard to expense, weather, or anything else. An amount of money has been invested in properties which frightens the manager and will astonish the public." Sometimes spectacular advertising devices were used to draw attention to the spectacle on the Bowery stages. To fan the fires of popular enthusiasm for Medina's adaptation of *Rienzi*, another of Bulwer-Lytton's novels, Hamblin covered the entire front of his theatre with a transparency depicting "the vast conflagration of the Palace of Constantine, with the fall of the Basalt Lion." According to *The Spirit of the Times*, "A fully-rigged schooner on top of a semi-used-up omnibus" announced an 1849 revival of Medina's *Wacousta*.[32]

The essence of the symbolic universe evident in performances of apocalyptic melodrama in Bowery theatres between 1835 and 1850 is vengeance, the motive force behind their structure and the quality that most clearly separates them from other types of melodrama in the antebellum period. From the point of view of these plays, the conspiratorial and demonic nature of villainy justifies any action that avenges past wrongs and destroys wickedness, even if innocent bystanders are drowned in the maelstrom. Since the stakes of the struggle ultimately involve forces beyond man's control, ritual actions, props, and slogans must be invoked to neutralize evil and to insure the triumph of vengeful justice. Mundane political or economic goals are clearly beside the point in this cosmic contest. The young male worker's desire for a final, earthshaking end to frustration and perceived exploitation and his need to purge the bile of bitterness through a spectacle of destruction is almost palpable in these melodramas. Rekindling his faith that "the mechanic is God's nobleman" was important too, but the smoldering resentment arising from this belief primarily served to add yet more fuel to the fires of revenge.

III

Mob violence burned over American cities in 1834 as it had not done since the days of the Revolutionary War, scorching New York thirteen times in that one year alone. Political, nativist, and antiabolitionist riots in New York City had their counterpart in similar disturbances in Philadelphia, Baltimore, Boston, and twelve other cities. The worst of the New York riots—destroying over sixty buildings and causing numerous injuries (though few deaths)—occurred during several days in July and was precipitated, in part, by an incident at the Bowery Theatre. On July 5, William Farren, the English-born stage manager at the Bowery, reportedly remarked, "Damn the Yankees; they are a damn set of jackasses, and fit to be gulled." D. D. McKinney, a disgruntled actor fired by Hamblin for refusing to learn his lines, used newspaper announcements and other means to gather together a group of men intent on avenging Farren's and Hamblin's purportedly unpatriotic behavior. At a benefit performance for Farren on

July 9, a mob of more than a thousand people, no doubt including McKinney and his gang, broke down the front doors of the theatre, stopped the performance, and demanded Farren's dismissal and an apology from Hamblin. Hamblin complied, but the mob, many of whom had gathered initially to protest an antislavery meeting in the nearly Chatham Street Chapel, proceeded to the home of abolitionist leader Lewis Tappen where they broke doors and windows and burned much of the furniture. During the next two days, mob violence against the homes, churches, and businesses of New York blacks and their perceived allies, the abolitionists, burned out of control, eventually necessitating the calling-out of the National Guard.[33]

The Astor Place riot in 1849 topped other disturbances of that year throughout the country in lives lost. It, too, began in a theatrical dispute, originating in rivalry between the English star William Charles Macready and the American actor Edwin Forrest who believed Macready's friends had hissed him in the theatre and villified him in the press on his London tour. Following three years of accusations, justifications, and counterplots on the part of the two rivals, Forrest's Bowery followers took advantage of Macready's scheduled performances at the Astor Place Opera House in New York to avenge the wrongs suffered by their hero. On May 10, 1849, some of the Bowery "b'hoys" occupied part of the theatre, intent on preventing Macready's performance, while others joined the mob outside the opera house. Stones were thrown at the building, Macready's *Macbeth* was temporarily halted by those inside, and the police were called to restore order. Their ineffective show of force, however, further inflamed the mob who set fires inside the opera house and threw paving stones through the windows. The arrival of the militia and their initial volley over the heads of the rioters momentarily quelled the crowd, which surged forward again in the mistaken belief that the military was using blanks. The result was twenty-three dead, many of them onlookers, and scores wounded. Crowds gathered the next day to protest this "murderous outrage," but military preparedness kept them at bay.[34]

The Farren riot of 1834 and the Astor Place riot of 1849, like many outbreaks of mob violence in antebellum America, conform to the general pattern of preindustrial urban riots discerned by historians George Rudé and Eric Hobsbawm. In these two riots, as in others of the type, the main participants were workers, not poor slum-dwellers or criminals. Rioters focused their attack on property rather than people, with the aim of demonstrating their hatred of specific villains and imposing their own rough form of "natural" justice on them. Unlike later mobs in Europe and America, these rioters were not animated by revolutionary goals, seeking instead the restoration of personal liberties, social relationships, or economic situations which they perceived had been lost through villanous conspiracy. Their protest invariably featured inflammatory slogans, stirring rhetoric, and a panoply of mystically charged actions. Often an individual, cast by the mob in the role of heroic Avenger, lurked in the wings, inspiring his followers to commit brave acts of revenge.[35] As this description suggests, preindustrial urban riots mirrored the essential structural elements of apocalyptic melodrama.

Although the social and economic composition of the mob in the Farren and Astor Place riots is difficult to discern, evidence suggests that most rioters were of the same class, age, and value orientation as the typical Bowery theatre audience. Of the twenty-three people who died in the 1849 riot, sixteen were listed in the anonymous pamphlet *Account of the Terrific and Fatal Riot of the New-York Astor Place Opera House on the Night of May 10th, 1849* as having working-class occupations. Only two were not workers, and the rest were not identified by occupation. Also at least thirteen were under twenty-five years of age (out of nineteen whose ages were listed). Although many of those who died were onlookers, the presence of such a great proportion of workers in the surrounding crowd in an upper-class square of the city suggests that many spectators came to cheer on their working-class friends and neighbors. Newspaper accounts, too, stressed the involvement of Bowery "b'hoys" in the violence.[36]

Regarding the Farren riot, the friends of the ousted actor McKinney who joined the antiabolitionist mob were doubtless Bowery theatre regulars, and the man who swore out a statement that Farren had damned the Yankees was a butcher by trade. Furthermore, the Chatham Street Chapel near the Bowery theatre was an initial target of the rioters, and most of the destruction to black homes and establishments occurred in the sixth ward, a predominantly working-class neighborhood. Sufficient circumstantial evidence exists, then, to apply cultural historian David Grimsted's conclusion that "rioters were predominantly lower middle-class people with a skill or some property and some position in the community; the majority also tended to be young, in their late teens or twenties, and to have ties with the Jacksonian equivalent of the modern urban gang, the fire house companies" to the Farren and Astor Place riots.[37] The audience for apocalyptic melodrama was virtually identical.

In both riots, as in apocalyptic melodrama, a conspiratorial web of villainy was perceived to be the root cause of evil. For several weeks preceding the Farren riot, many New York newspapers spread rumors linking abolitionism to "amalgamation," i.e., interracial marriage. It was alleged that abolitionist ministers were regularly conducting such ceremonies, that the prominent abolitionist Arthur Tappan had married a Negro, and that Negro "dandies" were attempting to attract white females. Even the *Evening Post*, generally a defender of anti-slavery activities, reported that abolitionists "had entered into a conspiracy against the human species by promoting marriage between blacks and whites." Following a minor scuffle between blacks and whites on July 7th, two days before the main rioting, the New York *Courier and Enquirer* reported that whites were beaten—"yes, beaten, fellow citizens, by the bludgeons of an infuriated and an *encouraged* negro mob." The newspaper then demanded, "How much longer are we to submit? In the name of the country, in the name of heaven, how much more are we to bear from Arthur Tappan's mad impertinence?'' In the mind of the mob, the supposedly unpatriotic actions of Hamblin and Farren linked these minor villains to the larger chain of amalgamationist evil threatening to surround and crush ''the human species.'' Breaking the chain, vanquishing Tappan and his minions, was the patriotic duty of every full-blooded American.[38]

Class antagonism between rich and poor defined conspiratorial villainy for the rioters in 1849. Macready, with his aloof acting style and English aristocratic connections, came ready-made for artisan nomination to villainy; an easier target would be difficult to imagine. An anonymous but typical ''American citizen,'' for example, dubbed Macready ''the pet of princes and nobles—the stately, but frigid representation of kings.'' The English actor, like Hamblin and his stage manager before him, came to represent an essentially transparent character through which the rioters perceived a more pervasive evil—in this case, the threat of aristocratic domination. ''Working men: Shall Americans or English rule in this city?'' warned posters put up before Macready's arrival in New York. With no basis in fact whatever, the poster further proclaimed:

> The crew of the *British Steamer* have threatened all Americans who shall dare to express their opinion on this night at the English Aristocratic Opera House!!!

> We advocate no violence, but a free expression of opinion to all public men!
> WORKING MEN! FREEMEN!
> Stand by your
> LAWFUL RIGHTS
>
> American Committee

The American Committee, a group of nativist politicians headed by E. Z. C. Judson, better known to the public as Ned Buntline, the dime novelist, fired broadsides of posters, pamphlets, and newspaper statements against aristocrats before and during the rioting. Drawing on precedents from the Revolutionary War, the committee urged citizens to ''own yourselves sons of the true hearts of '76'' by protesting the killings the day after the main riot. On the same day, Tammany politicians, many of whom were on the American Committee, told an assembled crowd that the policemen had been stationed at the Astor Place Theatre ''to avenge the aristocrats of this city against the working classes.'' As the anonymous *Account* reported after the riot, ''Macready was a subordinate personage, and he was to be put down less on his own account than to spite his aristocratic supporters. The question became not only a national, but a social one. It was the rich against the poor—the aristocracy against the people. Forrest's advocates looked upon it as a piece of retributive justice.''[39] Whatever the underlying social causes of the riot, including much justified bitterness by young workers against New York capitalists, there is no doubt that the rioters inflated out of proportion the extent of the evil forces ranged against them. Like the perception of wickedness held by antiabolitionists in the Farron riot, beliefs urged by the American Committee and apparently fastened on by the Astor Place mob were fundamentally within the paranoid style in their conception of a vast conspiracy and the ubiquity and power of the villains.

Both riots, too, featured wronged Avengers in starring roles. As Rudé notes, the heroes embraced by the preindustrial mob were sometimes reluctant to return the compliment by assuming leadership of the riot, though their presence in the background usually lent focus and direction to the violence.[40] Such was the case with Edwin Forrest and D. D. McKinney in the Astor Place and Farren riots. Forrest, believing himself the embodiment of American democratic principles, pushed his rivalry with Macready into the public limelight at every opportunity prior to the riot, stating in one published manifesto, "I most solemnly aver and do believe that Mr. Macready, instigated by his narrow envious mind and his selfish fears, did *secretly*—not openly—suborn several writers for the English press to write me down." The American star vehemently denied that he had organized opposition to the English actor (though he probably had) and stoutly stood by his belief that Macready had conspired with others to damn his acting (a point never proven). Forrest's vindictiveness stopped short of actual participation in the rioting, however; the actor apparently never contacted the American Committee or other leaders of the mob who acted in his name to avenge his purported insult.[41]

McKinney, like Forrest, was an active Avenger before the riot but disappeared up stage behind the mob when the violence began. Like Marteau in *The Carpenter of Rouen*, the disgruntled actor gathered with his compatriots to counter Hamblin's evil power with a rituallike resolution ringing with the rhetoric of the Revolutionary War:

Resolved, That the course pursued by Thomas S. Hamblin, proprietor of the Bowery Theatre, and his stage manager, Mr. Farren, in attempting to coerce people to conform to their private rules and regulations, which are often changed to suit their purposes, and in denying to the audience of that Theatre the right of expressing their approbation or disapprobation of an actor's performance, is contrary to all precedent, tyrannical and arbitrary in the extreme, and not to be tolerated by an American public. . . .

Resolved, That the expression made use of by the said Thomas S. Hamblin, that "he did not care a damn for the American public; that he did not value their approbation, and that he would have things as *he* pleased," and various other expressions made use of by him, degrading the American character, shows a despotic, aristocratic and unprincipled disposition, by no means congenial to the feelings of American citizens. . . .

Resolved, That the conduct of the said Thomas S. Hamblin, in discharging Mr. McKinney, a favorite American Actor, from the boards of the said Theatre, without any just cause, and supporting the illegal and despotic conduct of Mr. Farren, the stage manager, towards Mr. McKinney, is a piece with the rest of his conduct, and proves, evidently, that success has made him proud and insolent, and that he has forgotten to whom he owes his present prosperity.[42]

Though these moralistic distinctions between the aristocrats and the people along with McKinney's personal sense of injustice were later subsumed in the rhetoric

and behavior of the antiabolitionist rioters, McKinney's conspiratorial perceptions and his use of a counterconspiracy to avenge the evil he saw identify him
as a conventional Avenger. The calculation and self-consciousness of the preceding resolution, in fact—coupled with what must have been McKinney's
knowledge that Hamblin was perfectly justified in firing him—suggests that
McKinney may have knowingly cast himself in that role.

Besides resolutions imitating the Declaration of Independence, other rituallike activities abound in these two riots, as in apocalyptic melodrama. According
to a contemporary, minutes before the start of Macready's *Macbeth*, the Bowery
"b'hoys" inside the Astor Place Opera House began their "regular 'tramp'
warning peculiar to the Chatham and the Bowery"—a noise made by clapping
together hands, seats, or any object within reach—and they built this racket to
a crescendo to force Macready's appearance. This ritual clearly signified the
power of the "b'hoys" and their contempt for the kid-glove manners of the
aristocrats in the audience. The theatre itself—"attended by the most wealthy
and fashionable people, who have made extravagant displays of luxurious adorn-
ment" as the anonymous *Account* correctly reported—represented a bastion of
privilege in the eyes of the mob. The rioters broke windows, chairs, and other
furnishings, attempted to batter down the door, and even set fires in the basement.
The main force of the riot, at least until the militia arrived, was directed against
the building, not against the aristocratic spectators or even against Macready.[43]
Clearly what the rioters had in mind was the sort of spectacular destruction they
had seen so often in Bowery melodramas: an all-consuming fire that would burn
away their bitterness by toppling an image of villainy and oppression.

The rioters gained their imitation apocalypse in the antiabolitionist violence
of 1834, breaking into, burning, or pulling down over sixty residences and
churches. In the theatre riot preceding it, wealthy New Yorker Philip Hone
reported in his diary that "poor Hamblin" was "hissed and pelted" at the Bowery
despite "the talisman which he relied upon, the American flag, which he waved
over his head." The rioter's respect for ritual objects (Hamblin's pelting not-
withstanding) occasionally took an ironic, even comic, turn. In the midst of
destroying the house and possessions of Lewis Tappan, several people in the
mob paused to rescue a portrait of George Washington from the flames, gently
setting it aside and guarding it from accidental harm.[44]

As in other typical preindustrial riots and in apocalyptic melodrama too, the
destruction wrought by retributive justice was generally planned in advance.
Although some of the initial destruction of the antiabolitionist mobs in 1834
may have been spontaneous, the longer the rioting continued, the more me-
thodical it became. Meeting places were chosen ahead of time, battle plans
agreed upon, and targets carefully specified. Rioters on July 11th in the Five-
Points district adopted a system of biblical signification to distinguish white from
black homes by spreading the word that white families were to keep candles lit
in the windows so that the riotous plague might pass over them.[45] Similar planning
and battle strategy occurred in 1849. Nativist politician "Captain" Rynders

confessed later at a trial to having purchased and distributed fifty tickets among his Bowery followers to hiss Macready off the stage. His American Committee must have been organized weeks before Macready's arrival in New York, because it began cranking out propaganda as soon as the English actor stepped ashore. For all their perspicacity, however, Rynders and Buntline, his first lieutenant, did not foresee and clearly did not welcome the arrival of the military and the ensuing deaths. As Rudé remarks, traditional riots rarely appeared entirely ready-made; instead they often assumed "a dimension and momentum that no one, not even the most experienced of leaders, could have planned or expected."[46] The leaders of the 1834 and 1849 mobs may have designed a scenario similar in its sequence of primal activities and roles to the action and characters of apocalyptic melodrama, but accident and chance insured that their riots would never match their artistry.

In other ways, too, the fit between the melodramas and the mob violence proved more rough than precise. The plays, for example, were both more extreme and less complex than the riots. Macready and his aristocratic minions may have been powerful, ubiquitous, and conspiratorial from the rioters' point of view, but they were not seen as demonic forces possessing superhuman powers. The amalgamationists, too, were perceived as evil, but the rioters never believed that they consorted with witches and Egyptian gods, like Arbaces in *The Last Days of Pompeii*. Likewise the tramp warning used by the Bowery "b'hoys" to assert their control of the Astor Place Opera House and the candles in the windows lighted to signal good houses from evil ones in the antiabolitionist riots of 1834 may have been rituallike actions, but their purpose was too efficacious to define this kind of behavior as ritual, pure and simple. The indoctrination of the apprentice carpenter into the secret society in *The Carpenter of Rouen*, in contrast, had no instrumental value whatever in the "real" world of the play but stood instead as a symbolic rite performed to reaffirm the *Confrierie*'s transcendental purposes. Although the underlying intention of vengeance was similar in the plays and riots (as evidenced particularly in the hyperbolic, generalized rhetoric of both), the Avenger led the charge against villainy in the melodramas but merged into the crowd or lurked in the wings of the riots.

One difficulty in comparing these acts of mob violence to melodramas is that rioters became both actors and spectators in the same evening. Fate decreed that melodramatic Avengers die, but avenging mobs (if not the Avengers themselves) in preindustrial riots might enjoy the spectacle they themselves had created. In the 1834 riots, a spirit of Bacchanalian festivity seized the successful rioters, who drank and cheered while burning buildings and destroying property. Historian David Grimsted reports that this catharsis was not at all unique among antebellum mobs: "Once action began, [the anger in most riots] was replaced by joy and release if the mob was not seriously opposed."[47] The rioters at Astor Place, however, never made the full transition from actors to spectators because the authorities intervened before the scenario had reached its climax. From a dramaturgical point of view, the 1849 riot was a failure; it aroused expectations of emotional release and then frustrated them when the pyramid of dramatic action was truncated by the arrival of the militia. This, as much as anything, may help to account for the barricades, bonfires, and further assaults on the opera house on the night following the principal riot. The actors-spectators in the 1834 riots, on the other hand, simply exhausted themselves and stopped—a more logically dramatic denouement.

As is clear from the foregoing discussion, rioters also directed their own disturbances, sometimes improvising staging and at other times following the directions of professionals like Rynders and Buntline. The organization, limited goals, and collective consciousness evident in most pre-Civil War, working-class riots, as in the 1834 and 1849 episodes, have led many historians to view antebellum mob violence as a generally rational response to real grievances. Grimsted, on the other hand, emphasizes the often irrational hopes and fears released in a riot and the volatility that anonymity in a surging crowd induced in the rioters. The similarity between the riots and the plays suggests a third conclusion, one that synthesizes the dominant aspects of the other two. Just as a theatrical performance of apocalyptic melodrama had to be clearly delimited in its goals and well planned in its execution to purge the audience of its momentary paranoia through staged actions of vengeance, so, perhaps, was it necessary to plot a riot to achieve a similar catharsis among its participants. Looked at in this way, the rational intentions and structure of the riot provided a necessary framework for its irrational affect. Certainly, rioters in 1834 and 1849 who frequented the Bowery theatres would have understood the emotional release the pursuit of vengeance and destruction might bring. Though there is no direct historical evidence for it, some antebellum workers may have hoped that their man-made riots might anticipate and speed up a providentially-ordained apocalypse, dooming forever the villains of their lives. As Eric Hobsbawm, historian of European mob violence, remarks, "There are moments [in a riot] when the apocalypse seems imminent; when the entire structure of existing society whose total end the apocalypse symbolizes and predicts, actually looks about to collapse in ruins, and the tiny light of hope turns into the light of possible sunrise."[48] Rioters responsive to the formula of catastrophic melodrama would likely find several such moments of imminent apocalypse.

The millennial symbolic universe of apocalyptic melodrama as a source of social justification for many antebellum riots calls into question the applicability of Grimsted's conclusion that an optimistic notion of individual freedom legitimated rioting during the Jacksonian period in the eyes of working-class mobs. According to Grimsted, "The ideological tenets and political emotions of the age of Jackson, focusing on the centrality and sovereignty of the individual, both encouraged riotous response to certain situations and made it difficult to put riot down when it broke out." To be sure, social values elevating individual rights over legal restrictions may indeed have influenced the response of the general public to mob violence. But the popularity of apocalyptic melodrama among workers and its general congruence with two widely different working-class riots suggests that righteous vengeance was motive and justification enough for instigating and enjoying a riot among traditional workers. Moreover, their thirst for revenge was grounded in a rather rigid perception that others were conspiring against them, not in a generally optimistic estimation of man's moral nature. As we have seen, working-class rioters sometimes appealed to vaguely Lockean ideas of freedom to justify their vigilante mob violence to others—as indeed did some protagonists in the plays—but moralistic vengeance informed the fundamental roles and actions of each.[49]

Recent scholarship has emphasized the extent to which antebellum class and ethnic differences motivated mob violence and helped to shape the response of one group of Americans to the riotous behavior of another. In particular, Theodore Hammett's "Two Mobs of Jacksonian Boston: Ideology and Interest" gets at the often sharp contrasts between the structure of one working-class riot and that of an instance of elite mob violence.[50] Hence it is likely that the sources of legitimacy for one group of rioters differed from that of another, especially if the rioting group was perceived as a deviant subculture by most antebellum Americans (as tradition-oriented urban workers increasingly were). This being the case, it is necessary to go beyond the often dressed-up statements the rioters made to justify their actions after the fact and into the real experience of members of a subgroup to understand the underlying sources of legitimacy for their mob violence. In this regard, theatrical performances enjoyed by a particular class or ethnic group provide insight into the roles and actions—indeed, into the entire symbolic universe—of members of that subculture.

NOTES

1. *New York Tribune* (May 9, 1849), p. 2; bank clerk quoted by David Grimsted, "Rioting in Its Jacksonian Setting" in *The Underside of American History: Other Readings*, ed. Thomas Frazier, 3rd ed. (1972; rpt., New York, 1978), p. 177; "theatre of the mob" quotation in Paul Boyer, *Urban Masses and the Moral Order in America* (Cambridge, 1978), pp. 69–70.

2. See Kenneth Burke, "From *Lexicon Rhetoricae*," in *Terms for Order*, ed. Stanley Edgar Hyman (Bloomington, Indiana, 1964), pp. 20-21, 124, and *The Social Construction of Reality: A Treatise in the Sociology of Knowledge*, 2nd ed. (Garden City, New York, 1966), pp. 92–128. On Burke's "dramatistic approach," see his *A Grammar of Motives* (New York, 1945) and an overview of the theory by William Rueckert, *Kenneth Burke and the Drama of Human Relations* (Berkeley, 1982). Many structuralists, of course, have argued along similar lines but without Burke's Aristotelean framework, whose conception of *mimesis* I continue to regard as helpful. These structuralists include Elizabeth Burns, *Theatricality: A Study of Convention in the Theatre and in Social Life* (New York, 1972); Jean Duvignaud, "The Theatre in Society: Society in the Theatre," in *Sociology in Literature and Drama*, ed. Elizabeth and Tom Burns, Penguin Modern Sociology Readings (Harmondsworth, England, 1973), pp. 82–108; Jeffrey L. Sammons, *Literary Sociology and Practical Criticism* (Bloomington, Indiana, 1977); and Hayden V. White, "Structuralism and Popular Culture," *Journal of Popular Culture*, 7 (1974), 759–75.

Despite my reservations about the ahistorical nature of structuralism and my refusal to adopt their theoretical assumptions, I have used several ideas, including binary opposition, the centrality of paradigms, and the relative unimportance of a positivist causality from these articles and books.

3. *Rites of Modernization: Symbolic and Social Aspects of Indonesian Proletarian Drama* (Chicago and London, 1968), pp. 6, 246.

4. See, for example, Michael Feldberg's, "Urbanization as a Cause of Violence: Philadelphia as a Test Case," in *The Peoples of Philadelphia: A History of Ethnic Groups and Lower-Class Life*, ed. Allen F. Davis and Mark H. Hall (Philadelphia, 1973), pp. 53–70; and Maurice Willson Discher's *Blood and Thunder: Mid-Victorian Melodrama and Its Origins* (London, 1949), passim. The rather narrow functionalism of Feldberg's article, however, is not repeated in his later work, *The Philadelphia Riots of 1844: A Study of Ethnic Conflict*.

5. Theodore Shank's, "The Bowery Theatre, 1826–1836," (Diss., Stanford University, 1956) is the most reliable source on the Bowery Theatre during its early years. For developments after 1836, see George C. D. Odell, *Annals of the New York Stage*, 15 vols. (New York, 1927–1949), especially vols. 4–6. Bowery fires occurred in 1836, 1838, and 1845. Hamblin managed the Bowery throughout the period except for two years between 1837 and 1839 when William Dinneford ran the theatre.

6. See Claudia Johnson, "Burlesques of Shakespeare: The Democratic American's 'Light Artillery,' " *Theatre Survey*, 21 (May 1980), 49–62. *The City and the Theatre: New York Playhouses from Bowling Green to Times Square* (Clifton, New Jersey, 1973), p. 69.

7. *The Spirit of the Times: A Chronicle of the Turf, Field, Sports, Literature and the Stage*, 16 (February 6, 1847), 590; Whitman quoted in David Grimsted, *Melodrama Unveiled: American Theater and Culture, 1800–1850* (Chicago, 1968), p. 55; *Brother Jonathan*, 6 (May 9, 1843), 47; William K. Northall, *Before and Behind the Curtain, or Fifteen Years' Observations Among the Theatres of New York* (New York, 1851), p. 152.

8. See Howard B. Rock, *Artisans of the New Republic: The Tradesmen of New York City in the Age of Jefferson* (New York, 1979), pp. 135–43, passim; quoted in Michael Feldberg, *The Philadelphia Riots of 1844: A Study of Ethnic Conflict*, Contributions in American History, No. 43 (Westport, Connecticut, 1975), p. 68.

9. Quoted in Norman Ware, *The Industrial Worker, 1840–1860: The Reaction of American Industrial Society to the Advance of the Industrial Revolution* (Cambridge, 1924), p. xiv; quoted in Rex Burns, *Success in America: The Yeoman Dream and the Industrial Revolution (1825–1860)* (Amherst, Massachusetts, 1976), p. 118.

10. See Burns, pp. 91–127; W. Elliot Brownlee, *Dynamics of Ascent: A History of the American Economy* (New York, 1974), pp. 85–168; and Rock, pp. 237–88. Susan E. Hirsch, *Roots of the American Working Class: The Industrialization of the Crafts in Newark, 1800–1860* (Philadelphia, 1978) and Sam Bass Warner, *The Private City: Philadelphia in Three Periods of its Growth* (Philadelphia, 1968) provide useful information on working-class conditions in Newark and Philadelphia during the period. See Robert Ernst, *Immigrant Life in New York City, 1825–1863* (Port Washington, New York, 1949) for a discussion of immigrant neighborhoods.

11. See Edward Pessen, *Most Uncommon Jacksonians: The Radical Leaders of the Early Labor Movement* (Albany, 1967) on the development of working-class political

parties and labor unions. Joseph G. Rayback, *A History of American Labor* (New York, 1966) and Ware are also helpful.

12. Herbert G. Gutman, "Work, Culture and Society in Industrializing America," in *Work, Culture and Society in Industrializing America* (New York, 1976), pp. 3–78 and Bruce Laurie, "Nothing on Compulsion: Life Styles of Philadelphia Artisans, 1820–1850," *Labor History*, 15 (Summer 1974), 337–66 are particularly useful in delineating the social life of the typical antebellum urban worker. Regarding working-class fire-companies, see Stephen F. Ginsberg, "Volunteer Firemen in New York City, 1836–1837," *New York History*, 50 (April 1969), 165–86 and Bruce Laurie, "Fire Companies and Gangs in Southwark: The 1840s," in *The Peoples of Philadelphia: A History of Ethnic Groups and Lower-Class Life*, ed. Allen F. Davis and Mark H. Hall (Philadelphia, 1973), pp. 71–87. Herbert Asbury, *The Gangs of New York: An Informal History of the Underworld* (New York, 1928), pp. 21–117 and A. F. Harlow, *Old Bowery Days* (New York, 1931), pp. 170–218 provide interesting impressionistic histories of working-class society and the fire house companies.

13. For details, see Leonard L. Richards, *"Gentlemen of Property and Standing": Anti-Abolition Mobs in Jacksonian America* (1970; rpt., New York, 1977) and Paul O. Weinbaum, *Mobs and Demagogues: The New York Response to Collective Violence in the Early Nineteenth Century*, Studies in American History and Culture, No. 3 (UMI Research Press, 1979). Probably the best report on the Astor Place riot remains the *Anonymous Account of the Terrific and Fatal Riot at the New York Astor Place Opera House, On the Night of May 10th, 1849* (New York, 1849). Chevalier, "Symptoms of Revolution," in *Ideology and Power in the Age of Jackson*, ed. T. Rozwenc, Documents in American Civilization Series (Garden City, New York, 1964), p. 183.

14. Greeley quoted in Ware, p. 33. Ticket prices at the Bowery and Chatham for most of the period were seventy-five cents for a chair in one of the boxes, thirty-seven-and-a-half cents for a place on a backless bench in the pit and twenty-five cents for a bench in the balcony. These prices were halved during the depression years of the early 1840s. See Ware, pp. 26–70, for an account of the wages typical of the period. Day laborers were generally paid less than a dollar a day for their work.

15. See *The Spirit of the Times*, *Brother Jonathan*, and Northall, quoted above. Several issues of *The New-York Dramatic Mirror* also comment on Bowery audiences, notably vol. 13 (December 12, 1835), 191; vol. 13 (August 20, 1836) 63; and vol. 19 (January 23, 1841), 31. Northall and others refer to Mitchell's audience at the Olympic Theatre, an audience probably similar to those at the Bowery and Chatham, as predominantly youthful (pp. 220–30).

16. "Cultural Aspects of the Industrial Revolution: Lynn, Massachusetts, Shoemakers and Industrial Morality, 1826–1860," *Labor History*, 15 (Summer 1974), 367–94 and Laurie, p. 344. "Loyalists" and "rebels" are Faler's terms, pp. 391–92. On the continuing usefulness of Faler's ideal-type classification of antebellum workers into traditionalists, loyalists, and rebels, see Alan Dawley and Paul Faler, "Working-Class Culture and Politics in the Industrial Revolution: Sources of Loyalism and Rebellion," *Journal of Social History*, 9 (June 1976), 466–80 and Friedrich Lenger, "Class, Culture and Class-Consciousness in Ante-Bellum Lynn: A Critique of Alan Dawley and Paul Faler," *Social History*, 6 (October 1981), 317–32.

17. *The New-York Mirror*, 15 (April 28, 1838), 351. Mrs. M. Clarke, *A Concise History of the Life and Amours of Thomas S. Hamblin, late Manager of the Bowery Theatre As Communicated by His Legal Wife Mrs. Elizabeth Hamblin* (New York, 1838

[?]), p. 28. Elizabeth Hamblin apparently hired Mrs. Clarke to do an exposé of her former husband and his mistress, Louisa Medina.

18. *The Last Days of Pompeii: A Dramatic Spectacle*, French's Standard Drama, Acting Edition No. 146 (New York: S[amuel] French, [n.d.]); *Ernest Maltravers* (188–; rpt., New York: Readex Microprint, 1966); *Nick of the Woods*, New York Public Library of Performing Arts, MS, NCOF (the promptbook of E. H. Taylor using the Boston: W. V. Spencer, [n.d.] edition of the script). Further information on Medina and her plays may be gleaned from Rosemarie K. Bank's "Theatre and Narrative Fiction in the Work of the Nineteenth-Century American Playwright Louisa Medina," *Theatre History Studies*, 3 (1983), 54–67, an article that appeared after the present essay was completed. In contrasting the novels of *Ernest Maltravers* and *Nick* with Medina's melodramas, Bank makes two observations which emphasize Medina's interest in foregrounding the motive of vengeance and in thrusting the action of these plays toward final judgment. Bank states that the Avenger in *Ernest*, "Richard Darvil, the role played by Hamblin and a minor presence in the novel, becomes a central figure in the play" (p. 60). In the novel of *Nick of the Woods*, "the Jibbenainosay moves on to other frontiers, while in the play, his revenge complete, he dies" (p. 59).

19. *The Carpenter of Rouen*, New York Public Library of Performing Arts MS, NCOF (The promptbook of J. B. Wright, prompter for Pelby's National Theatre in Boston, 184–); *The Surgeon of Paris* ([1856]); rpt., New York: Readex Microprint, 1966); *Captain Kyd, or the Wizard of the Sea*, New York Public Library of Performing Arts MS, NCOF (a prompter's copy using the Boston: W. V. Spencer, [n.d.] edition of the script, probably used by J. B. Wright). Subsequent editions of *The Carpenter of Rouen* by Samuel French delete two pointedly anti-Catholic scenes in the play and append the subtitle *The Massacre of St. Bartholomew*, a publishing error since the massacre actually occurs in *The Surgeon of Paris*.

20. I am indebted here to John G. Cawelti's discussion of formulaic literature in chapter 1 of his *Adventure, Mystery and Romance: Formula Stories as Art and Popular Culture* (Chicago, 1976), pp. 5–36. Also of use is Cawelti's earlier article, "The Concept of Formula in the Study of Popular Culture," *Journal of Popular Culture*, 3 (Winter 1969), 381–90.

21. *The Life of the Drama* (New York, 1964), p. 202.

22. *The Paranoid Style in American Politics and Other Essays* (New York, 1966), pp. 29, 30, 32. See also David Brion Davis, "Some Themes of Counter-Subversion: An Analysis of Anti-Masonic, Anti-Catholic and Anti-Mormon Literature," in *The Fear of Conspiracy: Images of Un-American Subversion from the Revolution to the Present*, ed. David Brion Davis (Ithaca and London, 1971), pp. 9–22.

23. From the point of view of stage realism, of course, this scenario is completely unbelievable. The conventions of realism, however, are incapable of signifying what literary historian Peter Brooks terms the melodramatic realm of "the moral occult": "the domain of operative spiritual values which is both indicated within and masked by the surface of reality. The moral occult is not a metaphysical system." Brooks continues, "It is rather the repository of the fragmentary and desacralized remnants of sacred myth. . . . The melodramatic mode in large measure exists to locate and to articulate the moral occult" in *The Melodramatic Imagination: Balzac, Henry James, Melodrama and the Mode of Excess* (New Haven and London, 1976), p. 5.

24. For a short history of the development of melodrama in revolutionary France, see

Frank Rahill, *The World of Melodrama* (University Park, Pennsylvania, 1967), pp. 7–29.

25. "Aesthetic of Revolution: The Marxist Melodrama," *The Kenyon Review*, 10 (Summer 1948), 437.

26. See Brooks, pp. 24–55.

27. *The Spirit of the Times*, 6 (January 21, 1837), 387. The remainder of the spoof reads, "founded on fact, entitled *The Black Nunnery of Bagdad, or The Blood-Drinking Monk* which has been for some time preparing."

28. "The Boys of the Bowery Pit," a printed copy of the song by "W. C.," in Joseph Ireland, *Extra-Illustrated Records of the New York Stage*, Harvard Theatre Collection, ser. 2, 6. See Odell, vol. 4, 250, for contemporary reports of Kirby.

29. *The New-York Mirror*, 12 (June 24, 1835), p. 243. Booth played this villain at Pelby's National Theatre in Boston in 1850, according to a list of performances in the frontispiece of the Samuel French edition of the script. An undated newspaper clipping in the Harvard Theatre Collection file on *Nick of the Woods* notes that "Porter, the giant," appeared in the initial Bowery production of the play and frequently afterward.

30. Melodramatic rhetoric, as Peter Brooks notes, "represents a victory over repression": "The melodramatic utterance breaks through everything that constitutes the 'reality principle;' all its censorships, accomodations, tonings-down. . . . Desire triumphs over the world of substitute formations and detours; it achieves plenitude of meaning" (*The Melodramatic Imagination*, p. 41).

31. *The Carpenter of Rouen* IV, 4, MS, New York Library of Performing Arts.

32. Program for *Ernest Maltravers*, May 14, 1839, in Ireland, *Extra-Illustrated Records of the New York Stage*, ser. 2, 6; *Scrapbook of Theatre Clippings*, MS, New York Library of Peforming Arts; *The Spirit of the Times*, 9 (March 16, 1839), 13; *The New York Sun*, quoted in Odell, vol. 4, 83; *The Spirit of the Times*, 18 (January 20, 1849), 576.

33. See Richards, pp. 113–22, for a brief summary of the Farren riot. Shank, pp. 378–84, emphasizes the significance of Hamblin, Farren, and McKinney in the riot. Weinbaum, pp. 2–41, places the Farren riot in the context of other, similar riots in New York in 1834.

34. Grimsted, pp. 68–75, provides a useful summary of the riot and Richard Moody's *The Astor Place Riot* (Bloomington, Indiana, 1958) paints in its theatrical backdrop.

35. See George Rudé, *The Crowd in History: A Study of Popular Disturbances in France and England, 1730–1848* (New York, 1964), pp. 237–57, passim; Eric J. Hobsbawm, *Social Bandits and Primitive Rebels: Studies in Archaic Forms of Social Movement in the 19th and 20th Centuries* (Glencoe, Illinois, 1959), pp. 108–25, 150–74; and David Grimsted,"Rioting in Its Jacksonian Setting." Richards, pp. 111–13, notes the similarity of the Farren riot to contemporary lower-class riots in European cities.

36. *Account*, pp. 28–29. The occupations of most of the wounded were not listed.

37. "Rioting in Its Jacksonian Setting," p. 178.

38. The *Evening Post* and the *Corrier and Enquirer* quoted in Richards, pp. 115, 117. See also p. 115n for Richards's assessment of the extent of the rumors.

39. "American Citizen," *A Rejoinder to "Replies from England" Together with an Impartial History and Review of the Lamentable Occurrences at the Astor Place Opera House* (New York, 1849), p. 68; poster quoted in Northall, p. 143; reprinted in Montrose J. Moses, *The Fabulous Forrest: The Record of An American Actor* (Boston, 1929), p. 260; quoted in Moody, p. 187; *Account*, p. 19.

40. Rudé, pp. 247–48.

41. *Account*, pp. 12–13. Forrest had close ties to Rynders and others in the Tammany organization. A lifelong Democrat, Forrest contributed to the party, spoke at rallies, and almost ran as a Democratic candidate from New York City in 1838.

42. Quoted in Shank, pp. 379–80.

43. Northall, pp. 133–36, provides a thorough description of Bowery "b'hoy" behavior at the Opera House; *Account*, p. 5. The testimony of several eyewitnesses cited in the *Account*, (pp. 20–26) supports this conclusion.

44. Philip Hone, *The Diary of Philip Hone*, ed. Bayard Tuckerman (New York, 1910), p. 100. See Harlow, pp. 290–92, for his report of the Farren riot.

45. Richards, pp. 118–20. Richards concludes, "During the two nights of intense rioting, then, the New York rioters behaved neither spontaneously nor capriciously. They displayed as much rhyme and reason, as much purposefulness and singlemindedness, as the rioters whom Rudé describes."

46. Rynders quoted in *Account*, p. 16; Rudé, p. 242.

47. Grimsted, "Rioting in Its Jacksonian Setting," p. 176.

48. Irving J. Sloan, *Our Violent Past* (New York, 1970) and Ovid Demaris, *America the Violent* (New York, 1970), for example, stress the organization and general rationality of most antebellum mobs. Hobsbawm, *Bandits* (New York, 1969), p. 22. See also, *Social Bandits and Primitive Rebels*, pp. 57–174 for Hobsbawm's relevant comments on millenarianism and labor sects in Britain. Hobsbawm concludes that apocalyptic religion among nineteenth-century British workers was truly "the opium of the people."

49. Grimsted, p. 160. Ironically, Grimsted pays close attention to what I, borrowing from Hofstadter, have been calling the paranoid style of the rioters but does not see in their fear of conspiracy a main source of legitimacy for mob violence. It may be that Grimsted's disinterest in separating working-class from other kinds of riots and in distinguishing the general public repsonse to mob behavior from the specific values of the rioters lead him to his overly general and misleading conclusions.

50. Hammett's essay in *Journal of American History*, 62 (1976), 845–68. See also Feldberg's *The Philadelphia Riots of 1844*, Weinbaum's study and Paul A. Gilje, "The Baltimore Riots of 1812 and the Breakdown of the Anglo-American Mob Tradition," *Journal of Social History*, 13 (Summer 1980), 547–64.

2

The Plebeian Moment: Theatre and Working-Class Life in Late Nineteenth-Century Pittsburgh

Francis G. Couvares

From the 1850s through the 1880s stage entertainment was an important part of a flourishing plebeian culture in Pittsburgh. Working people—especially the highly skilled and well-paid iron and glass craftsmen—made up the bulk of the audience and set tastes for the city. By the turn of the century, however, the theatre and its audience had fragmented. In addition to a sharp class division that marked "New York theatre" from lower-class amusement, new kinds of mass entertainment, especially movies, generated new audiences. This chapter describes plebeian theatre and its social context and suggests the causes of its transfiguration and demise in the face of emergent mass culture.

Like the industrial craftsmen[1] who comprised its core audience, plebeian culture[2] occupied a distinct historical moment. Neither artisans nor proletarians, the craftsmen partook of pastimes that were not simply inheritances of folk tradition or commodities produced and distributed for mass consumption. Mediated by small-scale, aggressive "merchants of leisure," plebeian culture was at once intensely local, rooted in the vernacular life of the walking city[3] and highly responsive to local tastes and expectations. Yet the culture was open to the growing variety of professional sports and entertainment that riverboats and railroads had begun to deliver to the American hinterland.[4] Before detailing this historical juncture, however, it is necessary to account for the peculiar lack in Pittsburgh of a viable elite alternative to the developing plebeian culture.

The absence of genteel or cosmopolitan culture in Pittsburgh reflected the dour provinciality of the iron elite. In the words of one visitor in 1868, the iron-masters were

mostly of the Scotch-Irish race, Presbyterians, keen and steady . . . singularly devoid of the usual vanities and ostentations, proud to possess a solid and spacious factory, and to live in an insignificant house. There are no men of leisure in town. . . . The old men never think of "retiring," nor is there anything for them to retire to. . . . Until very recently, in Pittsburgh, it would have boded ill for a man to build a handsome house a few miles out of the smoke; and to this day it is said that a Pittsburgh man of business who should publish a poem would find his "paper" doubted at the bank. "A good man, sir, but not practical."[5]

Local commentators and visitors agreed that luxury was a sin to which the ironmaster seldom had to confess.[6] A deeply Puritan and utilitarian sensibility made the fussier sublimations of Victorian respectability seem out of place in Pittsburgh. Neither home, nor manners, nor civic duty distracted the businessman from his main business: the pursuit of wealth and family security.

The ironmaster lived in a small, provincial world. His factory was staffed by sons and nephews. His children usually married within the local elite and seldom went to finishing schools or to Ivy League colleges.[7] To them the ironmaster transmitted a dual message: pursue wealth yet disdain its enjoyment. Some elite Presbyterians in Pittsburgh still pledged "to abstain from the opera, the theater, the circus, and card playing," and Methodists condemned even more persistently "the frivolous and sometimes filthy thing which is to-day called . . . theater."[8] Thus, children of the iron elite recalled later in life having grown up in a "purely material" world where civilization was measured "in tons of pig iron."[9]

For example, Elizabeth Moorhead, daughter of a leading transportation and iron magnate, remembered Pittsburgh as "a barren and unlovely place . . . dom-inated by our industries." With some emotion she recalled her own and her friends' repeated efforts to legitimize their interest in drama in the face of strong disapproval. Their Shakespeare Reading Club was finally allowed to exist, though its performances were "strictly censored."[10] Even those, like the family of William G. Johnston, who shared little of the Presbyterian prejudice against amusement, felt its disapproving weight upon the conscience. Sitting in his cheap seat at the theatre, young Johnston suspected that "there was something ominous . . . in the name of the place in which I sat—the pit." He too threw himself into "private theatricals, set up in the cellar of my father's house."[11] Thus, when the Pittsburgh Opera House opened in 1871, its management saw to it that the son of a leading Presbyterian minister (with the impeccable name of Knox) composed a verse oration in defense of the "Gods of Drama." Read during opening ceremonies, it presumably eased the transition to the melodrama *Ruy Blas*, though it won for its author "the condemnation of pulpit and church."[12]

The ironmasters demonstrated little inclination to participate in the forging of a distinctive bourgeois cultural order or to link themselves spiritually with their class.[13] Indeed they regularly frustrated those who called upon them to assume cultural responsibilities. Thus the *Daily Gazette* lamented on February 23, 1850 that "our city lacks, exceedingly, those more healthful and proper sources of amusement, which render other cities so attractive, such as galleries of pictures, museums, public institutions, and Libraries, &c." For more than forty years such laments continued to sound and to elicit little response from the ironmasters. Until the 1890s prosperous Pittsburghers who sought genteel recreation had little to choose from: an occasional concert organized by local talent, a church Christmas concert, a performance by one of the German singing societies. The Pittsburgh Female Academy and a few private teachers offered musical training to their children, but few musicians, music teachers, or dealers survived long in Pittsburgh.[14] Literary diversion was even scarcer: an almost bankrupt library association, an occasional lecture, and a small Philomathic Club which debated topics of moral and political concern.[15]

Perhaps elite culture was not utterly austere, but neither was it full or free. With no museums or galleries, no orchestra or musical societies, no night life or club society, no literary or artistic circles, opportunities for establishing bonds of sociability and solidarity among the "natural kings of Pittsburgh"[16] were severely limited. With neither the trappings of elegant culture nor the customary duty to serve as patrons of plebeian culture, the elite lacked local status commensurate with their wealth. With a few notable exceptions, Pittsburgh's leading industrialists remained simply rich men. The very ethic which bound them to hard work, self-discipline, and competitive individualism as marks of moral superiority prevented them from seizing upon the marks of cultural superiority which might have confirmed their class advantage. The Presbyterian elite was ill-suited to the role of patriciate.

However austere the cultural life of the upper classes, the bulk of Pittsburgh's citizens endured no such deprivation. On the contrary, plebeian culture was rich, varied, and relatively uninhibited. Especially after the iron works let out on Saturday afternoon, downtown Pittsburgh became the scene of "a decent carnival": "The principal streets are given over completely to the workman and his wife and sturdy little ones, who sally forth in their washed-up best to make their purchases and amuse themselves."[17] Noting the same scene, journalist James Parton added some detail to the picture: "They stroll about; they stand conversing in groups; they gather in semicircles, about every shop-window object; especially do they haunt the news-stands, which provide a free picture-gallery for them of Illustrated News, Comic Monthlies, and Funny Fellows."[18]

In addition to the newsstands, a number of art shops provided public galleries of original art. Pittsburgh was the center of a rather lively regional art network whose most talented figure was David Blythe. Blythe's genre renditions of local scenes—"humorous interiors and other kindred subjects"—appealed both to wealthy collectors and to the artist's cronies in the volunteer fire companies and the ironworkers' union, the Sons of Vulcan. His pictures regularly appeared in the window of J. J. Gillespie's art shop, where they became "the talk of the town and attracted such crowds that one could hardly get along the street." Similarly, Gillespie's announcement that "our fellow townsman W. C. Wall, Esq., has just completed a beautiful picture of Pack Saddle Gap" drew crowds to his window for days.[19]

Beyond the art shops, the Pittsburgh Exposition displayed an entire hall of local paintings once a year, which attracted large audiences. Moreover, ever-popular dioramas, panoramas, and cycloramas—painted scenes mounted on rolls or panels, usually portraying spectacular landscapes or historical events—filled halls for days at a time. Finally, at least one fire company maintained an art gallery open to the public.[20]

Music was as readily accessible as painting. Since the 1840s Pittsburgh had been "band conscious."[21] Soirees organized by fire and militia company bands were well-advertised and attended. On the banks of the Monongahela rival steamboats played calliopes and offered brass-band concerts. After 1860 the demand for band music was strong enough to support numerous professional bands. Some were hired for picnics, expositions, or Fourth of July celebrations, others for special subscription concerts. Bandleaders were men of humble origin, among them a barber turned saloonkeeper, a glassblower, a wood turner, a jeweler, and a man who was successively a tobacconist, foreman, and shoemaker. Although the trend was toward professionalization, most music making was performed by amateurs through the 1880s. Indeed, some kinds of amateur music making, such as barbershop singing, grew in popularity as the century wore on. Union balls, testimonials, and fund raisers always included music, usually traditional ballads, catches, and topical songs. On such occasions participant and spectator were often one and the same. Many members composed as well as sang, though some lodges had a special bard who turned out tunes on request. Some of these local songwriters and poets reached a wider audience through the newspapers, especially the *National Labor Tribune*, which regularly published poems and ballads written by and for workers.[22]

Within this plebeian culture, the local theatre occupied a central place. It was vernacular, full of variety, and responsive to local demand. In the midst of a welter of concert saloons, billiard halls, bowling alleys, and freak shows, the theatre served as a source of common imagery and an occasion of common experience for the city's plebs.[23]

The most striking feature of the theatre was its overwhelmingly plebeian and masculine audience. One account of the Saturday night theatre crowd emphasized both its size—an "army of ten thousand men"—and its social composition—"these workers in iron and steel and glass." Parton's description was, as usual, full of detail:

Not a woman was present. The place was packed with brawny men and noisy boys, all washed, all well-disposed, though half mad with joyous excitement. On the walls were posted such admonitions as these: "Hats off," "No hallooing or whistling allowed," "Applaud with your hands," . . . [but] the audience paid no heed to them whatever. The performances consisted of farces raised to the fiftieth power, comic songs, and legs. Never have we seen an audience so amusable. . . . We discovered here what the playbills mean when they speak of "roaring farces," and of farces that are "screaming."[24]

At a price of twenty-five cents or less, the variety show was the staple of the Pittsburgh stage. Offered at the legitimate houses as well as at the varieties, it appealed to a mixed, though predominantly lower-class, audience. Until the 1890s no theatre, legitimate or otherwise, could survive unless, as one manager explained, it drew regular support from "the working classes."[25] No theatre in Pittsburgh catered exclusively to a refined audience. However, the manner in which the *Pittsburgh Post* anticipated a local performance of Gounod's *Faust* on the night of May 11, 1863, suggests the existence of a delicate and informal code which allowed the elite occasional use of the public theatre: "In Pittsburgh— without wishing to make any invidious comparisons between different classes— there is a class who understand and thoroughly appreciate the difficult music of the opera. Their tastes are cultivated and refined." As if on cue, a "large and fashionable audience" attended the following night. But such events were rare. The few distinguished citizens who chose to attend the theatre had normally to sit alongside, or nearby, an audience of craftsmen, laborers, and "urchins" of all kinds. And they had to take their Shakespeare—if that is what they sought— with a large dose of spectacle, melodrama, and farce.[26]

Intended to provide something for everyone, theatre programs were exceptionally varied. To compete with the caravans, circuses, and menageries which regularly came to town, the theatre offered plenty of spectacle. To compete with the dioramas and panoramas, it offered historical tableaux. To compete with the saloon, it filled its bills with songs, comic skits, and farces, and opened its own bar at intermission. Finally, it offered what only the theatre could provide, the staple of the nineteenth-century stage, melodrama.

There was some differentiation in programming between the varieties and the legitimates. At the former the emphasis was on "low"—song and dance, farce, and the likes of "M'lle Marie Zoe, the beautiful Cuban Sylph." At the latter "high" drama appeared with some frequency, but even the most respectable houses varied the programs and filled them with the same sketches and mimes that dominated the variety show. A look at programming in the months of October and November 1882 reveals the variety and scope of entertainment in the legitimate theatres in Pittsburgh.[27] Within that period Library Hall ran successively high-toned melodrama (including the inevitable *East Lynne*), comic opera, minstrels, and melodrama again. At the same time the Opera House went from Haverly's Consolidated Mastadon Minstrels to *King Lear*, with the usual assortment of varieties in between. In both these houses short comic skits and musical routines opened, closed, and punctuated the bills. Mixed programs allowed them to compete with Trimble's Varieties and Harry Williams's Academy of Music. Moreover, the legitimates made their melodramatic offerings as sensational as possible. Execrated by critics, those "cut-throat dramas" filled with "railroad collisions and steamboat collisions" and with "women in unmentionables" satisfied the plebeian taste for action and excitement. Special effects, animals, and numerous female extras bolstered the legitimates' appeal to audiences which might otherwise choose such amusement as that offered at Harris's Mammoth Museum. Opened in 1883, the museum programmed an occasional melodrama or comic opera in a schedule packed with "Midgets," "YOUNG AJAX, the Boy Serpent," "MARVELLE, Prince of Magic," "Hurtt's Baby Quartette," "Charles Tripp, the armless wonder," and the like.

If the exotic and spectacular drew plebeian audiences, however, so did the homely and familiar. Indeed, among the more distinctive features of theatrical programming in the years between 1860 and 1890 was the extent to which melodrama and comedy were based on local and working-class themes. They were, like London music hall fare, "both escapist *and yet* strongly rooted in the realities of working-class life."[28]

"The pieces are local" was an advertisement that most theatres counted on to draw an audience.[29] Comedies like *Two Brides of Allegheny* and *Did You Ever Send Your Wife to Oakland?* (shown at the Pittsburgh Theatre in 1876) and melodramas like *Pittsburgh by Gaslight* (shown at Trimble's in 1867) successfully adapted well-known formulas to local tastes. Local playwrights such as Bartley Campbell and David Lowry portrayed the lives of mill owners, craftsmen, and laborers. In so doing, they often provoked cries of recognition and delight from the gallery.

Ethnic characterizations enjoyed wide appeal. Specialists in Irish and German types regularly presented their sympathetic, if sometimes ridiculous, portrayals at the legitimates, varieties, and saloons. In so doing they ratified the fact that these immigrants, who had faced nativist hostility as recently as the 1850s, had become better integrated into the city—its skilled trades, commerce, and politics. Far less sympathetic was the treatment of Negro characters—although outside the minstrel show and with the notable exception of *Uncle Tom's Cabin*, any treatment of blacks was rare.

In *The Story of a Coal Miner*, *The Workmen of Pittsburgh*, *The Boss*, and *Our Boarding House*, Pittsburgh's working man saw not only familiar types but also familiar settings. For example, *The Workmen of New York; or, The Curse of the Drink* retold the familiar temperance story of ruin and resurrection with attention to the everyday conditions of industrial work. As staged at the Pittsburgh, "the interior [was] of an extensive machine shop, in which are shown huge furnaces, glowing with heat, crowds of busy workmen, and the ponderous machinery . . . complete in all its details." Such shows were not realistic—indeed, the light they cast on ordinary life was often absurdly sentimental. Nonetheless, for the materials with which to inhabit the moralistic formula and the romantic cliché, they turned not to antiquity or to exotic locales but to the recognizable milieu of the working-class city.

Pittsburgh theatres hewed closely to the tastes of their plebeian audience in part because of the nature of theatrical organization in the era before the rise of national syndicates. Managers like William Henderson and John Ellsler were actor-entrepreneurs whose sole business was local or regional entertainment. They maintained resident stock companies whose stars claimed loyal followings and whose familiarity with the common life around them gave their skits and characterizations special appeal. Actors were well known about town, and they often incorporated into their acts suggestions heard on street corners or in saloons and barber shops. Such managers and actors are perhaps best seen as craftsmen. They were capable of putting together topical shows, such as those dramatizing events of the Civil War, at a few days' notice. The distinction between manager, actor, and stagehand was slight or nonexistent. The Ellsler family, which dominated theatrical entertainment in Pittsburgh and Cleveland in the 1870s, performed at one time or another almost every function required of the company on and off stage. Members of Henderson's Pittsburgh Theatre company did likewise.[30]

Nothing illustrates the character and function of the plebeian theatre better than the 1878 production of Bartley Campbell's *The Lower Million*. The play depicts events of the great riot of 1877. Its setting is a Pittsburgh iron mill. When the mill owner treats a workers' committee with contempt, the workers strike and join the crowd in the streets. The play's hero, Frank Farwell, is a mechanic and aspiring inventor who is loved—and whose inventions are financed—by the mill owner's daughter. The villain is Gilbert, who wants to seize control of both the mill and the mill owner's daughter. These are stock characters, as are Gilhooley, the Irish worker, and Geister, the German. But their very simplicity and conventionality allowed men like Ellsler to set them in motion in such a way as to register, with extraordinary immediacy, the state of public judgment upon questions of great moment. Thus Farwell and his ethnic comrades "stand up for the workingmen's rights" at the same time that they expose Gilbert's plot and save the mill owner from ruin. In the end Farwell wins not only the mill owner's daughter but also his respect and, not least, his concession to new terms in the mill. Among the numerous judgments made along the way, one stands out: the skilled craftsman is the key to the industrial system in the iron city; he is the link to all varieties of working men and the savior of honest management as well.

The Lower Million was John Ellsler's major production of the 1878 season at the Fifth Avenue Lyceum, and it was a big success. Elaborately staged, employing the full stock company and scores of extras (including, by one account, "veteran rioters from the strike"),[31] it was one of the fullest expressions of the plebeian theatrical taste which Pittsburgh's working class cultivated and helped shape in the post–Civil War years. It displayed many characteristics that made the theatre so central a part of the plebeian culture: an intimate acquaintance with local events and personalities; an idealization of the common man and a sympathy for republican and craftsmanly values; and an inclusiveness and accessibility that made each theatrical event itself, regardless of content, an enactment of plebeian community.

By the end of the century, the plebeian theatre had vanished along with the plebeian community that had nurtured it. Already in the late 1870s, the local managers and stock companies had begun to feel the competition of traveling shows and nascent syndicates. In 1879 the last company disbanded, and John Ellsler, who had referred to it as his "acting school," left the city for Cleveland.

In his place, two successors eventually emerged: first, the managers of new and fancier theatres, who funtioned essentially as booking agents for legitimate and vaudeville syndicates; and second, marginal entrepreneurs who relied on cheap liquor and free-lance acts of an inferior stripe. To make sense of the fluid and chaotic theatrical scene in the latter decades of the century, however, one must note the social and economic changes that were remaking the audiences for entertainment in Pittsburgh.

The growth of cities and of railroads and other industries created vast new markets for iron and steel in the post–Civil War period. By the late 1870s and 1880s, that expansion had generated immense new fortunes and a more intense search for productive methods. While the former phenomenon meant more surplus capital for bourgeoise Pittsburghers to spend on leisure, the latter meant the end of the craft-dominated iron era and the onset of the steel era, in which proletarianized work was performed by new immigrants and supervised by a growing army of clerical, technical, and supervisory personnel.[32] The heightened disparity in wealth, the relative decline of the craft elite, and the flood of southern and eastern European immigrants spurred a rapid spatial reorganization of life in Pittsburgh. Most of the professional and clerical middle class followed the steel barons to new streetcar suburbs while the old wards turned into proletarian slums surrounding a commercial core.[33]

Among the first cultural consequences of this social reorganization was the emergence of a more class-conscious and expressive bourgeois culture.[34] In their new professionally decorated east-end homes, the wealthy rapidly abandoned their old austerity. They installed Pittsburgh's first generation of such modern conveniences as indoor plumbing, gas furnaces, electrical appliances, and telephones. They also began to give gracious, catered parties and to entertain themselves with Merry Twelve Socials, Tuesday Musical Clubs, euchre parties, and the like. Elizabeth Moorhead traces the evolution of one form of domestic entertainment, the amateur theatrical, from the "strictly censored" Shakespeare Reading Club to the "more frivolous" Crusaders and, finally, around 1890, to the Tuesday Night Club, which was "more elaborate than the Crusaders, for Pittsburgh society was progressing in sophistication and made greater demands."[35] Beyond the domestic sphere, the elite erected great Gothic churches and hired professional organists and directors who not only revived the great traditions of church music but also transformed the secular music life of the city. In response to such demands "New York" theatres were built in the 1890s and the early twentieth century.

The theatrical building wave represented a cultural step beyond the creation of an "Edenic circle" in the bourgeois suburbs. Like the erection in 1895 of the Carnegie complex—music hall, art institute, and library—and the transformation of the Pittsburgh Exposition from a plebeian fair into an agency of corporate boosterism, theatre building gave institutional expression to a growing ambition on the part of upper- and middle-class Pittsburghers to impress cosmopolitan and progressive standards on the city and to link themselves with translocal networks of authority and consumption.[36] Industrialist Henry W. Oliver organized the financing and building of Pittsburgh's first elite theatres because he insisted that "the theater should be commensurate with the importance of Pittsburgh as he saw it."[37] The first fruits of this effort, the Nixon and Alvin theatres, gave Pittsburgh's steel masters and aspiring suburbanites what they wanted: "New York theatre," i.e., syndicated shows and great stars such as Maggie Mitchell, Laurence Barrett, Thomas Keene, and Sarah Bernhardt. Moreover, like the Gothic churches and the *belle epoque* Carnegie center, the new theatres offered architecture and design that was suitably foreign and grand: Moorish and rococo embellishments, velvet, gilt, and mahogany appointments, and no galleries. Unlike the inclusive plebeian theatre, which mixed touring shows and local productions and served a varied audience a varied fare, the new theatres served an exclusive audience intent upon the decorous but conspicuous consumption of "culture."

What happened to the older theatres and their audience?[38] Some of the managers tried to straddle the social cleavage which was fragmenting their audience. To maintain and expand their appeal to the respectable, they renovated the halls, introduced fancy decoration and electric lights, and advertised the virtues of vaudeville—the sanitized successor to the variety show. The latter was especially important in attracting women to the theatre. As managers tried to expand their market, however, they tried to hold on to skilled workers, shopkeepers, and other plebs who had always constituted the bulk of their audience. They fought a losing battle to keep ticket prices at twenty-five cents in the face of increased costs for renovations, celebrity acts, and escalating downtown rents. Whenever possible, they tried to identify themselves with the cause of organized labor (at least until the Homestead strike of 1892). Thus, during the Black Diamond strike of 1887–1888, the manager of the Grand Opera House granted free use of his theatre to the leaders of the Amalgamated Association of Iron and Steel Workers and donated the proceeds of a "first-class performance" to the strike fund. At the same time a rival manager—who liked to call his Bijou "the people's theater"—convinced several other managers to offer publicly "all assistance in their power" to the strikers.[39]

Despite these efforts, however, the older theatres could neither compete with their new rivals for the elite audience nor survive on the patronage of the increasingly hard-pressed and economically marginal skilled craftsmen and shopkeepers. Nor, finally, could they hope to attract to a more respectable and more expensive show the poor alien habitués of the saloons and ten-cent houses. While most of the Slavic immigrant communities rapidly developed the churches, lodges, and clubs that offered familiar and inexpensive entertainment to workers and their families, the bulk of Pittsburgh's unskilled labor force remained male, unattached, transient, and insecure. Whatever consolation they derived from ethnic festivals and organized activities was supplemented only by the few drinks and the bit of song and dance available for ten or twenty cents at the saloon.

Toward the end of the century, the few old theatres that were left in Pittsburgh faced additional competition from progressive leisure reformers who sought to lure immigrants and other workers into settlement houses, playgrounds, library extensions, YMCAs, and churches, and from welfare capitalists like Carnegie and Heinz, who sought to uplift the spirits and insure the loyalties of their employees by supplying a wide range of sporting, literary, musical, and theatrical entertainment free of charge. To most immigrants and workers, however, reformed leisure appeared anything but free. Preferring not to be "civilized" by Protestant reformers, they spent their precious leisure time with their countrymen and their precious money at the "free-and-easy."

By the end of the century, however, some of the immigrants who had first arrived in Pittsburgh in the late 1880s had won a limited foothold in the industrial city. They and their children comprised a large majority of the city's population and, in the eyes of a new breed of leisure entrepreneurs, a vast, potential market. But it was not a market for the old melodrama or for vaudeville, or even for burlesque, despite its militantly libertine and anti-elitist appeal. It was a market for the movies.

The historian Asa Briggs has noted that "the cinema did not so much divert an older audience from other kinds of entertainment as create an enormous new one."[40] Such was the case in Pittsburgh. With startling rapidity several new or transformed pastimes, including professional baseball and amusement parks, attracted the small change and the loyalty of the urban working class, but none so powerfully as the movies. When the *Pittsburgh Survey* investigated the lives of workers and their families in the first decade of the twentieth century, field investigators found themselves astonished at "the part these shows play in the life of the community." They were less surprised that children were "always begging for five cents to go to the nickelodeon" than that men and women of all ages, singly, as couples, and in family groups, regularly spent a few nickels or dimes on the moving pictures. However "hot and tired and irritable" they appeared on the long lines outside movie houses, they were "willing to wait" and "determined to be amused."[41]

Such determination did not escape the notice of the ambitious, small-time operators who invested a little capital in the storefront, a few nickelodeons, and as many one-reelers as they could get their hands on. More prosperous entrepreneurs, such as John P. Harris, whose museum had been the most successful ten-cent house in Pittsburgh (and who would soon be elected to the state senate), quickly sensed the trend and erected "the first all-motion picture theater" in America. Newspapers began advertising and reviewing movies, and in 1905 the Pittsburgh *Post* ran a series explaining to an interested public the process of filmmaking. And by 1915, the *National Labor Tribune* of Pittsburgh was celebrating Charlie Chaplin as "a national hero, whose funny hat, walk, cane, and mustache are now better known than the prayer book."[42]

Movies drove the final nail into the coffin of popular theatre in Pittsburgh. The syndicates had driven out the local stock companies and managers, the new bourgeoisie had withdrawn to respectable palaces, and the core audience of craftsmen and shopkeepers had been overwhelmed and fragmented by industrial and spatial reorganization. Finally, the new immigrants were won over to a new form of entertainment that was immediately comprehensible, fast-paced, escapist, and, at least for a time, unreformed.

The infant medium could not offer spectators the advantages of the old plebeian theatre, namely, responsiveness to local and everyday experience, a sense of community between audience and performers, or the sheer variety of performances, from Shakespeare to slapstick, from topical melodrama to farce, from jugglers to minstrels. On the other hand, these virtues can be exaggerated. The plebeian theatre never included the lowest ranks of the working class. Furthermore, as entertainment or inspiration, the bulk of melodrama, comedy, song and dance may have offered its audience little that was deep or lasting. Moreover, the movies quickly revealed their own virtues. Certainly in Charlie Chaplin the new, urban working class must have recognized its own hero. His absurdly unconquerable dignity—in the face of reformers, bosses, and cheats, and in spite of the caprices of chance and his own ungovernable impuses—must have given hope to an audience badly in need of a sense of possibilities. And this was a task that neither the plebeian stage, which had been shaped by a very different audience, nor its theatrical successors, which catered to a fragmented one, could perform as well.

NOTES

1. On industrial craftsmen in the nineteenth century, see David Montgomery, "Workers' Control of Machine Production in the Nineteenth Century," *Labor History*, 17 (Fall 1976), 485–509; Francis G. Couvares, "Work, Leisure and Reform in Pittsburgh: The Transformation of an Urban Culture, 1860–1920" (Diss., University of Michigan, 1980), chapter 1 (a revised version is forthcoming from the State University of New York Press); in "Beyond Class: The Decline of Industrial Labor and Leisure," *Telos*, 28 (Summer 1976), 55–80, John Alt overstates the autonomy of craft-related culture within the industrial city, in an otherwise enlightening discussion.

2. Couvares, chapter 2; see E. P. Thompson, "Patrician Society, Plebeian Culture," *Journal of Social History*, 7 (Summer 1974), 382–405. I use the term *plebeian* because what I am describing is a culture that is neither bourgeois nor proletarian, though it does include a "horizontal solidarity" whose center of gravity is among industrial craftsmen and the bulk of whose members are workers. While I borrow the term from Thompson, I need to qualify its usage here. The term connotes here, as in Thompson's article, the predominance of vernacular as opposed to refined forms of expression, and the importance of customary pastimes (more so in eighteenth-century England than in nineteenth-century America, however) and commercial amusements. Also like the eighteenth-century English variety, Pittsburgh's plebeian culture was neither "protorevolutionary" nor "deferential." Unlike the former, however, the latter was not "the other side of the medal" of hegemonic elite culture. Indeed it was toward hegemony that the steel elite was moving in the latter years of the century, but until that time there was nothing resembling a patriciate in Pittsburgh.

3. On the walking city, see Sam Bass Warner, *Streetcar Suburbs: The Process of*

Growth in Boston 1870–1900 (Cambridge, 1962), pp. 15–21; on Pittsburgh, Joel A. Tarr, *Transportation Innovation and Changing Spatial Patterns: Pittsburgh, 1850–1910* (Washington, D.C., 1972), pp. 1–5, and Couvares, chapter 1. On merchants of leisure, see Gareth Stedman Jones, "Class Expression versus Social Control? A Critique of Recent Trends in the Social History of 'Leisure,'" *History Workshop*, 4 (Autumn 1977), 163–70.

   4. See Neil Harris, "Four Stages of Cultural Growth: The American City," *Indiana Historical Society Lectures: History and the Role of the City in American Life* (Indianapolis, 1972). Harris's second stage corresponds closely to this description of plebeian culture in Pittsburgh; see also Russel Nye, *The Unembarrassed Muse: The Popular Arts in America* (New York, 1970), introduction and part 2.

   5. In James Parton, "Pittsburgh," *Atlantic Monthly* (January 1868), 31–32.

   6. Ibid., p. 19; George H. Thurston, *Pittsburgh as It Is* (Pittsburgh, 1857), p. 37; Ralph Keeler and Harry Fenn, "The Taking of Pittsburgh . . . Part IV," *Every Saturday* (25 March 1871), 274.

   7. John N. Ingham, "The American Urban Upper Class: Cosmopolitans or Locals?" *Journal of Urban History*, 2 (November 1975), 70–75, and "Rags to Riches Revisited: The Effect of City Size and Related Factors on the Recruitment of Business Leaders," *Journal of American History*, 63 (December 1976), 618–21, 624–27, 634; see also Parton, p. 32; Elizabeth Moorhead, *Whirling Spindle: The Story of a Pittsburgh Family* (Pittsburgh, 1942), p. 208.

   8. Clarence E. Macartney, *Right Here in Pittsburgh* (Pittsburgh, 1937), pp. 32–33; *Christian Advocate*, 12 July 1877, 10 November 1887. See also C. F. C. Arensberg, "The Pittsburgh Fire of April 10, 1845," *Western Pennsylvania Historical Magazine* (hereafter *WPHM*), 28 (March–June 1945), 13.

   9. Pittsburgh Central High School, *Class Book of 1880* (Pittsburgh, 1906), pp. 77–80.

   10. Moorhead, pp. 262–69.

   11. William G. Johnston, *Life and Reminiscences from Birth to Manhood* (New York, 1901), pp. 114, 162, 166–71.

   12. Moorhead, pp. 251–56; Shakespeare Reading Club Programs, Historical Society of Western Pennsylvania (hereafter HSWP).

   13. The unassertiveness of Pittsburgh's social elite is in contrast with the large public role played by other urban elites. In Boston at midcentury, for example, "no serious disagreement as to the utility of culture for business families" hindered the shaping of "a durable (and worthy) upper class within a capitalist order": Ronald Story, "Class and Culture in Boston: The Atheneum, 1807–1869," *American Quarterly*, 27 (May 1975), 178–99. On the decline in the public role of older mercantile elites, see M. J. Heale, "From City Fathers to Social Critics: Humanitarianism and Government in New York 1790–1860," *Journal of American History*, 63 (June 1976), 21–41. By 1880 Philadelphia possessed Academies of Fine Arts, Music, and Natural Science, a library, Philosophical Society, and the famous Franklin Institute: Edwin Wolf II, *Philadelphia: Portrait of an American City* (Harrisburg, 1975), p. 248. Yet these were the product of an old elite whose cultural and political functions had already splintered by 1860: Sam Bass Warner, *The Private City: Philadelphia in Three Periods of Its Growth* (Philadelphia, 1968), chapter 5.

   14. A review of city directories from 1860 to 1880 reveals very little occupational or residential persistence among such musical personnel. On the Pittsburgh music scene see

the early chapter of Edward G. Baynham, "A History of Pittsburgh Music, 1758–1958" (Manuscript, Carnegie Library of Pittsburgh, 1970).

15. Records of the Philomathic Club may be found in the George L. Hailman Family Papers, HSWP; Donald M. Goodfellow, "Centenary of a Pittsburgh Library," *WPHM*, 31 (March–June 1948), 21–25.

16. Parton, p. 35.

17. Keeler and Fenn, p. 274.

18. Parton, pp. 35–36; see also *Post*, 27 May 1863. Robert Layton, of the Knights of Labor, decried the Sunday draping of these windows since they constituted an important part of working-class recreation: U. S. Senate Committee on Education and Labor, *Report Upon the Relations Between Labor and Capital* (Washington, D.C., 1885), 1:31.

19. On Blythe see Bruce W. Chambers, *The World of David Gilmour Blythe (1815–1865)*, exhibition catalog (Washington, D.C. 1980); Dorothy Miller, *The Life and Works of David Blythe* (Pittsburgh, 1950); John O'Connor, Jr., "David Gilmour Blythe, Artist," *WPHM*, 27 (March–June 1944), 29–36; David G. Wilkins, *Art in Nineteenth-Century Pittsburgh*, exhibition catalog (Pittsburgh, 1977). See also Dorothy Daniel, "The Sanitary Fair," *WPHM*, 41 (Summer 1958), 154–60; Thurston, p. 202; *Post*, 14 June 1863.

20. Charles T. Dawson, *Our Firemen: A History of the Pittsburgh Fire Department* (Pittsburgh, 1889), p. 120; *Daily Gazette*, 23 February 1850; *Commercial Gazette*, 18 October and 16 November 1886; Nye, pp. 186–88; *National Labor Tribune* (hereafter *NLT*), 8 July 1876; *Christian Advocate*, 19 July 1877.

21. Couvares, pp. 69–71.

22. See the famous "March of the Rolling Mill Men," by Reese E. Lewis, published 30 March 1875 ("Rouse, ye noble sons of Labor/ And protect your country's honor,/ Who with bone, and brain, and fibre,/ Make the nation's wealth."). There were other ways to circulate poetry in Pittsburgh. For example, one finds the case of "John (Jack) McKee, an eccentric character well known throughout Pittsburgh as the Poet of Bayardstown. If you refused to buy his poems, usually printed on long strips of paper, he became angry and berated you as illiterate and no good," in P. W. Siebert, "Old Bayardstown," *WPHM*, 9 (April 1926), 92. See also George Korson, ed., *Pennsylvania Songs and Legends* (Philadelphia, 1949) pp. 426–27; John W. Bennett, "Iron Workers in Woods Run and Johnstown: The Union Era 1865–1895," (Diss., University of Pittsburgh, 1977), pp. 119–25; *NLT*, 1 April 1876 and 10 February 1877; *Commercial Gazette*, 15 November 1886.

23. See Nye, pp. 149–68, and David Grimsted, *Melodrama Unveiled: American Theater and Culture, 1800–1850* (Chicago, 1968), for a general discussion of the development of American theatre in the nineteenth century. The following account of theatre life in Pittsburgh draws heavily upon James A. Lowrie, "A History of the Pittsburgh Stage, 1861–1891," (Diss., University of Pittsburgh, 1943), especially pp. 1–142 and appendix I; another useful source is the file of nineteenth-century Pittsburgh theatre programs in the Pennsylvania Division, Carnegie Library of Pittsburgh. See also regular reviews in the *Post, Gazette, Commercial Gazette*, and *Evening Telegram*.

24. Parton, pp. 34–35; Keeler and Fenn, p. 274.

25. See comments of Harry Ellsler, treasurer of the Opera House quoted in Lowrie, p. 178; Johnston, pp. 112–14; *Gazette*, 17 August 1866.

26. See Andrew Carnegie, *Autobiography of Andrew Carnegie* (New York, 1920), pp. 26–50. On street urchins, see *Peoples Monthly* (February 1872), 143. See also Nye, pp. 188–91; *Post*, 27 May 1863, 24 June 1867.

27. *Commercial Gazette*, 13 October, 6 November, 7 November, and 8 November 1882; for further documentation see Couvares, pp. 72–79; for an interesting outsider's view of the nineteenth-century American stage, see Knut Hamsun, *The Cultural Life of Modern America* (Cambridge, 1969; originally published in Copenhagen, 1889), pp. 90–103.

28. Gareth Stedman Jones, "Working-Class Culture and Working-Class Politics in London, 1870–1900; Notes on the Remaking of a Working Class," *Journal of Social History*, 7 (Summer 1974), 491.

29. Concerning nineteenth-century melodrama, David Grimsted in *Melodrama Unveiled* has said: "It took the lives of common people seriously and paid much respect to their superior purity and wisdom. It elevated them often into the aristocracy, always into a world charged with action, excitement and a sense of wonder" (p. 248).

30. On Henderson's Pittsburgh Theater company see the A. B. Palmer Papers, HSWP; *Post*, 28 April 1863, 24 June and 28 June 1867; on the Ellslers see John A. Ellsler, *The Stage Memories of John A. Ellsler* (Cleveland, 1950), pp. 142, 144, 146, 157–58; William G. Rose, *Cleveland: The Making of a City* (Cleveland and New York, 1950), pp. 228, 259–60, 368, 382, 404–5, 479.

31. Cited in P. S. Klein and A. Hoogenboom, *A History of Pennsylvania* (New York, 1973), p. 354; see James J. Davis, *The Iron Puddler* (Indianapolis, 1922), pp. 68–70, for a description of popular involvement in the local theatre of Sharon, Pennsylvania.

32. See David Brody, *Steelworkers in America: The Nonunion Era* (Cambridge, 1960), chapters 3 and 4, and Couvares, chapter 4.

33. On the suburbanization of Pittsburgh, see Tarr, pp. 17–27, and Couvares, chapters 4 and 5; see also Robert J. Jucha, "Anatomy of a Streetcar Suburb: A Development History of Shadyside, 1852–1916," *WPHM*, 62 (October 1972), 301–20.

34. Couvares, chapter 5.

35. Moorhead, pp. 265, 269; see also Samuel J. Fisher, *Our Suburb* (Pittsburgh, n.d.).

36. Couvares, chapters 5 and 6. This ambition is reflected in the fact that, as the century progressed, children of the Pittsburgh elite increasingly attended finishing schools and Ivy League colleges and began marrying spouses from beyond the western Pennsylvania region; see Ingham, pp. 70–75.

37. Henry O. Evans, *Iron Pioneer: Henry W. Oliver, 1850–1905* (New York, 1942), p. 302.

38. See Couvares, chapter 6.

39. *Post*, 3 September 1887; *NLT*, 29 October, 19 November, 26 November 1887.

40. *Mass Entertainments: The Origins of a Modern Industry* (Adelaide, Australia 1960), p. 18. On Pittsburgh, see my essay, "The Triumph of Commerce," in *Working-Class History*, ed. D. Walkowitz and M. Frisch (Urbana-Champaign, 1982).

41. See especially Margaret Byington, *Homestead: The Households of a Mill Town* (New York, 1910), pp. 110–11, and Elizabeth B. Butler, *Women and the Trades* (New York, 1909), pp. 324, 333.

42. *NLT*, 11 November 1915; *Post*, 24 December 1905; Lowrie, pp. 170–74; George T. Fleming, *History of Pittsburgh and Environs* (Pittsburgh, 1922), 2:636–37. On the early history of film, see Robert Sklar, *Movie-Made America: A Cultural History of American Movies* (New York, 1975), chapters 1 and 2.

3

German-American Socialist Workers' Theatre, 1877–1900

Carol Poore

If we look beyond commonly held stereotypes of the German immigrant as being easily assimilable into a mainstream American society, we find another rich tradition of German-American history embodied by socialist immigrants whose political, economic, and cultural goals found strong resonance among German immigrant workers. From the radical-democratic forty-eighters, to political emigrés fleeing the repression of Bismarck's anti-Socialist laws, to immigrants radicalized by their disillusionment with America, German socialists constituted by far the most significant group of radicals in the nineteenth-century United States.[1]

These German-American socialists became involved in politics, trade union organization, and cultural activity both within and outside of the German community. Although they could claim only negligible success in electoral politics, they were extremely influential in the development of trade unionism because of the large base of skilled German immigrant workers. The socialist subculture which flourished in urban German-American working-class districts attested to their wide-ranging goals for social transformation.

This socialist subculture was composed of many elements. Its most important component was the thriving German-language socialist press which not only analyzed world, national, and local events from a socialist perspective, but also provided a communications network that tied the various elements of German socialist activity together. Socialist schools for children and adults (*Arbeiterbildungsvereine*) and labor lyceums were founded in many cities to counteract bourgeois religious and political doctrines, spread familiarity with socialist thought, and perpetuate the German language. Workers' singing societies, often begun out of dissatisfaction with the "philistinism" of other groups and a desire to perform songs of the workers' movement, eventually united to form regional branches of the *Arbeiter-Sängerbund von Nord-Amerika*, attracting thousands to their festivals held around the country. Finally, festivals, demonstrations, benefits, and commemorations helped to create an alternative sense of history and a perception of solidarity with workers of other ethnic groups.

German-American socialist workers' theatre should be viewed in the context of this socialist subculture as part of a general effort to create alternatives to the mainstream of German-American society. Plays by socialist authors were part of a large body of literature that was closely connected to socialist politics. It was a drama which differed fundamentally from that large portion of German-American literature which centered around the private sphere and affirmed existing social relationships. At the same time, these plays were not only examples of alternative literary expression, but they were also part of the more general effort to establish a socialist cultural movement in the German-American community.

The 1880s mark the high point of this socialist subculture, which diminished in extent and importance after the turn of the century because of the Americanization of the socialist movement, the decrease in the number of German immigrants, their assimilation into the English-speaking world around them, and finally, anti-German attitudes brought on by World War I.

The first indication of amateur theatrical activity among German-American socialists occurred in the spring of 1877. The New York *Volkszeitung* reported that the *Arbeiter-Bühne* (Workers' Stage), directed by August Otto-Walster, was performing Max Kegel's *Preßprozesse* (*The Press on Trial*) and Otto-Walster's *Die Staatsretter* (*Saviors of the State*).[2] Performances by local socialist theatre groups soon became a popular feature of mass meetings and festivals in other large cities such as Brooklyn, Cincinnati, Louisville, Chicago, St. Louis, and Milwaukee and in many smaller towns too numerous to mention.[3] These theatre groups were affiliated in various ways with socialist political organizations, either as local sections of the Socialist Labor party or as politically more heterogeneous groups sympathetic to socialism. Most were small clubs of a dozen or so members who met once or twice a month in the evenings to give dramatic readings, skits, comic routines, and productions of short plays which demanded a minimum of acting talent and stage props. Like the amateur theatrical activity which was a popular pastime in non-socialist immigrant circles, these theatre groups served to provide entertainment in the small amount of leisure time remaining after work to both actors and audience—entertainment which provided an enjoyable distraction from the rigors and conflicts of the working day. Accordingly, the majority of plays in the repertoire of these theatres were the same second-rate farces and comedies that could be seen any evening in immigrant clubrooms, and these plays were performed for the entertainment of relatives and friends during a social evening. For example, one dramatic group reported that in order to satisfy everyone's taste, it would perform two "political plays," two "popular plays," and two "farces"during the season—a typical repertory.[4]

Building on the popularity of productions aimed mainly at entertainment, German socialists established workers' theatres to spread fundamental ideas of socialism in an entertaining way and to offer models for action and images of a better future. They hoped thereby to attract an audience that might be less receptive to political lectures, that perhaps did not read the socialist press, and that would be difficult to approach in other ways. These goals set socialist theatrical groups apart from other amateur theatres of the time as well as from professional German-American theatre troupes. As an article on "The Amateur Stage" in the New York *Sozialist* stated in 1892:

We are of the opinion that such political plays are of the greatest value for spreading our ideas to larger groups of the population who, for obvious reasons, do not and cannot show *such* an interest in and comprehension of theoretical lectures, as we might wish for the sake of the cause.[5]

Other reports also mention the desired agitational effect, and statements can be found in the socialist press that new members joined party sections after seeing such performances.

Most often, for reasons of convenience, these groups chose simply to perform the small number of available plays by German Social-Democratic writers such as J. B von Schweitzer or Max Kegel. Some party members and performers, however, wrote and produced their own plays. A survey of the German-American socialist press reveals approximately fifty such plays written before 1900, almost all consisting of one act and a minimal number of characters to suit the needs and talents of the small amateur groups. Unfortunately, most of the manuscripts received no distribution to other socialist groups beyond the circle of their authors' immediate activity, so only the titles or very brief descriptions can be found.

In addition to these short plays, festival plays (*Festspiele*), including Ludwig Geißler's *Allegorisches Weihnachtsfestspiel* (*Allegorical Christmas Festival Play*, ca. 1880) and the anonymous *Die Nihilisten* (*The Nihilists*, 1882), performed to commemorate the Paris Commune, were written for special occasions. While the festival plays as a form can be traced to the Middle Ages and were often used to serve patriotic, nationalistic purposes in the nineteenth century, socialists wrote their own festival plays to reinterpret traditional festivals such as Christmas or to celebrate historical events of significance to the working class.

Finally, tableaux (*lebende Bilder*) often formed a popular and important part of festivals and celebrations. These tableaux were particularly well suited for dramatizing blatant social contrasts or providing schematic representations of historical progress. Thus, they often illustrated themes such as the life of the poor and the life of the rich, the proletariat in the past, present, and future, historical subjects such as the Paris Commune, or the exploitation of black and white wage workers.[6] Like the festival play, tableaux dated from the Middle Ages, when they were employed to portray religious subjects such as the manger scene. In the eighteenth and nineteenth centuries, they enjoyed popularity in aristocratic circles in Germany. In all of these instances, socialists took over traditional forms and adapted them to suit their own purposes.

Several prominent German-American socialists took an interest in developing theatre as a means of political agitation, including August Otto-Walster, Wilhelm Rosenberg and, perhaps surprisingly, the Social-Democrat-turned-anarchist Johann Most. In the late 1870s and early 1880s, Otto-Walster, delegate of the German Social Democratic party to the final conference of the First International held in Philadelphia, traveled to New York, St. Louis, and Cincinnati establishing workers' theatres and providing them with his own one-act plays.[7] His dramas, including *Ein verunglückter Agitator* (*The Misfortunes of an Agitator*), *Die Staatsretter* (*Saviors of the State*), and *In eigener Falle* (*In His Own Trap*), were among the most popular selections in socialist workers' theatres. Rosenberg, head of the Socialist Labor party for a time in the 1880s and the most prolific German-American socialist author, wrote approximately a dozen short plays, some meant expressly for workers' theatres and situated in an American context.[8] Johann Most helped to develop amateur theatre through his activities as an actor and producer.[9] Having always had an ambition to act, Most undertook to establish workers' theatres, which he called *Freie Bühnen* (free stages), in his travels to New York, Chicago, and San Francisco. The first play performed by these groups was always Gerhard Hauptmann's *Die Weber* (*The Weavers*), with Most himself playing the role of Old Baumert. In New York and Chicago, these amateur theatres were able to sustain themselves for several years by continuing to give performances of *Die Weber* and other naturalist dramas. Most's reputation as a dangerous anarchist led to the only discoverable instance of police interference in German-American socialist theatrical activity at this time. In an article captioned "*Die Weber* a Threat to the State," the New York *Volkszeitung* reported on October 29, 1894, that a Newark performance by the New York *Freie Bühne* had been forbidden by the Newark police. The police chief explained his motivation:

We are living in a time of great upheaval. In the fourth precinct 1000 strikers have been out of work for nine weeks, their families are starving, and therefore I think it is dangerous to allow an agitator like John Most to stir them up any more. If he dares to speak here, I will arrest him.[10]

The majority of plays by German-American socialist writers did not deal with a specifically American milieu. Instead, playwrights continued to take their material from European situations or to portray generalized conflicts applicable to any industrializing country. Preferred techniques to enlighten their audience included long, didactic monologues on political and economic themes and the stereotyping of opposing characters—the good worker versus the evil capitalist, for example. These plays, then, were often like well-prepared lectures. Also, the stereotypical or allegorical depiction of conflict was often based on moralistic criteria which did not reflect specific social situations. The opposition of good and evil forces and the frequent use of images taken from nature to characterize capitalist oppression (night), revolution (storm), and the socialist future (day) meant that the process of social change was presented more as an inexorable development independent of human activity than as a process that was initiated by people proceeding from their understanding of history, their present needs, and their visions of the future.

Although most of these plays did not deal concretely with situations that their audience faced in daily life and remained abstract in their theoretical expositions and appeals for action, there were, however, a few plays by German-American socialist writers that dealt with significant issues in American society. These include Wilhelm Rosenberg's *Crumbleton* (1898), concerned with corruption in business and industry, and Gustav Lyser's *Congreß zur Verwirrung der Arbeiterfrage in New-York* (*Congress for the Muddling-Up of the Labor Question in New York*).[11] This latter dramatic sketch, published in the Chicago newspaper *Vorbote* in 1878, vividly expresses the disillusionment felt by many immigrants in the New World and attempts to expose the economic foundations of the inequities they encountered. However, such plays remained the exception in the repertoire of the amateur socialist theatrical groups.

Of all the plays written by German-American socialists, the one that was reviewed most extensively in their press was *Die Nihilisten* (*The Nihilists*), a festival play written for the Commune Festival of Social-Revolutionaries in Chicago in 1882. In their list of proscribed publications, authorities enforcing the anti-Socialist laws in Germany attributed this play to August Spies, but it seems more likely that two journalists living in Chicago, Wilhelm Rosenberg and Paul Grottkau, were the authors.[12] Rosenberg and Grottkau were active socialists, and the Chicago actors in the production, including the Haymarket martyrs August Spies and Oskar Neebe, were also connected with socialist groups. The play was the main event at the yearly Paris Commune festival sponsored by the Socialistic Publishing Company for the benefit of its press. This was a typical use of such festival plays and theatrical presentations—to raise money for the party, the press, election funds, or comrades in need.

The Chicago socialists had a special admiration for the Russian Nihilists, who formed a nucleus of opposition to czardom and finally assassinated Alexander II in 1881. The festival play *Die Nihilisten*, written and performed one year later, deals with this group of revolutionaries. In the first act, which takes place in their secret headquarters, the Nihilists are printing their proclamations and discussing their vision of Russia after its liberation from tyranny. Members of the aristocracy and the military gather to plan the suppression of the nihilists in act 2. Next, the Nihilists, having been arrested, their leaflets confiscated, are placed on trial. Accused of treason, they make speeches to the court, accusing the accusers and explaining how their perception of social injustice drove them to nihilism. Finally, in the last act, the Nihilists have been condemned to exile and are on their way to Siberia through the desolate winter landscape. Just when they are beginning to lose hope, their comrades rescue them, killing the cossack guards and announcing that Czar Alexander has been killed according to the will of the people. Amid cheers for the Nihilists, the play closes with the following appeal:

Rise up, brothers, from the humiliation of bondage, close your ranks, and go forward like heroes, with common resolve. And when you all sharpen the sword of revenge on the sorrow of your sufferings, the spirit of freedom will hasten the hour of social revolution and the coming of a new era.[13]

According to the socialist press, performances of this play were meant to serve several functions. The first was didactic; to transmit historical information and to educate the audience about the nihilistic movement.[14] In this regard, the audience was encouraged to make connections between the goals of the revolutionaries portrayed on stage and their own situation. This connection was shown concretely in the performance by casting members of the armed socialist organization of Chicago, the *Lehr- und Wehr-Verein* (Educational and Defense Society), as the armed rescuers of the nihilists in the last act.[15] Thus the appeal just quoted takes on the character of a direct address to the audience, and the call to raise the "sword of revenge" is given a contemporary ring. The defense speeches of the Nihilists in the court, their attacks on tyranny and their program for the future, were also meant as statements of the Chicago socialists' goals. According to one of the main socialist newspapers of Chicago, the *Arbeiter-Zeitung*, "The defense speeches of the prisoners are completely objective and nevertheless have an idealistic tendency, which moves the spectator involuntarily to indignation at prevailing injustice and enthusiasm for the cause of humanity."[16]

Finally, these socialists also understood attendance at the presentation of *Die Nihilisten* as a public statement of commitment to revolutionary goals and as furthering the creation of an alternative, progressive view of history. As the announcement for this 1882 Commune Festival states, it was important that all friends of progress and freedom attend the production, "so that the ruling classes come to understand that the spirit of those martyrs, who met an untimely death at the hands of the executioner, pervades humanity with ever increasing intensity and power."[17] Groups associated with Johann Most and the anarchist International Working People's Association, who understood the message of the play as a call to carry out acts of terrorism, continued to perform the play at festivals in Chicago and elsewhere.[18]

German-American socialist workers' theatre never went beyond the level of amateur performances, and, unlike the development in Germany after about 1900, no groups of socialist authors began to write plays which might have been performed by professional theatres.[19] There were only scattered efforts by socialist groups to engage professional theatre companies to perform plays such as Schiller's *Die Räuber* (*The Robbers*) or contemporary, naturalistic dramas like *Die Weber* for a working-class audience. German-American amateur theatres continued to exist into the 1930s within the framework of the Socialist party. These groups selected most of their plays from the standard non-socialist repertoire for amateur theatre, or they chose political plays that were being published in Germany.[20] This amateur socialist theatre, then, remained a matter of local initiative involving small numbers of participants with the consequence that the production of original plays declined. It was only with the formation of the *Prolet-Buehne*, an agitprop troupe associated with the Communist party performing in New York in the late twenties and early thirties, that a German-American workers' theatre was formed which created its own material collectively and entered into productive contact with other troupes, including native-American ones.[21]

The importance of this immigrant socialist workers' theatre in its own time as well as for our rediscovery of it today lies not so much in the individual works it produced as in its place within the multi-faceted effort to create alternative possibilities for cultural expression involving the restructuring of daily life and political participation. The German-American socialist movement advocated the democratization of theatre and other previously elite areas of cultural activity such as literature and classical music. Even as immigrants were mostly prevented by the language barrier from entering into debate with the dominant English-speaking majority, these socialists still developed alternatives to the cultural institutions of the more prosperous and establishment-oriented German-Americans.

NOTES

1. See my dissertation on *German-American Socialist Literature in the Late Nineteenth Century* (University of Wisconsin, 1979). For analyses of socialist workers' theatre in Germany and reprints of works, see the following: Friedrich Knilli and Ursula Münchow, *Frühes sozialistisches Arbeitertheater, 1847–1918* (Munich, 1970); Peter von Rüden, *Sozialdemokratisches Arbeitertheater, 1848–1914* (Frankfurt, 1973); Gerald Stieg and Bernd Witte, *Abriß einer Geschichte der deutschen Arbeiterliteratur* (Stuttgart, 1973); Zentralinstitut für Literaturgeschichte der Akademie der Wissenschaften der DDR, *Textausgaben zur frühen sozialistischen Literatur in Deutschland*, ed. Ursula Munchow (Berlin, 1964).

2. For reports on the *Arbeiter-Bühne*, see the New York *Volkszeitung*, January 28, February 25, March 25, April 15, April 22, May 6, 1877.

3. The best source on the local activities of party sections around the country is *Der Sozialist*, the official organ of the *Sozialistische Arbeiter-Partei* (Socialist Labor party).

4. This was the "Dramatischer Verein 'Fortschritt,' " (Dramatic Club "Progress") in Newark. New York *Volkszeitung*, August 7, 1895, p. 4.

5. *Der Sozialist*, April 2, 1892, p. 3. I have translated this and all other quotations from the original German.

6. The following is a description of an elaborate tableau presented in Chicago at a workers' Fourth of July festival in 1876 on the occasion of the centennial:

The high point of the festival was the tableau on a revolving platform 28 feet high which depicted the old and the new world, the present situation of exploitation of man by man, and the goal of our efforts, the free, social people's state.

On the one side, the old world was portrayed as follows: On the first step, enslaved labor, workers of all kinds, some in chains, some bursting their chains and looking with longing over the sea, where a ship (socialism) with two sailors approaches them. The sailors hold a banner, equality and justice. On the second step, 7 feet higher, poverty and misery, a needy woman and child (poverty), and a woman (misery) pleading with an exploiter. The exploiter is setting a dog on the miserable figures. On the third step, 7 feet higher, the rule of money and priests. Two exploiters sitting on their moneybags, and above them a priest, blessing their shameful undertaking.

On the other side, separated by a wall from the old world, is the new world, the future of work. On the first step: agriculture (farmer with plow and horse) and family happiness, the family life of liberated humanity, glowing with happiness and content, free of need and cares. On the second step, 7 feet higher, industry, art and science as the common property of liberated humanity, portrayed by 3 women in Greek robes. On the third step, 7 feet higher, as the greatest good of humanity and the fundamental principle of the new world, justice and equality, portrayed by two women. Justice holds the scales and the sword, and freedom holds the red flag and the Jacobin cap.

The source for this description is the Chicago *Vorbote*, July 1, 1876, and July 8, 1876.

7. See *August Otto-Walster, Leben und Werk*, ed. Wolfgang Friedrich (Berlin, 1966).

8. I was able to locate the following plays by Rosenberg: *Crumbleton* (Cleveland, 1898), *Die Macht des Aberglaubens* (Cleveland, n.d.), *Der Spion* (Cleveland, n.d.), and *Vor der Wahlschlacht* (New York, 1887). I found references to the following plays by him which I could not locate: *Die Antwort dem Kaiser, Auf der Moralwage, Der Erfinder, Der Friedensstifter, Der Held von St. Juan Hill*, and *Wer trägt die Schuld?*

9. For Most's biography, see Rudolf Rocker, *Johann Most* (Berlin, 1924).

10. New York *Volkszeitung*, October 29, 1894, p. 1.

11. Cf. the translation of this play published by Heinz Ickstadt and Hartmut Keil, "A Forgotten Piece of Working-Class Literature: Gustav Lyser's Satire of the Hewitt Hearing of 1878," in *Labor History*, 20 (Winter 1979), 127–140.

12. I am indebted to Hartmut Keil for this information.

13. *Die Nihilisten* (Chicago, 1882), p. 19.

14. *Fackel*, March 12, 1882, p. 8.

15. Ibid.

16. Chicago *Arbeiter-Zeitung*, March 20, 1882, p. 4.

17. *Fackel*, March 12, 1882, p. 8.

18. St. Louis *Parole*, March 1885, p. 1.

19. For the development of workers' theatre in Germany during the Weimar Republic, see Ludwig Hoffmann and Daniel Hoffmann-Ostwald, *Deutsches Arbeitertheater 1918–1933*, 2 vols. (Munich, 1973).

20. An example of a socialist workers' theatre which performed almost solely those plays for workers' theatre which were published in Germany, was the group in Milwaukee. The Heinrich Bartel Collection at the Milwaukee County Historical Society contains listings of its repertoire.

21. Cf. Daniel Friedman, *The Prolet Buehne* (Diss., University of Wisconsin, 1978).

4

The Yiddish Theatre in New York: 1900

Mel Gordon

The relationship between the worsening social conditions brought about by the industrial revolution and the growing popularity of the stage melodrama in the first half of the nineteenth century is a relatively new concern. To be sure, the new working class's general acceptance of increasingly inhuman working and living circumstances—especially between 1810 and 1840—is well known. Overcrowding, disease, child labor, seventy-five-hour working weeks, cut wages—these are all trademarks of urban life in Western Europe and North America in the 1800s. Yet the resulting cultural shock and social malaise led not only to the disruption of communal ties and familial patterns that we would expect but also to an unending obsession with the melodrama.

Mediating between what working people wanted and what they experienced, the melodrama released a powerful psychic spring in the working-class imagination. Although its efficacy differed in various cultures, the melodrama shared a similar and ironclad format whenever it appeared: the forces of morality would always triumph over those of capital. And in the melodramatic ethos, the struggle of classes would be forever linked not just with property but with sexuality.

Most of our information about performances of melodramas is from the published texts themselves or descriptions of much later middle-class varieties. The few documents we have that describe the working-class melodramas, or penny gaffs, are usually illuminating as to the stage and audience behavior and deserve to be looked at more carefully.[1] But if actual scenic documentation of English, French, and German cheap melodramas is scarce, then material on Yiddish melodrama seems relatively abundant.

Begun in the 1870s in Rumania just when the industrial revolution started to make itself felt among eastern Europe's seven million Jews, the Yiddish melodrama reached its apogee around the turn of the century in New York's Lower

Like all contemporary writers on Yiddish theatre, I am indebted to Wolf Younin for original materials.

East Side, which became a ghetto to over 300,000 Yiddish-speaking Jews who were trapped by poverty and language. Working in garment factories, little industry sweatshops, in restaurants and brothels, and peddling on the streets, even the most unhappy Jews accepted the Lower East Side as their home because returning to their countries of origin was unthinkable. While the majority of the Jews came from small villages where the synagogue held cultural sway, once in the Lower East Side, the Yiddish theatre suddenly became their object of extreme—almost religious—devotion.

Presenting real-life detail within a fantasy structure, the Yiddish melodrama began to dominate the subconscious life of the Lower East Side. Writing in 1901, Hutchins Hapgood reported that "many a poor Jew, man or girl, who makes no more than $10 a week in the sweatshop, will spend $5 of it on the theatre."[2] For a great many Jews, the viewing of the Yiddish theatre, almost entirely devoted to melodramas then, became as important as the eating of bread. Both the intelligentsia and mass audiences spoke of theatre constantly. Even the editor-in-chief of the most influential Yiddish newspaper, the *Daily Forward*, doubled as a play reviewer.

Ted Thomas, the son of two well-known Yiddish actors, described this early melodramatic period of the stage: "The Yiddish theatre made the Left Bank of Paris look like a convent. There was every form of degeneration you can imagine: murder, suicide, drugs, sex deviations of all kinds. There were the emergent Jews, after years of living a Torah-cloistered existence, suddenly free—and drunk with it."[3]

But if melodrama was the single most popular genre on the Yiddish stage, historians, scholars, and translators at that time and after have downplayed its social and artistic merits. They called it *shund* (aesthetic trash) or "onion plays," because of its ability to draw tears, and nearly all of the Lower East Side's intellectuals and leading performers fought a life-and-death struggle against the cheap, "three-hankie" melodrama. By 1925, the literary, "thought-minded" performance won out, but at a terrible cost—the loss of the average Yiddish theatregoer.

Essentially, the Yiddish melodrama, like its English, French, and German counterparts, fell into one of several distinct varieties. The earliest kind—the historical spectacle, a mix of local color, adventure, threatened innocence, sacrifice, tangled sexuality, and tragedy—was also the most lavish in terms of costuming, stage effects, music, and language. Typically set in ancient Palestine or at the courts of Renaissance princes, the historical melodrama pitted the Jewish protagonist, usually a well-known figure, and his lover against a superior Gentile force. Much of the performance's pathos and irony was dependent on the spectators' historical knowledge of disaster. For instance, in Avrom Goldfadn's successful melodrama, *Bar Kokhba; or, The Last Days of Jerusalem*, written in 1883, the tragic hero, Bar Kokhba, battling the Romans, makes a prayer, "O, Lord of my fathers, we pray that you do not help our enemy. As for ourselves, we need no help!" Knowing the catastrophe that will follow, the normally noisy audience members cluck their tongues, sigh an "oy," or whisper to no one in particular, "Ah, this will end badly!"

After 1900, domestic subjects were the focus of most Yiddish melodrama. The very short runs for most domestic plays necessitated rather extensive repertoire. Several dozen of those early texts were not written at all but were, according to the terminology of the time, "baked." A baked or constructed drama was formed by altering scenes from other—usually obscure classical—plays, but only slightly amending plot and characterization. In other words, a baker-playwright would outline his story on paper: (1) A henpecked husband and wife arrive in the big city for the first time (funny scene); (2) a young woman shows her retarded son the grave of his grandfather in a potter's field (pathetic scene); and so forth. Then the playwright would search through volumes of world literature to find vaguely appropriate scenes and dialogue. So, frequently a Yiddish audience would hear an illiterate shoemaker, who in the first act sounded like a poor Hauptmann character, suddenly lament like a worried Macbeth in the second, and finally commiserate in the words of Ivan Karamazov in the last.

Often the domestic melodramatic characters started off in Russia and by the second or third act found themselves in America. As in the English penny gaffs, the protagonists regularly went through the process of being orphaned, abandoned, humiliated, beaten, raped, cheated, and impoverished. Joseph Lateiner's *The Jewish Heart* (1908) contains many typical elements of this variety.[4] A Jewish art student in Rumania, Yankev, discovers that his archenemy, the anti-Semitic Viktor, is his half-brother. By the end of act 1, Yankev realizes that his long-lost mother ran away after his birth, married a Rumanian aristocrat, and bore him a child, Viktor. The play ends with Yankev murdering Viktor to save his "Christian" mother, who later takes the blame for the killing. In the last scene, Yankev marries a Jewish girl before emigrating to America, as his mother, watching and in chains, dies of heart-rending joy. Just as the curtain falls, Yankev breaks into a song about mother-love, about the Jewish mother.

Most of these melodramas were fueled by standard character types with identifiable accessories and musical themes: the student (with his ubiquitous open book and skullcap), the marriage broker (and umbrella), the synagogue sexton (and snuffbox), the landlord, the righteous Gentile, the wife-beating Christian count, the political radical, the idiot child, the self-deprecating proletarian father, and of course the Jewish mother. In the last act of each play, at least one protagonist had what was called "the tablecloth speech"—an emotionally charged outburst that summarized or changed every aspect of the plot.

A third kind of melodrama dramatized recent news stories from the Yiddish and English-language press. The most sensational of these portrayed trials of innocent Jews accused of ritual murders in Russia, Hungary, and the American South. Others documented natural and man-made disasters such as the Johnstown flood and World War I battles. Interestingly, many of the *zaytstucke* (time plays) from the non-Yiddish newspapers revolved around malpractice by Christian doctors.

Another form of Yiddish melodrama consciously took classical and foreign-language plays and fit them into nineteenth-century Jewish settings. The *Yiddish Medea*, the *Jewish King Lear*, and *The Rabbinical Student (Hamlet)* were the best known of this variety. In these versions, ancient Greek and Elizabethan characters once again appear as Yiddish theatre stereotypes: Hamlet as the young scholar, Claudius as a lecherous and wealthy rabbi, the ghost of Hamlet's father as a vengeful dybbuk, Ophelia as the deranged Esther, and so on. Even Boris Tomashevsky's *Uncle Tom's Cabin*, "Where One Persecuted Race Portrays the Hardships of Another," substituted a red-bloused cossack for Simon Legree. Curiously, if the mix of Jewish elements in the world repertoire seems comical today, many typical spectators at the turn of the century were not even aware that Shakespeare was a seventeenth-century English writer.

The single most unusual feature of the Yiddish melodrama did not involve the plays themselves as much as it involved the audience-actor relationships. Jewish spectators were obsessed with not only the personalities but also the working styles of the actors. As distinct from Irish and Italian theatregoers of the same social status in New York, the Jewish spectators applied strict critical yardsticks for both comic and melodramatic acting. More than any other aspect of the Yiddish theatre, this deeply impressed the non-Jewish writer Hapgood:

The spectators laugh at the exact reproduction by the actor of a tattered type which they know well. A scene of perfect sordidness will arouse the sympathetic laughter or tears of the people. "It is so natural," they say to one another, "so true." The word "natural" indeed is the favorite term of praise in the Ghetto. What hits home to them, to their sense of humor or of sad fact, is sure to move, altho sometimes in a manner surprising to a visitor. To what seems to him very sordid and sad they will frequently respond with laughter.[5]

Hapgood further explained how plays even with bizarre plot developments, unvarying characters, twisted dialogue, and shoddy properties and costuming still remain effective:

The Yiddish players, even the poorer among them, act with remarkable sincerity. Entirely lacking in self-consciousness, they attain almost from the outset to a direct and forcible expressiveness. They, like the audience, rejoice in what they deem truth.[6]

As the taste for literary melodramas grew, many of the Yiddish performers found themselves more and more dependent on the prompter—who was, oddly enough, usually a musician. This created a new kind of acting style on the Second Avenue stage. Whenever a performer needed a forgotten line, he crossed in front of the prompter in studiously measured strides, polishing his glasses or playing with a coin or looking into the distance as if he were lost in thought. After being fed the remaining dialogue, the actor returned to his place. All of which caused the audience to remark to one another, "What an actor! He thinks!"

or "Such a deep play!" Sarah Adler called this puffing technique "pecking corn."

The most celebrated feature of the Yiddish theatre concerned the audience's fanatical involvement with the performances and the actors. Spectators frequently interrupted the plays to comment on the acting or to warn the protagonists of the coming deluge. Nahma Sandrow even records an instance: after Jacob Adler as the Yiddish King Lear is refused soup by his ungrateful daughter, a spectator stepped into the aisle, shouting, "Leave those rotten children of yours and come home with me. My wife is a good cook, she'll fix you up."[7] And since the majority of spectators were familiar with the real-life melodramas of the performers, whenever a similar situation occurred on the stage, audiences exploded in applause and psychological analysis.

The stars of the Yiddish theatre usually had large and sometimes violence-prone fan clubs, or *patriotn*. Members of *patriotn* followed their idols everywhere, occasionally even taking their names or acting as their house servants. Rival fan clubs brawled and often ridiculed the performances of their idol's challengers, shouting during the play or carrying signs in front of the theatre. On some occasions, this escalated into even more direct action: *patriotn* drugged a horse on which Tomashevsky was to ride at the play's finale, which caused the horse to get sick on stage. Certainly, the greatest and best documented events in the Lower East Side before 1920 were the gigantic processional funerals of the Yiddish actors. Even the sweatshop operators understood that these were holidays of epic proportions.

While few historians have attempted to explain the phenomenal popularity of Yiddish melodrama and its performers between 1900 and 1925 and its subsequent decline, except in purely linguistic terms, one explanation may have to do with the lack of Jewish leadership and the ghetto's general political impotence. Until the power of trade unionism was firmly established in New York and elsewhere, until working and living conditions allowed for more intellectual and aesthetic activity, the Jewish masses sought solutions on the natural but melodramatic stage.

NOTES

1. See *Theatre Quarterly* (October–December 1971).
2. Hutchins Hapgood, *The Spirit of the Ghetto* (rpt., New York, 1966), p. 118.
3. Jerome Lawrence, *Actor: The Life and Times of Paul Muni* (New York, 1974), p. 40.
4. Partly translated in Nahma Sandrow's *Vagabond Stars* (New York, 1977), pp. 116–21.
5. Hapgood, p. 138.
6. Ibid., p. 137.
7. Sandrow, p. 102.

5

Shakespeare, Sardou, and Pulcinella: Italian-American Working-Class Theatre in New York, 1880–1940

A. Richard Sogliuzzo

Italian-American theatre came to New York City in the 1880s with the first wave of Italian immigrants. Over the years, five million Italians emigrated to America, the great majority of them settling initially in large cities. Many found immediate employment in construction, helping to build New York's vast subway system, its streets and skyscrapers; eventually they entered other industries and trades.[1] Italian-American theatre was the primary form of entertainment for these mostly poor laborers in New York.

Although this theatrical activity, which peaked in popularity during the 1930s and declined in the late 1940s, constituted a major ethnic theatre, its history was neglected and remained virtually unknown to historians outside the area of Italian-American studies. Production books, actors' diaries, and letters are scarce or lost. Many of the late-nineteenth-century issues of the *Eco d'Italia* and *Il Progresso Italo-Americano*, the two leading newspapers, are missing.[2] Moreover, neither newspaper had an official dramatic critic at that time; thus newspaper coverage was sporadic and minimal, often limited to advertisements of performances. Consequently, observations of American critics interested in the Italian-American theatre provide the primary basis for this chapter.

During the 1860s, many northern Italians, a number of whom had fought with Giuseppe Garibaldi in Italy's fight for independence from Austria, emigrated to America. The venerated general himself lived for several years on Staten Island. Predictably, the first Italian-American theatrical events were patriotic spectacles commemorating Italy's fight for independence. For the season of 1868–1869, the *Eco d'Italia* announced that the *Associazione Italiana del Trio al Bersaglio—Guardia Columbo* (a rifleman's club) held its second annual ball at the Germania Assembly Rooms at 291–293 on the Bowery. On September 10, 1868, the same club celebrated the disembarking of Columbus in the New World.[3] The exact nature of the celebration was not specified, though it is likely that a spectacle reenacting this famous moment augmented the speeches, parades, songs, and dances.

The first significant theatrical activity began in the 1880s with the establishment of amateur theatre clubs, prototypes for the professional theatres in the Italian-American community. The clubs frequently performed on saints' days or on American and Italian holidays. Among the first groups were the *Circolo filo-drammatico italo-Americano* (1885), *Compagnia Galileo Galilei* (1890), and the *Compagnia filodrammatica napoletana* (1891).[4] The high-sounding nomencla-ture is a manifestation of the Italianization that occurred in America in response to the bitter prejudice against Italians, a ruthlessly exploited and detested mi-nority.[5] To defend themselves against "the gratuitous insults of the majority group," immigrants with slight knowledge of their national history suddenly embraced their heritage and proudly declared the names of Galileo, Dante, and Columbus.[6]

The performers were probably literate members of the working-class com-munity, possibly emigrés from the large cities who had previously attended the theatre in Italy. The establishment of amateur theatre clubs was a manifestation of the prowess of ethnocentricism characteristic of all immigrant groups. Arriving in a foreign country, initially unable to cope with the language and mores of the new society, immigrants formed ghettos and reestablished their cultural patterns as a means of psychological survival.[7] The festivities on holidays and the drama clubs were among the few forms of entertainment available to Italian immigrants. The amateur theatre clubs performed in halls and church basements on New York's Lower East Side. The earliest record of a dramatic performance in one of them is an announcement in the *Eco d'Italia* of May 6, 1882: Carlo Goldoni's *La locandiera* (*The Mistress of the Inn*) and a farce, *I due sordi* (*The Two Deaf Men*), at the Concordia Hall on Avenue A.[8] Later programs indicate a long and varied evening's entertainment, from thrilling melodramas and commedia dell'arte skits to songs and dances, frequently performed in Neapolitan or Sicilian, the two major dialects of the immigrant population after 1880. A typical evening is that of May 25, 1890, at the Bowery's Germania Assembly Rooms, with the *Compagnia filodrammatica napoletana*, performing *Nu muorto Chi non e Muorto* (*The Lively Corpse*), a commedia parody in two acts featuring Pulcinella and directed by Signor Francesco Riccardi, and a "most brilliant" comedy titled *Pasca' si Porco* (*Pasquale You're a Pig*).[9] In addition to plays written in dialect, there were also performances of the works of popular writers such as Victorian Sardou and Paolo Giacometti and major playwrights such as Schiller and Vittorio Alfieri. However, the most popular plays were the farces featuring Pulcinella and the "potboiling" melodramas.[10]

American critic Hutchins Hapgood described a production of a melodrama he attended in 1900. The play was set in a seamy cafe in Naples where three ragged young men were drinking together. One of the bosom friends called the other a bastard, claiming that a certain priest would confirm his accusation. Knives were immediately drawn, but others parted the two enraged friends. The young man's mother begrudgingly admitted the truth of his illegitimacy but refused to reveal the identity of the "man with whom she had sinned." The priest arrived, a quarrel ensued between him and the young man, and just as the latter was about to shoot the priest, the mother revealed the priest as his father. The horror-stricken son rushed from the scene and went to his friend who had first revealed to him the nature of his illegitimate birth. The two friends vowed to die together. They embraced and shot each other. The other personages of the drama rushed on, but it was too late. The old priest announced that he was the cause of the tragedy. Hapgood thought that "the situation throughout was simple and intense, and the actors so thoroughly in an emotional atmosphere natural to them that there is no trace of the unreal effect of melodrama."[11]

Italians regarded the theatre as a place to socialize and be entertained. House-lights were always partially lit during performances to allow for a ready exchange of conversation among members of the audience. There was eating, drinking, and the accompanying din of pop bottles rolling under seats. One journalist provided a vivid description of the Italian-American audience in 1919:

The theatre [the Bowery] is filled with all sorts and conditions of men and women, working men in their shirt sleeves for it is summer, women with slick hair parted over their oval olive faces suckling their babys [sic], or with half-nude infants lying over their knees. Boys in white coats, with baskets of multi-colored pop and other forms of soda water pass up and down the aisles seeking customers, and you see young mothers, young girls with their young men, grey-haired grandmothers tightly bound in thick black shawls in spite of the heat sipping the red and pink and yellow pop through long straws directly from the bottles . . . all this observed in the smokey half light of the darkened theatre for the performance going on is to the highest degree picturesque . . . a man and a woman have just finished singing a duet from the *Count of Luxembourg*.[12]

Italian audiences were boisterous: talking to the actors, singing, laughing, weeping, and hissing the villain. The line between the reality of life and the illusion of the stage was sometimes imperceptible to them. Almarinda Migliaccio, daughter of the great comedian Eduardo Migliaccio, recalled that on one occasion a group of spectators waited outside the theatre to beat up the actor playing the villain for his abusive treatment of the innocent family portrayed in the drama.[13] In another instance, an actor-manager's defense of an unacceptable script was met with yells, hisses, insults, popcorn, old hats, apple cores, candy, and bottles. As a spectator in one of the boxes was about to throw a chair, the *capocomico* jumped for his life.[14]

John Corbin of *Harper's Weekly* observed that the theatres located south of Grand Street were "as crude and bare as ever an Elizabethan playhouse on the bankside." Attending a performance of *Othello* at the Bowery Theatre in 1898, Corbin noted that the scenery consisted primarily of signs indicating locales: "Venice, A Council Chamber; Cyprus, Before the Castle." The settings were poorly constructed: "Desdemona and Emilia could be plainly seen through the aperture in the castle wall where they were quietly awaiting their cues." Italians were unperturbed by such primitive scenery; the play was everything, and they willingly imagined the palaces and battlements suggested by the signs and simple settings.[15]

In the 1890s the Italian-American theatre began its professional phase, as actors, lured by the popularity of the *circolo filodrammatico* groups, emigrated to America. Perhaps the first manifestation of professionalism occurred in the *cafes chantants*, Italian music halls with cheap variety performances. No admission fee was charged; the actors shared the profits from the drinks sold. The *cafes chantants* dotted the Italian community. Usually bearing the name of the *capocomico*, the companies performed in theatres and halls throughout New York and in the Italian communities of neighboring states. Frequent intermarriages among actors produced a remarkable homogeneity in the Italian troupes. Children and grandchildren and successive generations of intermarriages further strengthened the cohesion of the troupes. Younger actors were trained by older members of the company or by the *capocomico* and often inherited their parents' roles, thus perpetuating acting traditions.[16]

The first important professional entertainer to arrive in the United States was Gugliemo Ricciardi,[17] a Neapolitan who had played secondary roles in a company of actors touring South America. His intention was to remain only long enough to earn his passage back to Italy. Ricciardi began performing comedy sketches in little theatres and *cafes chantants* and became so successful that he soon abandoned all plans of returning to Italy. His first recorded performance in the United States took place on April 18, 1891, when he directed and probably acted in a comedy, *Maria Giovanne e la famiglia dell'ubriacone* (*Maria Giovanna and the Drunkard's Family*).[18] He was the quintessence of the charming Neapolitan, a lively personality with a robust face dominated by a large nose, possessing a loud yet pleasant singing voice. A critic for the *New York Times* described him as "one of those protean actors in whose rapid change of wigs and costumes European audiences so delight."[19]

Ricciardi's production of the *Executed Man* at the Grand Eden, his own *cafe chantant*, demonstrated his gift for improvisation. The play ended with the central character about to be executed, but the spectators at its premiere were angered at the brevity of the drama and demanded more. Ricciardi called up the curtain, and a scene was instantly improvised: the man's execution was fortuitously prevented by a pardon from the governor. The curtain descended, but the greedy spectators would not be satisfied. The curtain was raised again, and a tender scene between the pardoned hero and his overjoyed mother was enacted. Still the spectators demanded more. The fiancée rushed into this scene of maternal bliss and embraced her lover. Anticipating his customers' expectations, however, Ricciardi raised the curtain again for a final *tableau vivant*, a joyous wedding involving the entire cast. Cheers from the audience![20]

The *Executed Man* is also interesting as an example of early Italian-American drama. During the first years of immigration, when ties to Italy were still strong, Italian plays were performed almost exclusively. Gradually, the Italian-American experience evolved, and the *Executed Man* was a parable of that experience. It suggested the hardships of working-class immigrant life and the difficulties of adjustment with a note of optimism: a poor Italian had been unjustifiably condemned to die, but Ricciardi's improvised ending implied that in America justice was available to rich and poor alike. The governor, symbol of America, was a benevolent father-figure who saved an innocent man from death and so assured the continuance of the sacred institution of the family, represented by the joyous mother and the triumphant wedding.

Although Ricciardi was the first professional actor in the history of the Italian-American theatre, Antonio Maiori (1868–1938) was the first to establish a company. He arrived in 1892 and began performing as a ballet dancer and mime with Kiralfy's Circus. Maiori's first recorded dramatic performance was Schiller's *The Robbers* at Turn Hall on May 9, 1892.[21] Determined to provide the Italian community with a classical repertory company, Maiori leased the Irving Street Theatre in the Bowery and recruited additional professional actors from Italy. He was, however, unable to maintain his theatre since his weekly expenses amounted to $700, his receipts to only $300.[22] Embittered by the lack of support from the Italian community, he confessed to a journalist:

It is a shame, an outrage! Here are we Italians posing to all the world as apostles of fine arts, and yet it is impossible to get enough backing among the one-hundred and fifty thousand people of my nationality in this city to maintain a theatre which would rank with those of the other foreign-tongued races. Instead of being encouraged by those who could well afford it, they had asked . . . "What is there in it for me?" Art? Why these rich people do not care for the art of their nation—they are money-mad.[23]

Several factors accounted for Maiori's difficulties in attracting an audience. Culturally, Italy had more of a musical than a theatrical tradition; opera, not theatre, was the popular art form. The opera and the variety theatre, with its Neapolitan songs and dances, had greater appeal for Italian-Americans. Although the wealthy attended the theatre in Italy, the "rich" that Maiori referred to were nouveau riche, who were not theatregoers. Maiori eventually drew his support from working- rather than merchant-class Italians.

In order to cut operating expenses, Maiori converted the ground floor of a building at 24 Spring Street into a theatre. Two drawing rooms became the lobby and auditorium; an outdoor stage was erected in the backyard. Seats were priced from ten cents to fifty cents to attract working-class theatregoers, and the gross receipts finally enabled him to maintain his small company. One contemporary journalist noted that the audience of bootblacks and barbers was transported by art to the Venetian palace of Othello, unperturbed by such "trifling details" as Desdemona "gasping her last breaths" amid the "clouds of fried onions" wafting over the fence from the nearby Hotel Garibaldi.[24]

Maiori performed melodramas, but his great love was the classics, particularly Italianized adaptations of Shakespeare. His *Hamlet* was intensely passionate.

Hapgood noted that in the bedroom scene between the Dane and his mother, "Hamlet tramples violently under foot the picture of his uncle, and at the burial of Ophelia breaks into passion long before the lines warrant. In the scenes with the Queen, the tenderness and sentiment is exquisitely rendered, always minimizing in translation and in action Hamlet's pale cast of thought."[25]

Maiori's favorite Shakespearean role was Othello, and apparently it was the company's tour de force. In an ethnocentric remark, Hapgood observed that the emotions on stage were "native to the actors and characteristic of the play."[26] Maiori was a congenial but demanding director, a rigid taskmaster. The company rehearsed daily with Maiori explaining motivation, demonstrating business, and training the company in voice and diction—striving for perfect Italian pronunciation. Much of what American critics believed about the Italian actors' gift for improvisation was achieved through careful planning and repetition.[27] A popular society artist of the period, William Santini, accidentally discovered Maiori's theatre on Spring Street. Impressed with the young actor's extraordinary talents, Santini encouraged his friends to attend one of Maiori's performances. "Coming first to be amused by the novelty of the thing and the surroundings, they realized ere long, that a genius of no mean order was spouting away to audiences barely able to appreciate him. The attendance of society folk became more frequent and Maiori himself became a fad of the most surprising permanency."[28]

In 1907 Maiori became a partner with Marcus Lowe (later of MGM), and brought additional talent from Italy, and formed a new company in Brooklyn's Royal Theatre. In 1909, the company embarked on a national tour, performing several tragedies by Shakespeare and Italian plays by D'Annunzio, Goldoni, and others. Although a superb actor, Maiori was a terrible businessman, losing three fortunes between 1902 and 1912. In 1913 he decided to recoup his losses by dissolving his dramatic repertory company and establishing a chain of variety theatres throughout New York City. From 1898 to 1913 Maiori had been the foremost exponent of the classic drama in the Italian-American theatre and its leading actor.[29]

Maiori's successor for a brief period was Giovanni De Rosalia, a versatile actor but lacking Maiori's powerful figure and voice. Ultimately, De Rosalia also abandoned the legitimate theatre and became a popular comedian, creating the character of De Nofrio, a Sicilian caricature on the order of Pulcinella. The character was played without a mask but with shabby clothes and a large false nose.[30]

Two other leading theatrical personalities were the husband-and-wife team of Silvio Minciotti and Esther Cunico, who were among the few Italian-American actors ultimately to succeed on Broadway and in Hollywood. Formerly a member of Maiori's company, Minciotti was *capocomico* of his own company from 1901 to 1906. He finally settled in San Francisco where he and his wife formed their own company and remained for a number of years.[31]

Maiori and Minciotti were highly accomplished actors, but they performed for audiences that preferred the comic, dialect theatre to the legitimate. Thus they never enjoyed the enormous popularity and adulation of such tragedians of the Yiddish stage and Boris Tomashevsky and Maurice Schwartz. Jews of all social classes regularly attended the legitimate theatre,[32] but vaudeville was the popular art of the Italian-Americans, and their idol was the brilliant comedian, Eduardo Migliaccio, commonly known as Farfariello. His depiction of the *cafone*, the country bumpkin helplessly adrift in the New World, was comparable to Chaplin's Tramp; the little guy full of good intentions and ambitions but victimized by both society and his own ineptitude. Rich and poor alike attended Migliaccio's theatre, and his popularity was unparalleled by any other Italian-American artist.

Migliaccio was a *machiettista*, a vaudeville comedian, whose art, derived from the commedia dell'arte, consisted in burlesquing social stereotypes. His comic sketches, *machiette*, provided a vast panorama of characters drawn from the life of Little Italy: the undertaker, the watchman, the soldier, the patriot, the domineering wife, the anxious bride, and the inevitable *cafone*. Writing for *Theatre Magazine*, American critic Van Vechten chronicled Migliaccio's virtuosity in 1919:

A transformed Farfariello enters, from hair to shoes he is a French concert-hall singer of the type familiar at Coney Island. He has transformed his eyes; his nose is new; gesture, voice, all his powers, physical and mental are moulded in a new metal. He shrieks his vapid ditty in a raucous falsetto; he flicks his spangled skirt; he winks at the orchestra leader, and shakes his buttocks; his bosom has become an enormous jelly. Again he is gone but soon the figure of an Italian patriot appears, a large florid person with heavy hair and moustache. Across his chest, over his shoulder, and ending in a sash at his hip, he wears a tricolor of Italy. Farfariello paints the man in action; he is forever marching in parades; he is forever making speeches at banquets; he is forever shouting Viva l'Italia. Like all good caricatures this is not only a comment on the thing; it is the thing itself and as this portrait is essentially provincial it thereby passes easily in universal apprehension. We all know this man in some guise or other. Farfariello goes on singing, acting, impersonating. Perhaps next he is one of the Bersagliere, perhaps a Spanish dancer, perhaps a funeral director, or a night watchman. He may sing *Pasquale Basciamento, Rosolina, Quanno Spussia Francisco*, but always at the end he is the iceman.[33]

Migliaccio was a keen observer of immigrant life, and his *machiette*, published in *La Follia* of New York, constitute a major contribution to American ethnic literature.[34] As social documents, they afford, perhaps, a more complete insight into the life of Little Italy than the Italian-American novels that often focus on the bitter poverty of ghetto life. Migliaccio's *machiette* were gentle satires depicting the foibles of the first generation of Italian-Americans, their guile as well as their gullibility which often made them victims of unscrupulous opportunists.

Migliaccio was born in 1880 at Cava dei tireni near Naples. His family had emigrated to Pennsylvania in 1898 to speculate in coal mining, but lost a fortune. Having received an excellent formal education in Italy, Migliaccio easily found employment in New York's Italian community. He obtained a position in a bank on Mulberry Street, advising immigrants on financial matters. During his lunch hours, he frequently attended the nearby *cafe chantant*, Vittorio Emmanuele, and one afternoon, quite spontaneously, entertained the audience with a song and a comic sketch based on a character called Farfariello (Little Butterfly). His success was instantaneous, and he became a regular performer at the Vittorio Emmanuele, much to the chagrin of his family who considered it a dishonor to have a son as an entertainer.[35]

Prior to his arrival in America, Migliaccio's only theatrical experience had been as a theatregoer, regularly attending the performances of the great Neapolitan *machiettista*, Maldacea, thus familiarizing himself with the art of the comic theatre.[36] In addition to being a natural performer, Migliaccio was a skilled craftsman. Rehearsing long hours before a mirror, Migliaccio precisely planned and executed every gesture, dance step, line delivery, and vocal inflection. He maintained a workshop at home, where he taught himself the art of wig and mask making. When constructing a mask, he began by carving a potato to serve as a mold for the nose that usually dominated the mask.[37] Since Migliaccio performed as many as six sketches in a half-hour routine, he devised a method for quick costume changes: the entire costume was constructed as a unit with snaps at the back. In later years, he was asssisted by his son, who waited in the wings with wigs, costumes, and props. All was carefully synchronized, so that the costume changes were orchestrated into the entire act. During the interlude for the costume change, the band began the musical introduction for the next sketch.[38]

Migliaccio's sketches were based on his observations of immigrant life. While sitting at a cafe, he mentally recorded the emotions, gestures, and idiosyncracies of his countrymen. The dialogue for Migliaccio's sketches and lyrics was a combination of standard Italian, Neapolitan, and Italian-American argot. For example, in one sketch, an immigrant is knocked unconscious in a bar by several Americans for having uttered, "*Orre'* Italy!" They throw him out on the sidewalk, where he is subsequently picked up for vagrancy and brought to court. The judge asks him, "Watzo maro laste naite?" ("What's the matter last night?"). The Italian replies, "No tocche nglese" ("No talk English"). The judge quickly retorts, "No? Tenne dollari" ("No? Ten dollars"). The immigrant is forced to pay a fine: "*E quello porco dello giorge nun scherzava perche le diece pezze se lo pigliaie*" ("And that pig of a judge wasn't joking; he took the ten dollars").[39] Between the laughs, one senses the injustices suffered by Italians at the hands of Americans.

Migliaccio had a deep concern for the plight of the uneducated immigrant. His sketches sometimes contained an element of criticism of Italy and America for their unfair treatment of the poor. One of Migliaccio's songs (recorded by RCA Victor)[40] tells the story of an immigrant named John who expected to find the streets paved with gold and discovered, instead, a society prejudiced against him. Unable to earn an adequate income, John became a bootlegger, made a fortune, and earned the respect of both Italians and Americans. Those who had previously disdained him, now addressed him as "Mr. John," and for a thousand-dollar bill "the wretches" accorded him more respect than they did the President of the United States.

John became an American gentleman. He bought a house on the Brooklyn shore so close to the beach that he could leap into the sea from his front porch; he smoked expensive cigars and drank "rock and rye." His wealth enabled him to humiliate those who had previously treated him with scorn. John bought a limousine and ran over hypocrites who greeted him in the streets. Returning to Italy for a visit, John was honored with a banquet by his village, which had once considered him less than an animal. They expected him to modernize the town: repairs for the church, new roads, a hospital, fountains. John informed them that although he was not deaf (*sordo*), he could not hear a word they said, and so would not give them a cent (*surdo*). The banquet ended abruptly, and the village once again scorned him. Such an action merely confirmed John's belief in man's treachery. He returned to his joyous life in America: thousand-dollar bills in his pockets, "stars in his eyes"—thanks to the "moonashina."

Although the references in the song are dated, it retains the impact of a Brecht-Weill number: joyous music paradoxically contrasted by sombre lyrics, and a sardonic, world-weary quality that was uniquely Italian in its cynicism yet universal in appeal. The song was Migliaccio's denunciation of a society's cruelty and hypocrisy, which forced honest men into dishonest professions.

The Italian-American theatre grew in popularity through the 1920s. Migliaccio appealed to native American as well as to Italian-American audiences, when he performed in English at such major theatres as the Palace on Broadway. While his variety theatre thrived, artists such as Maiori and Minciotti were forced to abandon their hopes to establish permanent repertory companies regularly performing the classics. Italian-American audiences preferred popular melodramas, farces, or the variety theatre. Though productions of the classics diminished[41] Italian-American theatre continued its success, achieving its zenith in the 1930s as a result of the impact of Italian-American radio.[42]

In the 1940s the theatre declined in popularity and eventually died in the 1950s. The reason was obvious: with the passing of the first generation of Italian-Americans and the disinterest of the second who were anxious to become Americanized, the theatre had lost its Italian-speaking audience.[43] The Italian Actors' Union still exists but is inactive. A number of actors, particularly those who began their careers in the late 1930s, are still alive. Their theatrical life was brief but intense. One is reminded of the words of the Player in Tom Stoppard's *Rosencrantz and Guildenstern are Dead*: "We're actors . . . we pledged out identities, secure in the conviction of our trade that someone would be watching. And then, gradually, no one was."

NOTES

1. By 1880, there were 44,230 Italian immigrants in America, most of them from Southern Italy. See Robert Foerster, *The Italian Emigration in Our Times* (Cambridge,

1919), p. 323. By 1930, Italians constituted nearly one-sixth of New York City's population. See Nathan Glazer and Daniel Patrick Moynihan, *Beyond the Melting Pot*, 2nd ed. (Cambridge, 1970), p. 186.

2. The New York Public Library is the only repository for these two newspapers. *Il Progresso Italo-Americano* did not retain back issues of its early publications. Private collections may possibly contain some of these early issues. I have discovered programs and newspaper clippings in the personal collections of Italian-American actors.

3. George C. Odell, *Annals of the New York Stage* (New York, 1936), 8: 463.

4. Ibid., 12: 489; 14: 616, 618.

5. Jerry Mangione, "Half Bitter, Half Sweet," review of *An Excursion Into Italian-American History* by Alexander De Conde, *The New York Times Book Review*, 6 February 1972, p. 41.

6. Joseph Lopreato, *Italian-Americans* (New York, 1970), p. 171.

7. Ibid., p. 6.

8. Odell, 12: 78.

9. Odell, 14: 336. Signor Ricciardi's troupe must have been among the most popular during those early years. Frequent announcements of its performances appear in the *Eco d'Italia* (as indicated in Odell's *Annals of the New York Stage*). The author's debt to George Odell for recording these Italian activities is inestimable. Discussing the Italian season of 1890–1891, Odell wrote: "The reader and I agree in thinking this Italian record far from thrilling. I even wonder if it warrants, in these troubled times [1945], the expenditure of time, paper and ink involved. I commit the answer to posterity," (*Annals*, 14: 616). Many of the copies of the *Eco d'Italia* and *Il Progresso Italo-Americano* have been lost, I assume through disintegration. A number of the copies preserved on microfilm at the New York Public Library also show considerable damage. If Odell had not recorded these activities, much of the early history of the Italian-American theatre would have been lost.

10. The popularity of such simple theatrical fare was attributed to the Italian-American audiences being almost entirely composed of uneducated laborers and artisans. "The mass of immigrants are classed as unskilled laborers, or without defined training. This classification is passably correct, but it should be borne in mind that the great majority of immigrants from Italy have had some experience in gardening, farming, or home industries of some kind. The line is not so sharply drawn in our country between the artisan and the farm hand." Quoted from Eliot Lord, John J. D. Revor, and Samuel J. Barrow, *The Italian in America* (New York, 1950), p. 61.

11. "The Foreign Stage in New York," *The Bookman*, 11 (August 1900), 547.

12. "A Night with Farfariello," *Theatre Magazine*, 29 (January 1919), 32.

13. Interview, January 1972.

14. "The Bowery," *The American Mercury*, 9, No. 35 (November 1926), 368.

15. "Shakespeare in the Bowery," *Harper's Weekly*, 42 (12 March 1898), 244. "Figure e Scene del Teatro Popolare Italiano a New York," *Il Progresso Italo-Americano*, 3 May 1942.

16. Since the Italian companies had such large repertoires and only a few actors, doubling of roles was common, causing considerable reliance on the prompter. Actors mastered the technique of following the prompter; performances progressed at a regular pace. Laurence Estavan, "The Italian Theatre in San Francisco," *San Francisco Theatre Research*, NS 21 (San Francisco, Works Progress Administration, 1939), p. 17. Lorenzo Rondine, President of the Italian Actors' Union, recalls an instance where the actor-

manager, Alberto Compobasso, was writing a script during a performance—each completed a scene being handed to the prompter, who then related it to the actors on stage. The performance progressed without an interruption. ("Notes from a Radio Interview on Station WHOV," n.d. [probably 1941] MS provided by Carol Garuffi, member of the Italian Actors' Union). Rachel Maiori, daughter of Silvio Minciotti, recalls an instance when Frederick March witnessed a demonstration of the actor-prompter technique in her home. March was amazed by the almost instantaneous rendering of the lines by the actors (Interview, Rachel Maiori, September 1971).

17. No relationship to Francesco Ricciardi mentioned earlier.

18. *New York Times*, 17 March 1916; Odell, 15: 229.

19. "Figure e Scene," *Il Progresso* 17 March 1916.

20. Ibid. (The article did not give the Italian title for this play.)

21. Odell, 15: 111.

22. Owen Kildare, "Bowery Salvini," *New York Herald*, 1902, in clipping file: "Italian-American Theatre," New York Public Library.

23. Ibid.

24. Ibid.

25. Hapgood, p. 547.

26. Ibid., p. 550.

27. Interview, Marietta Maiori, daughter of Antonio and child-actress in her father's company, September 1971.

28. Kildare, "Bowery Salvini."

29. "Figure e Scene," *Il Progresso*, 28 June 1942.

30. Ibid. (*Il Progresso*, 13 September 1907, contains an announcement of the formation of De Rosalia's company with Paolo Cremonesi.)

31. "Figure e Scene," *Il Progresso*, 28 June 1942. Miss Cunico achieved international recognition for her portrayal of the mother in the film *Marty*.

32. David Lifson, *The Yiddish Theatre in America* (New York, 1965), pp. 166–84.

33. "A Night with Farfariello," 32.

34. Joseph Tigani, "Italian-American Pens," *Italian Heritage* (May 1971), p. 2.

35. Giuseppe Prezzolini, *I trapiantati* (Milano, 1963), pp. 323–25.

36. Ibid., p. 323.

37. Interview, Almarinda Migliaccio. I wish to express my gratitude to Mr. Francis R. Favorini, who introduced me to the Migliaccio family who allowed me to use their collection.

38. Interview, Teodorico Migliaccio (father's assistant), January 1972.

39. Prezzolini, p. 328.

40. Record contained in the Migliaccio family collection. The label is badly worn on the recording, making it impossible to discern its numerical identification.

41. There was a revival of the Italian and other European classics in the 1930s when the brilliant actor Giuseppe Sterni formed his Teatro d'Arte. He was the first to introduce Pirandello to Italian-American audiences, but he received little support and was also forced to produce popular melodramas. "Teatro d'Arte Opens Season," *New York Times*, 7 October 1935.

42. "The miracle that occurred during the epoch that followed the terrible depression . . . was caused by radio, whose programs brought out beautiful language into Italian homes and created such euphoria as to bring tears to one's eyes. Theatre profited from this enthusiasm. Radio drama had thousands of listeners, and these same dramas were

then presented at theatres with profitable results at the box office'' (Rondine, ''Notes from a Radio Interview''). A frequent device used to lure audiences to the theatre was to present the first two acts of a play on radio during the week and complete the last two or three acts at a theatre on Sunday (Interview, Rachel Maiori).

43. During World War II, immigration from Italy ceased. The Immigration Act of 1952 placed severe quota restrictions on immigrants from Southern Europe. These two factors, therefore, prevented any possibility of a revival of the Italian-American theatre.

6

The Paterson Strike Pageant of 1913

Linda Nochlin

> What is a labor victory? I maintain that it is a twofold thing. Workers must
> gain economic advantage, but they must also gain revolutionary spirit, in
> order to achieve a complete victory.[1]
>
> Elizabeth Gurley Flynn

On the evening of June 7, 1913, an important incident in the history of radical
self-consciousness and public art in this country took place. In the old Madison
Square Garden, in New York City, before an estimated audience of 15,000,
beneath bright red electric lights spelling out IWW in ten-foot-high letters above
the building, assembled a cast of about 1,500 striking silk workers—mainly
Italian, Jewish, and Polish immigrants. They reenacted the major incidents of
the strike then taking place in Paterson, New Jersey, under the aegis of organizers
Elizabeth Gurley Flynn, Carlo Tresca, Patrick Quinlan, and Big Bill Haywood,
dedicated leaders of the so-called Wobblies—Industrial Workers of the World.
The Paterson Strike Pageant itself had come into being mainly through the
efforts of the young John Reed, who was later to gain fame for his firsthand
account of the Russian Revolution, *Ten Days that Shook the World*, and who,
on his premature death in 1920, was to be buried in the Kremlin as a hero of
the revolution amidst pageantry even more impressive than that he had devised
for the striking silk workers.[2]

  At the time he undertook the organization of the Paterson Strike Pageant,
however, Reed was a relatively unknown if extraordinarily energetic writer for
the recently founded left-wing journal, *The Masses*. At Harvard, from which he
had graduated in 1910, Reed had been active in the Socialist Club and in the
Dramatic Club, which was closely related to Professor George Pierce Baker's
famous course in dramatic writing, English 47.[3] After a brief trip to Europe,
Reed migrated to Greenwich Village, then in its heyday as a center of radical

politics and artistic ferment, where he met such varied proponents of social reform as Lincoln Steffens, Max Eastman, Emma Goldman, and Ida Tarbell. His dramatic interests were expressed in a minor way in a skit he wrote in 1912–1913 for the Dutch Treat Club, an organization of successful and conservative writers and artists, for its annual dinner at Delmonico's. He maintained his Harvard connection by membership in the Harvard Club. At the same time, his politics were moving dramatically leftward: he had experienced the Paterson strike firsthand on an investigatory trip during the course of which he had been thrown into jail with the immigrant workers. He recounted his experiences in an article for *The Masses* called "The War in Paterson."[4]

In the short space of three weeks, Reed whipped up a theatrical spectacle that played the mass action of the striker-performers against stirring speeches by Flynn, Tresca, Quinlan, and Haywood. He rehearsed the cast in songs like "The Marseillaise" and "The International" from the little red song book of the IWW and in other songs especially composed for the occasion. Mabel Dodge, one of the major figures in the radical chic of the times (and then having an affair with Reed), pointed out: "One of the gayest touches . . . was teaching them to sing one of their lawless songs to *Harvard, Old Harvard*."[5] Reed's attachment to his alma mater was obviously an ambivalent one, but it played a role, however indirect, in his conception of the strike pageant. A classmate of his, Robert Edmond Jones, later to gain a major reputation as an innovative theatre designer, particularly for his starkly evocative sets for the dramas of Eugene O'Neill, was called on to stage the production and to design the poster of the militant workman that also served as the cover of the strike pageant program.[6] The simple but effective backdrop of silk mills was painted by John Sloan, then an active socialist and a major contributor to *The Masses*, for which he did over fifty drawings.[7]

The overtly political, propagandistic intention of the Paterson Strike Pageant was set forth in the introduction to the pageant program, edited by Frederick Summer Boyd, which included a history of the strike itself and a synopsis of the scenario: "The Pageant represents a battle between the working class and the capitalist class conducted by the Industrial Workers of the World (IWW), making use of the General Strike as the chief weapon. It is a conflict between two social forces—the force of labor and the force of capital."[8]

The actual performance, divided into six major episodes summarized in the pageant program, was vividly described on the front page of the *Herald Tribune* of June 8, 1913, under the headline, "Strike Realism Staged in Pageant":

The first episode of the pageant, entitled "The Mill Alive—The Workers Dead," represented 6 o'clock one February morning. A great painted drop, two hundred feet wide, stretching across the hippodrome-like stage built for the show, represented a Paterson silk mill, the windows aglow with the artificial light in which the workers began their daily tasks.

Then came the operatives, men, women, and children; some mere tots, others decrepit old people, 1,200 of them, trooping sadly and reluctantly to work the "oppression" of the bosses made them hate. Their mutterings of discontent were soon merged in the whir of the looms as the whistles blew and the day's work was on.

But that day's work did not last long, for the smouldering spirit of revolt suddenly burst into the flame of the strike, and the operatives rushed pell-mell out of the mills, shouting and dancing with the intoxication of freedom. The whir of the mills died down, and then rose the surging tones of the "Marseillaise" [in which the entire audience was invited to join] as the strikers marked defiantly up and down before the silent mill.

"The Mills Dead—The Workers Alive"—that was the name of the second episode—is best described, perhaps, in the words of the scenario of the pageant: "Mass picketing, every worker alert. The police interfere with peaceful picketing and treat the strikers with great brutality. The workers are provoked to anger. Fights between the police and strikers ensue. Many strikers are clubbed and arrested. Shots are fired by detectives hired by the manufacturers, and Valentino Modestino, who was not a striker or a silk-mill worker, is hit by a bullet and killed as he stands on the porch of his house with one of his children in his arms."

Episode three represents the funeral of Modestino, a scene that, with all the accessories of sombre realism, worked the actors themselves and their thousands of sympathizers in the audience up to a high pitch of emotion, punctuated with moans and groans and sobs. A coffin, supposed to contain Modestino's body, was borne across the stage, followed by the strikers in funeral procession to the heavy tones of the "Dead March." As they passed, the mourners dropped red carnations and ribbons upon the coffin, until it was buried "beneath the crimson symbol of the workers' blood."

And, as if this were not enough of realism, Carlo Tresca himself appeared, and outdid Marc Antony's funeral oration, with a repetition of his own famous "Blood for Blood" speech that got him into jail in Paterson when he delivered the original.[9]

The fourth episode, a mass meeting of 20,000 strikers, featured speeches by the IWW organizers and songs by the strike composers in German, Italian, and English, as well as the singing of "The Internationale", "The Marseillaise," and "The Red Flag," with audience participation invited once more. In the fifth episode, the performers marched through the audience in a reenactment of the May Day Parade and were addressed by Elizabeth Gurley Flynn; this episode featured the handing over of the strikers' children, appropriately dressed in red, to their "strike mothers" from other cities. The final episode was the strike meeting. In the words of the program synopsis: "The Strikers, men and women, legislate for themselves. They pass a law for the eight-hour day. No court can declare the law thus made unconstitutional. Elizabeth Gurley Flynn, Carlo Tresca, and William D. Haywood made typical strike speeches."[10]

Almost all the eyewitness accounts of the Paterson Strike Pageant praised it for its simplicity, its aesthetic innovations, and its dramatic as well as political effectiveness. It had evidently been a highly emotional theatrical experience combining stark realism and daring stylization: "There was no plot—no more than in the crude Elizabethan history plays," observed the critic of *The Independent*, who went on to describe the performance:

There was no play acting. . . . The strikers were simply living over, for their fellows to see, their most telling experiences. No stage in the country had ever seen a more real

dramatic expression of American life. . . . In its own fashion it was as simple as the
primitive drama of the 16th century. "Jack" Reed . . . stood in front of the crowd and
stage-managered with a megaphone. There was no curtain; the stage, unlocalized save
for the drop, became in turn the street, Haledon (a nearby village) and Turn Hall in
Paterson, quite as freely as a pre-Elizabethan innyard.[11]

The writer in the New York *World* praised its simple effectiveness—"Need
can speak without elocutionists and unison of thought in a great mass of highly
wrought-up people [which] may swell emotion to the point of tears." The reporter
in the New York *Tribune* connected the dramatic success of the pageant quite
explicitly with avant-garde aesthetics in this, the year of the armory show: "There
was a startling touch of ultra-modern—or rather of Futurism—in the Paterson
strike pageant. . . . Certainly nothing like it had been known before in the history
of labor agitation."[12] Several observers stressed the effectiveness of the staging
that led the striker-performers in procession back and forth through the audience
itself: "It is an unequalled device for clutching the emotion of the audience,"
wrote *The Independent*, "this parade of the actors through the center of the
crowd. The dramatic liturgy of the Roman Church, in which our English drama
had its rise, the processional in the Episcopal Church too, and even the familiar
wedding march recognize its value. Rarely has it been used in New York theatres
. . . but never with more effect than in this performance, where actors and audience were of one class and one hope."[13] Mabel Dodge also commented on
the modernism of the device, although in somewhat more exaggerated terms:

Our Bobby Jones . . . insisted on making it a Gordon Craig affair, and having a long street
scene right through the audience and up to the far end of the hall, and the funeral procession
marched through it, so that for a few electric moments there was a terrible unity between
all those people. They were one: the workers who had come to show their comrades what
was happening across the river, and the workers who had come to see it. I have never
felt such a high pulsing vibration in any gathering before or since.[14]

The pageant as an art form enjoys a unique status in its relation to politics.
First of all, it is the mass art par excellence. Percy MacKaye, one of the leaders
of the vigorous but little-known pageant movement in this country at the beginning of the century, termed pageantry "the poetry of the masses," but it is of
course more than poetry. A combination of visual spectacle and dramatic performance, the pageant can weld together two seemingly disparate forces, the
subject and object of the dramatic metaphor. In reenactments, like the Paterson
Strike Pageant, the "actors" remain themselves yet at the same time play their
roles as symbols of broader issues. In the same way, the farm laborers in Hitler's
Nuremburg Rally of 1934 played—and were—themselves but at the same time
stood for the masses of agricultural workers throughout the country. In like
manner, the vast crowds that reenacted in Moscow in 1919 the storming of the
Winter Palace were revolutionaries themselves yet also played the role of vaster
revolutionary Russian forces.

For leaders of revolutionary movements, as well as for ideologues consciously or unconsciously intent on maintaining the status quo, the pageant was a potent weapon in forging a sense of communal identity for the hitherto inarticulate and unself-conscious lower classes. A pageant could function in the realm of participatory *dramatic* action rather in the way Diego River's Mexican murals did in the realm of public *visual* art: to forge a sense of contemporary purpose, self-identity and social cohesion out of a vivid recapitulation of historical fact heightened by symbolism.

But the pageant was also a unique political instrument in another way: the effects it had on the performers were as important as those it had on the audience. This can be said of no other performance art form. In the case of the *Paterson Strike Pageant*, the choice of significant incidents—the walkout, the martyrdom, the funeral of the martyr, the May Day Parade, the sending away of the children, the strike vote—the repetition of the speeches of the strike-leaders, and the dramatic simplification and compression of events which may have been unclear when experienced in actuality all made the striking workers conscious of the meaning of what they had lived through. In participating in the pageant, they became conscious of their experience as a meaningful force in history and of themselves as self-determining members of a class that shaped history. Reed's radical pageant, although it evidently failed in its fund-raising mission, was nevertheless a potent instrument in raising political consciousness and forging a sense of working-class solidarity. Although Jacques-Louis David's great pageants organized for the French First Republic obviously have historical precedence over Reed's *Paterson Strike Pageant*, and Europe had its own rich tradition of public political performance, still we can see what John Howard Lawson was getting at when he maintained in 1967 that the Paterson pageant had been a major event in the history of radical theatre: "The audience participation, the living-newspaper technique, the working-class point of view, foreshadow the work of Mayakovsky and Meyerhold in the Soviet Union and Brecht and Piscator in Germany, as well as the New Playwrights' Theatre in New York and the social drama of the 1930s."[15]

Where did Reed get the ideas for his *Paterson Strike Pageant*? While his production was stunningly effective as drama, spectacle, and political propaganda, it was by no means unique at the time. One might indeed say that the whole country was in the throes of a vigorous pageant renaissance, often referred to as the new pageant movement, sometimes as community or civic theatre. The year of the Paterson pageant saw the founding of the American Pageant Association, an organization with a *Bulletin*, a series of conferences, and a solid educational program. The bulletin listed almost fifty performances coast to coast in 1913 in addition to Reed's, including such varied fare as the *Pageant of the Nations* in Newburyport, Massachusetts, the *Pageant of American Childhood* in Worcester, Massachusetts, the Historical Pageant at Carmel, California, the *Suffrage Allegory and Pageant Parade* in Washington, D.C., a Greek Festival in Nashville and, perhaps particularly significant given Reed's Harvard background, both the Hollis Hall Pageant at that university (organized by George Pierce Baker, a strong proponent of civic theatre) and *Sanctuary, A Bird Masque*, directed by Percy MacKaye, Harvard 1897, leader of the civic-theatre movement and pageant-master extraordinary.[16]

For all those involved in the promulgation of pageantry in the United States at the time, the notion of civic uplift was primary; lurking in the background, often unarticulated, of course, were both a fear of and an altruistic wish to do good for the vast, unprecedented waves of immigrants arriving on our shores. The pageant could serve as an instrument of pacification, Americanization, and patriotic indoctrination for the supposedly unwashed and, in many ways, unwanted foreigners flooding our cities. John Collier, speaking in the pages of the *American Pageant Association Bulletin* in 1913, only hints at the problem of immigrant education in his impassioned defense of "the new Pageantry," seeing in it "the birth of a new educational ideal" and "the forerunner of a distinctly different and distinctly higher civic and social life" resting "on community consciousness and brotherhood" and creating them in its turn.[17] However, Esther Willard Bates, in her pioneering study of 1912, *Pageants and Pageantry*, had been more explicit about the pageants' function vis-à-vis the recent immigrants:

American pageantry will be so ordered as to possess a constructive influence on the people. . . . The spectacle will stimulate pride in town, state and nation; a broad sympathy for all lands and peoples will underlie and dominate the scenes; and finally there will be a definite educational aim to make real the great deeds of the fathers and to quicken the aspirations of the sons for right living and for devotion to country. In this last appeal the need of our immigrant population will be kept fully in mind.[18]

Many of the pageants immediately before and after World War I featured preludes of Italians, Poles, or Irish singing and dancing in colorful native costumes, generally followed by symbolic or actual obeisance to personifications of America and the singing of the national anthem. Nowhere was this integrative function of pageantry made more overt than in Percy MacKaye's *The New Citizenship: A Civic Ritual Devised for Places of Public Meeting in America*, published in 1915. This pageant was intended to accompany the naturalization ceremony and to underline through mass movement, song, and dance the transformation of the foreigner into the patriotic American citizen.[19]

The vast scope of MacKaye's achievements in mass participation and civic patriotism can be gathered from the *Pageant and Masque of St. Louis*, which he helped to create in 1914 in celebration of the 150th anniversary of the founding of that city. Performed out-of-doors in Forest Park on a mammoth, specially constructed stage by a cast of 7,500 citizens of St. Louis before a total of half a million spectators for five performances, the historical pageant and civic masque offered its awestruck audience what must have been a heady mixture of New-World symbolism, prophetic of Rivera and its harking back to pre-Columbian mythology and art forms. It was a premonition of Cecil B. de Mille in its ambitious crowd spectacles—choruses and Pioneers, World Adventurers, and "multitudes of men and women, garbed in the native costumes of all nations"—and reminiscent of Longfellow's *Hiawatha* in its speech (for example: "Ohè, Ohè, Ohè!/Our chief is cold—he is dead./Ohè, ohè, ohè!'').

The masque ended on a note of super spectacular patriotic exaltation in which the assembled throngs—including the cities and states of the Union, the distinctive industries, arts, sciences and professions, George Washington, St. Louis, personifications of Gold, Imagination, and the Great Bear, choruses of Wild Nature Forces, the Stars and Earth Spirits—joined together in a choir of hope for the future, as a gigantic eagle soared over their heads, "scattering wild sparkles of fire in its wake." In a footnote, MacKaye proudly explains that the bird, while "in configuration and color an eagle," is, of course, "an aeroplane, serving thus for the first time [1914] the symbolism of dramatic poetry." Yet perhaps even more revealing of the unexpressed function of the St. Louis spectacle was the fact that the "historic pageant" preceding the masque had ended with the entry of German immigrants into St. Louis, laden with boxes, satchels, and bundles, singing heartily in German and immediately becoming incorporated into the bosom of the city.[20]

Reed's Paterson Strike Pageant assumes its full importance only in the context of the more general pageant movement of its time in the United States. Reed may be said to have turned the patriotic rhetoric, the well-meaning melting pot psychology of the do-gooder civic-theatre leaders, back upon itself, revealing its idealistic vision of the immigrant workers' place in their new land for the sentimental cant it was. The patriotic pageants were all too often merely spectacular rationalizations of the status quo, filling the workers with false promises and false consciousness at the same time. In the Paterson Strike Pageant, it was made dramatically clear that the new citizens were contributing more than their dances, their songs, and their folk traditions to this country: they were being forced to contribute their health, their hopes, their honor, and their children and to live lives of wretchedness and squalor so that WASP capitalist society might flourish.

Percy MacKaye's pageant for the new citizens ended with a stirring proclamation about the joys of labor during which a symbolic figure of Liberty unfurled the American flag above the nationalized immigrants' heads.[21] The Paterson strikers, on the other hand, had replied to their employers' hypocritical eulogy of the American flag by saying about themselves that "they wove the flag, they dyed the flag and they refused to scab under the flag."[22] Reed's pageant, among other achievements, articulated the hollowness of the symbols of the American dream of freedom, democracy, and prosperity—for the oppressed immigrant workers of Paterson and, by implication, for the nation as a whole. In the words of Elizabeth Gurley Flynn, speaking of the strikers: "They have no more use for the state. To them the Statue of Liberty is personified by the policeman and his club."[23]

NOTES

1. Elizabeth Gurley Flynn, "The Truth About the Paterson Strike" (speech delivered January 31, 1914, at the New York Civic Club Forum), manuscript from Labadie Collection of Labor Materials, University of Michigan Library, p. 1. I am grateful to Professor Marilyn Blatt Young for providing me with a copy of this manuscript and for her generous assistance in other aspects of the preparation of this article.

2. The most inclusive discussion of the Paterson strike, including publication of important source material, is contained in Joyce L. Kornbluh's *Rebel Voices: An IWW Anthology* (Ann Arbor, 1964), pp. 197–226. A far more personal account of the pageant is to be found in Mabel Dodge Luhan's *Movers and Shakers (Intimate Memories, III)* (New York, 1936), pp. 200–12.

3. While Baker himself was anything but a political radical, one of his students, a Radcliffe woman named Elizabeth MacFadden, was the author of the first play about child labor, *The Product of the Mill*, performed in Boston at the Castle Square Theatre in 1912. See Percy MacKaye, *The Civic Theatre in Relation to the Redemption of Leisure* (New York, 1912), pp. 222, 275. For a more thorough examination of Baker and his work at Harvard, see Wisner Payne Kinne, *George Pierce Baker and the American Theatre* (Cambridge, 1954). Baker was associated with pageant-master Percy MacKaye at Harvard and himself produced the Peterborough Pageant at the MacDowell Colony in 1910, the year of Reed's graduation; in the same year he planned a grandiose commemorative pageant, which never took place, for the settling of Oregon and a decade later actually carried out an ambitious pageant reenacting the landing of the Pilgrims for the tercentenary of the founding of Plymouth Colony. See Kinne, pp. 138–42.

4. Originally published June 1913. Reprinted in *The Education of John Reed: Selected Writings*, ed. John Stuart (New York, 1955), pp. 39–47.

5. Luhan, p. 204.

6. Kornbluh, p. 201, attributes "the poster of the crouching workman" to Jones.

7. Kornbluh, p. 201. Sloan and his wife Dolly were active socialists at the time. Not only did he devote major energies to his drawings for *The Masses*, of which Dolly was business manager, but he ran as Socialist party candidate for the New York State assembly as well. See Van Wyck Brooks, *John Sloan: A Painter's Life* (New York, 1955), pp. 84–100.

8. Booklet, *The Pageant of the Paterson Strike*, Madison Square Garden, Saturday, June 7, 1913, 8:30 P.M., *p. 16. Reprinted in Kornbluh, p. 210.*

9. *New York Herald Tribune*, June 8, 1913, pp. 1, 4.

10. Pageant booklet, p. 17, and Kornbluh, pp. 210, 212.

11. *The Independent*, 74 (June 19, 1913), 1407.

12. Cited in Kornbluh, p. 212.

13. *The Independent*, pp. 1406–7.

14. Luhan, p. 204.

15. John Howard Lawson, intro. to John Reed, *Ten Days That Shook the World* (1919; rpt. New York, 1967), p. ix.

16. "List of Pageants of the Year 1913," *American Pageant Association Bulletin*, No. 2 (February 1, 1914).

17. John Collier, cited in *American Pageant Association Bulletin*, No. 1 (May 15, 1913).

18. Esther Willard Bates, *Pageants and Pageantry* (Boston, 1912), p. 18. Also see Ralph Davol, *A Handbook of American Pageantry* (Taunton, Massachusetts, 1914), pp. 88–91, for emphasis on pageantry's duty to reform and Americanize immigrants.

19. Percy MacKaye, *The New Citizenship: A Civic Ritual Devised for Places of Public Meeting in America* (New York, 1915).

20. Thomas Wood Stevens and Percy MacKaye, *The Book of Words of the Pageant and Masque of St. Louis*, 2nd ed. (St. Louis, 1914). The simple dialogue is actually from Thomas Wood Stevens's portion of the event. MacKaye often employed what appears to be native American in his script. ''Pooloopooloonool Hiloha!'' is the opening line of the chorus of Wild Nature Forces (p. 69) in his text.

21. MacKaye, *The New Citizenship*, p. 86.

22. Cited in the booklet, *The Pageant of the Paterson Strike*, p. 22.

23. Flynn, p. 30.

7

"Let Them Be Amused": The Industrial Drama Movement, 1910–1929

Hiroko Tsuchiya

During the progressive era and into the 1920s, American industrial enterprises built company auditoriums, subsidized drama clubs, and staged company vaudevilles to entertain their workers and occupy their leisure time. To further extend their influence over their workers' lives, industrialists financed community-sponsored plays and pageants involving workers and their families. Employers, concerned with maximum production through the elimination of a fraction of second of waste in workers' motion, were unlikely patrons of theatrical productions that demanded long hours from their employees. What motivated management to hold theatricals on factory sites and in industrial communities? An analysis of the industrial drama movement promises to anwer this question and, in the process, to deepen our understanding of the complex relationship between modern capitalism and culture.[1]

The early company drama movement was part of an industrial recreation campaign that had become fashionable after 1890 among larger corporations. From the 1880s to the 1910s, engineers discovered that the "overuse of human machines," to use their jargon, diminished productivity. By conducting numerous fatigue and efficiency surveys, management consultants demonstrated that workers could achieve higher production rates in shorter hours; eight hours a day could be at least as productive as nine or ten. Employers, convinced of the profitability of shorter hours of work, now proclaimed that leisure pays. Hours of work gradually shortened after 1890, from an average of sixty hours a week to fifty-one in 1920. By 1921, eight hours a day had become common practice in larger companies. Although employers instituted shorter workdays in the hope of increasing productivity, the resulting new leisure caused anxiety among employers and their consultants and among government policy makers and civic leaders. Many believed that workers, inevitably bored by their highly regulated, monotonous work, were particularly susceptible to "peculiar temptations during their leisure hours [which] too often [led] them into immorality and crime." Instead of eliminating the cause of this boredom in work, managers attempted to manipulate workers' leisure-time activities by establishing "directed recreation" programs in factories. These programs, common in the industrial North after 1900, began to appear in southern mills, mining, and lumber camps and even in Hawaiian sugar plantations after 1910.[2]

Industrial recreation programs were designed to replace existing working-class street institutions: saloons, dance halls, and vaudeville theatres. Saloons and theatres not only offered entertainment to workers but provided back rooms for union meetings after hours too. Also, in dance halls and vaudeville theatres young women working fifty hours a week for ten dollars were open to the temptations of easy money, or so it was believed. Convinced that city streets generated strikes, alcoholism, and prostitution, industrialists and civic leaders crusaded against such "immorality and crime" by attacking street institutions. Some companies went so far as to discourage employees from going outside the company site during lunch. In their eagerness to replace working-class institutions, companies offered hygienic versions of popular concert saloons with features such as bars, restaurants, bowling alleys, billiards, pool tables, theatres, dance halls, small meeting places, and occasionally roof gardens.[3]

Organizers of industrial theatricals were clearly conscious of the enormous popularity of commercial variety shows that were accessible to their employees. The live theatre was a vital entertainment for urban workers at least until the early 1930s. A survey made in 1912 showed that more than one-third of New York working men visited a live theatre of some sort in the week they were interviewed. More than 20 percent of the married men working over eleven hours a day said they had visited a theatre during the week. Employers were fearful of the moral consequences to their work force of such theatregoing. The City Club of Milwaukee, financed by over 900 manufacturers and other local elites, reported that theatre problems were more serious than those caused by the saloons. In order to investigate the extent to which the working class patronized the "dangerous" vaudevilles, the secretary of the City Club nightly attended vaudevilles in the winter of 1913 and rated the "moral influence," "appeal" ("emotional," "sexual instinct"), "artistic value," and the nature of the applause of each of the acts.[4]

Since company theatricals were intended to compete with and finally to substitute for existing working-class entertainment, company shows of necessity imitated and sanitized the most popular forms of working-class theatre. Vaudevilles and minstrel shows were seen as particularly suitable for industrial workers for two reasons. First, variety shows did "not require very extensive preparation" in "shops where the workers' time for recreation is limited," to quote the Industrial Department of the Young Men's Christian Association. Second, the messages of mindless gaiety and childlike innocence that the company variety shows were expected to promote appealed to management fearful of the radicalization of their employees and of impending strikes. Before 1920, the qualities that employers wished to inculcate in their work force were based on two sets of criteria. At work, good workers were machine parts or "intelligent gorillas" capable of repeating prescribed motions. After work, employers urged their "human machines" to transform themselves into happy-go-lucky, Sambo-like characters. Andrew Carnegie, for instance, espoused "laughter and frolic" and showed a keen interest in "trifles" as important virtues for his workers. "Life must not be taken too seriously," preached the steel magnate. People involved with trifles and indifferent to serious things—like politics—were unlikely to strike. "Jolly and clean" vaudevilles seemed to be a perfect instrument for creating such an atmosphere after work.[5]

The Goodyear Greater Minstrels, performing on two evenings in March 1917 at Akron's Grand Opera House, exemplified the notion of easygoing, carefree industrial relations desired by the company. Sponsored by management and directed by an employment officer, the cast consisted of 100 employees, ranging from salesmen and stenographers to factory hands. The show included comic skits in blackface, ragtime and dixieland music, acrobatic acts, a skit entitled "A Night in the Factory Lunch Room," and a finale called "The Midnight Cakewalk Ball." The Goodyear Minstrels typified company shows during the 1910s. Composed mostly of song and dance acts, these productions rarely developed a story line, unlike many shows of the 1920s.[6]

The entrance of the United States into World War I provided recreation campaigners with a vast opportunity for experimenting with organized adult recreation. Wartime mobilization inevitably created temporary communities of strangers made up, many feared, of unattached and footloose workers and soldiers. In camps, shipyards, ammunition industries, and governmental bureaucracies, these strangers appeared to create a perpetual preriot situation in the minds of company and government managers. Industries and the United States government introduced adult recreation into these new communities as a pacifying and unifying measure in their war effort. In creating national agencies for catering to adult recreational needs, the government solicited expert advice from industrial welfare directors, progressive reformers, and recreation organizations. Industrial recreation advocates regarded this governmental call as an ultimate sanction for organized recreation and, with an eye on their groups' future expansion in postwar society, responded enthusiastically.[7]

To meet the recreational needs of the soldiers, the federal government constructed thirty-four "Liberty Theatres" within a year after the declaration of war. Four dramatic and four vaudeville companies performed at these theatres along with other volunteering professional performers. The proclaimed objective of the liberty theatres was to "compete" with the "vicious influence" of commercial establishments by offering soldiers "wholesome" and "clean" entertainment. The nature of the shows was more recreational than educational, keeping the soldiers "in a happy mood." In large cities, where soldiers visited on weekends, the Playground and Recreation Association of America (founded in 1906), under the Commission on Training Camp Activities in the Department of War, secured the cooperation of local theatre managers and professional entertainers along with the State Women's War Relief. These women helped the Playground Association to provide soldiers with professional vaudeville on Sunday afternoons, entertaining the young men "in leisure hours when loneliness and homesickness are most dangerous." For the civilian workforce, the Playground Association advocated constructing industrial community centers.[8]

Corporations not only sought to control their work force by limiting outside influence, they also wanted to increase their authority over the outside community itself. Industry, according to the managers of International Harvester Company, was groping for "a possibility of extending [their] influence largely into the community" to find a "remedy for many neighborhood social evils."[9] The industrialists' sense of corrupting outside influences grew keener during the 1920s when the majority of industrial workers worked an eight-hour day. Management was aware that it was impossible to cordon off such influences during the sixteen hours of workers' lives outside factories and shops. Adding to the industrialists' sense of alarm, company reports and governmental surveys indicated that workers tended to avoid company recreation facilities. This, too, led management to relegate some of their attempt to control employees' nonwork time to outside organizations which shared their views. In addition, industries abhorred their being labeled as paternalistic organizations. A manager of Studebaker, for instance, said at an engineers' convention that paternalism would breed "servile" employees, a result incompatible with the American ideals of independence and individual ambition. Besides, he added, paternalism smacked of "socialism or communism." Finally, the passage of the prohibition amendment created a vacuum in working-class leisure previously occupied by the saloon. Consequently, industrial recreation advocates felt a "greatly intensified" need for working-class meeting places where management and employees "may come together in their leisure time in a friendly manner." Primarily for these reasons, many companies chose to finance community activities, gradually reducing the number of their own organized recreational programs. As early as 1921, virtually all large industrial cities and more than 300 smaller towns operated community centers with the cooperation of local industries.[10]

The Playground Association, having gained national prominence through its wartime service, expanded its work from the prewar children's playground movement to industrial community recreation. In 1919, the Association formally established the Department of Industry and the Department of Drama to reorganize the lives of workers in peacetime industrial communities. The Association served as a link between local governments and industrial concerns, sending field workers to industrial communities—often at the request of local chambers of commerce and industrialists—to lobby for more community centers. The military-camp theatrical provided a model for community drama during the postwar years. Advocates called community drama "the supreme method" of social engineering in peacetime, since it was "the art, *par excellence*, of resolving the estrangement and conflict of social elements into harmony." The Association ran a summer drama school and trained recreation directors for industries and communities.[11]

Reflecting the xenophobia of the postwar red-scare era which held foreign-born residents responsible for much of the violence and radical ideology in America, the Playground Association emphasized the Americanization of immigrant workers. One purpose of stage productions, according to the Association, was "to increase the *esprit de corps*" of newly arrived workers. To further specify their goals, the Association printed model scripts for pageant presentation. The values propagated in these scripts are demonstrated in this typical scene.

America: Who is it that knocks?

An Immigrant: We, the people of other lands, who are seeking Liberty.

America: I bid you enter.

Immigrant Leader: We have been oppressed. We are bowed under heavy burdens.

America: I will lift your burdens.

(At a sign from America, Liberty lifts the burden from off the back of the immigrants.)

Immigrants: We have been starved.

America: If you work I will give you bread. . . . And what will you give me in return for what I have given you?

Immigrants: We will give you loyalty, devotion and gratitude.[12]

The Association's campaign to Americanize immigrant workers through pageants caught on. In the *League of Nations* pageant at Chester, Pennsylvania, the figure of Chester held out her arms to all foreign-born residents. The governor of Pennsylvania, appearing in the pageant, urged the newcomers to offer the community "the contribution of their best" through "united effort." This speech was translated into several languages so that everyone in the audience could understand it. Then, "responding to the outflung arms of Chester, the foreign born marched through the entrance arch of the city" and proceeded to demonstrate their cultural roots in crafts, songs, and dances. At the finale, "all the foreign flags were brought to the center of the stage and grouped about the flags of Chester and the United States, while the whole assembly sang the national anthem." According to the writer of this report, similar Americanization pageants had been "successfully staged at numerous other industrial centers."[13]

The Playground Association was working in close cooperation with industrial and business firms, and their model scripts were in compliance with corporate ideology and standards. Their Americanization theme was no cruder than that of a pageant staged by the Ford Company's compulsory English school for immigrant workers. In the Ford pageant, a long line of immigrants wearing their national costumes marched into a great melting pot and emerged in identical suits, each worker carrying a little American flag.[14]

Complementing Americanization, the glorification of hard work was another theme of industrial community productions. The Playground Association's model pageant for Labor Day (1921) sanctified breakneck speed and strenuous toil. In the pageant, the figure of America proclaims,

> Work,
> Thank God for the pride of it,
> For the beautiful conquering tide of it,
> Sweeping the life in its furious fold,
> Thrilling the arteries, cleansing the blood,
> Mastering the stupor and dull despair,
> Moving the dreamer to do and dare . . .
> Work, the power that drives behind,
> Guiding the purpose, taming the mind,
> Holding the runaway wishes back,
> Reining the will to one steady track,
> Speeding the energies faster and faster . . .
> What is so kind as the cruel goad,
> Forcing us on through the rugged road?

The closing poem, also read by America, depicts Labor "clamouring," "hammering," "thundering," "shaping the earth,"—in short, tearing the world apart with the flaming "passion of labor."[15]

Besides the glory of work, this Labor Day pageant taught workers their position in the existing industrial hierarchy. The civil engineer, for instance, cuts an imposing figure: "he's a nervy, wiry divil,/ with his notebook, and his livil,/ Ah! he doesn't seem to know the name of fear." In contrast to the independent engineer, the steel worker is subjected to an abusive foreman who shouts: "Hey you! Watch the way you're doin' there! Use your blooming head." The steel worker remains silent. "Costumed properly," the steel workers, civil engineers, Panama Canal labor gang, and other occupations were clearly distinguished from each other. The pageant concluded with the participants' reciting their work songs while marching in procession to place flowers on the altar of America.[16]

Pageants had been important means of communication, education, and entertainment for working-class audiences and participants since the late nineteenth century. Workers organized their own pageants on picnics, rallies, and sometimes on strikes. Although the form was similar to those of industrial community pageants, the messages were quite different. Compare, for instance, the *Paterson Strike Pageant* staged by the Industrial Workers of the World in June 1913 with later industrial pageants. The IWW pageant opened with a scene of the silk mills that prospered by exploiting their employees. Workers were described as neither giggling buffoons nor pathetic victims: they were alert and intelligent. A speech preceding the pageant stressed workers' independence and their "passion for solidarity." After episodes of police brutality and the death of a worker by a stray bullet, the show closed with a mass strike for the eight-hour day. Corporate theatre programs were devised, in part, to counteract this trend in genuine work-ing-class theatre. Clearly, industrialists were fearful of the "new ideals of the proletarian masses given strong, unequivocal expression through the drama," in the words of Rose P. Stokes, a socialist.[17]

Although the trend of company recreation shifted from individual, in-factory programs to community organizations, some large industries continued to stage their own shows in the early twenties. The Western Electric Company's Haw-thorne Works (hiring about 20,000 employees) presented a company show in February 1920. The show, entitled *Hawthorne Follies*, ran for a full week in downtown Chicago. The *Follies* opened with the Hawthorne Minstrels, a cast of sixty-five white employees in blackface with Liberty in the center of their minstrel half circle. This was followed by a comic skit depicting a day in the company medical clinic during the height of the then-recent influenza epidemic. The *Follies* included numerous songs and dances, ranging from pseudo-ragtime to patriotic numbers. The costumes were as varied as the songs: an enormous American flag to clothe a goddesslike figure, silk hats, vaguely Chinese dresses, and a "wild Malay" costume worn by a man swinging a saber. The *Follies* closed with a "Rush-in Ballet," presenting twelve male employees in wigs and female ballet outfits. The costumes, skits, and songs followed the current fashions of commercial vaudevilles.[18]

What differentiated the 1920s company shows from the simple vaudeville acts in the 1910s and from the deadly serious industrial pageants were their acceptance of conventional commercialism and their benign indulgence of jazz-age fads. The description of the *Follies* in the company magazine for workers stressed professional stage sets and glamorous costumes. Comparing their *Follies* with Ziegfeld's, the company writer noted that the lighting effects were so fantastic that they "could make the electrician of the Winter Garden cringe with envy." Furthermore, the espousal of fun and mindlessness on the stage was more frantic than the plea in 1910 for innocent smiles and childlike gaiety. The *Follies*, it was said, tickled the "funny bone" of workers; in fact the actors were so amusing that people would shake off the flu with laughter. Persistent allusions were made in pictures and cartoons to women employees on stage with their legs exposed in flapper costumes.[19]

The de-emphasis of hard work and avoidance of explicit moralism reflected changing industrial management techniques which increasingly relied on psy-chological theories. According to Hugo Muensterberg, William James's protégé and a founder of industrial psychology, "All business is ultimately the affair of minds." During the postwar red-scare years, the pseudo-Freudian analysis of the cause of social unrest appealed to management fearful of a revolutionized working class. Industrial psychologists described the strikes and the alleged revolutionary movement of the period as the result of "balked instincts" or as explosions of the "subconscious." Management had to "deflect" instincts into "useful channels" to prevent workers from becoming Wobblies and bolsheviks. "Provisions must always be made," wrote G. Stanley Hall, "for every kind of wholesome *convivium* vents and releases [of] strain and tension which may break out in riotous form." The industrial drama movement was influenced by the popularity of this new management theory of instincts, repression, and expression. Leisure and recreation would provide pacifying agents in the "mental underworld" of workers. Psychological jargon came to permeate the vocabulary of the recreation organizers: "Recreation must be vital enough to affect the subconscious," said Howard S. Braucher of the Playground Association. The Association stressed that theatricals in industrial communities would be "particularly valuable" for taming the misplaced instincts of the working class and thus securing an efficient, strikeless society.[20]

Psychologized management theories of the 1920s transformed the employers' conception of work and play. In the earliest industrial recreation campaign, play and work had been distinctly and rigidly segregated. Workers in the progressive era were encouraged to be amused in auditoriums and recreation rooms, but not in the work place—work remained a serious task of life and was not to be confused with play. During the twenties, however, management became interested in merging the hitherto clearly separated spheres of work and play. One of the factors that caused this shift was a general acceptance within management that routinized, segmented work was necessary to businesses geared to maximizing profit. Consequently, it became ludicrous to demand that workers thrive on simple tasks and repetitive motions. Employers were aware that the staggeringly high turnover and unprecedented number of strikes from 1914 to 1922 were workers' responses to the new management and production techniques. In addition, industrial psychologists, as we have noted earlier, were proselytizing the danger of repression caused by monotonous work. How could management induce employees to accept work? The glorification of work, exemplified in the Playground Association's model pageants, appeared unpersuasive and almost outdated. Instead, introducing play elements into work was considered a more effective alternative. "If work can be made into play, so much the more powerful its appeal," wrote Professor Harry A. Overstreet of the City College of New York. Flapper employees on the Hawthorne stage symbolized the emergence of a new work ethic. A model worker was no longer hard-driving and serious-looking since seriousness in work implied "repression . . . ,the fertile soil of unrest for the agitators, the radical, the bolsheviks." The ideal worker of the roaring twenties was a playful one, a creature of "free spirit," according to Overstreet.[21]

Playful workers, however, were not to stray far from the company backyard in their leisure time. The second *Hawthorne Follies* staged in 1922, demonstrated that workers' lives revolved around the company. The show this time was a semimusical romance performed by thirty-six men and forty women. Captain Jack, a World War I veteran, falls in love with the "girl with the golden voice" over a telephone, and they become engaged. (Western Electric was a subsidiary of the American Telephone and Telegraph Company.) A villain named Switch, desiring the "golden voice" for himself, persuades the father of the girl to demand that the captain save $5,000 as a precondition for the marriage. So Captain Jack finds a job at the Hawthorne Works, which is coincidentally offering a $5,000 prize in a slogan contest at the Hawthorne Club. After some complications created by the vicious Switch, the captain prevails, winning the prize and the girl. The dialogue is full of Hawthorne with several scenes at the Hawthorne Works, characters who are Hawthorne employees, and workers singing "Made in Western Electric" on the stage.[22]

It is quite possible that these shows temporarily aroused interest among workers. The Hawthorne Works was located in the western part of Chicago, a dismal industrial district characterized by "a few patches of soot-coated crab grass, and littered streets." The extravagant costumes and dazzling lighting effects might have given its work force a temporary illusion of glamour and luxury. However, the Hawthorne management failed to increase its output through amusement. Two years later (1924), the company started a series of efficiency experiments which continued well into the 1930s. There is no record of a third *Follies*.[23]

A 1922 show of the Goodyear Rubber and Tire Company provides another example of mock playfulness, imposed conviviality, and company solidarity. The show, entitled *A Day at the Goodyear* and presented by the company's Prune Street Players at the "Generally Offul Restaurant," dramatized the activities of the Akron plant managers and workers. Although the script has not survived, short descriptions of characters in the program indicate job hierarchy as well as personality stereotypes attributed to each post. To tie the plot together, an ambitious messenger boy ("He may be president some day") visits various departments. The first character to appear is the spirit of Charles Goodyear, "an inventer." Paul W. Litchman, vice president and author of the welfare plan at Akron, is "the workingman's friend." Other managers are tough characters: Elbert Bark ("His bite is even worse"), one called "a terror with the graph," and another characterized as "a Monarch of all he surveys." Others are fussy: Hal Cammel is "always worrying about costs," and someone else is "an efficiency enthusiast." In contrast to these silly authoritarians and self-involved managers, the rank and file are portrayed as "blithesome" workers who "come merrily to work." Only one woman is given a distinct role: a stenographer ("She's no lady."). The show ends in a finale called "A Manufacturing Milestone." The program notes promised the spectators "the most smiles per dollar," inviting the workers in the audience to laugh at the managerial caricatures on stage.[24]

In contrast to the professionalism in stage setting and costumes that the organizers of industrial shows stressed, acting excellence was not a priority in industrial stage production. According to a pamphlet put out by the Metropolitan Life Insurance Company: "It should be remembered that amateur productions are often most successful when enthusiasm, rather than art, is predominant." More bluntly, the Playground Association advocated a double standard of theatrical quality, maintaining that industrial community theatres should provide lower-quality production for their "less sophisticated public." The main goal

of industrial theatre should be "not art, but life . . . ,not esthetic, but sociological." Sociological here meant exactly what the International Harvester Company
intended when they established their sociological department. It was a "scheme,"
as the executive wrote, to keep workers complacent and efficient. A guest teacher
of the Association's drama school advised future directors of industrial theatres
to "forget . . . whatever professional standards" they might have. The teacher
concluded, "The amateur and the professional follow parallel roads, perhaps,
but we must never forget that parallel lines, even if infinitely extended, can
never meet." This attitude contradicted the occasional advice given to industrial
community theatres by promoters of classical arts. Otto H. Kahn, chairman of
the Metropolitan Opera Company, had proclaimed: "Aim high. The higher you
aim, the more likely you are to hit. Don't think you have to play down to an
assumed level of your public."[25]

In 1925, Metropolitan Life issued its policyholders a pamphlet entitled "Drama
in Industry," demonstrating that drama had become an accepted medium of
management propaganda and education. It suggested four possible uses of industrial drama. The first use involved demonstration skits for sales employees
to show the proper method of selling merchandise. The second was to "impress
upon employees the prestige and stability of the establishment for which they
work." The third was "solely to entertain: a step toward happier contact between
employer and employees." And the fourth involved educational material on
particular merchandise. Some companies developed an additional function for
industrial drama: public relations. For instance, Western Electric's *Hawthorne
Follies* entertained a street crowd gathered for the opening of a Chicago bridge,
and the company ran a charity show in Chicago's largest theatre for the benefit
of an old-age home. In 1925, Dan River Mills in Danville, Virginia (employing
5,000 workers), produced a show called *The Story of Cotton*. The management
came to regard the annual pageant as an effective advertisement as well as "a
builder of morale." Pleased with their success in "visualizing the function of
[mill operatives] as one of the cleanest and most useful occupations in the
industrial world," the company made a portion of the story into a five-reel
motion picture for use in their public relations campaign.[26]

By sponsoring employees' shows and industrial community pageants, American industries, for the first time, practiced the role of providers of mass entertainment. Ralph Parlette, a popular public lecturer, summarized the new mode
of corporate thinking by proclaiming, "Community is just a larger playground.
Business, industry, commerce are just larger games with finer toys and tools.
Let us not take ourselves so seriously. Not one of us is indispensable. Every job
. . . is just another opportunity for us to have a good time, play the game, kick
up our heels."

If life was a playground, its residents were obliged to "have a good time"
there. The new sense of obligation to participate in company-supported activities
was reinforced by management's presupposition that it owned the workers' leisure hours. Companies wanted to convert spare time "into an asset which will

yield large dividends,'' in the words of George Eastman of Kodak to the president of the Playground Association. True American workers had to have the "energy with which to enjoy it."[27]

In 1924, President Calvin Coolidge announced his intention of establishing a coordinated federal recreation policy to generate "perennial gladness" and a play spirit among the people. Reflecting the national interest in obligatory happiness and joy, the Metropolitan Life Insurance Company issued a "SUB-POENA" to its employees in the "Name of his Royal Highness, the Prince of Merriment." The Prince ordered Metropolitan workers to "appear before the high court of JOYFULNESS," meaning the company's annual party, the "Society Circus." There, in the "Court of JOYFULNESS," the insurance company employees would be transformed into subjects of the "State of Amusement" and citizens of the "City of Laughter." If workers found it hard to keep laughing, then a Playground Association activist told them to "pretend." The essence of drama was "pretending they are someone else," said a drama organizer. "It is indeed a great land of 'Let's pretend,' '' she concluded with approval.[28]

In the characterization of managers and in the description of routine work in the company show, we note incipient bitterness and a touch of cynicism. However, these negative feelings, safely channeled into dramatic expression, remained unthreatening to the industrial order. Resignation to the status quo, if not acceptance of it, was the dramatic catharsis of company theatricals in the 1920s. Indeed, industrial dramas may have served, for a short time, as an expedient outlet for many workers' pent-up "emotions"—to use management jargon. The gaiety of company shows concealed some essentially chilling and demeaning messages: life is merely a game to play, and all players are replaceable. The incessant insistence of recreation propagandists to "have fun" was equally degrading because coerced amusement is a form of labor and enforced happiness is a mode of oppression.

NOTES

1. As for the elimination of waste, see H. K. Hathaway (vice president, Tabor Manufacturing Company, Philadelphia), "Elementary Time Study as a Part of the Taylor System of Scientific Management," in *Scientific Management*, ed. Clarence B. Thompson (Cambridge, Massachusetts, 1914), pp. 521–79.

2. See fatigue and efficiency studies by Frederick W. Taylor, Josephine Goldmark, and Frank B. Gilbreth, and Lillian M. Gilbreth; National Cash Register, "The Beginning of a New Era" (1899); "Interview with Miss Elia M. Haas (National Cash Register)" on August 3, 1901, National Civic Federation Papers (NCF Papers), Box 113, New York Public Library; Resumé of Report, "Condition of Employment: 22 New York Concerns Affiliated with the New York Retail Dry Goods Association," July 15, 1913, NCF Papers, Box 111, pp. 9–10; Ida Tarbell, *New Ideals in Business* (New York, 1916), pp. 163–70; Charles A. Prosser, "The Training of the Factory Worker Through Industrial Edu-

cation,'' a speech before the Fifth Annual Convention of the National Society for Promotion of Industrial Education, Cincinnati, November, 1911, p. 7.

3. Theatre and saloon designs and activities can be located in "Police Reports concerning Licensing of Theaters, Halls, . . . " Box 6172, Mayor's Papers, prior to 1898, Municipal Archives of New York City. Typical antistreet attitudes were Lee K. Frankel (Metropolitan Life Insurance), Remarks, May 29, 1916, NCF Papers, Box 113; J. M. Giddings to Gertrude Beeks, April 17, 1911, NCF Papers, Box 120.

4. The 1912 survey is in George E. Bevans, *How Workingmen Spend Their Spare Time* (New York, 1913), tables 4, 5, 12, 13, 15, and 24. Also see, Irving Howe, *World of Our Fathers* (New York, 1976), pp. 460–96; *Leisure Time Activities of 5,000 Individuals* (New York, 1933), pp. 1–11. Regarding Milwaukee vaudevilles, see "Tentative Outline for Recreation Exhibit," 1913, The City Club of Milwaukee Papers, Wisconsin State Historical Society, Box 4, p. 2. According to the secretary's survey notes, the "economic status" of the majority of the audience was either "struggling" or "poor."

5. YMCA, *Among Industrial Workers* (New York, 1919), p. 111; Frederick W. Taylor, *The Principles of Scientific Management* (New York, 1916), p. 40; Sidney McCurdy, "Present Scope of Welfare Work in Iron and Steel Industry," May 22, 1914, NCF Papers, Box 109; Andrew Carnegie's speech in *Dedication of the Carnegie Library at the Edgar Thomson Rail Works* (1894), a pamphlet in New York Public Library, p. 27.

6. Goodyear Rubber and Tire Company, *Goodyear Greater Minstrels* (1917), a nine-page program, Goodyear Rubber and Tire Company Archives.

7. U.S. Department of War, Council of National Defense, *Bulletin,* no. 7743, October 29, 1918; Newton D. Baker, "Liberty Theater," a speech before the commission on Training Camp Activities, War Department, 1918, p. 4.

8. War Department, *Report of the Chairman on Training Camp Activities* (Washington, D.C., 1918), pp. 20–21; *New York Times Magazine*, November 4, 1917, p. 129; Baker, "Liberty," p. 5; War Department, *Report*, p. 5; separate evaulation sheets inserted in *Report*; "Trouping for Uncle Sam and His Boys," *New York Tribune*, 5 May 1918, a clipping from a Stage Women's War Relief scrap book (n.c. 5461), Lincoln Center, New York Public Library; *Evening Sun*, 31 May 1918, SWWR scrapbook. The War Department had its own organizers. Nineteen "able dramatic directors" were training soldiers to perform on their own. The government printed and distributed light comedies for their use (Department of Dramatic Activities Among Soldiers, War Department, *Service Edition*, no. 15). The YMCA was involved: YMCA, *Service with Fighting Men* (New York, 1922), 1: 340–42.

9. J. G. Wood to G. F. Steele, April 25, 1905, Cyrus McCormick, Jr., NCF Papers, Box 42; M. L. Goss to Cyrus McCormick, April 2, 1907, in the same box.

10. U.S. Bureau of Labor Statistics, *Bulletin*, no. 250 (1919), table 5, p. 70; "Notes Taken at the Group Meeting of the National Congress on Outdoor Recreation Papers," Box 1, National Archives. As for paternalism, see Charles A. Lippincott's speech at the twelfth National Convention of the Society of Industrial Engineers, Cleveland, May 1925, *Proceedings*, pp. 214–15. On a working-class meeting place: Community Service (Playground Association), *Community Buildings for Industrial Towns* (New York, 1921), pp. 5, 9. The number of the community centers is from "Industrial Recreation," *Playground*, 14 (1920), pp. 356–66.

11. Numerous accounts of industries' involvement in community center movements can be found in correspondence and minutes in the Playground and Recreation Association of America Papers, Social Welfare History Archives, University of Minnesota. The

quotation is from Percy MacKaye, *Community Drama: Its Method of Neighborliness* (Boston, 1917), pp. viii–xi.

12. Playground Association, *Community Drama* (November 1921), pp. 14–15; ibid., pp. 119–20.

13. "Industrial Recreation," *Playground*, 14 (1920), p. 480.

14. John Higham, *Strangers in the Land* (1968; rpt., New York, 1973), p. 248.

15. Mary Pashly Harris, "A Tribute to Labor: A Suggestive Program for Labor Day," (mimeographed), Bulletin, no. 224 (1921), Playground Association Papers, pp. 1–7.

16. Ibid., pp. 4–7.

17. Booklet, *The Pageant of the Paterson Strike* (Madison Square Garden, Saturday, June 7, 1913, 8:30 P.M.), reprinted in Joyce L. Kornbluh, *Rebel Voices: An IWW Anthology* (Ann Arbor, 1964), pp. 197–226; Frederick S. Boyd, "The General Strike in the Silk Industry," a pamphlet in the New York Public Library, p. 7; New York *Call*, 28 January 1920.

18. "Hawthorne Works Produces Great Play," *Western Electric News* (March 1920).

19. Ibid.

20. Hugo Muensterberg, *Business Psychology* (Chicago, 1920), p. 5. *Practical Psychology*, ed. Lionel Edie (New York, 1922), p. 57; Donald A Laird, *Increasing Personal Efficiency* (New York, 1922), p. 166; R. B. Wolf, "Making Men Like Their Jobs," in Edie, p. 113; G. Stanley Hall, "Scope of Psychology in Industry," address before Worcester Polytechnic Institute, June 10, 1920, in Edie, p. 21. As for community organizers, see Howard S. Braucher, "Recreation in Relation to Work," *Playground*, 23 (1929–1930), p. 443; Playground Association, *Community Buildings*, p. 506; "Organized Labor and Recreation," *Playground*, 18 (1924), pp. 125–26.

21. Harry A. Overstreet, *Influencing Human Behavior* (New York, 1925), pp. 38, 264. Also see Henry Elkind, "Practical Applications of Mental Hygiene in Industry," *Preventive Management: Mental Hygiene in Industry*, ed. Henry Elkind, (New York, 1931).

22. "*Hawthorne Follies* Again Proves a Big Success," *Western Electric* (April 1922); "Hawthorne Works"; "Kitty of the Chorus Lands Her Hammer on Chicago, But Sings the Praises of the New *Hawthorne Follies*," *Western Electric* (July 1920).

23. Loren Baritz, *The Servants of Power: A History of the Use of Social Science in American Industry* (Middletown, Connecticut, 1960), pp. 77–116.

24. *A Day at Goodyear: An Extravaganza in Three Acts*, presented on November 3, 1922, Goodyear Company Archives. A detailed seven-page program.

25. Metropolitan Life, "Drama in Industry" (New York, 1925), pp. 1–7, (mimeographed); Barrett Clark, "The Point of View," *Playground*, 19 (1926), p. 627; Frank Fricsson to S. M. Darling, August 5, 1904, McCormick Papers, Box 39; S. M. Darling to Cyrus Bentley, September 1, 1904, McCormick Papers, Box 40; Kahn, a speech given at the Drama League of America, February 9, 1915, in a scrapbook (n.c. 2273) in Lincoln Center Library.

26. Metropolitan, "Drama," pp. 1–7; "Kitty"; *Textile World*, 63 (June 2, 1923), p. 77, cited in Robert S. Smith, *Mill on the Dan: A History of Dan River Mills, 1882–1950* (Durham, North Carolina, 1960), p. 252; *Progress*, cited in Smith, p. 253.

27. Ralph Parlette, *The Big Business of Life* (Chicago, 1920), p. 84; Eastman to Joseph Lee, (n.d.), published in *Playground*, 16 (1922), p. 409; Metropolitan Life, *Are You a True American?* (1922), p. 2, Metropolitan Life Insurance Company Archives.

28. National Conference on Outdoor Recreation, *Proceedings* of National Conference

on Outdoor Recreation, held in Washington, D.C., May 22–24, 1924, (Senate Document, no. 151, 68th Congress 16: 8249), p. 14; Metropolitan, a program announcement, February 9, 1923, (mimeographed), Metropolitan Archives; Community Service Convention, "Report," (1919), (mimeographed), Playground Papers, p. 243.

8

A Brief Description of the Workers' Theatre Movement of the Thirties

Daniel Friedman

An indigenous workers' theatre movement developed in the early 1930s. It was the only grass-roots amateur movement in U.S. history in which workers created theatre for their fellow laborers. At its height, the movement involved hundreds of troupes and tens of thousands of workers who wrote, directed, performed and attended their own theatrical pieces. They did so with the deliberate intent of helping to create a distinct working-class culture which they hoped would reflect and inspire their fellow workers in their economic and political struggles. In the course of this activity, they adapted and developed a particular performance style and aesthetic attitude.

Although theatre by workers and for workers was to be found among numerous immigrant groups before 1930,[1] no such amateur theatre tradition existed among native-born, English-speaking workers. The only theatrical activity among English-speaking workers prior to the Great Depression were the skits and pageants performed in conjunction with various strikes by members of the radical union, the Industrial Workers of the World (IWW), between 1905 and 1920.[2] The most important of these was the *Paterson Strike Pageant* which was performed in 1913 by a cast of 1,200 striking silk workers who reenacted the major incidents of their strike before an overflow crowd in Madison Square Garden.[3] Such activity was very sporadic and brief and did not succeed in establishing a self-sustaining theatrical tradition among English-speaking workers.

Among the immigrant groups the theatrical activity at this time was not, for the most part, indigenous to the workers themselves. Instead it imitated standard plays from mainstream theatre.[4] Although most of the social and fraternal organizations which generated the immigrant theatre groups had at least vague left-wing sympathies, and many in the 1920s associated themselves with the Workers' (later Communist) party, they do not appear, on the whole, to have conceived of their function as the creation of a workers' theatre aesthetically and politically distinct from the traditional theatre. Rather, they saw their theatrical work as a way of bringing "high culture" to workers. The most frequently performed playwrights appear to have been Ibsen, Hauptmann, Shakespeare, and other established national playwrights.[5]

The ideological assumption at work in this type of workers' theatre was that universal culture transcends social class. Working on this assumption, the amateur worker-actors saw it as their duty to educate themselves in this universal culture. They brought this approach with them from the European Social-Democratic movement. These conventional productions of standard playwrights and the acceptance of the assumption behind them came to an abrupt end with the stock market crash of 1929.

Three important changes in the nature of workers' theatre in the United States can be ascertained after 1930. The first is quantitative growth: workers' theatre groups proliferated at a rate unprecedented before or since. The first attempt to establish contact between workers' theatres in 1930 succeeded in contacting twenty-one groups.[6] By 1934 there were 400 workers' theatre groups associated with a national organization called the League of Workers Theatres.[7]

The second change was a radical shift in the ethnic composition of the workers' theatre movement. While foreign language groups continued to grow in the early thirties, for the first time large numbers of English-speaking troupes composed of native-born workers sprang up. In 1929, only one English-speaking workers' theatre was functioning. By 1933 there were more English-speaking workers' theatres than there were of any other single ethnic group, constituting almost half the total of the workers' theatres in the country.[8]

The third major change was an ideological and aesthetic one. Prior to 1930 the majority of workers' theatres performed classics from the established professional stage in a conventional style. After 1930 the majority of groups created their own material that consisted, for the most part, of short political skits performed in a unique presentational style, which was intended to propagate the acceptance of radical political solutions among its audience and agitate them to act on those solutions. The style, quite logically, was called agitprop which was short for agitation and propaganda.

This shift away from conventional content and style reflected a movement away from the concept of universal culture toward the concept of a class culture. This concept presupposed that the conflicting economic and political interests between workers and their employers necessitated a different cultural expression by the conflicting classes.

The combination of these three factors—a qualitative leap in the number of workers' theatres, a major shift in ethnic composition with native-born workers in large numbers taking up theatre for the first time, and a common ideological and aesthetic approach—justifies terming the workers' theatre of the thirties a *movement*. In addition, these three characteristics, from a historical perspective, define that movement.

Two catalytic events, both initially outside of the theatre, helped to bring about these changes in the American workers' theatre. The first was the Russian

Revolution and the second was the Great Depression. While the Russian Revolution provided an inspiration and a living example of class culture at work, the depression economically and politically polarized America to such an extent that the class culture concept could find acceptance among a relatively large number of workers.

Much could be said about the Soviet amateur workers' theatre in the 1920s. Its growth and extensiveness were phenomenal. Numerous visitors to the Soviet Union at that time reported that every factory and every trade union had a theatre group attached to it.[9] By 1926 the Russian Federated Soviet Socialist Republic, just one of the Soviet Union's republics, has some 20,000 amateur dramatic circles, involving about 280,000 worker-actors who were performing for an audience of 25 million people per year.[10]

In the course of this feverish theatrical activity the Soviet worker-actors, basing themselves on the class-culture concept, developed a style and form that reflected both the political goals they set for their theatre and the physical and temporal limits they faced as amateurs playing in factories, meeting halls, and streets. Their style was characterized by radical political content; simplicity and mobility of set, costume, and makeup; the integration of dialogue with chanting, choral reading, singing, music, dance, and circus techniques; the consequent use of an extremely physical, presentational acting style; and the use of archetypal characters and symbolic dramatic imagery, which, tied together by political association in the form of montage, became the basic dramatic structure (as opposed to linear plot based on consistency of character, time, and action). These features came to characterize the agitprop movement internationally.

During the 1920s the agitprop style and class-culture concept spread with the Communist movement throughout the world. Germany, with its polarized economic and political environment, strong Communist party, and long tradition of workers' theatre proved particularly fertile ground for the agitprop movement. By 1928 agitprop troupes directly associated with the Communist party (which constituted only a part of the agitprop movement in Germany) reached an audience of approximately 3,600,000 workers.[11]

Although there were attempts at introducing agitprop techniques into American workers' theatres in the 1920s,[12] it was not until the American workers faced the polarized conditions of the depression that the concept of class culture and the mobile agitprop style took hold of the imaginations of American workers. The first group to adopt and consistently perform agitprop in the United States was, not surprisingly, a German immigrant group from New York's Yorkville section. They were called the *Prolet-Buehne*, which is a German contraction for Workers' Stage. Although the *Prolet-Buehne* was formed in 1925, it did not adopt agitprop techniques until sometime after 1928, when a number of recently arrived immigrants joined the group.[13] In April of 1930 it began to perform outside of the German immigrant community,[14] and the impact of its new performance style was immediate. There are numerous accounts, all of them excited and enthusiastic, of witnessing *Prolet-Buehne* performances for the first time.

What appears to have most impressed audiences was the group's energy level, its physical and precise performance technique, along with its ability to play anywhere, and the straightforward political content of its scripts.[15]

Almost simultaneously with the emergence of the *Prolet-Buehne*, an English-language workers' theatre calling itself the Workers' Laboratory Theatre (WLT) appeared in New York.[16] They were dedicated to performing political plays from a working-class perspective. When they encountered the *Prolet-Buehne* they immediately began to translate the former's scripts and adapted their performance style.[17]

Together the *Prolet-Buehne* and the WLT formed the vanguard of the workers' theatre movement. Not only were they the first to adopt the agitprop style, write their own skits, set performance standards, and advocate the concept of class culture, they also took the lead in organizing the various theatre groups into a movement. In the summer of 1931, they founded the Dramatic Bureau of the New York Cultural Federation. At its first meeting in July 1931, nine groups attended; in September fourteen groups were represented; by November the number had doubled to twenty-eight; and by April of 1932 there were 150 groups from all over the country associated with the Dramatic Bureau.[18] In 1932 these groups formed a national organization called the League of Workers' Theatres (LOWT) which distributed plays, held competitions, established a school to teach agitprop technique, and carried on a vast network of correspondence.[19]

Closely associated with the work of the Dramatic Bureau and the League of Workers' Theatres was the magazine *Workers Theatre*. Originally published as a mimeographed journal by the WLT, its first issue in April 1931 had a run of only 200.[20] Its editorial board was soon reinforced by members of the *Prolet-Buehne*, and its monthly circulation steadily grew so that by the end of its first year it had reached 1,000.[21] In 1932 it became the official organ of the LOWT, and by 1933 in that capacity its circulation had more than tripled to 3,500.[22] In September of 1933 the magazine changed its name to *New Theatre*, and by 1935 it reached a peak circulation of 18,000.[23] *Workers Theatre* magazine helped to consolidate the workers' theatre movement in two ways. First, it acted as a communications network through which groups throughout the country came into contact with each other and with the LOWT and through which skits were published. Second, it was the forum in which theoretical and technical questions were debated on a national level, thus creating a common political, technical, and artistic framework for the emerging workers' theatres nationwide. The success of LOWT and *Workers Theatre* magazine was such that the second national conference of the LOWT held in Chicago in April 1934 was attended by 1,500 people representing 400 workers' theatres in at least twenty-eight cities across the United States.[24]

The blossoming of the workers' theatre movement in the United States took place under the harshest conditions of the depression when unemployment, evictions, speed-ups, wage cuts, and hunger were facts of life confronted daily by the American worker. Facing these conditions the worker-actor used his theatrical activity to express his anger and present a hoped-for alternative to his present plight. The worker-actor therefore understood his theatrical activity as a continuation of his radical political activity by other means. In this regard the Communist party played an important role during this period in encouraging and supporting the workers' theatre. All of the members of the *Prolet-Buehne*, for example, were Communist party members,[25] and the Communist party press in all languages reviewed workers' theatre performances and in general encouraged the emerging workers' theatre movement. This is the economic and political background against which the concept of class culture flourished.

This class culture concept of the American workers' theatre of the early 1930s was most clearly expressed by John Bonn of the *Prolet-Buehne* in an address to the New York Workers' Cultural Convention in June of 1931. He wrote:

I. What is Workers' Theatre?

Workers' Theatre is NOT: a Theatre playing anything for workers
nor
a Theatre showing the dramatized world of the worker for anybody.

Workers' Theatre—like any form of art—is part of a culture,
reflecting (expressing) and promoting (impressing) this culture.

Workers' Theatre of today is part of the proletarian culture of today.

The proletarian culture of today is a culture in the beginning:
fighting *against* the bourgeois class
fighting *for* the proletarian class
it is a culture of Class-struggle.

Therefore:
Workers' Theatre of today is the theatre of Class-struggle.
Its *only* purpose is reflecting (dramatizing) the Class-struggle and promoting (propagandizing) the class-struggle.
Its *only* audience are the masses of workers.[26]

While Bonn's statement is an extreme expression of a general attitude, and while this attitude was never unanimously accepted by the workers' theatres of the thirties, the statement nonetheless serves as an accurate reflection of the class culture concept prevalent in the workers' theatre movement of the early thirties.

Within this aesthetic and political approach, the workers' theatres experimented with a wide variety of theatre forms and styles, including cabaret-style revues, vaudevillelike comedy routines, political circuses, mass pageants (usually at mass rallies and demonstrations), pantomimes (when the audience consisted of numerous nationality groups), and mass recitations.[27] This last, the mass recitation, proved to be the most popular and, for most people, characterized the American agitprop theatre. The mass recitation was basically just that: the mass recitation of verse by a chorus of workers within a dramatic context. The form originated in the workers' theatres of the Soviet Union in the early twenties and was also extremely popular in Germany where it was known as a *Sprechchore* (speaking chorus).[28]

The typical American mass recitation pitted a chorus of workers against a capitalist or a representative of the capitalist class, such as a foreman or policeman. In the beginning the chorus would be suffering oppression, but in the end they would succeed in vanquishing the capitalist in a reversal that usually included driving him physically off stage. The mass recitations, which were almost always in verse, usually rhymed couplets, made use of simple musical accompaniment and choreographed, almost dancelike movement by the actors. Virtually all of the workers' theatre of this period shared with the mass recitation the use of archetypal characters, revolutionary political content, a physical presentational acting style, and a minimal and mobile set.

Whether this theatre was successful in its goal of agitating and propagating among the mass of workers or whether it primarily served as a ritual communion among the already converted is a complex and challenging question which cannot be taken up here. Suffice it to say that the *goal* of the workers' theatres was to integrate their theatre activity with the economic and political struggles of American workers in such a way that the workers involved could learn more than they would have without the performance. The dramatic group of the Jewish Workers' Clubs of Chicago reported in the May 1934 issue of *Workers Theatre* on their involvement in a confrontation that exemplifies the type of political involvement sought by most of the agitprop groups:

The group was booked to present an eviction play written by one of its members before an Unemployment Council branch. Arriving at the hall, they heard news of an eviction taking place around the corner. They accompanied the Unemployed Council members to the scene of action, helped put the furniture back in the house, fought off the cops, and then proceeded to present the play. Thus, reality and make-believe were merged into a decisive educational experience for actors and audience.[29]

This "decisive educational experience" was precisely what the workers' theatres hoped to achieve through the nexus of politics and performance.

Although 1934 marked the height of the workers' theatre movement, it in no way marked its end. The successor to the LOWT, the New Theatre League, remained active until 1942.[30] However, after 1934 the nature of the workers' theatre movement began to change. The concept of a universal culture once again began to dominate over the concept of class culture. Realism and stationary theatres returned, instead of agitprop and mobile theatres. The movement began to concern itself more with the theatre professional than with the worker-actor.

There appear to be a number of interconnecting causes for the decline of the agitprop movement in the United States. First, the self-conscious class-culture approach to workers' theatre appears historically to flourish in a polarized social situation like the Soviet Union and Germany in the twenties and the United

States in the early years of the depression. Agitprop's strident agitational style is best suited to revolutionary or potentially revolutionary situations. The triumph of fascism in Europe, and particularly in Germany, was a tremendous setback for the political aspirations of the working class internationally. The assumption that revolution was imminent, which characterized the thinking of radical workers in the period of the agitprop theatre's initial growth, was gradually replaced after the Nazi seizure of power by the defensive policy of a united front with all parties and social forces that could be united against fascism. In this new political atmosphere agitprop techniques, designated to inspire an audience to revolutionary attitudes and actions, were gradually perceived as being out of place. The united front also led the workers' theatre movement to seek alliances with liberal theatre professionals, a situation in which the influence of the professionals grew steadily within the workers' movement to the detriment of agitprop attitudes. This resulted in a gradual reemergence of the concept of universal culture, which, in turn, led amateur worker-actors back toward imitation of the conventional theatre.

Converging with this united front policy of the workers was the Roosevelt administration's successful easing of the political polarization of the Hoover years through the policies of the New Deal. The Federal Theatre Project in particular played a significant role in the disintegration of an independent workers' theatre movement. Many of the most talented activists of the workers' theatre were offered paying jobs with the Federal Theatre. For example, John Bonn, the director of the *Prolet-Buehne*, was appointed by Hallie Flanagan and Elmer Rice to head the German section of the Project,[31] and no less than five members of the WLT worked in various capacities on the Federal Theatre's Living Newspapers.[32] The Federal Theatre Project decimated the ranks of the workers' theatre, filling the vacuum thus created by usurping the working-class audience that had been created by the workers' theatre movement.[33]

The American workers' theatre movement emerged, flourished, and died in less than a decade. Its most talented artists and most innovative techniques were absorbed by the mainstream theatre. By 1942 what remained of the workers' theatre movement ended as many of its members were drafted. What once had the potential to become a national, multiethnic workers' cultural institution disappeared leaving no living tradition behind it. Its history was vilified and covered up in the wake of the McCarthy-Truman repression of the 1950s.[34] Today it remains a virtually forgotten chapter in American theatre history.

Despite all this, the workers' theatre movement is obviously an important part of our American theatrical heritage. At no other time were regular American working people viewing plays, debating aesthetics, acting, and writing shows in such numbers or with such enthusiasm. Never, before or since, have we come so close to a truly democratic theatre.

Since the thirties there have been theatrical manifestations that hold much in common with the workers' theatre of that decade; in particular, the guerrilla theatre of the student movement of the sixties, and, most strikingly, El Teatro Campesino (the Farmworkers' Theatre) in its early days and other Chicano workers' theatres of the last two decades. But never has such a phenomenon been so widespread among the working class or so consistently radical in its aesthetic and political approach.

The workers' theatre movement of the early thirties remains the only movement in U.S. theatre history in which workers created theatre for their fellow workers with the express intent of building a distinct working-class culture. In this it remains a unique type of theatre for working-class audiences and one that deserves further study, particularly by those concerned with the relationship of cultural phenomena to social change.

NOTES

1. For evidence of theatre among German immigrant workers in the 1870s, see *The New York Volkszeitung*, January 28, February 25, March 25, April 15, April 22, and May 6, 1877, and *The New York Arbeiter Stimme*, February 25, 1877. For a more thorough discussion of nineteenth-century German-American immigrant theatre, see Carol Poore, "German-American Socialist Workers' Theatre 1877–1900," chapter 3 in this collection.

2. Ben Blake, *The Awakening of the American Theatre* (New York, 1935), p. 9. May Wells Jones, "A History of the Political Theatre in the United States from 1930–1970," (Diss., Tulane University, 1971), p. 9.

3. The only direct evidence of theatrical activity among the Wobblies comes from the extensive collection of IWW documents in the Labadie Collection at the University of Michigan Library. Included is a penciled program of an IWW "Entertainment" held on December 2, 1917, in the Cook County Jail, Chicago, where many IWWs were being held on sedition charges for opposing World War I. The program lists, along with numerous songs and poetry recitations, a stunt to be performed by Forrest Edwards as well as "Getting Acquainted With the Bull" and "The Little Bug" which, although not labeled as such, are apparently theatrical skits. There are relatively numerous references to Wobbly theatre pieces in secondary sources. See, for example, Richard Boyer and Herbert Morais, *Labor's Untold Story* (New York, 1955), p. 1974; and Alan Calmer, "The Wobbly in American Literature," in *Proletarian Literature in the United States*, ed. Granville Michs, et al., (New York, 1935), p. 340.

4. For a description of a typical production, see "Russian Branch Gives 'Return from Siberia' at Workers' Theatre," *Daily Worker*, 2 (13 November 1925). For discussion of this type of theatre among immigrant workers, see Blake, pp. 10–11; and Bernard Eines, "Our Widening Front," *Workers Theatre*, 2 (September–October 1932), 3.

5. Blake, p. 9.

6. L. A. DeSantes, "Workers' Drama," *New Masses*, 5 (March 1930), 20.

7. Mark Marwin, "Workers' Theatre Marches," *New Masses*, 11 (8 May 1934), 29.

8. See "Appendix D., U.S. Agit-Prop Groups Listed by Ethnic Groups," in my dissertation, "The Prolet-Buehne: America's First Agit-Prop Theatre," (University of Wisconsin, 1979), pp. 754–56.

9. See, for example, Marc Slonim, *Russian Theatre: From the Empire to the Soviets* (Cleveland, 1961), pp. 240–41.

10. Ibid., p. 281.

11. Report of the Central Committee of the Kommunistisch Partei Deutschlands to the Twelfth Party Congress, June 9–16, 1929. Quoted by Ludwig Hoffmann and Daniel Hoffmann-Ostwald, *Deutsches Arbeitertheater 1918–1933* (Munich, 1973), p. 38.

12. Nancy Markoff, "The Russian 'Living Newspaper' in Chicago," *Daily Worker*, 2 (21 December 1925), 5; and "Living Newspapers, Banquets, Music and Rescue Parties Will Feature California Celebrations," *Daily Worker*, 2 (7 January 1926), 5.

13. The first *Prolet-Buehne* production to contain agitprop influences was *Die enternationale*, performed on December 1, 1928. See, Ad, *Der Arbeiter*, 2 (27 November 1928), 5. Einem Arbeiter-Korrespondenten, "Prolet-Buehne—Ein Review," *Der Arbeiter*, 2 (11 December 1928), 6. The *Prolet-Buehne*'s total conversion to agitprop is variously dated by *Prolet-Buehne* members. M. Thorn, "The Artistic Life of the Prolet-Buehne, German Agit-Prop Troupe, New York," *Workers Theatre*, 1 (September 1931), 5, dates it from the fall of 1929. Margaret Haller, "The Organizational Structure of the Prolet-Buehne, German Agit-Prop Troupe, New York," *Workers Theater*, 1 (September 1931), p. 5, writes, "The sharp turn from the old type of Workers' Theatre to Agitprop work [was] made in the beginning of 1930."

14. "Kolektiv-Kritik (zum Fest der Prolet-Buehne)," *Der Arbeiter*, 4 (8 May 1930), 6.

15. See, for example, Blake, pp. 15–17; and Jay Williams, *Stage Left* (New York, 1974), pp. 36–37.

16. When the group was founded is unclear: L. A. De Santes, "Letter," *New Masses*, 5 (October 1929), 29, dates its founding in 1928. Blake, p. 18, dates the WLT from 1929.

17. For an account of the *Prolet-Buehne*'s influence on the WLT by a WLT member, see Harry Elion, "The Problems of Repertory," *Workers Theatre*, 3 (April 1933), 6.

18. The growth of the Dramatic Bureau during this period can be traced in the following articles: John E. Bonn, "New York Federation Drama section," *New Masses*, 7 (September 1931), 21; "News," *Workers Theatre*, 1 (October 1931), 31; and John E. Bonn, "Situation and Tasks of the Workers Theatre in the U.S.A. (A report to the First National Workers' Theatre Conference held in New York, April 17)," *Workers Theatre*, 2 (June–July 1932), 9.

19. Blake, p. 26.

20. Ibid., p. 21.

21. Ibid., p. 24.

22. Ibid., p. 41.

23. Ibid., p. 57.

24. Marwin, p. 29.

25. Fritz Hoffmann, former member of the *Prolet-Buehne*, in an unpublished interview with the author, January 1977.

26. John E. Bonn, "Workers' Theatre (Report given at the Workers' Cultural Convention in New York, June 14, 1931)," (Part I), *Workers Theatre*, 1 (August 1931), 1.

27. For a detailed description of the various forms and styles of the work of one group, the *Prolet-Buehne*, see my dissertation, "The Prolet-Buehne: America's First Agit-Prop Theatre," pp. 338–463.

28. For a discussion of the Soviet origins of mass recitation, see Serge Orlovsky, "Moscow Theatres, 1917–1941," in *Soviet Theatre, 1917–1941*, ed. Martha Bradshaw (Ann Arbor, 1954), p. 25; and Nikolaia Gorchakov, *The Theatre in Soviet Russia*, trans.

Edgar Lehrman (New York, 1957), pp. 143–44. For discussion of the German *Sprech-chore*, see Ludwig Hoffmann, "Einleitung," in *Deutsches Arbeitertheater, 1918–1933*, p. 31.

29. Alice Evans " . . . W.L.T. of Chicago," *New Theatre*, 1 (May 1934), 22.

30. Malcolm Goldstein, *The Political Stage: American Drama and the Great Depression* (New York, 1974), p. 217.

31. An outline of the German Unit's history is included in a memorandum from Alfred B. Kuttner to Hiram Motherwell, October 1, 1936, New York City National Office Correspondence, 1935–1939, Federal Theatre Project Records, Records of the Works Progress Administration, Bureau of Social and Economic Records, Record Group No. 69, National Archives, Washington, D.C.

32. Williams, pp. 234–35; and Douglas McDermott, "The Living Newspaper As a Dramatic Form," (Diss., University of Iowa, 1963), pp. 39–40.

33. Norris Houghton, *Advance From Broadway*, (New York, 1941), p. 274.

34. For an example of this bias, see the first book-length study of the political theatre of the 1930s: Morgan Y. Himelstein, *Drama Was a Weapon*, (New Brunswick, New Jersey, 1963).

9

The Workers' Laboratory Theatre: Archetype and Example

Douglas McDermott

Now that the fires of controversy surrounding the left-wing theatre of the American depression have guttered out, it is time to do some scholarly sifting of the ashes. Not only is reevaluation of this type of theatre possible, it is also imperative. New primary materials have become available about various groups and types of theatre, and it is now clear that political theatre in the 1930s was not confined either to this country or to the radical left. Moreover, the resurgence in the 1960s of theatrical activity that paralleled that of the previous generation suggests that social and artistic forces are at work in the creation of political theatre that are not the property of any particular era. Scripts and performance styles of political theatre have usually been unconventional and, therefore, frequently misunderstood. However, the continued popularity of political theatre suggests the possibility of a deliberate attempt to create a new genre that deserves to be viewed in terms of critical standards appropriate to it. This chapter is an attempt to do that by focusing on the Workers' Laboratory Theatre of New York, which, as the most successful agitprop group of the American radical left, now seems archetypal, and by analyzing its work in an enlarged theoretical framework and in an expanded chronological context.

In terms of political involvement there exists a broad spectrum of theatrical possibilities within which one may observe crucial clusters of activity. At one extreme is the commercial theatre, typified by the farce (*Charley's Aunt, A Flea in Her Ear*), which avoids political comment and effectively denies the significance of political structures. At this extreme, art and life are mutually exclusive. At one remove from this position is the theatre of social significance, typified by the domestic drama (*A Doll's House*), which deals directly with social issues and political tensions in society. The work of art is a comment on, and possibly a contribution to, a rational dialogue in real life. Removed even farther is the explicitly political theatre typified by the agitprop play (*Waiting for Lefty*), which not only identifies problems in the society but proposes specific political strategies for their solution. The work of art concludes the social discussion and agitates for direct action by the audience. Finally, at the opposite extreme from the commercial theatre, is the participatory theatre, typified by the ensemble piece and the mass spectacle (*Paradise Now*), which invites the audience to join in the theatrical performance as a mode of political action. At this extreme, art and life are no longer distinguished from one another.

Because this conceptual framework is provided as a way to understand political theatre, some qualifying comments are appropriate. First, this is a static description of existential possibilities, not a developmental scheme. Theatre in an era does not need to grow from one stage of political involvement to another in either direction. Rather, the theatre adopts the political postures that are appropriate and possible in its era. Second, in many cases more than one position on the political spectrum may be occupied. Third, the positions described are typical, not exhaustive. Fourth, while the spectrum is conceived in terms of modern theatre, older works may be understood in its terms. Finally, the expression of political posture may be comic as well as tragic or pathetic.

I am attempting to provide a scheme that allows for all theatrical postures in relation to the politics of the day. Unless we have such an understanding, we risk repeating the confusions of our major critics when, in the last two decades, they tried to grapple with agitational and participatory theatre.[1] Drawing on the work of George Szanto, Jacques Ellul, and Kenneth Burke, I am attempting to carry the discussion of politically committed theatre beyond Oscar Brockett's rational acceptance of the phenomenon. Once we have acknowledged that political theatre persists in various forms, we can attempt to understand it as a distinctive kind of performance that can be described, analyzed, and compared with other styles; and only after such an attempt may we legitimately draw our conclusions and make our value judgments.[2]

In these terms, then, we can approach the Workers' Laboratory Theatre (WLT) of New York, an agitational political theatre, whose performances attempted to influence audiences to put specific political strategies into practice in their lives. After we examine this group's work, we can compare it with the activity of other groups, both in its time and in ours. I hope this expanded theoretical and historical set of considerations will permit us to draw some conclusions about the nature and function of political theatre.

The WLT did not originate agitprop. Agitational performance began in a group called the Blue Blouses that was sponsored by the National Institute of Journalists in Moscow during 1923. Its original function seems to have been to indoctrinate an illiterate population with the correct political line by acting out current news headlines and editorial attitudes. From Russia the agitprop style spread to Germany where a tradition of working-class drama and theatrical societies traced their origins back to the previous century. A starkly simplistic style of staging political material had already been derived from the cabaret tradition by Erwin Piscator in his productions of *Russia's Day* (1920) and *Red Revue* (1924), and both the Communists and Social Democrats had developed choral-speaking groups

(*Sprechchor*) that indoctrinated workers through performances. A proliferation of agitational theatre groups resulted from the Moscow Blue Blouses' tour of Germany in the last three months of 1927. The Germans were shown new thematic and theatrical possibilities, and agitprop troupes of the Russian sort sprang up quickly in Berlin (The Red Blouses, The Red Rockets, The Red Megaphones, Column Left), and in Hamburg, Halle, Dresden, and Stuttgart. The tenth congress of the German Communist party in 1929 officially encouraged such troupes, and by the summer of 1930 there were over a hundred of them.[3]

In contrast to the agitprop activity, participatory political theatre also emerged at this time in both countries. Once they were secure in power, the Soviets sponsored mass historical pageants such as *The Storming of the Winter Palace*, which involved the spectators as participants in a reenactment of a historic revolutionary event. By means of such participation the average citizen identified with the revolution, thereby validating it through his own experience. Similar events occurred in Germany. In 1925 Piscator staged the mass pageant *In Spite of Everything*! for the Communist party conference in Berlin, and both the Communists and the Social Democrats made regular use of participatory events (marching, chanting, singing) and mass plays (*Massenspiele*) to create a sense of identity between the worker and the party. The most famous uses of pageant theatre, however, were those of the Nazis. Apart from their spectacularly effective rallies and their subversion of the Olympic ceremonies in 1936, they attempted to create a national form of participatory theatre, the *Thingspiele*, in which pageants based on the National Socialist mythology of race were designed to initiate people into the party's ideals. The existence of participatory and agitational theatre at the same time and at both extremes of politics supports the conceptual framework of this chapter.[4]

The first stirrings in America of what was to become a loosely coordinated workers' theatre movement came in 1913 in the pageant that sought to dramatize the conditions and concerns of striking textile workers in Paterson, New Jersey. Animated by the memory of that event, a group of experimental writers and political activists formed the New Playwrights' Theatre, producing eight plays between 1927 and 1929 at the expense of the capitalist Mycenae, Otto Kahn. These were essentially social dramas, but more agitational work soon appeared. The German language *Prolet-Buehne* split from its parent *arbeiterbund* in 1928, and in the same year the Workers' Laboratory Theatre was formed by the association of Alfred Saxe, Harry Elion, Jack Reines, Albert Prentiss, Will Lee, and Jack and Hiram Shapiro. Neither of these latter two groups had contact with the other at first, and their efforts seem to have been directed at the production of socially conscious but theatrically conventional short plays.[5]

Certainly, the *Prolet-Buehne* was the first to develop the agitprop style in the United States. Almost certainly, this new style was adapted from earlier Soviet and German work and was a response to the Communist International's strategy between 1928 and 1933. Calling for a radical turn to the left, the party exhorted members of the working class to emphasize class conflict and the inevitability of revolution. Artistically, the conventional representational theatre was rejected because it was the expression of bourgeois culture and capitalist economics. By 1930 the *Prolet-Buehne* was well known for its mass chants, and by 1931 the WLT was performing translations of such *Prolet-Buehne* pieces as *Tempo, Tempo* and clearly regarded itself as an agitprop theatre.[6] Between 1932 and 1934 it developed its own style and its own vehicles that made it the leading English-language group. The key to its success was its collective form of organization and the establishment in 1933 of the Shock Troupe. This group of twelve to eighteen members devoted itself full-time to theatrical training and performing. They were supported by the fifty or so members of the Evening Section, who held such jobs as they could and did theatre only at night. During this period their repertory expanded to include some eighty pieces that could be performed under almost any circumstances. The most famous of these was *Newsboy*, developed in the spring of 1933.[7]

The period between 1934 and 1937 was confusing and difficult for the WLT. They struggled to navigate both artistic and political crosscurrents that ultimately led to a drastic change in style, with fateful consequences. The first current was artistic. Many members of the WLT, most of them in the Shock Troupe, were artistically ambitious. Though relatively untrained and inexperienced, they wanted to make the artistic quality of their productions as high as possible to achieve the most compelling ideological results. Such ambition led them to inaugurate classes for their own development, and they turned to friends in the Group Theatre for instruction. The Shapiros had first done theatre with Lee Strasberg at the Chrystie Street Settlement House, and this friendship undoubtedly led to contact between the two groups. Group Theatre members like Morris Carnovsky, Robert Lewis, and Elia Kazan found in the WLT an outlet for their creative energies that was politically as well as artistically satisfying. Thus, the representational acting methods derived from the work of Konstantin Stanislavsky were introduced into the Shock Troupe, whose members passed them on to the Evening Section.

The move toward more polished representational production values was opposed by many in the Workers' Theatre Movement for two reasons. First, such a move was clearly an adaptation of techniques and methods from the established theatre of the bourgeoisie, and there was fear that ideological contamination would result. Second, greater emphasis on traditional production values conflicted with the demands of production under primitive circumstances at workers' meetings. Thus, some opposed the shift to representation because it clearly implied an abandonment of the original purpose and format of the group.

The second current of change tugging at the WLT was political, and by 1934 it coincided with the artistic ambitions of those who favored the use of bourgeois production methods. Not only had socialist realism become the official artistic style in the Soviet Union, but collaboration with the bourgeois left became the official strategy of the Communist party. Thus, art and politics coincided in the Popular Front Movement. Consequently, those members of the WLT like Al

Saxe and Harry Elion, who were clearly loyal party-liners, came to espouse representational production for political reasons. Thus, the artistic ambitions of some of the members united with the political goals of others, and the WLT entered the stylistic midstream of the American theatre.[8]

The crucial event in this process of change was the Group Theatre's production of *Waiting for Lefty*. A series of agitprop skits woven into a long play, it was finer than anything the WLT had done. Because it was set in a union hall during a strike meeting, it lent itself to mobile production, and its episodic construction lent itself to excerpting. Nevertheless, it was intensely representational and was best performed in a regular theatre. Its success led directly to members of the WLT collaborating with Arthur Vogel, a young man with no writing experience, on dramatizing his service in the Civilian Conservation Corps. Out of his rough draft, Saxe, Kazan, Peter Martin, and Charles Friedman hacked a full-length play, *The Young Go First*. For its production the Shock Troupe took the name Theatre of Action and opened in May of 1935 for forty-eight performances.

The Young Go First failed both artistically and economically. The result was the beginning of the end for the WLT. The Evening Section voted to disband in order not to place any economic burden on the Shock Troupe, which reverted to the mobile production of short plays to pay off the debt. By March 1936 the Shock Troupe was out of the hole, but its members were inevitably attracted by the relative stability and affluence of the Federal Theatre Project. They were absorbed into the FTP as the One-Act Experimental Theatre, produced one bill of short plays, and ceased to exist; its members were assigned to other FTP units in New York City.

Although the WLT came to an end in 1936, the movement struggled on. The Theatre Arts Committee was formed by theatrical professionals sympathetic to republican Spain, and their constantly changing, satirical *Cabaret TAC* entertained many during the summer of 1938. The American political left, however, was stricken by the Hitler-Stalin pact of August 1939, and the death blow came from the Russian invasion of Finland three months later. American disaffection with the left was subsumed in the imminent war effort, and without a political base the left-wing agitational theatre disappeared. Both politically and artistically the Popular Front coalition collapsed, and when the FTP came to an end, most WLT members seem to have left the theatre. Perry Bruskin, Will Lee, and Curt Conway had subsequent professional careers as actors, but only Al Saxe remained politically active. Between 1940 and 1943 he managed the Popular Theatre of San Francisco and by 1948 was back in New York leading the Jefferson Theatre Workshop. With the demise of that group in 1950, the WLT ended.

The performance style of the WLT was rooted in its ideals and in its mode of organization: class conscious, collective, and improvisational.[9] Certain given conditions existed throughout the group's life, and its work was a response to them. In the first place they were all amateurs, and what training and experience they had was diverse and not always directly applicable. This in itself impelled them to close cooperation and sharing, since no one of them had the ability to take complete charge of any aspect of their work. In the second place they were usually unpaid for doing theatre. Even after the Shock Troupe was organized, its booking fees barely covered production expenses. Thus, economically as well as artistically the group was necessarily a collective in its living and working arrangements. In the third place they desired to use their theatre as an instrument of social change. All of them were committed to a generally Marxist view of society and were sympathetic to the policies and programs of the Communist party. They perceived the world as made up of two classes, workers and bosses, and they accepted the inevitability of conflict between the two over the ownership of the means of production. Their primary goal was to persuade their fellow workers of the accuracy of this view and to show them appropriate solutions for their problems in this light.

These conditions carried certain consequences. The first was that a conventional kind of performance was impossible. It wasn't just that they were inexperienced amateurs. People with no more professional background had developed an entire theatrical subculture during the 1920s in the Little Theatre Movement. Rather, it was a case of the intended audience. Most working-class people were not used to going to the theatre in the 1930s, so even if the WLT had been able to afford a regular theatre, its audience wouldn't have come. Thus, it was necessary to go to the audience—to perform in locations and under circumstances where working people were already gathered, usually in union halls or in the open air. To meet the demands of mobile production under unpredictable and often adverse conditions, it was necessary to have scripts that were short and did not require elaborate scenery, costumes, or special effects. The second consequence was that existing scripts did not articulate the correct political line. However, in creating politically suitable scripts, the conditions of mobility still had to be met, and in a short, theatrically simple script it was not possible to engage in sophisticated analysis or elaborate dialectic. Thus, in addition to being short and simple, scripts had to be politically clear, which normally meant that characters and dialogue had to be exaggerated and stereotyped. Finally, performance conditions not only affected scripts, but scripts affected acting. Psychologically representational characterization was neither possible nor desirable in playing these scripts under these conditions. The result was an acting style that stressed clarity of voice and gesture and in which obvious effects were preferred to subtle ones.

The agitprop script was the result of these conditions. A failure to understand this has led to the conclusion that these theatre workers were simply untalented: "It was as if an 'artist' who could not draw a reasonable facsimile of the human body decided that he had better paint abstractions or draw cartoons."[10] Without pejorative connotation, abstractions and cartoons are accurate descriptions of these pieces. However, they were consciously created in response to a particular audience and set of performance conditions. To be sure, the plays have little literary value, and their politics are obvious, but both characteristics were virtues. Of thirty-eight scripts named in various sources, nineteen by the WLT survive, along with five by the *Prolet-Buehne*. All have certain things in common that permit generalization about agitprop scripts.

The first distinct type of script was the mass chant. It was popular because it made no specific demands for scenery, costumes, properties, staging, or characterization. It was simply an arrangement of slogans to be recited. The following excerpt from *Miners on Strike* is typical; the numbers at the left identify the speaker or speakers:

4. 1800 miners
5. In Kentucky and Tennessee
6. Strike
7. Against
1. Terror
2. Exploitation
3. Starvation
4, 5, 6. Strike
7. Against
1, 2, 3. The same capitalists
1. Who have thrown twelve million workers into the streets
2. Without a job
3. Who kill 1000 workers every day of starvation.[11]

When combined with group movement and musical or rhythmic accompaniment, this form of theatrical free verse was meant to have a galvanizing effect on audiences of workers already disposed to support strikes and strikers. Similar scripts were the *Prolet-Buehne*'s *Scottsboro* and *15 Minute Red Revue*. More sophisticated was *Fight Against Starvation*, in which a workers' chorus chanting a litany of problems on one side of the stage is combined with short scenes from the life of the striking Kentucky coal miners on the other. A certain unity of tone is maintained by the use of rough, doggerel verse. The mass chant was further developed by the *Prolet-Buehne*. In both *Tempo, Tempo* and *The Belt*, workers mime representational industrial activity while the Capitalist and the Foreman urge them on and keep them under control. In both scripts the workers spontaneously rebel and drive their masters from the stage.[12]

More common was the skit or sketch that combined mass chant with interaction among individual types. The simplest of these presented a general economic or political analysis. In the WLT's *Mr. Box, Mr. Fox, and Mr. Nox*, a group of workers watches while three capitalists set up competing hat companies. The workers see the results of competition: wages are cut and hours increased to compensate for price reductions, and finally when a profit is no longer possible, the factories close. The workers learn that they must take ownership of the factories themselves. Other scripts function to identify class enemies of the worker: the Minister, the Society Lady, the Labor Leader, and the Socialist. In such scripts as *Unemployed, Yoo-Hooey, The Fight Goes On, We Demand, Step on It,* and *The Big Stiff*, workers are shown that their only champion in the struggle is the Communist.[13]

The most fully developed skits attempt to provide some sense of place and situation as a vehicle for presenting the political point. Some, such as *It's Funny as Hell* and *Help the Miners*, are conveniently set in meeting halls. In both cases the Boss is meeting with his cohort of subservient types to devise strategies for controlling restive workers. Employees' delegations interrupt the meetings, scatter the oppressors, and address the audience as though they were co-workers with an exhortation to organize and fight.[14] A few of the sketches approach the full dramatization of conventional plays. In the first scene of *The Miners Are Striking*, for example, two miners trapped in a collapsing shaft call for help and try to escape as they are overcome by fumes. This vignette serves to motivate a strike, the progress of which is then treated in a series of parallel episodes in which the Boss uses the Priest, the Judge, and the Sheriff in attempts to break the strike. Each episode is rhetorically surrounded by a chorus of miners and their wives, who chant slogans that drive home the lesson of the play: the workers must organize and fight to achieve justice.[15] A similar structure is followed in *Lynch Law*, which deals with the famous Scottsboro trial. In a series of dramatic scenes, typical characters conspire to suborn witnesses to bring a rape charge against a group of Negro youths. At the end a chorus points out the obvious moral that this has been done to keep cheap Negro labor docile and that all workers, black and white, must unite and fight.[16]

Election scripts form a separate category and bring a refreshing note of humor to the agitprop scene. Their political point is that Republicans, Democrats, and Socialists are all on the side of the boss. However, this point is usually made through the use of comedy, song, and dance. For example, in the *Prolet-Buehne's Liberty U.S.A.*, Miss Liberty has five children, each represented by a doll. They all look alike, except the Socialist is cross-eyed and is always wetting himself, and the little Laborfaker has a wooden head. In this skit even the little Communist provides some humor, embarrassing his mother by his foolishness. He wants to live but has no money; and he extolls the virtues of the Soviet Union, which doesn't exist because President Hoover hasn't recognized it.[17] Similar exposures of the establishment political parties occur in *Vote Communist, Three of a Kind*, and *I'll Tell You How to Vote*.[18] The last is theatrically distinguished by its portrayal of Jimmy Walker as a song-and-dance man, somewhat before George Kaufman's use of a similar idea for a presidential candidate in *Of Thee I Sing*.

Certain characteristics of a dramatic form can be deduced from these examples. First, the action of an agitprop script is the arousal of the workers to a pitch of political awareness that leads them to take action by unifying and organizing on their own behalf. At the beginning of a script they are oppressed and docile. In the middle they become aware of their plight and begin to argue with and resist their oppressors. At the end they take symbolic action by uniting on stage and chasing off the characters who represent their enemies, turning to the audience in a final exhortation to do the same in real life. This action is always structured in a series of short episodes, each of which is followed by didactic commentary. In the moments of comment the audience is always addressed directly as though its members were characters in the play. Finally, the language of the scripts is usually a mixture of two styles: the rather formal rhetoric of the slogan and the attempts at idiomatically representational speech.

In the shift to full-length plays and stationary production, certain aspects of this dramatic form received more emphasis, and some were dropped altogether. Most of the Theatre Union repertory, for example, retained the basic pattern of the action, telling the story in more fully developed episodes by means of idiomatic dialogue and concluding with a scene of mass organization. But in line with the style of socialist realism, they omitted didactic commentary on the action and seldom addressed the audience directly.[19] Other scripts, however, more clearly retain their agitprop heritage and demonstrate that agitprop was capable of more sophisticated artistic use.

The most obvious instance of the elaboration of agitprop into fuller artistic form is Clifford Odet's *Waiting for Lefty*. Conceptually, it is an expanded series of agitprop episodes. It begins with a strike meeting in a union hall. Memory episodes in the lives of different kinds of workers alternate with episodes that recount the progress of the meeting itself. Each type of scene provides an implicit comment on the other, revealing that all workers have the same problems, whether they are taxi drivers, actors, or medical interns, and that their only hope is to organize. At the end as Agate shouts out the sloganized conclusions that can be drawn from the taxi drivers' experience, he seems to speak for all workers; and, as the stage is cleared of the corrupt union bosses, performers in the audience begin to participate in the action of the play, establishing a symbolic pattern for the nonactors to follow in real life. Although three different versions of the script are printed, each with a slightly different sequence of scenes, the action and impact are the same. Like any agitprop, it was written to be reshaped for various occasions.[20]

Irwin Shaw's *Bury the Dead* also shows its agitprop roots. It addresses the problem of war but is essentially a strike play which substitutes military classes. A group of dead soldiers (workers) refuses to be buried (goes on strike). The generals (bosses) attempt to get them buried (break the strike) by means of various forms of persuasion and coercion. At the end the dead arise and drive their oppressors from the stage. Although the episodes are in idiomatic dialogue, they contain didactic, sloganized commentary. Moreover, the soldiers' reason for refusing burial is a classic expression of basic Marxist rhetoric: since they have never possessed the earth or enjoyed the fruits of their labor, they refuse to be buried in the earth; and in rising from the dead, they are only taking possession of what is rightfully theirs.[21]

Finally, the use of music and humor, so much a part of agitprop, is fully developed in Marc Blitzstein's *The Cradle Will Rock*.[22] This strike play begins when, in the process of breaking up a mine-union meeting, the police mistakenly arrest the members of an anti-union Liberty Committee, which had come to disrupt the proceedings. All of the typical class enemies of the worker are thus brought into night court: Reverend Salvation, Editor Daily, Yasha (a musician),

Dauber (an artist), President Prexy and Professor Trixie of the local university, and Dr. Specialist. As each pleads his innocence, the action shifts, in the manner of *Lefty*, to a correlative scene. It is established that each of them is controlled by Mr. Mister, the mine owner. Two other characters make didactic comments on these scenes: Moll (a prostitute) and Harry Druggist (who lost his business because he refused to cooperate with Mr. Mister's frame-up of a worker for the dynamiting of union headquarters). The climax comes with the entrance of the meeting's speaker, Larry Foreman, who rejects Mr. Mister's attempts to co-opt him. At the end, thousands of workers mass off stage as Larry leads a final revolutionary chorus that parallels Agate's final speech in *Lefty*:

Agate (*crying*): Hear it boys, hear it? Hell, listen to me! Coast to coast! HELLO AMERICA! HELLO. WE'RE STORMBIRDS OF THE WORKING-CLASS. WORKERS OF THE WORLD. . . . OUR BONES AND BLOOD! And when we die they'll know what we did to make a new world! Christ, cut us up to little pieces. We'll die for what is right! put fruit trees where our ashes are!	*Larry*: That's thunder, that's lightning, And it's going to surround you! No wonder those stormbirds Seem to circle around you. . . . Well, you can't climb down, and "you can't sit still; There's a storm that's going to "last until The final wind blows . . . and "when the wind blows . . . the cradle will rock! . . .

In addition to the plays already discussed, *Pins and Needles, Parade*, and the Living Newspapers were strongly influenced by agitprop.[23]

The normative aspects of the WLT can be judged from the similar histories of various other agitational theatres in other countries during the 1930s. In particular, the tendency toward artistic sophistication can be seen at work, though the tensions thus created were resolved in various ways. Events in Germany have already been discussed, and the agitprop form was cut off by Hitler's accession to power early in 1933. Political opposition was quickly suppressed in all forms, and left-wing agitational theatre disappeared along with the parties that supported it.

Left-wing agitational theatre was also part of the scene in England and France, and while there were significant local variations, the overall picture of the activity resembles that of the WLT. As in Germany, there was a tradition in the English Socialist and Labor parties of both dramatic and musical performance as an expression of political attitudes. However, the bulk of activity before 1926 involved plays of social comment. The general strike of 1926 triggered the development of agitational theatre. That year Tom Thomas became a member of the Hackney Labor Dramatic Group, and the following year with about twenty others from the parent organization, he founded the Hackney People's Players, an agitational group that within a year was associating with similar groups in

London. By the time they made contact with German troupes in 1931, English agitational theatres had already developed their own form derived from the music hall tradition: satiric revues that were a mixture of song, dance, and skits similar to Piscator's *Red Revue* and to the WLT's election material. By mid-1932 there were some twenty-two groups in England, and by 1934 the movement toward longer plays in conventional theatres had begun. By 1936 a number of groups had combined to create Unity Theatre. While hard-liners like Thomas dropped out of the movement in its popular front phase, Unity managed the transition better than the WLT, by maintaining mobile agitational troupes while producing full-length plays. Unity survived the war and remained a force in English theatrical life until after 1950. Not only does the pattern of development parallel the American model, the style of performance seems to have been identical. The pieces were short, simple in both content and production, featured stock characters, eschewed illusion, espoused the party line, and were performed under whatever circumstances happened to exist at workers' meetings.[24]

Information in France is less complete. The only agitational group whose work survives is that of Jacques Prévert's Groupe Octobre, which in 1932 grew out of an earlier troupe called Premices. Groupe Octobre created its own uniquely comic form of agitprop, which was the product of Prévert's imagination, but descriptions of their most famous piece, an adaptation of Cervantes's *The Show of Wonders*, make it sound like a mixture of fairy tale and the WLT's election pieces. In performance the members wore unisex costumes and used a minimum of props on an otherwise bare stage. Prévert disbanded the troupe rather than make the transition to popular-front theatre in 1936.[25]

At this point it seems possible to offer two sets of preliminary observations based on the experience of the 1930s. The first set relates to historical development. In both American and British agitational theatres there was a tendency to move in the direction of more fully articulated and traditionally representational productions. This tendency did not preclude continued agitational productions, but the longer pieces dominated. Not only did they require more resources, but they appealed to a larger audience because their politics were less strident. Because of this appeal it was possible to fulfill both the artistic and political goals that gave rise to this tendency. However, only three groups succeeded in converting the political energies of agitprop into more broadly appealing plays that moved in the direction of social theatre: the Theatre Union of New York, and the Unity theatres of London and Glasgow. These facts lead to a second observation. Agitational theatre depended on an organized political party for economic and ideological support. The success of both Unities depended on their managing the problems of a more complex production style and also on the continuance of an active, leftist political movement in Great Britain. The demise of such politics not only doomed the American groups but also frustrated the possibility of such development in Germany.

The second set of observations relates to the style of production in all these groups. First, all agitational scripts shared certain common features, which have been described. Second, the manner of their production seems to have fit a similarly uniform pattern. Third, both script and production elements carried over from the agitprop pieces into longer, more traditional plays and into the productions of groups that made the popular front transition, and these elements also influenced commercial production work, at least in this country. Thus, the WLT and its associates in the 1930s provide two sets of norms: one for historical development, and another for the style of script and production.

With these norms in mind, we can now approach the political theatre of the 1960s. To a large extent the norms continued and thus provided a basis for understanding an apparently chaotic theatrical and political situation. Two groups have been particularly significant in this country. The first is the San Francisco Mime Troupe, founded by R. G. Davis in 1959. Davis found the most appropriate expression of his radical politics in adaptations from commedia scenarios and the plays of Moliere, Cervantes, and Goldoni; but the troupe's most successful and controversial piece was a political minstrel show, *Civil Rights in a Cracker Barrel* (1965). The Mime Troupe consistently used the basic techniques of direct address, audience involvement, a dialogue of mixed styles, and a sequence of short episodes with commentary to portray an action in which the oppressed awoke and threw off their oppressors. The difference was that they found all these characteristics in the conventions of commedia dell'arte, and they adapted the type characters of that form to the Marxist typology of bosses and workers. Davis resigned as artistic director in 1970, and out of necessity the troupe reorganized as a collective, in the manner of the WLT. Since reorganization, the style has been broadened to include character types and conventions of nineteenth-century melodrama, musical comedy, the movie western, and the comic strip. What has not changed is the simple comic style of playing politically agitational material dealing with American involvement in Vietnam (*The Dragon Lady's Revenge*, 1971), urban renewal (*San Fran Scandals of '73*), and the possibility of nuclear war (*Power Play*, 1975).[26]

The other significant modern American agitprop troupe, El Teatro Campesino, is an indirect outgrowth of the San Francisco Mime Troupe. Luis Valdez was, briefly, an actor with Davis. He left in 1965 to form his own group to support the strike of the United Farm Workers Union against the grape growers of the Delano area of California. Out of the strike and elements of Mexican-American culture, he developed his own agitprop form, the *acto*, "short scenes dealing with some specific element of the strike. The actors started with a real life incident, character or idea, and improvised around this in a commedia dell'arte fashion."[27] The farmworkers' struggle was replaced by the Vietnam War in the group's work between 1968 and 1970. Since then, from their permanent home in San Juan Bautista, the Teatro has developed a new form, the *mito*, which combines elements of Aztec mythology with the contemporary subculture of the urban *barrio*. The new form serves as a vehicle for the expression of a larger struggle in which the warfare of economic classes is subsumed within the conflicts arising from an attempt by an ethnic minority to establish its social and cultural identity. Most recently, Valdez has presented his protagonist (a streetwise punk called a *vato* or a *pachuco*) in both a full-length musical play, *Zoot Suit* (1978), and in a shorter piece, *Mundo* (1979), that has toured California and Europe.[28] El Teatro has made a successful transition from short pieces to long ones and appears to have abandoned agitational theatre for the theatre of social comment. In an explanation of his decision to abandon the *acto*, Valdez said, "We found we had to back away from Delano to be a theatre. Do you serve the moment [*sic*] by being just kind of half-assed, getting together whenever there's a chance, or do you really hone your theatre down into an effective weapon?"[29]

Agitational theatre was reborn in Europe about 1968. In England opposition to U.S. policy in Vietnam coincided with the abolition of stage censorship and resulted in a host of groups (Red Ladder, 7:84, Freehold Theatre Company, The Hull Truck, CAST, The General Will, and The Portable Theatre) who intended "to try and make the economic and social forces that so deeply affect our lives . . . visible and tangible so that they can be grasped and hopefully acted upon."[30] Using the familiar techniques of caricature and stereotype drawn from popular forms of entertainment, writers such as David Edgar, John McGrath, David Hare, and Howard Brenton developed agitprop pieces for performance in pubs, the traditional gathering place of the British working class.[31] Similar groups arose in France in the wake of the uprisings of May 1968, and at least one such group, Rote Rübe, exists in Munich.[32] Most of the influential European troupes, however, have transformed the traditional agitational techniques into more complex and fully articulated theatrical spectacles.

The influence of Bertolt Brecht is critical to understanding the development from strictly agitprop forms in the modern European theatre. In 1928 and 1929 Brecht experimented in his *Lehrstücke* with something like abstract agitprop. He combined the lessons he learned from producing these pieces with the example of the agitprop troupes to create the mature style of epic theatre. He concluded that an episodic form of writing enhanced the communication of political ideas, and a radically simplified style of staging made production easier within the limited resources usually available to interested groups.[33] However, the results of his achievement were not widely known or understood until after 1950, thus their impact has been relatively recent. What Brecht accomplished was the development of a style of theatre that stands somewhere between social comment and agitation. It seems to have the potential for both political effectiveness and artistic excellence, and the recent work of El Teatro Campesino and the English fringe playwrights as well as that of Dario Fo and of Le Theatre du Soliel seem to be elaborating the Brechtian solution to the tension between art and politics inherent in agitational theatre.[34]

At this same time, however, there was an alternative strategy of participatory theatre, as there had been in Germany during the previous era. In the turmoil between 1968 and 1970, many people rejected both the traditional political solutions of the orthodox left and the associated theatrical strategy of agitprop. Both Herbert Marcuse and R. D. Laing had perceived that language was oppressive because it was based on and perpetuated categories of thinking that inevitably led to bourgeois capitalism. So long as one spoke and though conventionally, one was trapped. The need was for a liberation of consciousness: at least the destruction of conventional language and thought, but ideally the creation of new modes of feeling, thinking, and expressing.[35] These political and psychological theories were congruent with the theatrical ideas of Antonin Artaud, which were popular at about the same time.

The work of Julian Beck and Judith Malina in the Living Theatre provided a crucial example of this theory in practice. The sage of the Becks' development from poetic to political radicals has been told often. As a result of what they perceived as their victimization by the American government, they moved directly from being primarily a theatre of social comment to becoming a participatory theatre of political revolution. In a work such as *Paradise Now* the aim of the performers was to persuade members of the audience to join the performance by committing subversive acts, such as publicly smoking marijuana or taking off their clothes.[36]

The appeal of participatory theatre can best be explained by the new political theatre's need for a party to support it. In rejecting the old left, the new-left radicals rejected the only existing organized movement. Their participatory theatre was an attempt to create alternative support by means of an expression of discontent so clear and so powerful that it would act as a magnet for the confused polarities of political turmoil. Briefly, especially in San Francisco in the summer of 1968, they seemed to succeed; but as the flower children wilted, the support for participatory theatre faded. Marcuse, the Becks, the Students for a Democratic Society (SDS), all rejected benevolent anarchy in favor of more orthodox Marxist attitudes, and agitprop pieces returned to the streets.[37] The atmosphere of participatory theatre was retained only by a few, such as The Performance Group, and in the rock musicals spawned by the success of *Hair*. So far as I know, the only survival of the participatory ideal is Augusto Boal's use of theatrical performance, in which the means of theatrical production are put in the hands of an audience of poor people as a rehearsal for taking possession of the means of economic production.[38]

A brief consideration of representative scripts will establish the similarity between recent agitational pieces and the WLT forerunners. *Song of the Mighty B-52*, performed by the University of Connecticut's SDS Radical Arts Troupe is typical of the scripts that opposed the Vietnam War. It begins with a mass chant by the ruling-class Americans that reminds one of "The Army Song" from Brecht's *Threepenny Opera*:

> The people need you
> The army'll feed you
> See the world you never saw
> We'll bring our way of life
> To countries torn by strife

If communist intervention
Spoils our democratic intention
We'll chop to bits
Because white America's rule is law.

After Black, Brown, and White soldiers have been recruited, their training is interrupted by a Vietcong, who argues with the Ruling Class about the justice of the war. The recruits are won over by the Vietcong arguments and turn their guns on the Ruling Class.[39]

The Big Top by the People's Street Theatre of the New York SDS is more complex and deals with several related issues. Using the convention of a circus performance, the play shows how the original ideas of government, education, and the labor movement have been systematically distorted in this country by the influence of big business. In the final scene a group of dissatisfied people from the previous scenes organizes in opposition to the satisfaction expressed by the Happy Family, which is supported by Business, Government, Education, and the Military. Gradually, the slogans of the dissatisfied overwhelm those of the opposition, and the audience is asked to join in chasing the oppressors off the stage.[40]

La Quinta Temporada (*The Fifth Season*) is a classic *acto* in which one can see Luis Valdez adapting agitational techniques to the particular situation of the California farmworkers. The play dramatizes the crucial effect of each season on the life of the farmworker (Campesino) as he is recruited by the labor contractor (Don Cyote) for the farmer (Patron). Summer, the best season because there is the most work, is depicted as a figure covered with dollar bills for the worker to pick. Winter, when there is no work, is the worst season and is depicted as a demanding, devouring monster. In each scene the worker is exploited by both the contractor and the farmer until the union intervenes. A strike forces the farmer to agree to a contract which frees the Campesino from economic victimization by creating a "fifth season." In the end only the contractor is left for Winter to despoil, and the audience joins the workers in a celebration of freedom and justice.[41]

The work of R. G. Davis and the San Francisco Mime Troupe, however, shows the full transformation of agitprop into something like a mature form. In *L'Amant Militaire*, adapted by Joan Holden from a play of the same title by Goldoni, the original situation becomes a comment on the Vietnam War.[42] The plot revolves around the efforts of two sets of characters to avoid the consequences of war. On the one hand, Alonso loves Rosalinda, Pantalone's daughter. Not only is he ordered to fight in a new offensive, but Pantalone is determined to marry his daughter to the commanding officer, Generale Garcia. At the same time, Rosalinda's maid, Corallina, is loved by Arlecchino, but he is drafted and sent to the front. In a series of broadly comic scenes both sets of lovers attempt to extricate the men from the military. Just as it appears that they will fail, that Rosalinda will have to marry the Generale and Arlecchino will be executed for desertion, Corallina appears disguised as the Pope. This divine intervention results in a happy ending. When Arlecchino can't believe his good fortune, Corallina turns to the audience and says, "You think this was a fairy tale? Listen, my friends—you want something done? Well, then, do it yourselves!"

The fabric of comment on America's involvement in Vietnam is sustained by a web of topical references to the Selective Service System, the modern weapons with which the armies are equipped, the fate of civilians in the war, and, above all, by the relationship between Pantalone, a business tycoon, and the Generale. As Pantalone observed, "When you think about it Generale, we're not doing so bad now. You're fighting, I'm making money, both of us is happy. Well, you take my advice, Generale: win a little, lose a little. That way nobody gets hurt." All topical references are reinforced, and the didactic antiwar tone is maintained by Punch, the traditional hand puppet, who pops up at the end of each scene to comment on the action. His observations on Arlecchino's joining the army are typical:

Listen—nobody *has* to go into the army. There are lots of ways to get out. You blow up the draft boards, commit a crime, go to jail, pour your blood on the records, stay in school for twenty-seven years—or you can psych out. Very easy—see you get yourself good and loaded and stay up for three nights. And then you go down there and write with your left hand (that's if you can still see the paper) then you let them know that *you* are a leading prevert [*sic*], you don't come right out and tell them—you just let them know. Then, when you finally get in front of the shrink, you put your head down on his desk and cry. [*cries: Wa-a-aah!*] You don't like that method, huh? Too all-American to be crazy? Just stand up and say "Hell, no—we won't go!" [*Corallina as pom-pom girl— off stage—leads audience in cheer.*] Some of you people don't know how to cheer! I know what you're doing: you're protecting your records, so you can have a civil service job when you're forty years old. There's nothing I can do for *you*—you're in the army already.

These more recent agitprop plays not only reflect the same dramatic practices as those of the WLT, but performance conditions and style are also similar. The plays of the various Radical Arts Troupes (RATS), the guerilla theatres of the SDS, were designed for performance in streets or parks, usually at antiwar gatherings. They require no scenery and few if any props, and the costumes are typical street wear for undergraduates. The symbolic costume pieces used by the WLT to identify characters by class are replaced by descriptive signs hung around performers' necks. El Teatro usually performed in halls, but many of the *actos* were done in parks, and some were done from truck beds in the fields. Their scenery, props, and costumes were similar to the RATS' pieces; symbolic elements from the culture are used for purposes of identification. Even the more elaborate staging of *L'Amant Militaire* shows its agitprop heritage. Although the Mime Troupe performed on a small booth stage and used traditional commedia costumes and masks, these items provided scenery and costumes for all scripts and occasions. Moreover, they were portable. In effect, then, in staging as in playwriting, the Mime Troupe found in commedia a set of colorful conventions that met the needs of agitprop performance.

The conclusions to be drawn from this survey of political theatre can be summarized. First, political theatre, understood as the relationship of theatrical work to the politics of its time, exists on a broad spectrum of possibilities that runs from the deliberate political nullity of the commercial theatre at one extreme to participatory theatre's commitment to involving the audience in the performance of political acts. The two most common political postures in the modern theatre have been the play of social comment and the play of political agitation.

Second, the agitational theatre arises at times of social unrest when rational dialogue no longer seems profitable or possible. Matters are so extreme that discussion is over. What remains are partisan conclusions and the necessity to motivate people to act on those conclusions. For agitational theatre to be possible, however, there must exist outside the theatre an effective party or movement that is dedicated to carrying out the actions that are the consequences of the conclusions articulated in the agitprop performance. When such a movement does not exist, agitational theatre cannot function, and the committed artist must choose either the social or the participatory stance in an attempt to create such a movement. The more severe the crisis seems, the more likely it is that the choice will be for the participatory form.

Third, agitational theatre can be identified as a discrete artistic form, possessing certain standard characteristics of both script and performance that are responses to political and theatrical conditions. These characteristics seem to exist most clearly in the work of the WLT, and available evidence suggests that they appeared also in groups in other countries during the 1930s and also a generation later. Typically, the agitational script embodies an action that shows characters of the audience's socioeconomic situation becoming aware of the cause of a problem, which leads to their deciding to take group action against their enemies, who are depicted by means of satiric reduction based on some form or forms derived from popular entertainment. The play ends with those enemies being driven from the stage in an action symbolic of the appropriate action in real life. Typically, these short scripts are meant for performance in nontheatrical spaces, and this results in a performance that uses minimal scenery, properties, and costumes and emphasizes simplicity and clarity in acting.

Fourth, artistic, economic, and political factors combine to create a tendency within agitational theatre groups to move in the direction of the theatre of social comment. The more complete and traditional forms of the theatre of social comment give the artistic impulses and ambitions of the artists greater scope, and this tends to reduce the intensity of the political message. A reduction in political intensity makes the plays and their performances appealing to a potentially larger audience, and this has both economic and political advantages. As R. G. Davis has pointed out,

Agitational propaganda is not revolutionary art. It supports rather than examines, explains rather than analyzes. It can be only a temporary form for the group that performs it. . . .

Didactic rather than dialectical, agitprop often skips over fundamental problems to fa-
cilitate immediate gains. Its very particularity limits its usefulness and longevity.[43]

Finally, it seems ironic, though perhaps dramatically appropriate, that the
most typical of all agitational theatres, the WLT, failed to achieve a more popular
style. They made a bad artistic choice in following the lead of the Theatre Union
into the style of socialist realism. The style failed them, not only because it
wedded them to complex illusionistic staging and acting, but because it compelled
them to falsify human motivation.[44] In part, the Theatre Union failed for this
reason also. Their unsuccessful production of Brecht's *The Mother* is a case in
point. They understood the play, as most Communist critics did, as socialist
realism. Brecht's presence at rehearsals and his futile attempts to explain his
intent only compounded the problems.[45] Ultimately, Brecht and others were
successful in finding a style of writing and performing that might have been
viable for the WLT had it been available to them. Certainly, the success of *The
Cradle Will Rock* and the Living Newspapers tends to support this hypothesis.
Consequently, the WLT remains the clearest example of a successful agitprop
theatre, and the example of their practice allows us to establish a descriptive
norm for agitational theatre as distinct from either the theatre of social comment
or that of political participation. Moreover, such distinctions allow us to locate
accurately the source and nature of the style of epic theatre.

One must still deal with the attitude that even if political theatre as such can
be taken seriously, the work of the Worker's Laboratory Theatre was only
Communist propaganda created by party professionals who had no real interest
in theatre. That, at least, was the line Elia Kazan took in his testimony before
the House Committee on Un-American Activities in 1952, and it shapes the
research and conclusions of Morgan Himelstein's *Drama Was a Weapon*.[46] In
the first place, it cannot be established who among the WLT's members belonged
to the Communist party, nor can it be established that any of them were ever
acting on direct orders from the party. As Jay Williams says, some of them were
Communists, and the history of the group is clear evidence that they always
tried to accommodate party policy.[47] However, that could be said of other groups
as well. There was in the 1930s a general sympathy with the left, represented
by the Soviet Union, as opposed to the right, represented by Hitler, Mussolini,
and Franco. One did not make fine distinctions among leftists. Antifascism was
a sufficient credential, and when the Hitler-Stalin pact deprived the Communists
of it, they lost most of their artistic adherents. But even if it could be shown
that every aspect of WLT theory and practice was the result of direct orders
from a commissar, and that everything was done for political rather than artistic
reasons, that would still be irrelevant. For whatever reasons, the result of the
WLT's work was a distinctive style of theatrical writing and performing that
had a significant impact in its own day and provides a norm for understanding
developments in our own time. Ultimately, we are free to dislike both the art
and the politics that shape it, but we are not free to ignore its existence as a

distinct theatrical genre that requires objective consideration by historians and critics.

NOTES

1. See the reviews in Eric Bentley, *The Theatre of Commitment* (New York, 1967); Robert Brustein, *Revolution as Theatre* (New York, 1971); Harold Clurman, *The Naked Image* (New York, 1966); Walter Kerr, *God on the Gymnasium Floor* (New York, 1971); and John Lahr, *Up Against the Fourth Wall* (New York, 1970).

2. For additional background on my approach, see Oscar G. Brockett, *Perspectives on Contemporary Theatre* (Baton Rouge, 1971), pp. 104–29; Jacques Ellul, *Propaganda: The Formation of Men's Attitudes*, trans. Konrad Kellen and Jean Lerner (New York, 1966); George H. Szanto, *Theater and Propaganda* (Austin, 1978); and Kenneth Burke, *The Philosophy of Literary Form* (New York, 1957). For a different approach to the critical problem, see Sam Smiley, *The Drama of Attack: Didactic Plays of the American Depression* (Columbia, 1972); and his "Thought as Plot in Didactic Drama," in *Studies in Theatre and Drama, Essays in Honor of Hubert C. Heffner*, ed. O. G. Brockett (The Hague, 1972), pp. 81–96.

3. On the Soviet Blue Blouses, see C. D. Innes, *Erwin Piscator's Political Theatre* (Cambridge, 1972), pp. 23–25. On developments in Germany, see Innes; Cecil W. Davies, "Working-Class Theatre in the Weimar Republic, 1919–1933: Part I," *Theatre Quarterly* [hereafter *TQ*], 10 (Summer 1980), 69–96; and Ludwig Hoffmann and Daniel Hoffmann-Oswald, eds., *Deutschesarbeitertheater, 1918–1933, Eine Dokumentation* (Berlin, 1961).

4. On Soviet mass plays, see Marc Slonim, *Russian Theater, from the Empire to the Soviets* (New York, 1961), pp. 231–34. On German *Massenspiele* and *Thingspiele*, see Henning Eichberg, et al., *Massenspiele, NS-Thingspiel, Arbeiterweihespiel und olympisches Zeremoniell* (Stuttgart-Bad Cannstatt, 1977); and Bruce Zortman, "The Theater of Ideology in Nazi Germany," (Diss., UCLA, 1969).

5. On the history of the WLT and the activity that preceded it, see Malcolm Goldstein, *The Political Stage, American Drama and Theatre of the Great Depression* (New York, 1974); and Jay Williams, *Stage Left* (New York, 1974).

6. On the *Prolet-Buehne*, see my article, "The Odyssey of John Bonn: A Note on German Theatre in America," *The German Quarterly*, 73 (May 1965), 325–34. On agitprop as a response to Communist party policy, see Raphael Samuel, "Workers' Theatre, 1926–1936," in *Performance and Politics in Popular Drama*, ed. David Bradby, et al., (London, 1980), pp. 213–30.

7. The WLT version of *Newsboy* is published in Williams, pp. 90–96. A much different and later version is in Karen Malpede Taylor, *People's Theatre in Amerika* (New York, 1972), pp. 55–60.

8. On the ideological conflict in relation to production style, see my article, "Propaganda and Art: Dramatic Theory and the American Depression," *Modern Drama*, 11 (May 1968), 73–81.

9. On the working methods and achievements of the WLT, see Goldstein, Williams, and my articles, "Agitprop: Production Practice in the Workers' Theatre, 1932–1942," *Theatre Survey*, 7 (November 1966), 115–24; and "New Theatre Schools, 1932–1942," *The Speech Teacher*, 14 (November 1965), 278–85.

10. Morgan Y. Himelstein, "Theory and Performance in the Depression Theatre," *Modern Drama*, 14 (February 1972), 426–35.

11. Workers Theatre [hereafter *WT*], 1 (March 1932), 9.

12. "Scottsboro," *WT*, 1 (April 1932), 14; "15 Minute Red Revue," *WT*, 2 (June–July 1932), 11–14; "Tempo, Tempo," *WT*, 1 (January 1932), 18–21; "The Belt," *WT*, 1 (March 1932), 6–8.

13. Will Lee, "Mr. Box, Mr. Fox, and Mr. Nox," *WT*, 1 (November 1931), 14–20; "Unemployed," *WT*, 1 (April 1931), 12–16; Harold Kotzer, "Yoo-Hooey," *WT*, 2 (August 1932), 14–15; B. Reines, "The Fight Goes On," *WT*, 1 (October 1931), 11–14; B. Reines, "We Demand," *WT*, 1 (February 1932), 21–26; Tric, "Step On It," *WT*, 1 (November 1931), 8–13; Tric, "The Big Stiff," *WT*, 1 (December 1931), 12–16.

14. "It's Funny as Hell," *WT*, 1 (May 1931), a-1 to a-7; A. Prentis, "Help The Miners," *WT*, 1 (August 1931), 9–15.

15. A. Prentis, "The Miners Are Striking," *WT*, 1 (February 1932), 15–20.

16. "Lynch Law," *WT*, 1 (June 1931), following p. 7.

17. "Liberty U.S.A.," *WT*, 1 (January 1932), 14–17.

18. "Vote Communist," *WT*, 2 (June–July 1932), 15–17; J. Shapiro, "Three of a Kind," *WT*, 1 (October 1931), 15–18; H. Elion, "I'll Tell You How to Vote," *WT*, 1 (September 1931), 15–23.

19. On Theatre Union plays, see Goldstein; also Smiley, *Drama of Attack*.

20. See *New Theatre*, 2 (February 1935), 13–20; William Kozlenko, ed., *The Best Short Plays of the Social Theatre* (New York, 1939), pp. 5–31; and *Sixteen Famous American Plays*, ed. Bennett Cerf and Van Cartmell (New York, 1941), pp. 423–47. The last is the most complete, and I refer to and quote from it.

21. Kozlenko, pp. 39–82.

22. Ibid., pp. 119–67.

23. On *Pins and Needles* and *Parade* see Harry Goldman and Mel Gordon, "Workers' Theatre In America: A Survey, 1913–1978," *Journal of American Culture*, 1 (Spring 1978), 169–81; and Harry Goldman, "When Social Significance Came to Broadway: Pins and Needles in Production," *TQ*, 7 (Winter 1978), 25–42. On the Living Newspaper, see Goldstein, and my article, "The Living Newspaper As a Dramatic Form," *Modern Drama*, 7 (May 1965), 82–94.

24. On Workers' Theatre in Great Britain, see the primary materials in "Documents and Texts from the Workers' Theatre Movement (1928–1936)," ed. Raphael Samuel, *History Workshop*, 4 (Autumn 1977), 102–43; Leonard Abraham Jones, "The Workers' Theatre Movement in the Twenties," *Zeitschrift fur Anglstik und Amerikanistik*, 14 (1966), 259–81; George Phillipson, "Workers' Theatre: Forms and Techniques," *Modern Drama*, 22 (December 1977), 383–89. On Unity Theatre, see Malcolm Page, "The Early Years at Unity," *TQ*, 1 (October–December 1971), 60–66. On related developments in Glasgow, see Douglas Allen, "Glasgow Workers' Theatre Group and the Methodology of Theatre Studies," *TQ*, 9 (Winter 1980), 45–54; and John Hill, "Towards a Scottish People's Theatre: The Rise and Fall of Glasgow Unity," *TQ*, 7 (Autumn 1977), 61–70.

25. On Groupe Octobre, see David Bradby, "The October Group and Theatre under the Front Populaire," in Bradby, et al., 231–42; and Susan Spitzer, "Prévert's Political Theatre: Two Versions of *La Bataille de Fontenoy*," *Theatre Research International*, 3 (October 1977), 54–65.

26. On the Mime Troupe, see Ruby Cohn, "Joan Holden and the San Francisco Mime

Troupe," *The Drama Review, 24 (June 1980), 41–50; R. G. Davis, The San Francisco Mime Troupe: The First Ten Years* (Palo Alto, 1975); Joan Holden, "Collective Playmaking: The Why and the How," *TQ*, 5 (June–August 1975), 28–36; Theodore Shank, "The San Francisco Mime Troupe's Production of False Promises," *TQ*, 7 (Autumn 1977), 41–52; and Richard Toscan and Kathryn Ripley, "The San Francisco Mime Troupe: Commedia to Collective Creation," *TQ*, 5 (June–August 1975), 22–25. Their recent scripts are in *By Popular Demand and Other Plays* (San Francisco, 1980).

27. John Harrop and Jorge Huerta, "The Agitprop Pilgrimage of Luis Valdez and El Teatro Campesino," *TQ*, 5 (March–May 1975), 31.

28. On El Teatro Campesino, see Beth Bagby, "El Teatro Campesino, Interviews with Luis Valdez," *The Drama Review*, 11 (Summer 1967), 70–80; Susan Bassnett-McGuire, "El Teatro Campesino: From Actos to Mitos," *TQ*, 9 (Summer 1979), 18–21; R. G. Davis and Betty Diamond, "Zoot Suit on the Road," *TQ*, 9 (Summer 1979), 21–25; Harrop and Huerta, pp. 30–39; Jeanne Wakatsuki Houston, "The Mundo of Luis Valdez," *California Living, San Francisco Sunday Examiner and Chronicle*, 23 November 1980, pp. 10–20; Nicolas Kanellos, "Chicano Theatre: A Popular Culture Battleground," *Journal of Popular Culture*, 13 (Spring 1980), 541–55; Francoise Kourilsky, "Approaching Quetzalcoatl: The Evolution of El Teatro Campesino," *Performance*, 2 (Fall 1973), 37–46; Theodore Shank, "A Return to Mayan and Aztec Roots," *The Drama Review*, 18 (December 1974), 56–70; and Carlos Morton, "The Teatro Campesino," *The Drama Review*, 18 (December 1974), 71–76.

29. Quoted in Harrop and Huerta, p. 32.

30. Richard Seyd of Red Ladder, quoted in David Edgar, "Ten Years of Political Theatre, 1968–1978," *TQ*, 8 (Winter 1979), 27.

31. On British fringe theatre, see Peter Ansorge, *Disrupting the Spectacle: Five Years of Experimental and Fringe Theatre in Britain* (London, 1975); Edgar, pp. 25–33; Ronald Hayman, *British Theatre Since 1955, A Reassessment* (London, 1979); John McGrath, "The Theory and Practice of Political Theatre," *TQ*, 9 (Autumn 1979), 43–54.

32. On France, see Francoise Kourilsky and Lenora Champagne, "Political Theatre in France Since 1968," *The Drama Review*, 19 (June 1975), 43–52. On Germany, see Denis Calandra, "Rote Rübe: Terror," *The Drama Review*, 19 (June 1975), 114–18.

33. On Brecht's *Lehrstücke* and their relation to agitprop, see Martin Esslin, *Brecht, The Man and His Work* (New York, 1961), pp. 22–58; and John Willett, *The Theatre of Bertolt Brecht*, 2nd ed. (New York, 1960), pp. 119–20.

34. On Dario Fo, see Suzanne Cowan, *Dario Fo*, Theatre Checklist No. 17 (London, 1978); and her "The Throw-Away Theatre of Dario Fo," *The Drama Review*, 19 (June 1975), 102–13. On Le Theatre du Soliel, see Arian Mnouchkine, "L'Age d'Or, The Long Journey from 1793 to 1975," *TQ*, 5 (June–August 1975), 4–14.

35. See Herbert Marcuse, *Counterrevolution and Revolt* (Boston, 1972); and his *An Essay on Liberation (Boston, 1972); also see R. D. Laing, The Politics of Experience* (London, 1967).

36. On the history of the Living Theatre, see Pierre Biner, *The Living Theatre* (New York, 1972); and Renfreu Neff, *The Living Theatre: U.S.A.* (New York, 1970). For descriptions of *Paradise Now*, see, *We, The Living Theatre*, ed. Aldo Rostagno (New York, 1970); *Yale/Theatre*, 2 (Spring 1969). The script is published as *Paradise Now, Collective Creation of the Living Theatre* (New York, 1971).

37. For an analysis of the failure of participatory theatre, see *Guerilla Street Theater*, ed. Harry Lesnick (New York, 1973); Arthur Sainer, *Radical Theatre Notebook* (New

York, 1975); Herbert Marcuse, *The Aesthetic Dimension, Toward a Critique of Marxist Aesthetics* (Boston, 1978); and Taylor, *People's Theatre*.

38. On the continuation of participatory theatrical experiments, see *The New Theatre, Performance Documentation*, ed. Michael Kirby (New York, 1974); and Richard Schechner, *Dionysus in 69* (New York, 1970); also his *Public Domain* (New York, 1969). On Boal, see Augusto Boal, *Theater of the Oppressed*, trans. Charles A. and Maria-Odilia Leal McBride (New York, 1979).

39. Lesnick, pp. 82–86.

40. Ibid., pp. 60–77.

41. Ibid., pp. 197–212.

42. The text is printed in Davis, *The San Francisco Mime Troupe*, pp. 173–93.

43. Ibid., p. 166.

44. On this aspect of socialist realism, see Abram Tertz, *On Socialist Realism*, trans. George Dennis (New York, 1969).

45. For an account of the Theatre Union's production of *The Mother*, see James K. Lyon, *Bertolt Brecht in America* (Princeton, New Jersey, 1980), pp. 6–20.

46. United States Congress, House Committee on Un-American Activities, *Hearings*, "Communist Infiltration into the Hollywood Motion-Picture Industry," Pt. 7, Testimony of Elia Kazan, 10 April 1952, p. 2410; Morgan Y. Himelstein, *Drama Was a Weapon, The Left-Wing Theatre in New York, 1929–1941* (New Brunswick, New Jersey, 1963).

47. Williams, p. 33.

Eduardo Migliaccio, "Farfariello," probably as *The Drunkard*. (Photo courtesy of Saul Mauriber, Photographic Executor of the Carl Van Vechten Collection, New York Public Library.)

Eduardo Migliaccio, "Farfariello," in costume as a French Concert Hall Singer. (Photo courtesy of Saul Mauriber, Photographic Executor Carl Van Vechten Collection, New York Public Library.)

A Chorus of Workers drives a Capitalist off the stage of history in a Prolet-Buehne production, probably *Tempo, Tempo*. (Photo from *The Workers Theatre*, 1932.)

The forces of Capitalism attack the Soviet Union in the Prolet-Buehne's production of *Fifteen Minute Red Revue*, first performed at the First National Workers' Theatre Conference, held in the Manhattan Lyceum in New York City on April 16, 1932. (Photo from *The Workers Theatre*, 1932.)

The Prolet-Buehne, America's first agit-prop troupe, provides a visual image of the struggle between Capitalism and Socialism in an unknown production, probably from 1932. (Photo from *The Workers Theatre*, 1932.)

El Teatro Campesino. *Las Dos Caras del Patroncito* (*The Two Faces of the Boss*). Luis Valdez as the Patroncito and Daniel Valdez as the Farmworker. (Photo by Theodore Shank.)

El Teatro Campesino. *La Carpa de los Rasquachis* (*The Tent of the Underdogs*). Saint Boss Church baptizes the babies. (Photo by Theodore Shank.)

Ramona Fisher and Wilson Hutton in The Iron Clad Agreement's *Out of This Furnace*. (Photo courtesy of The Iron Clad Agreement.)

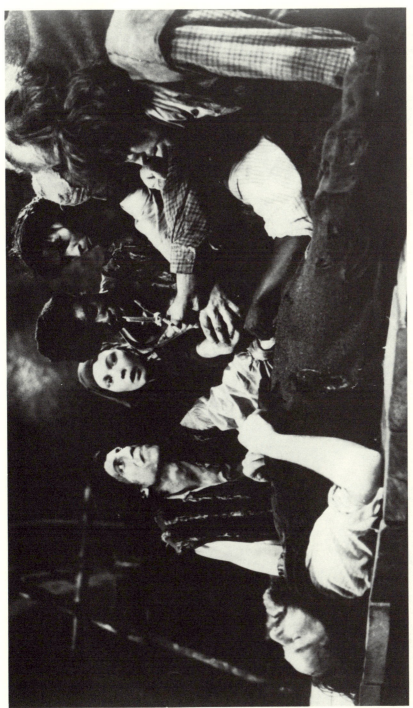

The New York Street Theatre Caravan's intense, emotional acting style is captured in this photograph of their production of *Molly Maguire*. (Photo courtesy of Marketa Kimbrell.)

149

The Everyday Theater of Washington, D.C., performing *Ghost Story*, a play about the consequences of "urban renewal." (Photo by Rick Reinhard, courtesy of The Everyday Theater.)

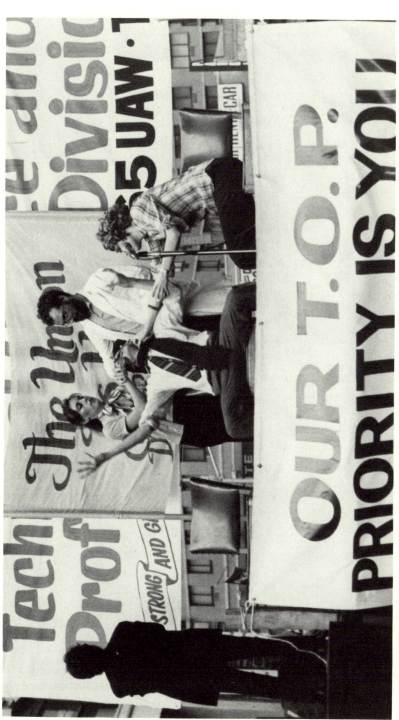

The vigorous, presentational performance style of Workers' Stage is demonstrated in this scene from the group's performance of *The Union Is Us* at a street festival sponsored by the Technical, Office, and Professional Division of District 65, UAW in New York City. (Photo courtesy of Workers' Stage.)

The New York Street Theatre Caravan performs a skit on the street. (Photo courtesy of Marketa Kimbrell.)

The Everyday Theater performs *The Begger and the Dead Dog* in a Washington, D.C., park. Mary Ann Ross is on stilts. Susie Solf plays the accordian. (Photo by Rick Reinhard, courtesy of The Everyday Theater.)

153

Joan Rosenfels seeks a room to rent from Peggy Pettitt in Modern Times' production of *The Bread and Roses Play*, a play about the Lawrence, Massachusetts, Textile Strike of 1912. (Photo by Steve Friedman, courtesy of Modern Times Theatre.)

10

Working-Class Theatre on the Auto Picket Line

Paul Sporn

I

The great organizing drive of automobile workers in the 1930s is an important but not well-known example of the stimulating effect of strikes on working-class theatre. The struggles that marked the drive's most concentrated years of effort, 1932 to 1938, constituted a series of conflicts whose complications, tensions, and denouements were eminently suitable as plots for the stage. Auto-strike plays were charged with a dramatic electricity that contrasted sharply with the tame contrivances usually favored by the commercial theatre. Moreover, since the drive clearly belonged to international and domestic events of the 1930s that were transforming social relationships and traditional ways of life, it offered working-class theatre the chance to portray an epic story of wide-ranging political significance.

The stimulus was not, by any means, a one-way affair. In seizing the dramatic raw materials that the organizing drive in the auto industry uncovered for it, working-class theatre transcended the limits of stage fiction and became politically significant—an instrument entering directly into the struggles of the workers. The plays that emerged relied heavily on auto workers for information and dialogue and, in one instance, for performers. Second, the scripts that reached the stage played to working-class audiences or to audiences with substantial contingents of workers in them, many of whom had been on strike only a short time before. Thus, in preparation and performance, the plays functioned as politically clarifying and inspirational instruments. They were able, in this way, to feed back to workers the inspiration they themselves had received from the union challenge to the giant auto companies.

Five plays grew out of the auto workers' challenge and reflect this cross-fertilization process. Although these plays represent responses in a variety of theatrical forms to a variety of events, the event motivating the most theatrical activity was the high drama of the sit-down strike against General Motors in Flint, Michigan. Two of the plays, *The Strike Marches On* and *Sit-Down*, are documentary retellings of this strike. The victory scored against General Motors in the Flint sit-down influenced workers elsewhere to do the same. *F.O.B. Detroit* centers on the events of the Ford hunger march in which demonstrating workers at the Ford River Rouge Plant were gunned down by the police. *Hoodwinked*, a musical skit, caricatures the notorious Black Legion, a Michigan-based armed association set up in part to oppose the unionization of the auto industry. *Million Dollar Babies*, another musical skit, deals with a strike against Detroit's main Woolworth outlet, whose female salesclerks (quite consciously modeling themselves after the Flint workers) decided to sit down in March 1937 for higher wages and better working conditions.

These theatrical responses to depression conditions in the Detroit area are not well known for two reasons. The playwrights were not close to the main centers of theatre in the United States. Although working-class theatre had rejected much of the bourgeois theatre, it was still most active where bourgeois theatre was primarily headquartered: in New York City, Chicago, and Los Angeles. The distance of these playwrights from these centers meant, therefore, that their work was not only ignored by much of the commercial press and by cosmopolitan audiences but also less publicized through the chief avenues of the working-class theatre. This distance also meant that their work had fewer opportunities for production. *F.O.B. Detroit* and *Million Dollar Babies* are cases in point. They were never produced. They are included here because they are bonafide responses to the auto drive; they are fairly good drama and clever entertainment, equal in quality to a number of plays that did reach New York or Chicago audiences; and they illustrate how theatre people, on the scene of events in Detroit, relied on workers for their dramatic material.

The second reason why these theatrical responses are not well known is that they have been lost, until recently, under the dust of time. This loss is attributable, in part, to the distance of these writers from the theatrical centers of the United States. The scripts were neither extensively noted nor reprinted in the usual newspapers and magazines for working-class theatre. Neither were they collected for safekeeping in the larger national repositories of historical documents; instead, they disappeared into private collections or smaller, less accessible archives. The generally conservative aesthetic and political attitudes that have prevailed in the United States since the end of World War II compounded the problem. Few historians of the theatre have been interested in rediscovering the 1930s. Those scholars who, in recent years, have written about working-class theatre in the Great Depression have concentrated their research in the major archives of the country.

Fortunately, much of the theatrical material related to the great auto workers' drive of the 1930s is now recovered.[1] These plays and the accounts of how they came to be written illustrate the use of working-class experience and working-class theatrical traditions to shape immediate events into presentations dramatizing political struggle. These plays are anchored in mass stage action, the use of ritualized chorus effects, the adaptation of popular songs to comment on social issues, improvised dialogue, minimal scenery and props, and interaction between the acting company and the audience. Those familiar with working-class theatre will recognize that this combination of techniques is part of a theatrical tradition dating from before the nineteenth century.[2] These techniques, particularly those that involve workers and audiences in the drama, are politically as well as aesthetically motivated: to heighten dramatic impact and to move the audience to action. All but one of the five plays belonging to the history of the auto drive offer good examples of this long-standing, dual motivation. But as much as working-class theatre tended to reject the bourgeois stage in theory, it never completely rooted out the influence of realism and naturalism. The theatrical response to the auto drive partly reflects this continued adherence to bourgeois forms. The musical skits draw on vaudeville and the movies—popular traditions of entertainment open to parody, satire, and comedy. Biting or gentle in humor, the skits clarified issues, while renewing the energies of the audience for battle through entertainment. Whatever forms they used, however, these plays thrived because they responded sympathetically to the struggles of the working-class drive to organize the auto industry workers.

II

F.O.B. Detroit is the one play of the group that is entirely in keeping with the realistic traditions of bourgeois theatre. This play is built around the massacre of unemployed workers who were demonstrating for food and jobs at Ford's River Rouge Plant on March 7, 1932. Maxine Wood, a native of Detroit, and Lou Falstein, who had worked for a short time at the Rouge, are its co-authors.[3] The title, which means "freight on board," is somewhat ironic for it implies that the auto industry delivers death. The story line of the play concerns two families, the Coreys and the Woodwards. The Coreys are a working-class family. Two brothers, Steve and Joe Corey, are engaged in organizing workers to fight the Frost Motor Company, Steve inside the plant and Joe among the unemployed. The Woodwards are a middle-class family who have fallen on hard times because of the depression. John Woodward, the son, has had to give up his medical school training to take a job with Frost Motor. The Coreys and the Woodwards respond differently to the march for food and jobs at the center of the play. Throughout much of the action, in fact, the conflict of outlook in each family parallels the conflict between the auto workers and the company. Steve's wife feels her husband should concentrate his energies on taking care of herself and their son rather than risking his job fighting for his class. In the Woodward family, the mother and her brother hang on to their middle-class ambitions, desiring status and money. John and his sister, on the other hand, view these aims as hypocritical in light of the problems facing ordinary people in the depression. The movement up and down this stacked set of contradictions—that is, the inner conflict within each family, the contrasting outlooks of each, and the frame of class conflict—embody the play's dialectical rhythm.

The play ends on a double note. The terrible outcome of the march, which kills Joe Corey, reunites his family. In contrast, the Woodward family disintegrates completely; only John manages to grow in the ordeal. He joins the remaining workers against the continuing harassment of the company and city officials. The other note is the optimism of the conclusion. Steve, who had fallen into despair at his brother's death, recovers from his malaise while a multitude of voices, embodying the thousands gathering to commemorate the dead, is heard singing offstage, with a determination to sweep away the murdering enemies of the working people. His are the last words of the play: "Listen to those voices. It's like a dam broke loose. Joe didn't die in vain. They know what he lived for—what he gave his life for! Where one falls ten will arise!" Clearly, happiness and social progress lie not in the self-seeking materialism of the middle class but in selfless devotion to working-class goals.

Wood and Falstein took many of the details of their play directly from the events of the workers' march on the Ford River Rouge Plant on March 7, 1932. Steve's description of the massacre, for example, matches the details of various eyewitness accounts. Joe Corey, twenty years old, a central figure in the march and murdered as a consequence, is patterned after Joe York, the twenty-year-old youth leader of the actual demonstration who was one of four people killed on March 7. The mass memorial at the closing moments of the play is based on two actual rallies. On March 11, 1932, about 8,000 people are reported to have met at Arena Gardens in Detroit where they pledged not to let the fight for jobs die out. The next day, 10,000 streamed down Woodward Avenue, the city's main thoroughfare, from the Institute of Arts to Grand Circus Park, where 30,000 others awaited them. From there, they walked five miles to Woodmere Cemetery, in easy view of the Rouge Plant, to bury the four victims in a common grave. The size of the funeral turnout—I have used a figure that falls midway between the lowest and highest reported estimates—was larger than the size of the crowd in the hunger march of the Monday before by a factor of ten—the same number, curiously, that Steve foresees rising to replace those fallen in battle.[4]

The other plays related to the organizing drive in the auto industry are episodic and abstract; they avoid realistic structural logic and the psychological conceptions of character embedded in the conventions of realism. Three of the plays rely extensively on song for a number of purposes. Song permeates them with a vein of satire expressing the auto workers' unawed, contemptuous feelings about established authority. At the same time that the songs convey information about the struggle and the aspirations of the working people in catchy, elementary terms, they also draw the audience into the entertainment through their general familiarity. Most songs used in these plays are adapted from contemporary popular music. The plays are deliberately episodic; the stress falls on the major events or attitudes affecting the final outcome rather than on the small, hidden nuances that endow them with texture but obscure their influence. Two of the plays, *The Strike Marches On* and *Sit-Down*, are documentary in the style of the Living Newspaper, a playwriting decision no doubt influenced by the success of that theatrical form in the Federal Theatre Project.

The specific ways in which these techniques are employed in *The Strike Marches On* are difficult to illustrate because this play relied almost entirely on improvised dialogue. A sketchy scenario in the labor archives at Wayne State University in Detroit is apparently all that remains of the play.[5] According to an account in that collection, Josephine Herbst, a novelist, and Dorothy Kraus, who headed up the daily operation of supplying the sit-downers with food, and Mary Heaton Vorse worked out the scenario.[6] Morris Watson, the national director of the Federal Theatre Project's Living Newspaper staff who happened to be in Detroit for a lecture the first week of February 1937, directed the play at the request of the three writers. Watson rehearsed the play for two days at strike headquarters with an audience of workers who shared in working out what was to be said and done with the eighty worker-actors. Helped by this improvisational interaction, the play, Watson later wrote, "served to clarify [the workers'] minds, to reduce to simple and understandable terms the purpose of the struggle of which they were a part. It stimulated them to inquiry and it fired them with new enthusiasm."[7]

The scenario of *The Strike Marches On* shows the extent to which the presentation relied on the creative improvising of the workers. It is nine pages long, but the last four suggest additional insertions without clear structural specificity. The face page reads "Outline for 'Living Newspaper' General Motors Strike in Flint, Michigan.—1936." Two Living-Newspaper devices used in the action were headlines shouted at key points in the plot by a newsboy and a radio loudspeaker in the last scene announcing news about the strike. The use of the strike's actual slogans and instructional tactics may also be considered part of the Living-Newspaper mode. Although the face page says 1936, the climax of the scenario is the taking-over of Chevrolet Plant 4, an event that occurred on February 2, 1937. *The Strike Marches On* was composed only moments after the events it depicts took place. It was written to be performed by members of the United Auto Workers and their families, who, because of the strike, were available in large numbers at union headquarters where the performance occurred.[8]

The five scenes called for by the scenario set up the bare-bones structure of the play, and bits of dialogue and stage direction suggest the point to be made in each scene or when action is to move from stage to auditorium. No scenery is designated for the play; the stage and auditorium are treated as a single space in which sound effects and simple props, such as plain cubes, suggest a specific setting. The first scene calls for monotonous, percussive music played at a faster and faster pace to evoke an assembly line and to suggest the company's speedup of production. A short dialogue is included between a worker and a foreman to illustrate how the company harasses union members. In the second scene, the assembly-line workers enter as if coming off their shift, discussing what to do about the union man fired in the first scene. The idea of a sit-down is introduced, and when one of the performers turns to the audience to ask for an opinion, the audience thunders back, "Sit down." When one of the performers suggests that someone in their ranks is a stool pigeon, a woman in the audience rises, advances toward the stage, and points a finger at one of the men: "There's your stool pigeon."

Scene 3 calls for all the performers to form a picket line, singing "Solidarity Forever." This scene takes place in front of Plant 9 and ends with a shout from the union sound car: "Everybody to Plant 4," the real object of attack. The next scene is at the Plant 4 gate, from which a worker addresses the women's emergency brigade which is singing "We Shall Not Be Moved." At the end of the scene, troops march onto the stage against the singing women, while offstage the union sound car is heard instructing the people inside the seized plant to "barricade the bridge . . . watch the roof . . . watch the tunnel between two and four." In scene 5, a radio announces that troops are pouring into Flint. While this announcement is being made, troops march on stage, and the radio suddenly addresses the audience: "Auto workers are you with us?" The audience is instructed to respond in full chorus: "Cadillac here, Chrysler here. Dodge is ready. Atlanta is watching. California is watching. England. France. Spain. THE WORLD IS WATCHING."

The play was originally intended to be part of an entertainment for an evening called AC Night, a special occasion for General Motors' spark plug workers, to be held Thursday, February 11. But early that morning, General Motors gave in to the demands of the sit-downers. The strike was over, and by midmorning and early afternoon processions of auto people filled the streets. That evening, Mary Heaton Vorse, making her way to union headquarters for the performance of *The Strike Marches On*, thought that no one would be there for the play. She reported later,

But the streets leading down to Pengalli [*sic*] Hall were so choked with people I could hardly get through. I could not fight my way up the stairs. In desperation I had climbed the fire escape and finally arrived where the cast was waiting for the pageant to begin. Every foot was crammed with people. The hall itself was choked. Another loudspeaker had to be rigged to address the crowd outside. Finally our little play went on. . . . We had taken the episode of sit-down which preceded Chevy Four. We proceeded with a picture of the Speed-up. But from on the meager skeleton the workers had taken it, enriched it, had added detail; made it their own.[9]

The play, designed for the lesser occasion of renewing the strike spirit, became instead a celebration of the workers' splendid victory.

Although William Titus's *Sit-Down* did not tread on the heel of events as immediately as *The Strike Marches On*, it followed a few short steps behind.[10] Less than two months after the strike ended, the play opened in New York City, on April 3, 1937. In the course of its career, it toured seventy-five cities, reaching Flint on May 30 and 31, for a two-night run. The Brookwood Labor Players, a troupe from the labor college in Katonah, New York, performed the show.

The record of their tour illustrates that they performed primarily to working-class audiences. After the New York premiere, they played New Bedford, Massachusetts, performing there on April 8 at Pulaski Hall. The Reverend Allen Keedy, chairman of the Civil Liberties Union educational committee which arranged the play's appearance in New Bedford, wrote that "this year we held the performance in the working-class district of North End, with the result that more workers came to see it." On April 10, *Sit-Down* played at the Peabody Playhouse of the Labor Lyceum in Boston. *The Sunday Post* reported that 150 people attended and stayed until midnight singing "Hold the Fort" and other "Soviet hymns of the C.I.O." According to *The Post*, the audience greeted the play with exceptional enthusiasm: "There was wild applause at times, hissing and booing at the company-union heroes and cheers for the CIO heroes." Next, the Brookwood company put the play on in Schenectady for Local 301 of the United Electrical and Radio Workers of America, where the audience consisted mostly of workers from General Electric. The Labor Players ran into trouble with their April 21 booking in Reading, Pennsylvania, when the local school board voted against the request of the Federated Trades Council for the use of the auditorium at Northwest Junior High School. The council had to rent a place called Eagle's Hall instead. The United Textile Workers of America, Local 1874, rented the Strand Theatre for an April 30 performance of *Sit-Down* in Cumberland, Maryland. There, *Sit-Down* shared a double bill with the film *Clarence* starring the comedian Roscoe Karns with all seats priced at thirty-five cents.[11]

The two performances in Flint had the added excitement of being presented to an audience that had firsthand knowledge of the strike. The May 25 issue of the *Flint Auto Worker* called the play powerful and a "true portrayal of the conditions in the auto industry which forced the revolt of the auto workers. It is a living document of the turning point in American labor history made by the courageous men and women of Flint and Detroit, based on actual facts in the great auto strike." The union paper also pointed out that the writer received a great deal of help with background material from many Flint workers.[12] The authenticity and heroic spirit of the play impressed the audience, reported the *CIO News*.[13]

From an announcement in the *Flint Auto Worker*, it appears that the play was divided into six episodes: "Start of the Strike," "Battle of Bulls' Run," "Capture of Chevy No. 4," "All Night Picket Lines," "Emergency Brigade in Action," and "Final Victory and Evacuation." The script itself has no divisions labeled. Brief blackouts indicate the end of each episode, suggesting that scenes move from one to another at a pace calculated to keep excitement and tension at a high, unrelenting pitch. The play begins with three brief sit-downs: at Fisher Body 1, General Motors in Atlanta, and Kelsey-Hayes in November and December—all preceding the major one at Flint. The initial episode, dramatizing the conflict between Mr. Parker, the manager of Fisher Body 1, and Simon, a plant worker, over the firing of several union members, captures the aggressiveness and humor of much of the dialogue. Parker, who insists that nothing will be settled until the men go back to work and that nothing will bulldoze him into making a concession, is informed, "We ain't bulldozing . . . we're just sittin'." When the manager learns that all the fired men must be rehired before the workers will return to work, he tries to hide behind an alleged lack of power to do anything about the company policy. The exchange then goes like this:

Simon: We ain't interested Mr. Parker. Do they go back to work?

Parker: All right. Monday. Yes.

Simon: Now! I guess the boys need the money. They go back today!

Parker: I tell you . . . now . . . yes!

Simon: 700 men to be paid for the time they've just been sittin'!

Parker: I tell you the company won't—I can't—all right! All right they'll be paid.

Simon: Well . . . I guess that's all ain't it boys?

Man: I been scratchin' my head Bud but they just don't seem to think of a nother thing [*sic*].

Step by step, with impish wiliness, backed of course by their power to keep production stopped, the workers face down the manager.

The workers' victory is greeted immediately with a song to the tune of "Hinkey-Dinkey, Parley-Voo": "We Union Men, are out to win, Parley-Voo,/We got old Parker on the run, Parley-Voo." The third and last stanza anticipates the battle to come:

Knudsen's just another man, Parley-Voo
Knudsen's just another man, Parley-Voo
Knudsen's just another man, who ought to be
      Kicked in the can—Hinkey-Dinkey, Parley-Voo!

The trifling humor of this doggerel should not obscure the workers' decision to take on all of General Motors, symbolized by the name Knudsen who at that time was second only to Alfred Sloan in running the company. Neither should it hide the irreverence with which he is treated, nor the idea that force should be used against him. The play's loudspeaker takes over at this point and, in rhythms echoing a *March of Time* narrator, elevates the implied meanings of the episode to its appropriate level of significance:

And thus on November the 14th, 1936, in Fisher Body #1, Flint, Michigan, the union wins one of the numerous first skirmishes in the struggle between the automobile workers and the Empire of General Motors! However, November the 18th, 1936, in the office of the plant manager of Fisher Body Atlanta, Georgia, the step that leads to decisive action is unconsciously taken—the step that opens the greatest American industrial war of the 20th century.

Although the styles are different, the movement in the three parts of this selection is the same, from limited demand to greater demand; from one level of managerial power to a higher one; from skirmish to war.

This pattern of dialogue-song-loudspeaker and of intensifying struggle is the basic structural and thematic unit of the play; it is repeated throughout as the conflict progresses. The intellectual content of the dialogue becomes more complex; the songs become more lofty in sentiment; and the actions and counteractions more physical, more violent, and, in the case of the workers, more subversive of the sanctity of capitalistic ownership. There is the Kelsey-Hayes sit-down where Ford guards, armed with guns to move out the brake drums made in the plant, are pelted with hinges by the striking men, who thus prevent the parts from leaving the plant. With the retreat of the Ford guards, the men sing:

> Comrades the bugles are sounding,
> Shoulder your arms for the fray.
> Boldly we'll fight for our freedom!
> Boldly we'll hew out a way!

The loudspeaker then announces that seven more plants are being held and five more are short of parts. The Battle of Bulls' Run episode is even more warlike. After the police use teargas on the workers and fire on the plant and the crowds in the street, the men inside counterattack with high-pressure hoses. When the emergency brigade joins the counteroffensive, the police break into a pell-mell retreat and the chorus sings:

> Cheer, boys, cheer,
> For we are full of fun,
> Cheer, boys, cheer,
> Old Knudsen's on the run;
> We had a fight last night
> And I tell you boys, we won,
> We had a hot time in the old town tonight!

Again the loudspeaker makes the significance of the action explicit: "For 4 heroic hours striking union men battled gas and guns! As the gas cleared 14 men lay, wounded, in the street! But the plants, the union forts, remained in the possession of the fighting union men!"

The episode dealing with the takeover of Chevrolet Plant 4 repeats the same pattern, but again at a higher level of dramatic intensity and political significance. The wiliness of the first section is duplicated, but it is of a much more sophisticated character—an elaborate war plan in which the company is completely outflanked because it is led to believe that the real object of attack is another plant. The seizure of Plant 4 also underscores the belief articulated earlier in the Fisher 2 episode that the rights of workers take precedence over the legal rights of industrial ownership. The takeover of Plant 4 is the strategic battle of the strike: it confirms that labor, not company officials, is the cornerstone of production. The episode is brought to a close with the men surveying what they have accomplished: "We beat the cops over at 9! 6 is in the bag!" "*And we got 4!*" "*Men we got everything!*" The takeover is so complete that the voice of General Motors agrees to the union demands. A huge crowd begins to sing in a low voice the words of "Solidarity Forever":

> In our hands is placed a power greater than their hoarded gold!
> Greater than the might of armies magnified a thousand fold!
> We can bring to birth the new world from the ashes of the old!
> *For the Union makes us strong*!

The speaker's voice then comes in over the singing crowd: "Stop and listen and you can hear 'em movin' now! Get to beatin' on a brake drum! Get to singin'! Stand up men and keep marchin'! *We the people are the power*! *Sing!*" And the whole crowd, and undoubtedly the audience too, breaks out with the chorus of "Solidarity Forever." Without violating the main historical details of what the workers had done, the play gives back to them their accomplishments in a form calculated to rouse the spirit and demonstrate the heroic, political nature of the sit-down.

The last two pieces connected to the auto drive, the musical skits *Hoodwinked* and *Million Dollar Babies*, are a complete change from the other plays. Though they are entertainment in the tradition of the lampoon or the spoof, designed mainly to evoke laughter, they are, nevertheless, thoroughly political in content. The political ideas and the contending characters are presented in the quick, unshaded strokes of caricature. The popular song hits of the period with lyrics suitably revised for the occasion provide a spirit of revelry, while summarizing what the political conflicts are all about.

Hoodwinked: or the Black Legion on the Pickert Line, whose author is Arthur Clifford, declares its political attitude and the mode of its funmaking through its title, which is anchored at each end by a pun.[14] The Black Legion, a reactionary group whose members came partly from the ranks of auto management and the police forces of the Detroit area, conducted night raids, wearing black hoods to escape identification, to terrorize militant auto workers, minorities, and left wingers.[15] Pickert was the name of Detroit's chief of police in the 1930s. Rumor had it that he was a member of the Black Legion. True or not, he was staunchly anti-union and had a record of making matters extremely difficult for picketing workers. One of his most notorious acts was his zealous pursuit of workers wounded in the Ford hunger march; he went right into hospitals to harass them. The puns of the title and their political significance were well known to the audience before which the skit played. *Hoodwinked* was put on by the Contemporary Theatre, the Detroit affiliate of the New Theatre League, at the Detroit Institute of Arts in 1936—the time of the Black Legion's greatest activity.

The skit is a farcical allegory that depicts the political realities of Detroit in the mid-1930s. Maiden, an innocent daughter of the working class, is courted by Leader, the head of the Black Legion. He wants to marry her in order to beget "a little stranger," whom they will raise to take "his rightful place in society behind a machine gun." Maiden refuses, whereupon Leader warns that she must either accept or die. Maiden and Mother are dismayed and seek help. They apply, in rapid succession, to Congress, the Roosevelts, Father Coughlin, and last to the police. All refuse, for one reason or another, to do anything. Leader then ties Maiden to a couple of chairs and places a bomb with a lighted fuse under her. As the fuse burns down to the exploding point, Maiden cries for help one last time, and in comes Farmer Labor to the rescue. Mother is overjoyed, while Leader slinks away in defeat.

The story is accompanied by song at every point. Soon after the skit opens, Maiden sings a WPA song to the tune of "Moon Over Miami": "Boondoggle, my mammy!/ Work hard and faithfully." When FDR enters wearing dark glasses, carrying a white cane and led by Eleanor, the spoof becomes even more sharply scornful. Mother, who has always wondered if FDR knew where he were going, concludes that he is lost. This is the cue for the Roosevelts to sing a duet:

Lost
My lovely NRA
   Lost
My darling AAA
Lost, my pet—a whole alphabet
Finders keepers, losers weepers.

This portrayal reflects accurately the current feeling among large sections of labor and the left that the liberal New Deal was basically a pretension. The reactionary forces, however, come in for the main share of spoofing. When the police enter the scene, led by their chief Pickertino, the Legionnaires convince them not to save the girl with a Gershwin tune:

She's a lady that's red
   A little bit crazy
In the back of her head.
   Wants higher wages
   Engages
In working-class activity.

The skit ends in a duet by Maiden and Farmer, summing up the true political road to salvation. It is based on a popular dance of the day:

If you're sick of watching Congress
   Do the boomalacka, boomalacka, lee,

>Just leave the Democrats and Republicans flat,
>   Build a Farmer-Labor Partee!

Million Dollar Babies Sit Down is written in the same spirit, although its political spectrum is much narrower.[16] The skit is based on the sit-down strike of Woolworth employees in Detroit, which began on February 22, 1937, sixteen days after the victory in Flint. It was one of the first sit-downs in the flood of plays that followed the Flint breakthrough.[17] The first page of the skit carries the information that it was written by the Entertainment Committee of the F. W. Woolworth strikers and Edith Segal of the Central Labor Body AFL Entertainment Committee for Sit-Down Strikers of Detroit. According to Segal, the skit never played to the public or, for that matter, to the striking Woolworth employees. She did send a copy to the Department Store Employees Union of Greater New York. A letter from this union to Segal, dated April 15, 1937, and signed by someone named Clarina, thanks her for the copy: "It is swell. Our dramatic department is using it as its first production. Everyone who has read it is strong for it."[18] Whether it actually played in New York and, if it did, to what kind and how large an audience are unknown.

Although there are ten scenes to *Million Dollar Babies*, its story is far simpler than *Hoodwinked*; the dialogue is cut to a minimum; and the songs fill more of the space. The first scene is a solo by Barbara Nutton, followed by a chorus of the entire cast:

>We're the million dollar babies
>Of Woolworth's five and ten cent store
>Oh we're the million dollar babies
>And we're sitting at the door.
>
>It may continue for a week girls
>And then again it may be more
>But we won't fall apart girls
>Till we get our ten cents more.

After this opening, with its ironic connection of millions to dimes, the story moves back in time to tell how the sit-down came about. Barbara Nutton applies for a job at Woolworth's. When she gets the job, having met the manager's approval of her looks and figure, she expresses her joy in these words to "Little Brown Jug":

>My troubles all are over now
>I've got a job, oh boy and how
>Down at Woolworth's five and dime
>Gee won't I have one swell time.

The cast, coming in from both wings, tells her the truth in a verse to the same tune. Discovering that they are right, Barbara sings "Am I Blue":

Am I tired
Do I ache
Hauling stock's more than any girl could take.

The girls consult a union representative, who promises to help. Barbara's spirits rise again and she picks up on one of the most popular hits of the time, "This Is My Lucky Day":

Oh, boy I'm happy,
Oh, joy I'm happy,
This is our lucky day,
We'll get together,
We'll stick together
Auto men showed the way.

The skit draws to a close when a customer applauds the girls for their spunk. The girls form a wheel, then march off stage in Busby-Berkeley fashion singing "Solidarity Forever." Less sharp or satirical than *Hoodwinked*, it is still a politicized divertissement, providing the relaxation of humor without losing sight of the fight workers are engaged in.

III

Strikes are extraordinary actions at all times; they pit large numbers of working people, who have no resources but themselves, against some very powerful institutions. Hence, strikes are inherently dramatic and theatrical. Few have been more so than the great drive to organize the auto industry workers in the 1930s. Before auto workers successfully forced the dismantling of the open shop system, they had to take on not only the most powerful business establishment of the country, but the courts, the police, the state militia, and an assortment of politically powerful anti-working-class vigilantes. With ingenuity and imagination, the auto workers created a remarkable unity of common effort, militancy, and purpose. In seizing plants, thought to be the major weapon of the drive, the workers disregarded the central economic and political orthodoxy of free enterprise. This implicitly subversive method of strike action coupled with the inventive community spirit called forth by the drive were resources of colorful spectacle and dramatic significance.

In an account she gives of a meeting held by the red-bereted Women's Emergency Brigade of Flint, Mary Heaton Vorse describes both the sense of collective purpose and the theatrical possibilities characteristic of the drive: "It was a wonderful meeting. Speaker after speaker told of the activities of the Women's Auxiliaries in the automobile towns. In brief speeches they told of activities that had a wide span: food, picketing, children, recreation, songs, music, plays. They spoke of the plays they acted, taken from strike activities. It might well be the germ of a workers' theatre." Mary Heaton Vorse was particularly sensitive to every sign of artistic imagination among workers, and she is right about the creative energies strikes release—that strikes are, in a certain respect, theatre, and that theatre is necessary to the life of strikes.[19]

The plays and skits that grew out of the auto drive responded instantly to the theatrical possibilities of its conflicts. They range in form from conventional realism to the Living Newspaper to musical skits reminiscent of vaudeville. What they all have in common is a power of expression inherent in the fundamental nature of the conflicts they dramatize and the language of the strikers they portray. Building on actual events and various popular forms, these plays drew significantly on the needs, the imagination, and the aspirations of the workers who performed in them and who made up the audience. Whatever their aesthetic approach, they produced competent political theatre and helped reinforce among the workers they consulted and the audiences they played to the class solidarity and fighting spirit required for the struggle.

NOTES

1. The sources from which these plays were recovered will be indicated in the second section of this paper at the point where each play is introduced for analysis. A considerable amount of detective work was required to locate various people who had scripts in their possession. The search grew out of a study, made possibly by grants from Wayne State University and the National Endowment for the Humanities, I have been doing of the Federal Theatre Project and the Federal Writers' Project. The Archives of Labor History and Urban Affairs (hereafter ALH) of the Walter Reuther Library at Wayne State University have proved an invaluable source of information for two of the plays and for background material on all the plays.

2. For accounts of working-class and other nonbourgeois theatre practices in France and Germany in the nineteenth century, see Frederick Brown, *Theater and Revolution: The Culture of the French Stage* (New York, 1980), chapters 2, 3, and 5; Peter von Rüden, *Sozialdemokratisches Arbeitertheater (1848–1914)* (Frankfort, 1973), chapters 1–4.

3. A copy of this play was kindly presented to me by Maxine Wood. In an interview at her home in New York, June 12, 1979, she described how she first became aware of the Ford hunger march while she was on a tour of the world. In India the ship's radio carried the story of the demonstration and the killing of four workers. Wood realized, on hearing the dreadful news, that she knew more about poverty in India than about working-class suffering in her native city, Detroit. She decided to return home to learn more of what was happening among auto workers.

4. Irving Bernstein, *The Lean Years* (Boston, 1960), pp. 432–34; Maurice Sugar Collection, ALH, Sub-Series C, Box 53, Folders 6 (Ford Massacre, 1932; Evidence, statements), 21, and 22 (Sugar, "Bullets—Not Food—For Ford Workers," *Nation*, March 23, 1932); Box 117 (Scrapbook on Ford Hunger March—Riot 1932, Ford Massacre—Publications and clippings); for the complete story in a single source, see Sugar's, *The Ford Hunger March* (Berkeley, 1980), p. 69 for a compilation of estimates.

5. Mary Heaton Vorse Collection, ALH, Box 109, File: Flint Sit-Down Strike, 1937, Outline for "Living Newspaper."

6. Dorothy Kraus writes that Vorse had the idea of doing the play like a Greek chorus. With no time to discuss the merits of the idea, Herbst, Kraus, and Vorse stripped the bed sheets from the hotel they were in, picked up some safety pins in a store on the way to Pengelly Hall, and from those items quickly improvised costumes. Letter to author, May 19, 1981.

7. Morris Watson, "Sitdown Theatre," *New Theatre and Film*, 4 (April 1937), 6.

8. Vorse Collection, Box 109, File: Flint Sit-Down Strike, 1937, MHV Pamphlet— typescript. See first page of chapter 12.

9. Ibid., p. 21.

10. Copies of this play are available in the Tamiment Library, New York University and the Lincoln Center for the Performing Arts branch of the New York Public Library. Lawrence Rogin, the last faculty member to leave the Brookwood Labor College, managed to find a copy in a private collection and generously sent me a copy of it for study. William Titus, the author of the play, joined the Lincoln-Washington Battalion of the International Brigade in Spain shortly after he wrote *Sit-Down*. He was killed at Segura De Los Baños, February 16, 1938. See Herbert L. Matthews, "American Brigade Head-quarters on the Teruel Front, Spain, *New York Times*, January 4, 1938, for an account of Titus at the front and Arthur H. Landis, *The Abraham Lincoln Brigade* (New York, 1967), p. 393 for the way he died.

11. Brookwood Collection, ALH, Box 96, Series IV, Folder: 96–13.

12. Henry Kraus Collection, ALH, Box 8, Folder: Labor in Literature-Drama and Brookwood Collection, Box 96, Series IV, Folder: 96–13.

13. *CIO News*, June 1, 1937.

14. The manuscript of this skit was sent to me by Arthur Clifford's widow, Margaret Clifford, who now lives in Australia. She has been extremely helpful in supplying me with other works by him, including one for a play called *1789: A Mass Play*, a very effective expressionist-constructivist play about the history of working-class struggles. By chance, a resident of Santa Barbara, where the Cliffords had settled after leaving Detroit in the late 1940s, saw a notice of my research and informed me of Ms. Clifford's present address.

15. Maurice Sugar Collection, ALH, Box 1, Series 1, Folder: 19; Box 7, Folders: 922 (Black Legion Activities); Boxes 18–23 (Clippings, membership lists, activities— 1936–37). Joe Brown Collection, ALH, Box 4, Folder: Black Legion; clippings pertaining to workers' efforts to organize in the automobile industry from August 2 to October 25, 1937 (Vol. 10): Vigilante Organizations in Auto Industry (Legion Hits at Sitdown and Legion's Role in Labor Rows, p. 11).

16. Edith Segal has in her possession the only script of the skit and kindly allowed me to copy it for my use. She had been in Detroit about a year, working as an actor and choreographer for the Michigan Federal Theatre Project, when the Flint sit-down occurred. She was an eyewitness to many of its events and immediately offered to work with the Woolworth sit-downers when they decided to follow the lead of the auto workers.

17. The Woolworth sit-down began on Saturday, February 27, 1937, sixteen days after the Flint victory. See front-page news story, "5 & 10 Girls Ban Officers," *Detroit News*, March 1, 1937. By mid-March, at least thirty business enterprises in Detroit were being struck by sit-downs or picket lines. These included several auto plants, a cigar factory, a food store, a bakery, several hotels, a shoe plant, and transportation and welfare

services. Police Chief Pickert put his force on a twelve-hour day to preserve law and order (*Detroit News*, March 17, 1937, p. 1), and the Michigan legislature prepared legislation to stop the outbreak (''2 Anti-Strike Bills Offered in Attempt to Stop Sit-Downs,'' *Detroit News*, March 18, 1937, p. 1). The Flint sit-down had become an epidemic.

18. Segal also allowed me to copy this letter from her private collection.

19. Vorse Collection, Box 109, File: Flint Sit-Down Strike, 1937, MHV Pamphlet—typescript. See second page of chapter 10.

11

The Federal Theatre Project's Search for an Audience

John O'Connor

The Federal Theatre Project's search for a working-class audience was part of a larger appeal to the many groups who generally did not attend plays. Whether because theatre was expensive or unavailable in their locale, or because radio and movies seemed more exciting and satisfying, many segments of the population—notably the working class—rarely went to the theatre. Also, the kinds of theatre that working people across the country had supported in the past—melodramas, vaudeville, and amateur theatrics—had been hard hit by the depression and the technological revolution in the entertainment industry. For Hallie Flanagan, the national director of the Federal Theatre Project, bringing theatre to thousands who had turned away from it or (as was more often the case) had not seen it at all was as much a goal of the Federal Theatre Project as putting needy theatre professionals to work again: "Our function is to extend the boundaries of theatre-going, to create a vigorous new audience, to make the theatre of value to more people."[1]

The Federal Theatre Project continually referred to itself as a people's theatre, and, while not defining who the people were, it clearly meant more than the traditional Broadway carriage trade. Residents of rural communities and industrial cities, children and the aged, blacks and foreign-language speakers were all considered important constituents of this new national theatre. Across the nation the Federal Theatre Project built not only on the high-class theatre of the universities and big-city companies, but also on community theatres, little theatres, and workers' theatres that were trying to appeal primarily to a working-class audience. The Federal Theatre could provide financial stability to such theatres as the Seattle Repertory, the Carolina Playmakers, the Cuban theatre in Tampa, and the children's theatre in Gary, all of which were committed to an alternative to the Broadway theatre and its traditional patrons.

During its four-year existence (1935–1939), the Federal Theatre Project (FTP) attracted over 30 million people to its productions, and Hallie Flanagan's desire to reach a new audience seemed to have been realized according to the statistics gathered by the FTP: 65 percent of the audiences were attending a play for the first time, and three-fourths of them listed "too expensive" as the reason they had not previously attended theatre. As was usual with the Federal Theatre, this accomplishment was a mixed blessing: it fulfilled its mandate from the administration to reach a new, national audience, but congressmen complained that the FTP "placed too much emphasis on poor audiences."[2]

When it was first organized as a relief program, the FTP did not charge admission to its performances. Instead the Federal Theatre distributed tickets to over 1,200 church, community, labor, and political organizations to reach its anticipated audience. In New York City, labor organizations consistently accounted for the largest block of tickets. Even when the Federal Theatre Project began to charge small amounts to cover increasing nonpersonnel costs, $1.10 was set as the highest possible price, yet large numbers of tickets were still distributed free. A simple example of the importance of price was the FTP production of *Swing Mikado*. With $1.10 as top price under the FTP, the productions in the enormous New Yorker theatre were sold out weeks in advance. It ran for sixty-two performances until commercial producers, notably Mike Todd, asked Congress to stop the government from competing with private enterprise. Once the *Swing Mikado* closed, Todd opened the *Hot Mikado* at a $2.20 minimum. The show played to considerably smaller audiences and closed after twenty-four performances.[3]

After it began charging admission, the Federal Theatre continued to attract working-class audiences by developing the policy of selling blocks of tickets to organizations at a discount and allowing the organization either to pass along the savings to its members or to make money by charging full price. These groups ranged from fraternal organizations like the Elks and Knights of Columbus, to civic groups such as community chest and police youth clubs. Unions and labor organizations were the largest category. They included the building and construction trades, heavy and light industry, and transport and communication workers; among the New York City clubs were the International Workers' Order and the League for Industrial Democracy.

When Margaret Larkin, former ticket manager for the Theatre Union, joined the Federal Theatre Project, she brought not only a familiarity with many New York City labor groups but a wealth of experience about organizing working-class community groups and generating appropriate promotional techniques. These techniques then became standard practice for publicity directors in other cities nationwide: invite representatives of labor organizations to rehearsals; send volunteer speakers or arrange discussions at meetings; encourage word-of-mouth publicity by passing out cards and heralds to patrons leaving the theatre, urging them to tell their friends; and combine events such as fund-raising dinners with a theatre performance. Such tactics were enormously successful. By 1939 over 12,000 organizations involving four million people had participated in Federal Theatre Project block sales. Block sales accounted for nearly half of all tickets, and some productions were almost completely booked through group sales. When *Pinocchio* opened in New York City in December 1938, it was nearly sold out for the next three months with group sales alone. Among the many groups buying blocks of tickets for this show (which became one of the ten biggest hits of the 1938–1939 Broadway season) were over 100 labor organizations and unions.[4] Group sales, incidentally, became such a successful way for the FTP to assure consistent audiences over a fixed run that it became a standard practice in the commercial theatre as well by the end of the thirties.

Working people were certainly attracted to the productions not only because of the free or cheap seats, but also because the Federal Theatre Project made performances remarkably accessible and because the FTP produced plays that appealed to these new theatre patrons. Besides reviving some of the older, popular shows, most notably vaudeville on tour, it also presented serious drama with entertaining flair—like the voodoo *Macbeth* and the magic light-show of *Dr. Faustus*. As Hallie Flanagan asked, "Is it sensible to believe that the great masses of people who have come to prefer movies and the radio are going to be suddenly reconverted to the same theatre from which they turned away? Rather it is up to us to study this vast new audience; to give this audience something which they cannot get in any other form of entertainment; and give it at a price which they can afford to pay."[5]

Because it could hire unemployed people as researchers, the Federal Theatre Project was able to study its audience in an unprecedented way. Project members passed out audience survey cards which asked about occupation, previous attendance at FTP and other plays, types of plays preferred (tragedy, comedy, farce, satire, social, historical, mystery, or musical), reaction to the play, attitude toward charging admission, and opinion about a permanent Federal Theatre. From these cards the audience research department determined which plays attracted new audiences, what type of people supported the FTP, and whether the theatres were developing regular patrons. For example, the surveys in Boston revealed that the audience wanted serious entertainment and classics, not "thin stuff" and nothing political or "economic." Not surprisingly, the audience in Boston was primarily from the professional class.[6] The audience research department also sent personnel (usually aspiring playwrights) to Federal Theatre plays to review the production and to analyze the audience reaction. The research was done primarily to prove that the Federal Theatre was appealing to a new audience—that it was not competing with private enterprise. But the surveys also helped directors see how their plays were being received and aided producers in deciding what plays to mount.

Despite such surveys, gauging the success of the Federal Theatre's efforts is difficult. Because the audience research department was cancelled when the first round of budget cuts hit in mid-1937, the basis for most analysis of Federal Theatre Project audiences is restricted to the first half of the project's life. In addition, although 45,000 questionnaires were collected from fifty-eight different productions, these were never all tabulated. Finally, later audience surveys were more haphazard and less detailed than the early ones. Thus, it is difficult to compare the composition of the early audiences with the later ones to see whether the Federal Theatre built a regular clientele (which the early returns suggest) and whether its attempts to reach new theatregoers continued to be effective.

Nevertheless, these theatre reports and surveys, though crude, present some important facts about the composition of the FTP audience: trades and office workers made up one-fourth of the audience, the largest single category; professionals (primarily teachers) were next with 21 percent.[7] However, these figures varied considerably from production to production and place to place. For instance, spot bookings in New York City boroughs were composed of over 40 percent trade and office workers. These two categories made up 36 percent of the audience in San Diego and San Francisco and 28 percent in Los Angeles. The Federal Theatre Project researcher in charge of audience surveys speculated that working-class attendance may have actually been greater, since people in this group, for one reason or another, frequently did not fill in the survey forms. Of the 34,000 cards tabulated, over 10,000 did not list the occupation of the respondent.[8]

The Federal Theatre Project also recognized that many people were either unable to attend the Broadway houses or their equivalents in other major cities, or that people unfamiliar with the theatre would be too intimidated to enter these bastions of high culture by themselves. The New York City project organized bus trips into the Manhattan theatres so that citizens could see some of the more elaborate productions with friends and neighbors. Also in New York City, a community theatre unit traveled through the boroughs staging plays requested by local audiences. Known as the Suitcase Theatre, it had over 600 bookings and an audience of over 900,000 in its first two years. The unit was supervised by Stephen Karnot, who had studied under Vsevolod Meyerhold in Russia and had been part of the Workers' Laboratory Theatre.[9] Among its productions were *The Comedy of Errors*, *Twelfth Night*, *The Miser*, *School for Scandal*, *She Stoops to Conquer*, and *Everyman*.

Not just in New York, but across the nation, the Federal Theatre took productions out of the theatre to where the people were. More than 37,000 performances were given in parks, schools, hospitals, public auditoriums, labor halls, prisons, orphanages, and homes for the elderly. Many of the units throughout the country took their productions to small communities in the surrounding area, using flatbed trucks for a stage. Over 350,000 people saw plays in the CCC camps, where the boys and men were incorporated into the action of some of the plays.[10] The Oakland, California, unit did not have an available theatre in town, so it loaded up and traveled on trucks and buses to play on the same bill with motion pictures in the small farm communities throughout the state. Most of their productions were vaudeville and melodrama.[11] In Florida the theatre had traditionally been part of the tourist industry—light comedies for the vacationing Northerners. The Federal Theatre Project decided to perform in the schools throughout the state, drawing both young people and adults into the auditoriums and gymnasiums. With each production they handed out an informational guide that offered some insight into the play and background on the author. The Federal Theatre Project joined the Farm Service Administration to bring theatre to resettlement and farm-labor camps. Nicholas Ray, who had been stage manager for the New York City Living Newspapers under Joseph Losey, produced plays on local conditions in Scottsboro and Birmingham, Alabama, and in Willard, North Carolina.[12] Unfortunately, state WPA rules made it financially very difficult for troupes to travel across state boundaries; when relief cuts came, the touring programs with their complex red tape and nonpersonnel costs were usually cut first.

In response to the personnel cuts and the travel restrictions, the Federal Theatre Project proposed a community drama program in August 1938 that would provide and encourage drama at a local level at a considerably reduced cost. A few professionals would be sent to a community to train and lead volunteers in original plays that would "draw color and background from the life, desires, and ambitions of the community itself."[13] West Virginia was chosen as an example of a state that would benefit especially from the proposal: it did not have an FTP unit, since not enough unemployed professional theatre people lived in the state, yet the state was filled with potential drama and untapped audiences. The West Virginia program was to be administered through local county recreation programs. Akron, Pittsburgh, and Seattle were listed as cities with significant labor populations that would support a local amateur theatre organized by the Federal Theatre Project. Unfortunately this program was still in the planning stage when the Federal Theatre had to turn almost all its attention to the mere survival of the project. If the Federal Theatre had been able to tour regularly in more Southern and Midwestern congressional districts, it might not have been so easy for Congress to drop the Federal Theatre Project from the WPA budget in 1939.

Other important sources of new audiences were blacks and foreign-language groups. The Federal Theatre established twenty-two black production units from New York to Seattle. Except for the Lafayette Theatre unit in Harlem, none of these units was surveyed, so there are no statistics on occupations of audience members. But given the economic and social state of affairs at the time, black patrons, if they had jobs, were overwhelmingly working class. The Harlem Lafayette Theatre drew a mix from the local black population and downtown, traditional, white theatregoers. Exotic shows like *Bassa Moona* and *Macbeth* in New York and *Swing Mikado* in Chicago and New York were such spectacular theatre that they drew an atypical audience. Other plays, like *The Trial of Dr. Beck* in New York and *Big White Fog* in Chicago, were clearly intended for a black audience. They explored some of the conflicts and prejudices within black communities. The characters were generally working-class people. Evelyn Quita Craig in *Black Drama of the Federal Theatre Era: Beyond the Formal Horizons* has written extensively about the appeal these plays had for black audiences.[14]

The Federal Theatre's black production units is another, quite remarkable example of its attempt to broaden the audience for theatre and to offer productions that explored the lives of working-class people.

Foreign-language projects included Yiddish units in New York, Boston, Chicago, and Los Angeles; Spanish in Tampa; German in New York; and French is Los Angeles. Since very few of the plays from these producing units were included in the audience surveys, there is no accurate, factual breakdown of the occupations of the audience. However, it seems reasonable to assume that these units played primarily to audiences from the neighboring working-class communities. The New York Yiddish and Tampa Spanish units were among the twenty-two production units to perform *It Can't Happen Here*, and the audience at a few of the Yiddish performances were briefly surveyed. The figures suggest that the Yiddish unit drew a greater percentage of working-class patrons than did English-speaking units.[15] Although the Yiddish unit mainly performed in Brooklyn, it also presented shows in the other boroughs and on Long Island. It produced a mixture of new shows like *Professor Mamlock*, *We Live and Laugh*, and a Yiddish *Awake and Sing*, together with traditional plays like *The Idiot*, *The Stranger*, and the Yiddish *King Lear* by Jacob Gordin.

The German-speaking unit performed most of its plays in the Yorkville section of the Bronx, which had a large German community. It was supervised by John Bonn, who had been head of the *Prolet-Buehne* before joining the Federal Theatre Project. Bonn planned productions of plays by Kaiser, Hauptmann, Schiller, and Shakespeare but had a difficult time getting production rights and finding appropriate actors. A typical production was *Einmal Mensch*, which was performed at the Yorkville Casino and at the Brooklyn Labor Lyceum. The audience breakdown was trades, 62; office workers, 14; professionals, 7; arts, 9; business, 6; housewives, 21; students, 1; not stated, 61. Other productions by this unit included *Die Apostel* by Rudolph Wittenberg, *Docktor Wespe* by Roderich Benedix, *Der Zerbrochene* by Heinrich von Kleist, and *Lokalbahn* by Ludwig Thoma.[16]

Because of the financial security offered to theatre artists, the Federal Theatre Project became an irresistible attraction for many participants of the small workers' theatres in New York and other cities across the country. Individuals like John Bonn or Stephen Karnot, or whole groups such as the Workers' Laboratory Theatre, found in the Federal Theatre Project a means of continuing their goal of creating theatre for the rank and file in such units as the community theatre, children's theatre, and the Living Newspaper. In turn, the Federal Theatre sponsored a conference to plan workshops for workers' theatre groups on producing living history plays. The workshops were to help select material, write scripts, train leaders, and solve organizational problems. Unfortunately, the Federal Theatre Project closed shortly after the first workshop.

The influence of small workers' theatres can be seen in the Federal Theatre play selection and in the production styles. As Hallie Flanagan hoped, many of the plays produced by the Federal Theatre were a stimulating alternative to the fare offered by the rest of the entertainment industry. They also reflected the choices expressed by the new audiences; when asked what kind of drama they preferred, most people asked for social drama, with comedy and satire a close second and third. George Sklar's *Life and Death of an American*, originally written for the Theatre Union in 1937 but never produced, was a good example of the social plays offered by the Federal Theatre Project and of the overlapping of workers' theatre groups and the FTP. The play dramatizes the life of Jerry Dorgan, the first American born in this century. Coming from a working-class family, Jerry (played by Arthur Kennedy) must quit school and go to work in the mill where his father has just died. Through hard work and some experience with airplanes in World War I, he becomes an aircraft designer in the boom twenties, only to lose his job during the depression. While walking to the park with his son to play football, Jerry is accidently killed in a labor demonstration.

The play is remarkable for its realistic depiction of everyday and small-town life. The first few scenes, which nostalgically dramatize life at the turn of the century, are similar to *American Way* and *Our Town*. The later, choric scenes capture the repetitive rhythms and debilitating routines of factory work:

(A factory whistle blows—the orchestra starts playing. A line of workers, shoulders bent, lunch box in hand [sic], trudges rhythmically across stage. Jerry gets up from the stairs and falls in with them. Suddenly we hear the whirr of machines. The time clock clangs. The line stops. The men turn front. To the accompaniment of the machine rhythms, which are accented by the music of the orchestra, they execute stylized work movements— repeating them monotonously. As they do, they keep up a steady chant of "one-two-three-four—one-two-three-four." Single voices come out of it.

First voice: In she goes and watch your finger—Bang! In she goes and watch your finger—Bang!

All: One-two-three-four—one-two-three-four.

Second voice: Monday, Tuesday, Wednesday, Thursday-Friday, Saturday, Monday, Tuesday.

First: On your toes, there, I mean you! Who do you think I'm talkin' to?

Third: Fourteen hours every day—Gotta work to get your pay!

Second: Monday, Tuesday, Wednesday, Thursday-Friday, Saturday, Monday, Tuesday.

First: In she goes and watch your finger—Bang! In she goes and watch your finger—Bang!

Fourth: Dirst and dust, and dust and dirt—Watch out there, or you'll get hurt!

Chorus: My bones are achin', my back is breakin', I feel so weary and blue.

Jerry: You're gonna punch that time clock and feed little Emma 14 hours a day, every day, at 18 per, until death do you part—yeah!—You're stuck, baby. You're stuck— you're free, white, and seventeen—but you're stuck and a Mack truck couldn't pull you out—Aw, what the hell! Quit you're [sic] squalkin'—O.K. Emma, here she comes—in she goes and watch your finger, bang! in she goes and watch your finger, bang! (The Chant grows louder.) 1-2-3-4—1-2-3-4—1-2-3-4—Yes, Sir, Dorgan, that's the life! Every day, 14 hours a day—Pound! Pound! Pound! Noise and dust and dirt—Breathe it in. Breathe it in.[17]

Jerry's frustrated ambitions and his vague awareness of the limitations imposed on him by class reflect the experience of many workers between the world wars. He is embittered by the lack of opportunity, especially for veterans, yet still plans to break out of a life with no future:

I don't believe in this fancy talk about ability and hard work getting you places anymore. We heroes came back and we couldn't get to first base. All the ability and will in the world couldn't get us jobs. . . . I'm not gonna take it on the chin like my ol' man and your ol' man and all the other suckers—the guys on the bottom who always get the dirty end of the stick. I got this break and I intend to make good on it—get up in the world where I'll be doing something I'll have some respect for and others'll respect me for.[18]

But every time Jerry gets a little ahead something happens—his father dies, the war breaks out, the depression hits. Early in the play Jerry's father plans a different future for his son: "One thing I know, you're not gonna work in the shop like your old man—You're not gonna stand over no acid vats, 14 hours a day and breathe it in and let it eat up your lungs, no sir, they could do it to your ol' man, but they're not gonna do it to you."

Near the end of the play Jerry, out of work during the depression, can only repeat these hopes for his own son: "We came here to enjoy life—get something out of it—something big and fine. And I'm gonna get it if I have to tear it out of the ground with my hands. At least Danny's going to have something, if we don't."[19] But, as Jerry's sudden death suggests, the cycle is likely to continue.

He is killed just after he has seen the light, the need for collective action. Jerry's ironic death is an effective variation of the popular conversion theme of many proletarian novels and plays of the thirties. The Federal Theatre Project produced its share of these plays, most notably Marie Baumer's *A Time to Remember*, Arthur Miller's *They Too Arise*, and Ted Ward's *Big White Fog*. They all have in common the sympathetic and realistic portrayal of working-class life in the thirties, with endings that stress the need for concerted, unified action.

I have quoted the play at length so that a sense of Sklar's style becomes apparent. Like Clifford Odets, he uses slang, obscenity, and colloquialisms not only to portray realistically working-class life, but also to make the theatre accessible to working-class audiences. Similarly, the production style was lively and fluid so that the play would compete with the cinema and popular theatre like vaudeville. The action is interspersed with such songs as "Hot Time in the Old Town Tonight," "Keep the Home Fires Burning," "You Can't Keep a Good Man Down," and "My God, How the Money Rolls In." Many of the speeches are like soliloquies and are addressed directly to the audience. The highly realistic and detailed costumes were counterpointed by a bare stage except for large symbolic drawings placed behind the action on two rollers like a giant scroll. When the scenes changed, a new drawing would be seen on the roll: a huge time clock, a factory on a hill dominating the town, row upon row of run-down houses on the far side of the railroad track, and so on. The panoramic sweep of time and the innovative staging made many of the reviewers label the play a Living Newspaper.

Life and Death of an American, opening on May 19, 1939, in the midst of the Congressional budget hearings on the WPA, was to be the last play produced by the Federal Theatre. The decision to go ahead with *Life and Death of an American* shows the project's commitment to working-class drama despite the intense political heat being generated in Washington.

Although only about 10 percent of its productions were social dramas, the Federal Theatre Project became known for its plays that dealt with immediate, provocative issues. Probably its best-known and most controversial social plays were the Living Newspapers. These documentaries on a current issue, presented with a strong editorial point of view, were explicitly addressed to working-class audiences. *One-Third of a Nation*—the most popular Living Newspaper—reflects its concern with the working class in its title. The play educates those not familiar with the living conditions in big-city tenements, and it also encourages people living in tenements to work together to force the government to respond to their needs. This combination of education and exhortation was a hallmark of the Living Newspaper.

Part of the popularity of the Living Newspaper was its flexible and lively staging. The form was experimental, and it varied considerably with each production. It borrowed heavily from popular theatre traditions and workers' agit-prop. The productions were noisy, frequently comic, and visually charged. The openings were highly theatrical and the pace rapid. *One-Third* begins with a tenement fire on stage, which claims the life of a child. *Power* opens with a power failure that leaves the theatre darkened except for flashlights on stage.

Exposition, usually limited to essential historical facts, was presented through dramatic metaphors rather than through speeches. In *One-Third*, for example, shortly after the opening fire, a history of how real estate became so highly valued in Manhattan is presented in terms of a green rug, representing grass. One person after another comes on stage, buys a section of carpet, and stands on it. Soon the rug is filled with people and a sign saying "this is mine, keep off." Now, anyone wanting to buy has to settle for less space at a higher price. The concept is presented with little dialogue and maximum visual effect. *Power* conveys the concept of the pyramidal holding company through a series of brightly colored building blocks stacked on top of each other in a pyramid.

To keep an audience attentive and alert as the factual material was presented, the whole theatre was used. In most of the plays an actor planted in the audience rose up to ask questions or challenge the ongoing action. Characters also frequently entered or exited by the aisles. At the start of the second act of *One-Third*, the loudspeaker asks where the "little man" who asked questions in the first act has gone. He responds, as he stumbles up the aisle, "Out for a beer. I just caught the end of that last scene. Tell me, why don't we tear down all those old-law tenements?"[20] Later is joined by his wife (entering from the back of the theatre) who wonders why he isn't home yet; by the end of the play she leads the rest of the cast in demanding that the state legislature investigate public housing. The Living Newspapers almost always concluded with speeches directly to the audience, which encouraged the audience to join with the actors (à la *Waiting for Lefty*).

The issues that the Living Newspapers chose to dramatize were important for the working-class audiences. Housing, health care, public utilities, labor organizing, and consumer unions were among the topic presented. These plays generally concluded that working people could (and should) solve the problems either by taking action themselves or by demanding that their elected representatives act for them. In *Triple-A Plowed Under*, the first officially produced Living Newspaper in New York City, much of the script details the common concerns and the interrelated problems of farm and industrial workers. The play then ends with a call for a farm-labor coalition to attack corporate power and a conservative judiciary.

The view that the courts are a tool of the corporations was developed more fully in another Living Newspaper, *Injunction Granted*, which is a history of labor's attempts to organize unions and capital's use of the courts to break them. In twenty-eight scenes, it recounts the challenges labor in this country has faced since the seventeenth century. The majority of the play focuses on the past ten years and the use of injunctions to stop strike action. The play ends with John L. Lewis shouting "Organized labor in America accepts the challenges of the overlords of steel." The play was directed by Joe Losey, who adopted many of the new staging techniques of the Russian directors Vsevolod Meyerhold and Nikolay Oklopkov. The set was composed of stairs, ramps, and platforms. The often bizarre but exciting visual aspects of the production were matched by a musical score by Virgil Thompson that relied on the bells, horns, motors, and the general noise of industry.

That the controversial Living Newspapers caused the Federal Theatre Project administration to balance precariously its desire for provocative theatre with realities in Washington is reflected in the fate of *Injunction Granted*. The play was produced in New York in the summer of 1936 when the Federal Theatre Project was filled with rumors about budget cuts and was busy defending itself against new criticism about New Deal boondoggles. After the production ran for three months, it was abruptly pulled for a revival of *Triple-A Plowed Under*. Hallie Flanagan and the New York City supervisor, Philip Barber, felt the play was too slanted and biased toward "the Party." In a series of memos to the producer and director, Flanagan objected to the noise, the political insinuations, and the conclusion which she felt relied too heavily on the clichéd agitprop call for unity in a strike action.[21] Unlike the other New York City Living Newspapers, *Injunction Granted* was not produced in other cities and was not included in a two-volume anthology of the Federal Theatre Project plays published by Random House in 1938, which did include all of the other Living Newspapers that were produced. Nevertheless, *Injunction Granted* spoke to the experiences of many of the people in the audience, who filled the house each night and greeted the play enthusiastically.

In contrast with the seeming suppression of *Injunction Granted*, the national administrators of the Federal Theatre Project were quite pleased with the controversy engendered by another play on labor organizing. *Altars of Steel* by Thomas Rogers was produced in Atlanta and Miami in 1937 and created enormous publicity, crowds, and Federal Theatre Project support. The play is about John Worth, the kindly owner of a small Southern steel mill, who faces labor agitation on the one hand and takeover by the vicious conglomerate United Steel on the other. While sympathetic to the family-style operation of Worth and small industry, the play clearly portrays the conflicting interests of labor and impersonal, absentee owners. Much of the strength and tension of the play comes from the conflicts in loyalties facing the foreman and the old owner who have generally "taken care of" the workers in the past but who must now give orders to speed up production, fire the weak and old, and ignore safety measures. When the men realize that the new bosses do not even care for minimal safety standards, they walk out.

The play has two endings. In one, the socialist labor organizer and Worth, the old owner, die along with sixteen workers in an open-hearth explosion, and the new heartless owner is convicted of murder for ordering the firing-up of a clearly defective hearth. In the alternate conclusion, the owner escapes prosecution after a rigged grand jury investigation. The Federal Theatre Project produced the latter version. The play incited a week of editorials in the Atlanta newspapers and filled the auditorium each night for its two-week run. The play was not as controversial in Miami, which did not identify so readily with the regional and industrial setting, but it was still a popular and critical success.

Life and Death of an American, Injunction Granted, and *Altars of Steel* all dramatize factory working conditions and the need for unions. Labor organizing, of course, was not the only topic that reflected and explored working-class lives. Nor did plays for working-class audiences always need to be serious. The statistics—as far as they go—indicate that subject matter was not as important as location or group sales promotions in drawing working people to the plays. Variety, which was the staple of many of the Federal Theatre units (and which is often associated with working-class audiences), drew the same percentage of trade and office workers (24 to 30%) as the average for all plays (26%).[22] Nevertheless, it is significant that the Federal Theatre Project did not equate entertainment with escape and that it chose to produce plays that challenged individual and institutional complacency.

Actually, the Federal Theatre's choice of plays, venues, and production styles was intended to attract not only the working class but the whole range of people who thought the theatre was alien to their own world. From all accounts, this new audience was enthusiastic and vibrant. Richard Lockridge, drama critic for the New York *Sun*, was moved to comment on the Federal Theatre audiences:

The Works Progress Administration has brought into the legitimate playhouse a new, vociferous and rather engaging audience. It is an audience which I suspect is not over-familiar with the stage of flesh and blood and it has had moments of rather startling naivete. But it is an engaging audience. Its face is not frozen. It is not sitting on its hands. When it hisses, it is not self-conscious and when it cheers, it means it. It is young, lively and I suspect hard up. Probably the low admission fees charged at the Works Progress Administration plays have had a large part in bringing it out of the neighborhood movie houses—it is an eager audience.[23]

The eagerness of the audience was something the actors especially felt and appreciated, an enduring memory of the Federal Theatre Project. According to Orson Welles, "The audience was fresh. It was eager. To anyone who saw it night after night as we did, it was not the Broadway crowd.... One had the feeling every night, that here were people on a voyage of discovery in the theatre."[24]

What effect the "voyage of discovery" had on the new audiences is debatable, but the Federal Theatre Project's desire to provide the opportunity for the voyage was clear. The Federal Theatre is an important historical precedent for a national theatre not only in its commitment to exciting drama on contemporary issues, but also in its commitment to bring this theatre to all ages, classes, and races.

NOTES

1. *Arena* (New York, 1940), p. 43.
2. Audience Survey Reports, National Service Bureau Office Files, Record Group 69, National Archives, Washington, D.C. *Arena*, p. 204.
3. Brooks Atkinson, "FDR'S WPA FTP," *New York Times*, May 28, 1939.
4. Iris Vinton, "Filling the Seats: A Report on Audience Building," Library of Congress, Federal Theatre Project Collection at George Mason University Libraries, Fairfax, Virginia.
5. "What Are We Doing With Our Chance?" *Federal Theatre*, vol. 2, no. 3, p. 6.
6. Flanagan, p. 230.
7. Audience Survey Reports. The categories the Audience Research Bureau used were arts, business, office workers (primarily clerks, secretaries, and stenographers), professionals (which was usually half teachers), trades (which was both skilled and unskilled labor with New York City audiences having a large percentage of garment workers), and miscellaneous (almost entirely composed of students and housewives).
8. Audience Survey Reports.
9. George Griggs, "Suitcase Theatre: Tradition Builder," *Federal Theatre*, vol. 2, no. 5, p. 14.
10. "Educational Aspects of the Federal Theatre Project," Library of Congress, Federal Theatre Project Collection at George Mason University Libraries, p. 24.
11. "California Now Has Its Own Circuit," *Federal Theatre*, vol. 2, no. 2, p. 25.

12. "Community Drama," National Office General Subject File, Record Group 69, National Archives.

13. Ibid.

14. (Amherst, 1980).

15. Audience Survey Reports.

16. Douglas McDermott, "The Odyssey of John Bonn: A Note on the German Theatre in America," *The German Quarterly*, 73 (1965), 325–44.

17. *Life and Death of an American*, typescript, I, 39–41. Library of Congress, Federal Theatre Project Collection at George Mason University Libraries.

18. Ibid., II, 8.

19. *One Third of a Nation*, typescript, II, 2.

20. Ibid., I, 27; II, 36.

21. Flanagan, p. 72.

22. Audience Survey Reports.

23. *Sun*, May 23, 1938, p. 16.

24. *New York Times*, May 10, 1937, L, 2.

12

El Teatro Campesino: The Farmworkers' Theatre

Theodore J. Shank

In 1965 Luis Valdez, then a theatre student in California, saw a commedia performance by the San Francisco Mime Troupe. He was so amazed by the vitality, color, and sound that he joined the troupe. It was about the same time that he began thinking of a theatre for farmworkers which would bring together his roots as the son of migrant laborers and his theatre training. He was convinced that if any theare would appeal to farmworkers it would be the lively, bawdy, outdoor style of the Mime Troupe.

Also in 1965 the National Farm Workers Association of Cesar Chavez, after three years of development, first began to test its strength by joining the Agricultural Workers Organizing Committee in a strike of field workers against the grape growers in Delano, California. Valdez says that he knew he had to do something, so he talked to officers of the union about the value of a farmworkers' theatre. They were encouraging, so he decided to go to Delano, where he was born in 1940, and attempt to start a theatre.

Nearly all of the field workers were Chicanos—that is, of American-Indian and Spanish ancestry—which made organizing very difficult. For most of them the only possibility for work was in the fields since they had poor or no formal education and limited English. Typically, they considered themselves fortunate to have a job, so they were reluctant to strike even though their low wages kept them at poverty level. Progress toward forming a viable union was slow. The situation was further aggravated by Mexican workers who illegally slipped across the border, often with the help of labor contractors, and were willing to work as scabs. These illegal workers were especially obliging in accepting whatever payment was offered. They could make no demands without the threat of deportation.

My conversations and interviews with Luis Valdez between 1965 and 1980 have greatly enhanced this article, for which I thank him.

The strike had been in effect for a month when Valdez arrived in Delano and met one evening in the house behind the union office with a group of workers and student volunteers who were helping the union. These workers and students spent their days attempting to persuade those who were still picking grapes to join the strike. Valdez had brought along some signs made especially for the occasion. He hung signs saying *Huelgista* (striker) on two of the men and *Esquirol* (scab) on a third who was instructed to act like a scab. The *Huelgistas* started shouting at the scab, and everyone began laughing.[1] It was the beginning of El Teatro Campesino.

For about three weeks the small group spent their days on the picket line, and at night they worked on skits. Then they gave their first presentation in Filipino Hall. Soon a pattern was established. The company would spend most of their time in the cities performing to raise money for the strike and return to Delano to provide entertainment for weekly union meetings. During the historic 300-mile, twenty-five-day march to Sacramento in 1966 which brought press attention to the union, the Teatro provided entertainment at each night's rally. In preparation for the election which would resolve the jurisdictional dispute between the United Farmworkers' Organizing Committee (UFWOC) and the Teamsters, the group was sent to the labor camps to perform and organize.

The theatrical form which had taken shape came to be called the *acto*. It was a short bilingual skit of perhaps fifteen minutes dealing in a comic way with situations in the lives of Chicano workers. They were short enough for use on a picket line, and three or four could be put together for a longer program. The style of performance was similar to that of the San Francisco Mime Troupe as adapted from commedia dell'arte. Taking the Mexican mime Cantinflas as their model, they used broad, energetic movement that could convey a situation without words, and some performers wore masks which highlighted the stereotypical characters. Because the audience consisted of monolingual Spanish and English speakers as well as those who were bilingual, the Teatro's plays were always a mixture of two languages—a practice which is common in the everyday language of the barrios.

Each *acto* made a specific point. In *Las Dos Caras del Patroncito* (*The Two Faces of the Boss*), first performed in 1965 on the picket line, the scab is shown as the second face of the boss. The Boss, wearing a piglike mask, attempts to persuade one of his scab farmworkers that it is better to be a worker than to have the burdensome responsibilities of being a boss. He is so persuasive that he convinces himself, and the worker and Boss exchange roles. The Boss discovers his mistake, but the Farmworker refuses to trade back. The performance ends with the Boss calling for the help of Cesar Chavez and shouting "Huelga!"

Valdez was finding it difficult to direct a theatre company that was part of the union. Troupe members who were working for the union were obligated to its immediate needs. And the strike needed everyone to help with such activities as organizing a grape boycott. The quality of performances suffered, and it was difficult to make plans. However, they managed their first national tour in the summer of 1967 to raise funds and publicize the strike. But when they returned, El Teatro Campesino became independent of the union and moved to Del Rey, a small suburb of Fresno about sixty miles north of Delano.

In their new location the group established El Centro Campesino Cultural (The Farmworkers' Cultural Center), and their objectives expanded. As in other minority movements, the Chicano movement (La Raza) was attempting to identify and emphasize its own unique cultural attributes. At the center Valdez and his associates taught classes in music, history, drama, English, Spanish, and practical politics. "Many of our people," wrote Valdez, "felt shame and loss of pride in their own Mestizo, mixed-Indian and European culture."[2] They set out to restore this pride. While they continued to support the union and to perform the *huelga actos*, the troupe expanded the subjects of their new plays to include various aspects of Chicano life, even though the union was still a rallying cause.

Los Vendidos (*The Sellouts*, 1967) was concerned with stereotypes and tokenism in appointing Chicanos to minor positions in state government. A secretary from Governor Reagan's office comes to Honest Sancho's Used Mexican Lot and Curio Shop to find "a Mexican type for the administration." She is shown several models. There is the Farmworker whom Sancho describes as the Volkswagen of Mexico: very economical, a few pennies a day is all it takes to keep him going on tortillas and beans. The secretary is impressed by the economical advantages, but when she discovers that he doesn't speak English, she moves on to Johnny Pachuco who runs on hamburgers, beer, and marijuana. Johnny has all of the necessities for city life—he dances, he knife-fights, and he steals. Other models include the Revolucionario—a geniune antique who has starred in all of the Pancho Villa movies and runs on raw horse meat and tequila. However the model that the secretary considers most appropriate is the Mexican-American who wears a business suit and tie. Sancho explains that he is just like the white model, but he comes in several colors. He is a bit more expensive to run because he requires dry martinis. He eats Mexican food only on ceremonial occasions. The secretary thinks he is perfect and makes the purchase. However, as soon as money changes hands, the Mexican-American shouts, "Viva la huelga," and all of the models chase the secretary away and divide the money.

In 1969 the company moved to Fresno, which had a metropolitan population of 300,000 including many Chicanos. In this urban environment they continued their objectives of education and agitation by presenting plays concerned with various aspects of Chicano culture. *No Saco Nada de la Escuela* (*I Don't Get Anything Out of School*, 1969) deals with the Chicano experience in schools from kindergarten to college. Through satire and stereotypes the play demonstrates the discrimination that white teachers display against Chicano students as they attempt to eradicate all but white, middle-class values. In *The Militants* (1969), a five-minute play, comes the first indication of the company's worries about the movement—the internal conflicts and the tendency of some Chicanos to engage in stirring rhetoric and rallies while leaving the boring and arduous door-to-door work to others. The play makes the point that the outward show of militancy can be assimilated by the system with no real changes resulting. A white professor greets the audience and explains how pleased he is to welcome a militant speaker who will "tell it like it is" and "sock it to us." It turns out that two militant speakers claim to be the one invited, so they take turns speaking in increasingly violent rhetoric. While each begins by agreeing with the other, they soon find fault with what the other has said. The professor assents to each of the disparaging comments about him and the establishment of which he is a part. In the end the two militants shoot each other. The professor announces the conclusion of the lecture, and through his laughter says, "I feel so guilty."

It was not long before the conflicts within his own company and the movement as a whole caused Valdez to shift the focus and style of the Teatro. But in the meantime they continued to use the *acto* style to present plays dealing with a variety of social, economic, and political concerns in the Chicano community.

Vietnam Campesino (1970) is a particularly complex *acto* touching upon several issues: the need to protect farmworkers from pesticides sprayed in the fields, the disadvantage Chicanos faced with respect to the draft, the problems of maintaining an effective boycott against non-union grapes when the Defense Department was buying such grapes for the military, the importance of recognizing that Vietnamese peasants and Chicano farmworkers have a common enemy in the American military-agribusiness establishment. The play draws parallels between the conditions of the farmworkers in the United States on one side of the stage and the peasants of Vietnam on the other, between the Grower and the military power figure, General Defense, who conspire to help each other. Because of the grape boycott, the Grower cannot sell his grapes, so General Defense buys them for the army. The Grower's Son, with a toy airplane and a can of talcum powder, sprays "pesticides" on the Chicano farmworkers in his father's fields; then he joins the Air Force and goes to Vietnam where the drops napalm on the peasants and is awarded the Distinguished Flying Cross and a vacation in Hawaii. A young Chicano is drafted and sent to Vietnam where he is killed, and General Defense presents his farmworker parents with the Purple Heart. General Defense explains to the Grower how he manages to keep the war going: "You get the Whites to pay for it, and the Chicanos, the Blacks, Indians and Orientals to fight it." The Grower wants to know, "What are you doing over there anyway?" To which the General replies, "We're buying your grapes."

In 1971 Teatro Campesino and its cultural center moved to a new permanent home in San Juan Bautista, a small town which is the site of a Franciscan mission built at the end of the eighteenth century by Indians under the direction of Catholic priests from Spain. Such a move had become important because of the urban distractions of Fresno and frictions within the group. Shortly before this Valdez had commented that although sloganeering was a necessary part of any political movement, he was beginning to hunger for something else—a "greater spirituality."[3] He had come to believe that the frictions among those in the company came from a misdirected anger. The more they "called for a fighting spirit, the more that same spirit manifested itself in terms of internal conflict." Hostility against an unjust system was vented on each other. It destroyed the unity that was needed to continue and was in opposition to the reasons for doing their work—the brotherhood of Chicanos.

While the company continued to support the union and to work for social change, they were searching for a deeper spirituality. Since the group consisted of Chicanos, who, of course, were part American Indian—Valdez is part Yaqui—it was natural that the search would lead them to Mayan philosophy and practices. The Mayas, whose culture dates back to about 2000 B.C., were the intellectuals of ancient America, developing glyph-writing and complex calendrix, and building ceremonial monuments, the earthly seats of their theocracy, in the jungles of Yucatan, Chiapas, Guatemala, and Honduras.

Their theatre work was influenced by their study of Indian philosophy and mythology. Like the Mayas, they came to believe that people must be in harmony with nature and other human beings or violence would result. No longer was the aim of their theatre work to rally the Chicano community against those who were seen as oppressors; they wanted to harmonize the individual with "the greatest cause that unifies all mankind and that is god," stated Luis Valdez. Thus, he continued, "The cause of social justice becomes tied to the cause of everything else in our universe and in the cosmos."

From the outset Valdez associated the realism of the dominant American theatre with the American "hang-up on the material aspects of human existence." In the published collection of Teatro Campesino *actos* (1971), he calls for a Chicano theatre that is "revolutionary in technique as well as content" which would educate the people "toward an appreciation of *social change*."[4] At first he had adapted the San Francisco Mime Troupe style based on commedia. But commedia, like the plays making up the dominant American culture, had a European heritage unlike that of the Chicanos whose Indian ancestry went back to the Toltecs, Aztecs, and the Mayas.

The *acto* had served the needs of the union for specific social issues, but the new interest of the company in their ancient American roots led to the development of a new form which they called the *mito* (myth). Nearly from the beginning of El Teatro Campesino some characters in their plays were nonhuman. In 1965 actors played the title roles in *Three Grapes*. The following year, in *Quinta Temporada (Fifth Season)*, the cast of characters included Winter, Spring, Summer, and Fall. And in *Vietnam Campesino*, El Draft, wearing a death mask, takes away the young Chicano farmworker. The company had also dressed as *calaveras* (skeletons) for various events, borrowing the image from Mexican folklore. The *mito*, however, went even further in its use of nonhuman characters.

In *Bernabe* (ca. 1969) mythological figures are used in a central way. The title character, a village idiot in a California campesino town, is confronted by Luna (moon) dressed as a 1940s *pachuco* who arranges an assignation with his beautiful sister Tierra (earth). She tempts Bernabe into trying to seduce her but is told she must ask her father El Sol (the sun) for permission to marry. El Sol appears as the Aztec Sun God, and the play is resolved through the Aztec ritual of offering a human heart to the sun god so that he can continue to feed life. Bernabe is sacrificed and resurrected as a cosmic man. La Tierra is again pure.

The work which most directly reflected their Mayan interests in the early 1970s is *El Baile de los Gigantes* (*The Dance of the Giants*, 1974). It is their most mystical work, yet it is intended to have social efficacy through ritual purification. The production is a re-creation of a ceremony that has been performed for at least a thousand years by the Chorti Indians of Yucatan. The Chorti ceremony, in turn, is based on the mythology of the Mayan sacred book, the *Popul Vuh* (*People's Book*), which is an account of the cosmogony, mythology, traditions, and history of the Mayan people. The ceremony, presented at noon on the summer solstice, is intended to assure the well-being of the community.

The performance concerns the gods before the first dawn and tells how the sun and moon of our ancestors were created, thus preparing for the creation of man. It is narrated by Valdez and performed by eight dancers and musicians playing drum, cymbal, flute, rattles, guitar, and conch shell. Frequently the performers accompany their movement with singing. The only props are sticks used in fighting and a ball that serves in turn as a severed head, the belly of a pregnant woman, a newborn child, and the object of a battle. The ball has a special significance because from the earliest evidence of Mesoamerican culture the ball game was associated with the movement of celestial bodies and was a ritual act involving human sacrifice necessary for life. The performance of this ceremony is intended to counteract the potentially violent effect of the summer solstice when the sun is directly overhead and the concentration of solar energy is the greatest. According to Valdez this tremendous energy can cause a person with spiritual impurities—say, someone given to anger or envy—to commit violent acts. Valdez adds,

So *El Baile de los Gigantes* is a purification for the performers and for the whole tribe as well. It shows the good forces against the bad forces, and by concentrating on the action, the people go through the struggle in a sense and it liberates them from their bad feelings. It is cathartic, but it is also in direct relationship with the Mayan mathematical knowledge of reality.[5]

The ceremony was created by El Teatro Campesino specifically for the Chicano and Latin American Theatre Festival held in Mexico in the summer of 1974. Unlike the major European festivals which are organized and supported by municipalities to attract tourists, this festival was sponsored by two alternative theatre organizations having an affinity with indigenous culture on the North and South American continents. The Chicano organization from the north, Teatro Nacional de Aztlan (TENAZ)[6] had come into being when Teatro Campesino organized the first annual Chicano Theatre Festival in 1970. The daily discussions during the Mexico festival made clear the extent of the philosophical and political distance that had come to separate Teatro Campesino from the other Chicano and Latino teatros, many of which had originally been modeled after the theatre of Valdez. While the focus of Teatro Campesino was becoming increasingly spiritual, most of the other teatros were developing a Marxist consciousness and, through their plays, presenting a sociopolitical analysis in terms of class struggle. They angrily accused Valdez of abandoning his proletarian roots and saw his spirituality as an opiate promoting the status quo by refusing to enter into combat against it. The conflicts that Valdez had recognized in his own company and in the Chicano movement and had written about in plays such as *The Militants* were present in the festival. The objective of unifying Chicano and Latino cultural workers by emphasizing their common indigenous roots and traditions had failed.

Never again did El Teatro Campesino perform a Mayan ceremony, although on their land in San Juan Bautista at least one Indian marriage ceremony has taken place, and they celebrate Christmas with reenactments of events surrounding the birth of Christ. Their subsequent major works were less mystical. They combined the acting style developed for the *actos*, some mythological characters from the *mitos*, and elements from a new style called the *corrido*.

The original *corridos* were narrative folk ballads often telling stories of love, heroism, and death. In the Teatro performances a small group of musicians at one side of the stage or at the rear sings ballads with new lyrics as narration for the action.

La Carpa de los Rasquachis (*The Tent of the Underdogs*, 1972) was the first production to use the *corrido* style. The *mito* elements in the play include El Diablo (the devil) who symbolizes human vices and La Muerte (a skeleton figure representing death) who, through the use of costume pieces such as a hat or a shirt, plays a variety of characters. The play has undergone many major changes reflecting changes in the focus of the group and in political circumstances. The length of the versions has varied from less than an hour to about two hours.

In one of the versions the play begins with a song and procession in which a large banner of the Virgin of Guadalupe is paraded. The Virgin of Guadalupe is a brown-skinned version of the Virgin Mary who appeared as an apparition to a poor Mexican peasant. She has become a religious symbol for Mexican and Chicano Catholics. This is followed by flashes from history showing such events as the conquest of Mexico by the Spaniard Cortes. In another scene Indian slaves with ropes around their necks are driven by La Muerte. Most of the play, however, deals with more recent events. La Muerte introduces the story of Jesus Pelado Rasquachi, a Mexican who came to the United States to work in the fields. Throughout his life he wears the rope of a slave around his waist. He falls in love and is married (a priest ropes them together), buys a cheap used car (a tire which he rolls around the stage), leaves his pregnant wife at home while he gets drunk with La Muerte dressed as a dance-hall girl, comes home and beats his wife who gives birth to seven babies who are baptized by "Saint Boss Church." Conditions are tolerable as long as he is young and strong. When a United Farm Workers organizer comes around, he agrees with his boss that they don't need the union. But suddenly he is forty-seven, worn-out and broke, and he wants to go home to Mexico. His children refuse to go. The skeleton shakes his hand, and he dies, humiliated by the system. The rope he has worn all his life is still around his waist. In one version there is a happy ending. Rasquachi comes back to life, joins the union, and goes on strike.

In an earlier version, the second act concerns Rasquachi's widow and sons who go to the city where they are caught up in hatred and violence which brings about the deaths of the sons. The final section is a kind of mystical pageant in which the Virgin of Guadalupe appears. One of the sons transforms into a figure suggesting both Christ and Quetzalcoatl, a Mayan man-god parallel to Christ. We hear, "You are my other self." "If I do harm to you I do harm to myself." "Against hatred—love; against violence—peace."

Despite the apparent pessimism of the story of Rasquachi and his family, the play, even when performed without the final section, is not bitter. The tremendous energy of the performance—the music, the dance, the acrobatic movement—projects a positive reaffirmation of life. It is this spirit, without the obvious Mayan and Christian spirituality, that has continued to characterize the work of Teatro Campesino. However the setting of subsequent plays shifted from the farm to the city, a transition first clearly seen in some versions of *La Carpa de los Rasquachis*.

In *Mundo* the change in focus from farmworkers to urban Chicanos is complete. Work on this play began in 1972, and it was first performed in 1975 as *El Fin del Mundo* (*The End of the World*). This highly abstract version, greatly influenced by Mayan studies, was envisioned as an event for the traditional Mexican celebration of El Dia de los Muertos (The Day of the Dead). The fourth version called *Mundo* (1980), which Valdez considers "definitive," eliminated the Mayan abstractions and developed urban Chicano characters and an elaborate plot. Although it was no longer considered specifically as a celebration of El Dia de los Muertos, the play is permeated by the Mexican concept of death which is a mixture of indigenous and European attitudes. The playwright-director describes the play as a twentieth-century "Mystery/Miracle play. . . . The Mystery is Death, the Miracle is Life." As with *La Carpa de los Rasquachis, Mundo* combines elements of the *acto* and the *corrido* in its fast-moving commedialike acting and in its songs and dance. The *mito* element is still present, but in an altered form. There are no characters borrowed directly from Mayan or Christian mythology, nor are El Diablo or La Muerte present. Instead, all of the characters are human, but with two exceptions their faces are made up to resemble skulls, and skeletal bones are superimposed on their costumes. The play is set in the world of the dead, which parallels the world of the living except that its values are inverted.

In *Mundo* the concept of death is even more central than in previous work. The skeleton figures derive from the Mexican concept that death is not something that can be avoided; instead, death is a reminder of the commonality that all people must eventually die. Material possessions and physical appearances are transitory. Underneath, all people are the same—merely skeletons. From the time of the Mayas, death was thought to be a phase in the cycle of life, which is continually being renewed. Human sacrifices were offered to the sun god so that human life could continue. It is a communal rather than an individual view of life.

Mundo (meaning world) follows the adventures of Mundo Mata, a kind of urban Chicano everyman, on his adventures into the other side of reality. There he finds things much the same. His family and friends are living out their deaths as once they had lived out their lives. The adventures of Mundo begin with an overdose of heroin. He is being released after serving his "life" sentence. A jail door is rolled from place to place with Mundo behind it as if he is going through long corridors. He takes a bus (represented by five women) to the end of the line. Arrested, he is taken to city jail for the night where he finds his father. His mother, he discovers, is a prostitute who takes him to her room and to bed in a coffin. Her pimp relieves Mundo of his wallet before he sets out to find his grandparents.

The staging is simple, but the bizarre costumes, the music, dance, and frenetic energy make it seem elaborate. Ten actors play thirty-six characters by changing costume pieces over their skeleton-painted body stockings. Props and two rolling scaffold units the size of large closets make up the setting. By rearranging these units, they serve as jail, the Department of Urban Housing Underdevelopment, a hospital, and other locales in the land of the dead. The easy movement from place to place is similar to the jump cuts, segues, and other transitions used in films. Because of these cinematic techniques and others, Valdez refers to the play as a *mono*, a *pachuco* word for movie.

In search of his grandparents, Mundo crawls through a tire and discovers the entire community lying in cemeterylike rows with tire gravestones at their heads. He comes upon a vendor selling balloons (drugs). Because Mundo has no money, he trades his knife for a balloon which the vendor uses to burst the balloon, scattering glitter which the vendor identifies as "bone dust" (a reference to the drug called angel dust).

With the help of a street-punk friend who has a bullet hole in his forehead, Mundo finds his pregnant wife, Vera, at the End of the World Dance. He kills a rival, Little Death, and together he and Vera go to the Department of Unemployment so he can find a job. He has no death certificate for identification, but when he shows them his arm, they are so impressed with his "track record" that they offer him a job as executive director of the Drug Abuse Center. Mundo and Vera are in an accident in their low-rider car. At the hospital Mundo is told there is good news and bad news. The bad news is that his wife is alive; the good news is that the baby was born dead. Mundo wants Vera to return to prison with him—that is, back to the world of the living. But Vera refuses to leave her skeleton baby behind.

In the land of the dead, characters can be killed over and over. Little Death, whom Mundo had killed at the dance, attempts to shoot Mundo, but kills Vera instead. The dead Vera wants Mundo to come home with her and the baby, but he is not yet ready to die. "It's my . . . world," he says, "and I'm going to make it survive." Eventually, skeletons from the land of the dead force him out of their world, and Mundo again finds himself behind bars, sentenced to life. Vera is alive and pregnant. When offered some dust, he refuses. He is through with all of that. He has learned something.

The ironic view of life in the Chicano barrios is recognizable through the caricatures and stereotypes. Although *Mundo* concerns working-class people, no specific issue is in focus. The work of El Teatro Campesino has moved farther from its identification with the farmworkers' union as it has become concerned with the urban Chicano. This new concern was also evident in *Zoot Suit* (1978), written and directed by Valdez for the Mark Taper Forum in Los Angeles and subsequently produced in New York where it was publicized as the first Chicano play to be presented on Broadway. *Zoot Suit* focuses on the historical trial of the 1940s in which seventeen members of a pachuco street gang were wrongfully convicted of murder.

Concerning the recent work of Teatro Campesino, especially *Zoot Suit*, Luis Valdez has been accused by more politically doctrinaire Chicanos and by some people identified with the new left of selling out because his work is no longer overtly political. It is ironic that in the view of Valdez the failure of *Zoot Suit* in New York was partly because critics perceived it as agitprop theatre. However, he believes that the apparent political advocacy of the play was simply implicit in the historical material. He does not consider the most recent work of the Teatro to be overtly political. The farmworkers are better organized now; there is no acute political cause. Now, according to Valdez, the purpose of their work is to sensitize the public to other aspects of the Mexican people, the history of California and of the United States. The focus is the Anglo-Hispanic relationship.[7]

El Teatro Campesino has nonetheless continued its commitment to the Chicano people as a whole, attempting to avoid divisiveness. And because he is a theatre artist, Valdez is especially concerned about the relationship of Chicanos to the theatrical profession. He is convinced that Chicano theatre must establish itself on a professional level—not only for the sake of its artistry but for the livelihood of its practitioners. The Broadway production of *Zoot Suit* and the projected Hollywood movie are, in his view, in keeping with this objective. He is annoyed that some Chicano intellectuals have criticized him for participating in these commercial productions. To Valdez these critics are inconsistent. Some of them have gotten Ph.D.'s and settled into comfortable university positions without worrying about becoming compromised.

No doubt the early work of El Teatro Campesino in support of the organizing activities of the farmworkers' union was useful especially in persuading scabs to leave the fields, in strengthening the strike, and in helping to make the boycott against non-union grapes and lettuce a success. But surely the union would have succeeded without the Teatro. The most important contribution of El Teatro Campesino under the leadership of Luis Valdez was its being the first Chicano theatre. Since 1965 when his Teatro began, approximately eighty others have been formed. For many of these theatres Teatro Campesino was their model; for others, while using the *acto, mito, corrido,* and *mono* forms pioneered by

Valdez, specific problems in their own communities and sometimes a more doctrinaire political perspective provided a focus. For Chicanos who have seen El Teatro Campesino or read about its successful European tours or know how Peter Brook in 1973 came to spend a summer working with the Teatro or how the director of the company was appointed by the governor to the California Arts Council—surely these people now know that it is possible for a Chicano to become a professional theatre artist.

NOTES

1. Beth Bagby, "El Teatro Campesino; Interviews with Luis Valdez," *The Drama Review*, 11 (Summer 1967), 74–75.

2. Luis Valdez, "History of the Teatro Campesino," *La Raza*, 1 (Summer 1971), 19.

3. Unless otherwise noted, all quotations are from my conversations with Luis Valdez, 1965 to 1980.

4. Luis Valdez, *Actos*, (San Juan Bautista, California, 1971), pp. 1–2.

5. For a more extensive discussion of *El Baile de los Gigantes* and the Mayan philosophy and science involved, see Theodore Shank, "A Return to Mayan and Aztec Roots," *The Drama Review*, 18 (December 1974), 56–70.

6. Aztlan is an Aztec word used by Chicanos to indicate the area now comprising the Southwestern United States—the homeland of Aztecs before they migrated south to Mexico.

7. An interview with Luis Valdez by Charles Pelton, "Zoot-Suiting to Hollywood: Teatro Campesino's Luis Valdez," *Artbeat* (December 1980), 28.

13

Contemporary Theatre for Working-Class Audiences in the United States

Daniel Friedman

INTRODUCTION

Theatre for working-class audiences in the United States, for all practical purposes, ceased to exist in the 1940s. This is not to imply that working people never attended the theatre, but that mainstream theatre, commercial and noncommercial, continued to reflect the lives and values of its primarily middle-class, professional, and well-to-do audiences as it had since at least the turn of the century. The continuing escalation in the price of theatre tickets made it increasingly difficult, even in the boom decades after World War II, for workers to attend the theatre with any regularity; and television furthered the trend, started by the movies, of supplying the dramatic needs of the working class in media other than live theatre. This situation has not been significantly altered by the proliferation of regional theatres over the last two decades. Regional theatres have succeeded in expanding the American theatre's geographic base, but have not affected its social base. The same social strata that support and attend the theatre in New York do so in the cities served by the regional theatres.

The result is that almost two generations of American workers have grown up without the theatre. At best, they have seen an occasional high school or community theatre production of a recent or classic Broadway show. At worst, they have never seen live theatre at all. In either case American workers since World War II have not seen plays concerned with their points of view and their aspirations because such plays were not being produced.

In the last ten years this has begun to change. From the coal mines of Kentucky to the wheat fields of South Dakota, from the streets of the Bronx to the barrios of Santa Barbara, theatre troupes have emerged that are dedicating themselves entirely to the creation and performance of theatre for working people. For the most part unacknowledged by the established press, ignored by academia, functioning on a financial shoestring, and often unaware of each others' work, these theatres have nonetheless proliferated in the last few years.

On the West Coast, theatre for working-class audiences can be found in Seattle, Portland, the San Francisco Bay area, Santa Barbara, San Juan Bautista, and Los Angeles. On the East Coast, troupes are active in Boston, New York City, Baltimore, and Washington, D.C. In between, theatre troupes are at work in Kentucky, Illinois, Michigan, and South Dakota. In addition to performances in their home towns, some of the more established troupes have toured extensively in every region of the continental United States as well as in Europe, Mexico, Cuba, and Nicaragua.[1] While not yet at the point where it can be termed a movement, the emergence, for the first time in forty years, of theatres throughout the country dedicated to performing for working people is a phenomenon of some significance to cultural historians, sociologists, social activists, and theatre artists. These contemporary theatres for working-class audiences—their histories, their artistry, and their politics—are the subject of this chapter.

This study makes no claim to being thorough and balanced. The process of gathering information on the theatres has been frustratingly slow and is still painfully incomplete. Starting with nine groups that I personally knew about, I mailed them a twenty-point questionnaire and asked them to inform me of the names and addresses of other troupes. The questionnaire is attached as appendix A. Almost every group that responded knew of two or three other troupes. Sometimes they supplied an address, or sometimes a newly named troupe had to be located by more roundabout methods. As soon as an address was secured, a questionnaire was mailed. As of this writing, I have been able to verify the existence of thirty-two theatres for working-class audiences functioning in the United States today. A list of the troupes and mailing addresses is attached as appendix B. These 32 troupes had been performing together for at least two years before 1983.

In addition, not every troupe that I contacted chose to respond, and the existence of others came to my attention too late to be interviewed for this study. Of the thirty-two troupes known to exist, only fourteen responded to the questionnaire—ten in writing and four in taped interviews conducted by myself or Bruce McConachie. The troupes that responded are also indicated in appendix B. It is impossible to say how representative these fourteen are of their sister theatres, but since they are the ones who supplied the data, this study is, by necessity, based primarily on their responses.

Finally, the reader should be warned that I have worked as an actor with two of the troupes discussed here and have been peripherally involved with a number of the others. It is probable then that while I have tried to be objective, my personal responses to the performances, politics, and personalities involved will be reflected to some extent in the study that follows. With all of these limitations in mind, I hope that this study can be of some value as a first attempt to describe and analyze the current growth of theare for working-class audiences in the United States.

Because the nature of their audiences is what distinguishes these thirty-two theatres from all the others in the United States, first it is necessary to define that audience and to clarify what criteria were used to determine if a theatre was to be included in this study. By "working class" in the contemporary American context, I mean that segment of the population which neither owns nor controls the means of production or reproduction in society: all those who survive primarily by the sale of their labor power or that of someone else in their family, whether that sale be to a private company or a governmental institution. It also includes people who are unable to find a buyer for their labor power, those on unemployment insurance or welfare, and their families. In short, a worker is anyone who survives by working for someone else, receives a wage or salary, and is not in a management position. This segment of society includes, of course, the vast majority of Americans, but in the twentieth century that group has been only a small percentage of the theatregoing public.

The theatres examined here all perform for or are striving to perform for an audience made up primarily of workers as I have defined them. Although the motivations of most of the theatres in striving to reach the working class are political, not all political theatres have been included. For example, the Bread and Puppet Theatre, one of the best known political theatres in the United States, who have performed at almost every major antiwar demonstration since the mid-sixties and whose plays have been consistently pacifist in content, write, "We attempt to reach the widest cross-section of people possible. . . . We tend to reach younger people, theatre-oriented people, educated people, left-wing people."[2] Because they do not attempt to reach a working-class audience, the Bread and Puppet Theatre does not fall within the scope of this study. The Iron Clad Agreement (originally of Pittsburgh, now of New York City), on the other hand, is not usually thought of as a political theatre and has received grants from, among others, Trans World Airlines, U.S. Steel, ALCOA, and Westinghouse Electric. Nonetheless, The Iron Clad Agreement has consistently produced plays on working-class subjects and performed for primarily working-class audiences, so they are included here.

The content of their plays and the intentions of the theatre troupes have also determined whether they are included in this study. While the majority of the theatres included have apparently been very successful in reaching their intended audience, there are a few exceptions. The San Francisco Mime Troupe, for example, writes, "We would like to reach everyone who works for a living, or who can't find work." But they add that on tour, "Our audience is mainly the white left." El Teatro de la Esperanza (Santa Barbara) also reports that they play "mostly in University theatres." However, the San Francisco Mime Troupe since the early seventies and El Teatro de la Esperanza since its founding in 1971 have consistently presented plays with working-class characters, conflicts, and themes. In addition, both have worked systematically to expand the working-class element of their audiences. Therefore I have included them in this study of contemporary theatre for working-class audiences.

A particular problem of audience definition was posed by the Dakota Theatre Caravan, which performs exclusively in the rural areas of South Dakota. When the Caravan performs in a small town, most of the town shows up. When they did a show in Wessington, South Dakota (population 375), they had 325 at the play. In Reva, South Dakota, which consists of a gas station and store combination and has a population of 9, 100 people came in from the surrounding ranches to see the show. Obviously most of the audiences in these towns are not workers as defined here. While some may have been farmhands working for a wage, most were self-employed farmers and ranchers. Doug Paterson of the Dakota Theatre Caravan writes, "The Caravan's audience is not a classically working-class one. Terminology might say it is a 'peasant' audience, meaning farm, rural or small town; but the term 'peasant' isn't particularly flattering and we much prefer 'rural.' " What binds the Dakota Theatre Caravan to the other troupes considered is their desire to create theatre that is relevant to the people who do the productive labor of this country and to whom theatre has not been widely available before (in this case farmers instead of workers). I have considered this general orientation more important than technical definitions and have included them. A similar orientation helps define the Roadside Theater of Whitesburg, Kentucky, which performs not only in coal camps but also in farming communities in the Appalachian region.

The New York Street Theatre Caravan offers a definition of the audience they are trying to reach that could serve as a working definition for all the theatres in this group:

Our aim is to bring theatre back to the people, those not included in the cultural mainstream of our country, and to make theatre a social force dedicated to the sacred rights of all those working people upon whom the hope and welfare of our country depends, be they factory workers, miners, field workers, construction workers, office workers or teachers.[3]

Probably none of the theatres to be examined would quibble with this as a general definition of those for whom they want to perform. Within this general definition a number of the troupes see it as their job to serve a particular segment of the working-class population. El Teatro de la Esperanza writes, "We are concentrating on working-class audiences of all races, but with a heavy emphasis to the Spanish speaking." The Irish Rebel Theatre (New York City) describes the audience they want to reach as "blue-collar American Irish." Word of Mouth Productions, an all-woman theatre from the Boston area, maintains, "We are attempting to reach a working-class audience, primarily women." The Everyday Theatre (Washington, D.C.) has approached working people primarily as tenants, performing plays on tenants' struggles for tenants' unions and community organizations. Workers' Stage (New York City) specializes in peforming for workers in situations of collective struggle such as strikes, organizing drives, contract negotiations, and so forth based on the thesis that "such situations provide the most fertile environment for interacting with the audiences' lives and connecting specific experiences to broader political concepts.''[4] All of the theatres discussed here perform for, or are attempting to perform for, an audience composed primarily of workers or others engaged in productive labor who are not a part of the traditional theatre audience. This is what makes these troupes unique in America today, and this is what, despite their many differences, binds them together.

HISTORY I: THE PIONEERS

Most of the contemporary theatres for working-class audiences in the United States have emerged since 1970, but there are three important exceptions: the San Francisco Mime Troupe (founded in 1959), El Teatro Campesino (founded in 1965), and the New York Street Theatre Caravan (founded in 1968). All three remain productive and influential today. El Teatro Campesino, however, has not been primarily concerned with working-class issues or with reaching a specifically working-class audience since the early 1970s. Its influence on the development of the Chicano theatre movement will be touched upon in the discussion of El Teatro de la Esperanza. Here the early histories of the two pioneer groups that are still functioning as theatres for working people will be examined.

The San Francisco Mime Troupe was founded in 1959 by R. G. Davis, a mime trained by Etienne Decroux and Paul Curtis. By the mid-1960s, under Davis's leadership, the Mime Troupe had left silent mime behind and was performing commedia dell'arte, updated to deal with contemporary social issues, free in parks throughout the San Francisco Bay area. By the end of the decade— through a combination of their exciting and highly skilled performance, the radical content of their plays, police harassment that turned many of their shows into demonstrations, and extensive touring of college campuses—the Mime Troupe had become *the* theatre of America's left-wing community. However, the leftist community at that time was made up primarily of white students and counter-culturists, not workers, and it was essentially this audience that they played for throughout the decade.

In the midst of the upheavals of the late 1960s, the Mime Troupe began to study socialist theory, as did much of the left at the time. Robert Scheer, an actor with the troupe on several tours, recalls that: 'frequently . . . a hard day and night of performing in Albuquerque or Fargo [was] capped off by a late night study session or just a serious discussion about Mao's redbook, the Panthers, or the Mideast.''[5] This study and the experiences of the sixties gradually led the group to a general consensus that it was the working class, not students or countercultural youth, who had the long-term potential to profoundly alter American society along more humane and democratic lines. From this political perspective, the Mime Troupe began a conscious attempt to become a theatre for the working class.

At the end of the decade, R. G. Davis left the San Francisco Mime Troupe. His departure roughly corresponds with the beginning of the Mime Troupe's protracted struggle to build a working-class audience. This struggle has included the exploration of popular American theatrical forms, the development of a clear working-class stand in the content of their plays, the racial integration of the troupe, and attempts to link up with working-class social, political, and trade union organizations.

The Mime Troupe in the seventies abandoned the commedia that had characterized its work in the sixties and experimented with such popular American forms as melodrama, vaudeville, and comic books, as well as the circus and Brecht. Their 1972 production of *High Rises and Frozen Wages* marked a turning point for the theatre because they dealt explicitly with working-class issues for the first time, a trend that has continued to this day. *False Promises/Nos Enganaron* (1976), a full-length epic drama that dealt with the Spanish-American War from the point of view of its American working-class characters, was a major breakthrough in achieving the troupe's stated goal of "doing a play from working people's point of view, in a popular style, about working people's problems."

Even more significant than the development of its performance style or changes in the content of its scripts has been the Mime Troupe's concrete attempts to better represent and reach out to the working class. Reflecting on the multiracial and multiethnic nature of the U.S. working class, the Mime Troupe concluded that if it was to be a national theatre for the American working class, it would need to be integrated: in their own words, "We think a multi-racial country needs a multi-racial culture." Since 1970, the Mime Troupe has transformed itself from an all-white company to a fully integrated troupe. This has not been a quick or smooth transition, but it has resulted in a definite broadening of their audience. The Mime Troupe reports, "Mexican and Latino themes in several of our recent plays has [sic] won us a considerable Hispanic following in California, and some dynamite black performers have started drawing a black audience." However, they have found that a multiracial cast and antiracist content do not guarantee an integrated audience. "The difficulty we have had in getting our audience's racial balance to reflect our own shows us how segregated cultural life in this country still remains."

The other important development in the San Francisco Mime Troupe's practice over the last decade has been its increasing tendency to perform for working-class organizations and to have such organizations sponsor shows. Despite all their other efforts, the troupe found that because American workers lacked a tradition of attending live theatre, free performances in the parks were not attracting the audiences they wanted to reach. They write, "In most of the country, if not all of it, the traditionally-defined working class doesn't go to the theatre. This means you can't reach those people with any kind of publicity, as individuals; you have to reach them through groups, organizations that they belong to." The Mime Troupe reports that they now "get more requests from organizations than we can handle." This has been a major way to broaden their audience. They write, "Often people are introduced to our shows first by their organizations, then become regulars.'' As a result, the Mime Troupe's Bay area audience now consists, in their words, of ''working people of every race, families, seniors, gays, as well as this area's very broad progressive community.''

This relative success in reaching the working class locally has not been matched on the national level where the audience remains ''mainly the white left, except in places where we are sponsored by community organizations.'' A major frustration for the Mime Troupe both locally and nationally has been its inability to establish a working relationship with the main mass organizations of the American working class, the trade unions. Their reputation as a politically radical group has preceded them into the unions, apparently providing a stumbling block to more conservative trade union leaders. In addition, the troupe has often performed, in its own words, for ''union insurgents'' on the West Coast, a factor that has probably contributed to what they term the ''unreceptive'' and ''openly hostile'' attitudes they have encountered among union officials. Their most recent work, however, indicates the development of a closer working relationship with the trade unions. In May 1983 they reported that they were working on a show about plant closings: ''We're working with union people as consultants and hoping to build some long-term relationships.''

Beyond its own work, the San Francisco Mime Troupe is important for the influence it has exerted on the other theatres. It is the one theatre for working-class audiences whose work all the others are aware of. In fact, in its almost quarter-century of activity, it has spawned at least two other theatres for working people. El Teatro Campesino (The Farmworkers' Theatre) was founded by Luis Valdez, a former Mime Trouper, as are Steve Friedman, Denny Partridge, and Greta Minsky, who founded Modern Times Theatre in New York City in 1977. There are also two circuses founded by former Mime Troupers: the Pickle Family Circus, which travels a circuit up and down the West Coast sponsored by community organizations, and the Big Apple Circus, which performs throughout the five boroughs of New York City during the summer. The Mass Transit Street Theatre, a theatre for working people based in the Bronx, New York, reports that their adaptation of the Mime Troupe's children's play *Androcles and the Lion* has probably been the most widely seen of all their plays and that kids throughout the Bronx ''know it by heart.'' While these are the most explicit examples of the Mime Troupe's impact on other theatres for working-class audiences, its indirect influence is widespread; only the Roadside Theatre claimed that the Mime Troupe ''had no discernable influence'' on their work.

The second oldest theatre currently performing for working-class audiences in the United States is nine years younger than the San Francisco Mime Troupe. Almost as well known and respected today as the Mime Troupe, the New York Street Theatre Caravan was founded in 1968 by Marketa Kimbrell and Richard Levy. They met when she was an actress with the Repertory Theatre of Lincoln Center and he was on its literary staff. Inspired by the political upheavals of the time and wanting to give political meaning to their work, both gave up their jobs at Lincoln Center to found the New York Street Theatre Caravan. To support themselves, they taught acting, Kimbrell at New York University's School of the Arts and Levy at New York's High School of the Performing Arts.

Because it was oriented toward the working class from the beginning, the New York Street Theatre Caravan was able to avoid many of the problems later faced by the Mime Troupe. For example, the Street Theatre Caravan has always been an integrated troupe, with black, Puerto Rican, and white actors, reflecting New York's ethnic composition. Over the fifteen years of its existence (though none of the original members except Kimbrell remain), the Caravan has remained integrated, and today it includes Mexican-American actors as well. Rather than perform on campus for the left, the New York Street Theatre Caravan took its shows directly to the working class. One of its first performances was for the poor people's tent city erected in Washington, D.C. by the Southern Christian Leadership Council and others. Kimbrell and Levy realized that American workers had no tradition of going to the theatre, even free theatre in the parks, and so were determined to find a way to bring theatre to the people. They did this by performing on the street in working-class neighborhoods. In their first years, they performed in working-class areas of New York, particularly Brooklyn, where they had rehearsal space. Since 1970, they have been touring the country almost every summer with a flatbed truck (that doubles as a stage) and a van full of actors.

The Mime Troupe reports that it learned through experience that workers today are most successfully interested in plays "through groups, organizations they belong to." The New York Street Theatre Caravan realized this very early, and their street performances were rarely random; previous contact had almost always been made with a local community group or political organization, which did advance publicity and helped turn out the audience. In the late sixties and early seventies, the groups that sponsored their shows, both in New York and nationally, ranged from federally sponsored "poverty program" and VISTA offices to the Black Panthers and Young Lords. Since the mid-seventies much of their work, especially in New York, has been sponsored by unions.

The Street Theatre Caravan's relationship with the trade union movement goes back at least to 1970. On their first national tour that year, they performed for the United Farm Workers, both in Delano where they did a show for Philippino grape pickers in their union hall and in Salinas where they performed for a rapt audience of 3,000 at an open-air union meeting on the second night of the now-famous Salinas Valley lettuce strike. During the same tour they did a number of performances in West Virginia for the Retired Miner's Association, a group that played an important role in the movement that eventually ousted Tony Boyle's corrupt leadership of the United Mine Workers and replaced it with the reform administration of Arnold Miller. This work with the unions apparently remained erratic, however, until the mid-seventies when, the Caravan writes, "We began performing for the membership of many of New York's unions." They credit this development with allowing them to tour more extensively. Based on the union correspondence that the Caravan included with their questionnaire, they have performed most extensively for the International Ladies Garment Workers Union (ILGWU) and Local 1199 (Hospital Workers) in New York, and for the United Auto Workers throughout Michigan. They have also done shows in conjunction with the Amalgamated Clothing and Textile Workers Union's (ACTWU) attempts to organize J. P. Stevens in the Southeast.

The New York City Street Theatre Caravan writes that they have been "remarkably successful in remaining artistically and physically in contact" with the working class. They define their current audience as "the poor and dispossessed, and the working people," although they add, "We have also picked up, over the years, a very valuable audience of political thinkers and artistic sophisticates, who support us for their own reasons in what we do." In 1977, the Street Theatre Caravan "began to be invited to theatre festivals in Europe, which earned us enough money to eventually become full-time." The Caravan formed a coalition with Modern Times Theatre and the New York Labor Theatre in 1979 to convert a parish hall in New York's Chelsea area into the St. Peter's Performing Arts Center where they shared a season and subscription lists until 1983. It was here and in Europe that they primarily attracted the "political thinkers and artistic sophisticates" in their audience. It is through their touring in literally every region of the continental United States that the New York Street Theatre Caravan reaches its primary audience. Although there is no way to substantiate this, it is very likely that in its fifteen years of existence the Street Theatre Caravan has reached a larger audience of poor and working people than any other theatre in the United States since the 1930s. Certainly the variety of their working-class audience is unmatched. They have performed for workers of virtually every racial and ethnic group, for farmworkers, miners, industrial, office and service workers, and for prisoners. It should also be noted that they are the only current theatre for working-class audiences that makes it a point to perform on Native American reservations whenever possible. They have done shows for the Hopi, Navaho, Northern Cheyenne, and Santo Domingan peoples.

During its first two years of existence, the Caravan did short skits and playlets. In 1970, in conjunction with their first national tour, they created their first full-length piece, *Come On In My Kitchen*. The play, based on the old German folktale of "The Bremen Town Musicians," was created through extensive improvisation over a six-month period. In it, the various animals of the original story come to represent various segments of the American working-class who, after being thrown out of work, converge on Washington and drive the "robbers" out of the White House. Interestingly, this same piece, with a much tighter script, far more sophisticated use of music, and higher performance level, re-emerged in 1981 as *Hard Times Blues*. This eleven-year incubation period indicates the slow and careful creative process the Caravan uses. On the average, they finish a major new work only once every two years.

In addition to *Come On In My Kitchen/Hard Times Blues*, the Caravan's major works have been *The Mother*, their original adaptation of Gorki's novel that not only sidestepped Brecht's but, with its highly emotional and quasi-religious tone (the son is crucified), might well be considered an "answer play" to Brecht's version; *Bitter Harvest*, based on Steinbeck's *The Grapes of Wrath*; *Sacco and Vanzetti (The Passion of a Poor Fisherman and a Good Shoemaker)*, about the famous radical martyrs of the 1920s; and *Molly Maguire*, which dealt with the Irish migration in general and the "Molly Maguire" labor organization of immigrant Irish miners in particular. Since Richard Levy's departure in the early 1970s, all major works have been credited as "conceived and directed by Marketa Kimbrell." In addition to its full-length plays, the Caravan keeps an active repertory of short skits that can be performed for specific situations (such as rallies) or put together to provide "a two-hour evening of theatre." The Caravan writes, "In the skits we've taken the themes of working people's reality and made them into short, visual pieces of theatre . . . designed to be performed in union halls or in the streets."

The San Francisco Mime Troupe and the New York Street Theatre Caravan can accurately be credited with reviving the tradition of performing theatre for working-class audiences in the United States. They took the first experimental steps toward the working class and have since been followed by at least thirty other theatres. In this regard they have been true pioneers. Their historical contribution and current practice continue to inspire and inform their younger siblings across the country.

HISTORY II: THE EARLY SEVENTIES

With the exception of the two pioneer groups, America's contemporary theatres for working-class audiences have all emerged since 1970. Historically, they can be divided into two groups: those that were founded in the early seventies as the radical fervor of the sixties peaked, and those that were formed in the late seventies and early eighties as the economic decline accelerated and the focus and composition of America's life shifted from the campus to the working class.

In the early seventies there were scores of politically radical guerrilla street theatres in the United States. Most of them were student-based, either directly, as were the numerous Radical Arts Troupes (RATS) that were associated with Students for a Democratic Society (SDS), or indirectly, in that they performed on campus or at mostly student-attended rallies and demonstrations. Most of these troupes proved to be as impermanent as the student movement that gave them birth. They would perform together for a semester or two or just for a particular event, and then the members would go their separate ways. Even those campus-based groups that achieved a life span that could be measured in years instead of months (the Pageant Players, N.Y.C.; Rapid Transit Guerrilla Theatre, Chicago; San Francisco Red Theatre) disappeared as the war in Vietnam and the draft ended and the student movement faded away.[6] The radical theatres from this period that have survived are those that early in their histories sought their audience among the working class.

Both the Mass Transit Street Theatre (New York City) and El Teatro de la Esperanza (The Theatre of Hope, Santa Barbara) were founded in 1970. Mass Transit was begun by a group of young modern dancers who wanted to do an outdoor piece for the first Earth Day. The founders of El Teatro de la Esperanza were students at the University of California, Santa Barbara, where they were active in the Movimiento Estudiantial Chicano de Aztlan (Chicano Student Movement for Aztlan; Aztlan is an Aztec word used to indicate the area now comprising the Southwestern United States). So while the origins of both these troupes were typical of the guerrilla theatres of the time, neither remained typical for very long.

Within a year of its founding, Mass Transit had to decide between taking an antiwar skit to a major peace demonstration in Washington, D.C., or remaining in New York that weekend and performing their play in working-class neighborhoods. After an intense internal struggle, they decided to stay in New York. "It was a very important decision about who our audience was to be," recalls Jerry Cofta of Mass Transit, and he adds, "It wasn't easy." The decision was a turning point for the group; from then on, the content of their plays began to deal explicitly with working-class issues, and they began to seek out working-class audiences.

After a year as the cultural arm of the Movimiento Estudiantial Chicano de Aztlan, El Teatro de la Esperanza moved off campus to La Casa de la Raza (The House of the People), a community center on the working-class east side of Santa Barbara. This move needs to be understood in the context of the Chicano theatre movement. El Teatro Campesino (The Farmworkers' Theatre) was founded by Luis Valdez in 1965 to help with the strike of the United Farm Workers and sparked an unprecedented Chicano theatre movement that spawned approximately eighty Chicano theatre troupes since its founding. Most of the troupes drew their artistic and political inspiration from the early work of El Teatro Campesino when it performed short *actos* (skits) on working-class problems for an audience of farmworkers. By 1971 however, when El Teatro de la Esperanza moved off campus, El Teatro Campesino had, for the most part, abandoned its working-class concerns and taken up a mystically informed Chicano nationalism.[7] Nonetheless, it was the working-class *actos* that inspired the students from Santa Barbara and many others throughout the Southwest.

During their first year at La Casa de la Raza, El Teatro de la Esperanza reports that they performed many "of the Actos written by El Teatro Campesino" at the community center and "throughout the county of Santa Barbara." The next year, 1972, they were given a larger space at La Casa and began to create their own plays. At the same time it is important to note that El Teatro de la Esperana did not limit itself to theatre work but played an active role in building the community center. In their own estimation their work in these early years was "instrumental in the general development of La Casa." Their theatre work was just a part—an integral part to be sure—of their organizing work in the community.

At about this same time, Mass Transit Street Theatre also began the process of linking themselves with a community center and setting down roots in a working-class neighborhood. They had become dissatisfied with their random approach to performing in the streets and wanted to be in a situation where "people could see us more than once." In 1973 they began a ten-month search for a home.

They performed in working-class neighborhoods in all of New York's boroughs (except Staten Island), "looking for connections and a feeling we belonged." Eventually they chose the northwest Bronx, centering themselves in the area around St. James Park, then a white (predominantly Irish), working-class neighborhood. There were two primary reasons for this choice. First, as an all-white group, Mass Transit did not feel that they could do effective work among minority people. Secondly, there were at least two community-based organizations in the area with whom they wanted to work. The first was the Northwest Community Clergy Coalition, a broad, church-based housing coalition, and the other was White Lightning. White Lightning had originally been formed by "a bunch of white working-class guys" who, inspired by the Black Panthers, were attempting to bring the spirit of streetwise radicalism to the neighborhoods they had grown up in. By the time Mass Transit encountered them, they were, in the theatre's estimation, putting out a very good political newspaper called *White Lightning* and doing a lot of effective tenant organizing.

In 1974 the members of Mass Transit moved into the neighborhood, established themselves in a local community center, and began to work closely with White Lightning. Mass Transit would perform its tenant-organizing play, *Ursula Underdog vs. the Money Grabbers; or, Tenant Go Round*, on the street while members of White Lightning circulated through the crowd selling their newspaper. After the show, White Lightning would provide on-the-spot tenant counseling. In the community center, Mass Transit developed and performed, among other plays, *What Makes Daddy Run?* a play about "growing up working-class in America," and *Women's Right To Choose*, a proabortion play. The years of 1975 and 1976 marked the height of Mass Transit's community-based work. The second Bronx People's Fair, which they organized, drew, according to police estimates, 10,000 people to St. James park for a day of Bronx ethnic food, dance, music, and theatre, with community and political groups from the borough represented at tables and booths throughout the park.

Two other working-class theatres emerged early in the decade. The Irish Rebel Theatre of New York City has operated out of An Claideamh Soluis (The Irish Arts Center) in New York City's Hell's Kitchen area since 1972. They perform plays that they feel "genuinely depict the experience of the Irish people," with particular emphasis given to those that present a clear working-class or Irish nationalist perspective. Although the neighborhood is no longer predominantly Irish, the theatre continues to draw its audience of "Irish immigrants [and] blue-collar American Irish" from throughout New York City. The year 1972 also marked the beginning of Peggy Ings's struggle to convert an old firehouse into a theatre in the mostly Irish-American working-class town of Charlestown, in the Boston metropolitan area. In 1975, with the help of neighborhood people, she realized her dream as the Charlestown Working Theatre opened its first show, *The Lottery*. Since then it has been presenting plays by, among others, Sean O'Casey, Brecht, Lady Gregory, as well as an original play or adaptation every year.

The Irish Rebel Theatre and the Charlestown Working Theatre are different from all the other theatres discussed here because they are much closer to the traditional idea of a commuity theatre. Unlike the other theatres for working-class audiences in the United States today, they are not troupes in the sense of being a relatively permanent group of actors working together over an extended period. Each show is cast anew from the general community at the Charlestown Working Theatre and from "dues-paying performers and tech staff" at the Irish Rebel Theatre. What differentiates these theatres from other community theatres is their perception of and commitment to their audience as a group with distinctly working-class interests and aspirations. Peggy Ings of the Charlestown Working Theatre defines the group's goals as doing "shows about the people in Charlestown, by and for the people of Charlestown," plays that the working-class audience can "reflect on, [and] identify with."

While the Irish Rebel Theatre and the Charlestown Working Theatre have remained essentially working-class community theatres, both Mass Transit and El Teatro de la Esperanza had, by the second half of the decade, felt the need to expand beyond their neighborhood base. In the case of Mass Transit, this expansion of horizon was precipitated by New York City's fiscal crisis. In 1976 the community center where they rehearsed and which provided the base of their community audience had its city funds cut and was forced to close. Although Mass Transit soon affiliated itself with another Bronx community center (on whose executive committee it still sits), the loss of their original home was an initial setback. To make matters even more difficult, White Lightning, the community group whose work had helped attract Mass Transit to the neighborhood in the first place, fell apart. These upheavals led to a major personnel turnover within Mass Transit. Those who remained decided that if they were to survive as a theatre for working-class audiences, they would have to look beyond their neighborhood. "Our focus in terms of audience began to be to seek out whoever could use our performance." At the same time they didn't want to return to the random and disconnected performance patterns of their earliest years.

Their new approach led them to Marge Alberts and Julie Kushner, two dynamic organizers for District 65 (then an independent union, now affiliated with UAW), who were attempting to organize the office workers in the corporate headquarters of J. P. Stevens. Mass Transit, in consultation with the organizers, began to perform skits on the street in front of the J. P. Stevens Building at lunch time that were tied directly to the grievances of the workers and to specific reservations they had about organizing. Although the campaign failed, the value of theatre as an organizing tool had been demonstrated to District 65 which has continued to work with Mass Transit and other theatres.

For Mass Transit the experience was their first with unions, but not their last. In recent years unions and inter-union health and safety organizations have provided the group with a good deal of its audience. While Mass Transit still performs regularly in the northeast Bronx, they have performed in Staten Island, New Jersey, upstate New York, and as far away as Boston for unions and other mass organizations. Continuing to perform short street pieces for unions, they have concentrated since 1976 on creating longer indoor plays that can be used by organizations at fund-raising and consciousness-raising events. Among these longer works since 1977 has been *You've Got Nothing to Lose But Your Job*, about New York's fiscal crisis, and *Hasn't Hurt Me Yet*, a piece on occupational health and safety.

By mid-decade El Teatro de la Esperanza had also shifted from short *actos* to longer pieces best suited for indoor performance. In 1974 El Teatro completed its first full-length work, *Guadalupe*, based on a report by the California State Advisory Committee to the United States Commission on Civil Rights entitled *The Schools of Guadalupe—A Legacy of Educational Oppression*. The play dealt with "the struggles of a small community and their efforts to end brutality in their school, establish bi-lingual education and organize as concerned parents, their subsequent arrest and trials." With the help of the National Endowment for the Arts they toured the show throughout the Southwest for eighteen months, including a performance for the people of the town of Guadalupe itself. That tour established El Teatro de la Esperanza as "an important contributor to the Chicano theatre movement" and set the basis for their continued existence as a touring company.

Their next major work, *La Victima (The Victim*, 1976), concerned itself with "the undocumented workers and how they are pawns of the economic forces in this country," according to the theatre. It followed the story of one family from the time of the Mexican Revolution of 1910 to the present. *La Victima* proved to be immensely popular and established El Teatro de la Esperanza as a leading light in the Chicano theatre movement and among American theatres for working-class audiences. Louis Torres, in *Nuestro* magazine, wrote, "El Teatro de la Esperanza . . . is the hottest new group around—second only to the Campesino in its professional level and in the quality of its artistic development."[8] *La Victima* toured for two years both on college campuses and in community centers and union halls. Jorge Huerta, a founding member of El Teatro, describes its effects on a group of striking Chicano factory workers:

A scene in *La Victima* depicts an Immigration raid during a strike in a factory, and when the group performed this scene for . . . actual strikers, the audience was moved to tears. Thus actual events inspired a dramatic document which in turn encouraged the strikers to continue the struggle. The scene in which the aged mother, Ampáro, convinces her son to join the strike elicited shouts of approval from the workers.[9]

Since 1978 El Teatro de la Esperanza has created three major works: *Hijos, Once a Family*, which centers on the choice faced by a young Chicano worker whether to continue his father's work as a union militant or to become a strike-breaker; *The Octopus*, described by the theatre as "an analysis of the Right[ward] shift in this country in Allegorical-cabaret style"; and *The Tecolote Visions*, a combined production with the Provisional Theatre of Los Angeles.

In 1978 El Teatro de la Esperanza was invited to bring *La Victima* to Europe where it toured Yugoslavia, Poland, and Sweden, making Esperanza the first Chicano theatre and the first American theatre for working-class audiences to perform in the socialist countries of Eastern Europe. In recent years, in addition to touring extensively in California and the Southwest, El Teatro has performed in Mexico at least twice a year and has toured as far north as Minnesota and as far east as New York City, where it appeared most recently as the only Chicano theatre at the Third Latin American Popular Theater Festival at New York's Public Theater. While El Teatro de la Esperanza has continued to serve its home base in Santa Barbara and to create plays about the lives and aspirations of Chicano working people, it has also evolved into a professional touring theatre with a national and international reputation. Among American theatres for working-class audiences, the extensiveness of Esperanza's touring has only been matched by the two pioneer groups, the San Francisco Mime Troupe and the New York Street Theatre Caravan.

The Roadside Theater of Whitesburg, Kentucky, and the Little Flags Theatre Collective of Boston have been touring theatres from the time of their founding early in the decade. Like the founders of other theatres for working-class audiences established in the early seventies, their founders were inspired by the political fervor of the period. Maxine Klein, founder and artistic director of Little Flags, was a college theatre professor who emerged from the radical campus atmosphere of Boston in 1973 to found a theatre dedicated from the beginning to doing plays "about and for working people and people struggling for social change." Herb Smith, one of the founders of the cultural center Appalshop, with which the Roadside Theater is a part, recalls, "It was different times back then; the Vietnam war was going on and we were all a little wild-eyed."[10] Roadside Theater member Dudley Cocke writes, however, that the theatre, founded in 1974, "did not set out for philosophical, theological, or ideological reasons to perform for working-class audiences. It set out to perform for its own people. One characteristic of its people is that they are, by and large, 'working class.' "

Whatever its motivation, the Roadside Theater has been touring, in a tent, "the hollows, coal camps, and small farming communities" of the region since 1976. Their plays are based on "the area's oral history and heritage of traditional tales, many of which deal with the transformation of Appalachia's economy from subsistence farming to industrial mining." In addition to performing in the mountains, the Roadside Theater also visits the Appalachian communities in the industrial cities of the Midwest, performing for thousands of workers and their families who migrated from the mountains in search of work over the last three decades. Michael V. Perri reports in the weekly, *In These Times*,

A woman in one of Chicago's Appalachian ghettos . . . broke down and cried after seeing [the Roadside Theater's play] *Red Fox/Second Hangin'*. She told Roadside Manager Dudley Cocke that she had always been ashamed of the way her daddy talked until she heard actors [Don] Baker, Gary Slemp, and Frankie Taylor tell the story of "Doc" Taylor who was condemned by a judge eager to bring the mining companies' law and order to the mountains even if it meant sacrificing justice and hanging an innocent man.[11]

The Roadside Theater has been affiliated since its inception with Appalshop, an Appalachian cultural center that also includes Appalshop Films, which has produced thirty-six films since 1969; June Appal Recordings, which records both the traditional and new music of the region; Mountain Photography Workshop; and Headwaters Television, a weekly half-hour people's television program that is broadcast in prime time over NBC affiliate WKYH in Hazard, Kentucky. With a combined annual budget of almost one million dollars, Appalshop is a unique cultural institution that has played an important role in making theatre, film, TV, music, and photography for working-class audiences available in the southern Appalachians.

While the Roadside Theater is concerned with a specific geographical and cultural constituency, the Little Flags Theatre Collective has, like the San Francisco Mime Troupe and the New York Street Theatre Caravan, aspired to become a national theatre for working-class audiences. Founded in 1973 by Maxine Klein and her composer husband, James Oestereich, Little Flags drew its actors from the radical campus communities of the Boston area. During their first few years, Klein recalls, "All it did was turn over; so I didn't know if we would survive because you can't go back and re-do every thing every year. But gradually the core began to form." That core evolved in the context of almost constant touring. Klein says proudly that "one hundred percent" of their shows are toured. Little Flags neither has nor aspires to a permanent rehearsal or performance space, preferring "to perform in as many different neighborhoods as possible." They do, however, make a point of returning every year for a run at the Charlestown Working Theatre, whose founder, Peggy Ings, often performs with Little Flags. Most of their performances are in the Boston area, although they do tour extensively throughout New England and northern New York. They have also toured in the Southeast and Midwest and have even appeared as far west as Oregon.

Like the San Francisco Mime Troupe, Little Flags found much of its initial support on college campuses and among the left community in general. Its early plays reflect this constituency. Among the earliest of the shows they toured were David Hare's *Fanshen*, based on William Hinton's account of the transformation from feudalism to socialism of a small Chinese village, and *Tania*, an original play that tells the story of a young East German woman who moves to Cuba to help with socialist construction, becomes politically and romantically involved with Che Guevera, moves throughout Latin America as a spy for the revolutionaries, and is finally martyred along with Che in the mountains of Bolivia.

With *The Furies of Mother Jones* (1977), about Mary "Mother" Jones, the famous American union organizer of the late nineteenth and early twentieth centuries, Little Flags began to appeal to a broader working-class audience. Moving back and forth between Mother Jones at the turn of the century and the struggle to oust Tony Boyle from the United Mine Workers presidency in the late 1960s, the play proved popular both among leftists and trade unionists. For example, when performed for striking coal miners from Sterns, Kentucky, *The Furies of Mother Jones* provoked comments from the strikers such as "It was like being in the mines. I knew exactly what you were doing. I'd sure love my dad to see this play." "That's just the way it is, just exactly. Tonight I saw my life on that stage."[12]

The Furies of Mother Jones proved to be Little Flag's most popular play to date, and since its production their plays have continued to deal directly with the history and struggles of America's working people. Accompanying this change in content, the number of their performances for, and support from, the unions and their memberships has steadily increased. Among the unions they have performed for in the Boston area are Local 880, Service Employees International Union (SEIU); Local 470 of the American Federation of State, County and Municipal Employees (AFSCME); District 65 (Boston University Clerical Workers); and Local 426, State Hospital Workers. On the national level they have worked with the International Brotherhood of Electrical Workers (IBEW) and the United Mine Workers (UMW).

All of the theatres for working-class audiences that emerged in the early seventies were initially inspired, directly or indirectly, by the campus-based upheavals of the late sixties and early seventies. Unlike numerous other politically radical theatres of the period, they turned, more or less rapidly, to the working class for the content of their scripts and for an audience. All of them, with the exception of Little Flags, attempted at first to reach the working class through community and neighborhood organizations and to root themselves in a particular geographic or cultural community. Two of them, the Irish Rebel Theatre and the Charlestown Working Theatre, have taken on the form of traditional community theatres. For the others, the trend in the second half of the decade was to seek an audience beyond their immediate community and to play for whichever working-class audience could "use" their performance. This has resulted in an increased tendency toward touring and performing for unions. While Little Flags toured from their inception, they initially relied on the campus-based left-wing commuity that existed at the time. Since 1977, they too have worked more extensively and consistently with the trade union movement. Jon Weissman of the Massachusetts Organization to Repeal the Taft-Hartley Act, a multi-union group, wrote to tell Little Flags after a show what the theatre had done for them:

"The people rallying to revive the labor movement are also seeking a new kind of "culture"—a linking of today's working-class demands, daily life, and history. And a culture that puts the little people on center stage."[13]

The theatres for working-class audiences advanced this "new kind of culture" in the early seventies, and, along with those that were to follow later in the decade, are attempting to articulate it in the community centers, union halls, and streets across the nation.

HISTORY III: THE LATE SEVENTIES AND EARLY EIGHTIES

The theatres that have emerged since 1976 have been founded with the clear intent of locating themselves in the working class. Unlike their predecessors earlier in the decade, these theatres did not have a significant student or countercultural movement to use as a base or to react against. The student movement was in sharp numerical decline; most of the radicals who remained active had adopted a socialist perspective of one variety or another and were moving, through a combination of natural attrition and conscious political choice, from the academy to the working class, becoming involved in trade-union and other work-place organizing. This same period was marked by the first protracted overall decline in the living standards of American workers since the depression of the 1930s, which forced the trade unions and their membership into a more active political role. Within the context of this combination of factors the emergence and continued existence of theatres for working-class audiences in the late 1970s can be best understood.

The Iron Clad Agreement was founded in Pittsburgh in 1976 by Julia Swoyer and Wilson Hutton, both of whom left promising academic careers at Carnegie-Mellon University to devote themselves to the building of theatre for working-class audiences. From the beginning, the Iron Clad Agreement sought the realization not only of what it terms "the populist artistic idea" of bringing plays about work and industrial history to a working-class audience but also of creating "a situation in which all of us were employed full-time at equal salary levels." They achieved this within a year and a half. The Iron Clad's ability to pay its actors a living wage and to commission playwrights and songwriters and pay them professional fees indicates a level of financial viability and stability that might well be envied by every other theatre for working-class audiences in the United States today. Its production history is equally impressive: in the first five years of its existence, the Iron Clad Agreement produced over thirty original plays for a steadily increasing audience. During the 1979–1980 season, it produced five plays with a total of 158 performances for approximately 15,000 people. In 1980–1981, it staged seven new plays for 180 performances for about 30,000 people.

There are several reasons for their success. To start, the company has always been small, rarely exceeding four performers at a time. Over the last six years, a total of twelve actors have moved in and out of the company. Second, the Pittsburgh area is essentially a one-industry town. Once the theatre had established a working relationship with the United Steel Workers on the international, district, local, and rank-and-file levels, it had in fact established a working relationship with the area's labor movement. Many of their performance schedules refer to performances at "United Steel Workers, Local 1219, Braddock, Penn.," "United Steel Workers, Local 1397, Homestead, Penn.," and so on. In addition, the Iron Clad Agreement has held "special steelworker performances" at reduced prices; a leaflet for one such performance exhorts union members to "come in force!"[14]

The general blue-collar nature of the Pittsburgh area makes plays about labor history and industrialization of interest to the area's churches, colleges, town councils, and community organizations. In the public schools, in which labor history is not taught, there has been a great interest among teachers and students in the Iron Clad's plays. The theatre has performed in forty-six school districts in western Pennsylvania over the years. The Iron Clad Agreement's close association with *The Millhunk Herald*, an independent newspaper with a working-class readership edited by Larry Evans, also played an important role in establishing the visibility and reputation of the theatre for Pittsburgh area workers and others.

Julia Swoyer's skill as a fund raiser and her location within the mainstream of the arts establishment of western Pennsylvania should not be discounted as a contributing factor in the company's financial stability. Before founding the Iron Clad Agreement, Swoyer was a drama critic for *The Pittsburgh Forum* and was selected as a critic fellow to the National Critic's Institute at the Eugene O'Neill Theatre Center. She served on the Theatre Advisory Panel for the Pennsylvania Council on the Arts, as literary adviser for the Pittsburgh Public Theatre, and as a production associate for the segment on Andrew Carnegie in the nationally televised series, *American Life Style*. These credentials and connections undoubtedly contributed to the Iron Clad Agreement's ability to secure funding from sources ranging from the United Steel Workers to the United States Steel Corporation, as well as government and private foundations.

The generally nonpolemical content of their plays may also have helped them to secure broad-based financial support. The Iron Clad Agreement describes its areas of concern as exploring "the age of America's industrial revolution—its inventors, industrialists, workers, feminists and labor leaders." In addition to plays about workers and labor struggles, they have also done plays about Henry Ford and Thomas Edison. These plays were not, however, homages to the inventors but dramatic examinations of how their inventions and industrial innovations affected the work and lives of everyday Americans. Whatever the subject of the play, the Iron Clad Agreement presents its audience with information on labor history and positive images of themselves as industrial workers that they would not otherwise see. Their funding tactics have allowed them to build a full-time professional theatre company and bring plays on labor history and worker's concerns to literally tens of thousands of working people in western Pennsylvania and in "steel and textile towns throughout the eastern and southern United States."

For most of its history, the Iron Clad Agreeement has been solidly based in the steel country of western Pennsylvania. They have also performed as far north as Boston and as far west as St. Louis for festivals and other special events. In the summer of 1979, they toured *My Dear Sisters*, a play about Angelina and Sara Grimke. The Grimke sisters were abolitionists and women's rights activists who were driven from their home state of South Carolina in the 1820s.

In the autumn of 1981, the Iron Clad Agreement moved from Pittsburgh to New York City and reorganized itself "from a traveling theatre group to a production company of theatre, film, and television with national focus."[15] The Iron Clad Agreement, like Appalshop of Whitesburg, Kentucky, intends to produce programs in various media, but on a national rather than a regional scale. Among their hopes for the future are "film/video, television, cable, radio and print." They have already produced *Thread/Work*, a half-hour film documentary about the closing of a textile mill in Newberry, South Carolina. It has been broadcast by educational television in South Carolina and is being used as an organizing tool by the Amalgamated Clothing and Textile Workers Union. In addition, they are currently marketing five television treatments. They do not, however, intend to give up theatre. In fact, their first project as a "program producing entity" was a tour of England's industrial midlands with a live theatre piece, *Virgins and Dynamos, or How Many Robber Barons Does It Take to Screw in a Lightbulb?*, described as "a vaudeville in the style of the Marxes— Groucho and Karl."[16] This tour was part of an exchange program Iron Clad initiated with the Major Road theatre of Yorkshire, England, which resulted in further artistic collaboration and personnel exchange. Tom Hearn of the Iron Clad Agreement recently directed Major Road's *Echoes from the Valley*, an oral-history project based on textile workers' reminiscences of mill life in the Aire River Valley. The Iron Clad Agreement planned to present this production on tour in the United States in textile regions in South Carolina and Connecticut in 1984. While it is still too early to assess the success of the Iron Clad's expansion, if successful, it could be a major institutional boost to the development of working-class culture in the United States.

In 1977, a year after the Iron Clad Agreement had begun its work in Pittsburgh, two other theatres for working-class audiences were founded, one in New York City and the other in South Dakota. In New York, two former members of the San Francisco Mime Troupe, Denny Partridge and Steve Friedman, founded the Modern Times Theatre. Their first season was at the School for Marxist Education, a nonaccredited school that offers courses in history and Marxist theory and provides a forum for various Marxist groups to discuss their differences. The first season included *Two by Brecht* (their adaptations of *The Unseemly Old Lady* and *The Exception and the Rule*); Tillie Olsen's *Tell Me a Riddle*; and their first original work, *The Last Day*, "a dramatized oral history of the 10,000 person demonstration in Union Square the day the Rosenbergs were executed." *The Last Day* was performed at the Elizabeth Irwin High School before thousands of people commemorating the twenty-fifth anniversary of the Rosenbergs' deaths. As the content and context of this first season indicates, Modern Times began as a theatre for the left and reached the working class only to the extent that the left was beginning to build a base among New York's poor and working people. It has continued to fulfill the function of a professional theatre for the left in New York, while attempting to reach out to the city's and, more recently, the nation's working class.

The Dakota Theatre Caravan faced no such dichotomy. The left in South Dakota was not large enough to support a theatre group so the troupe went directly to the people it wished to perform for: the farmers and rural working people of South Dakota. It was founded by six people (five actors and a musician) in the summer of 1977 under the leadership of Doug Paterson. Paterson, a native of South Dakota, was, at the time, a tenured theatre professor at Willamette University in Salem, Oregon. He wanted to create theatre for and about the people of his home state. For their first play, the Theatre Caravan interviewed dozens of South Dakota townspeople, creating a drama called *Dakota Roads: The Story of a Prairie Family* which traced five generations of a South Dakota family, "hypothetical, but entirely typical," from Europe in 1856 to South Dakota in 1977. It took them less than five weeks to create the play, which they then performed twenty-two times in twenty towns throughout the state in twenty-seven days. The following summer, they remounted the same show and toured twenty-six more towns for a total of forty performances in forty-four days. The popularity of these performances and the enthusiasm of the South Dakota Arts Council led them by 1979 to quit their jobs and attempt to become a full-time company.

Back in New York, Modern Times Theatre was also achieving relatively rapid success. In their second year, they produced *Homeland* by actor-playwright Steve Friedman and exiled South African playwright Selailo Maredi, a "comedy about South Africa and the U.S.A." It was "performed all over New York City and the northeast," received five Audelco (black off-Broadway) nominations and three Villager Awards. It ran off-Broadway for sixteen weeks to much critical acclaim. *The Village Voice*, for example, called it "a biting comedy about race relations . . . hilarious, delightful."[17]

The following year (1979), building on the reputation and audience they had established with *Homeland*, Modern Times joined with the New York Street Theatre Caravan and the (New York) Labor Theater to form the Shared Season, which they described as "a place for leftist theatre in N.Y.C. at St. Peter's Hall in Chelsea." The three theatres pooled their mailing lists, shared office and administrative duties, and alternated shows in the performance space. The Shared Season lasted for four years and did much to consolidate the New York audience for all three troupes and, according to Denny Partridge of Modern Times, was "a source of both great comraderie and increased audience revenue." In 1983, however, St. Peter's Church raised the rent significantly, making the space unaffordable to the three theatres, which, while retaining close ties, went their own ways.

At this point, some mention should be made of the Labor Theater, although they did not respond to the questionnaire. They have been a significant force among theatres for working-class audiences in the New York City area during the later seventies and early eighties. They say of themselves, "We aim to bring relevant theater to working people, whose lives we portray."[18] The Labor Theater has strong ties with a number of unions,[19] and often tours under union auspices. Essentially a two-person operation of husband and wife, Chuck Portz and Bette Craig, the Labor Theater casts each show anew and is thus not a troupe of actors working together over an extended period of time as are most of the theatres discussed here. They have been able to attract relatively well-known actors such as Rip Torn and have produced for the first time in the United States such important English working-class scripts as J. Bentley Campbell's *Ragged Trousered Philanthropists* and an adaptation of John McGrath's *Yobbo Nowt*. They have also produced important American plays that otherwise would not have found a place on the American stage, including *The Wobblies* by Stewart Bird and Peter Robilotta and *The Dodo Bird* by former United Electrical Workers organizer and neglected American playwright, Emanuel Fried. In 1983 they produced a film, *Staus* starring Theodore Bikel, that explored the problems faced by a retired blue-collar worker. Finally, the Labor Theater played a catalytic role in bringing the three theatres together into the Shared Season.[20]

While the Labor Theater, the New York Street Theatre Caravan, and the Modern Times Theatre were establishing the Shared Season in New York, the Dakota Theatre Caravan was starting its first year as a full-time professional troupe. Doug Paterson writes, "We resigned our jobs . . . and hit the road with a new play in the fall of 1979 called *Dusting Off the 30s*." They toured *Dusting* and *Dakota Roads* throughout the 1979–1980 season, taking them to Minneapolis–St. Paul, Los Angeles, Bakersfield, San Francisco, and Eugene and Salem, Oregon, in addition to "blanketing the South Dakota area." The audience and critical response wherever they performed were enthusiastic. However, at the beginning of their second full-time year, they decided not to continue year-round "because most of us had life plans we'd shelved to do this work that we were missing, and because we kept being behind in management." They continued full-time until January 1981, with *Dusting* and a new show for schools called *Theatricks!*, at which point they "headed for more regular jobs."

The Dakota Theatre Caravan has continued to create and tour a new play for the rural population of South Dakota each summer, bringing plays about rural working life to the independent farmers, ranch and farmhands and other working people of the Great Plains. During the rest of the year, Doug Paterson teaches at the University of Nebraska at Omaha where he is developing "a focus area" in "people's theatre" in the graduate program in theatre and playing an active role in encouraging and coordinating alternative theatres throughout the upper Midwest.

Modern Times Theatre's first year with the Shared Season marked a major step for the group in terms of reaching a working-class audience. Turning to the tenants' organizations in the Chelsea area, where St. Peter's Hall is located, to gather background for their next play, the theatre produced *The Eight Million*, penned by Steve Friedman. It is the story of a group of tenants who refused to be evicted when their landlord tried to get rid of them so that he could jack up the rent for a new set of tenants. It reflected, as Modern Times says, "the housing horrors" that were happening all over Manhattan as landlords, encouraged by city tax policies, "gentrified" working-class neighborhoods. Not only did *The Eight Million* enjoy a successful run at St. Peter's, where it played for a primarily leftist audience, it also toured, through the New York City Department of Culture and the United Neighborhood Houses of New York, to community centers, settlement houses, and tenant union meetings throughout New York City.

Their next work, *The Bread and Roses Play*, again by Steve Friedman, which opened in late 1980, was even more successful in reaching a working-class audience. *The Bread and Roses Play* was the first of their pieces to deal directly with the labor movement. It is a love story set against the background of the famous Lawrence, Massachusetts, textile stike of 1912, a strike that succeeded in uniting thousands of immigrant workers speaking dozens of languages, many of them women, under the leadership of the radical Industrial Workers of the World (IWW). Dealing as it does with labor history and a strike situation, it is not surprising that *The Bread and Roses Play* generated more interest among trade unionists than any Modern Times play to date. Modern Times relates, "We performed for many labor unions and women's groups as well as a general audience." Among the general audience were junior high school students throughout Harlem and the South Bronx. Perhaps the most interesting performance of the piece was in Lawrence itself where they did the play for an audience of 1,800, including veterans of the strike and many children and grandchildren of the strikers.

Modern Times followed in early 1982 with *Hibakusha* by Steve Friedman. *Hibakusha* is also a love story, this time between two survivors of the bombing of Hiroshima. A remarkably powerful and moving piece that avoids the sentimentality that is the danger of such a subject, *Hibakusha* continues Modern Times' practice of creating scripts of unusual complexity in structure and character, an accomplishment for which actor-playwright Steve Friedman deserves much credit.

Modern Times had been able to support three of its members full-time since 1981, and in 1983 the theatre was able to become a "full-time, year round collective" of five actors and director Denny Partridge. This transformation came about when the Shared Season broke up and Modern Times increased its touring to a full-year, nationwide activity. Between January and July of 1983, they logged 18,000 miles, playing primarily in small cities (such as Ames, Iowa; Lincoln, Nebraska; Louisville, Kentucky; and Olympia, Washington) for low fees. Their audiences in these cities have been, by their estimate, 90 percent working class. Although they are on the road most of the time, since their eviction from St. Peter's, the troupe has moved its base of operations to the Lincoln Houses, a low-income housing project on New York City's west side, where they continue to build a production record and repertory that is truly outstanding among contemporary theatres for the working class.

Three of the most recently formed groups, though working in different cities (Boston, New York, and Washington, D.C.), have a number of important attributes in common. Each either works with a specific segment of the working-class population or performs primarily in specific working-class situations or both. Each places great emphasis on their theatre as an organizing tool. And finally, because of their relative newness or their political choices, none of the groups formed since 1978 is yet able to earn even a partial living for their members. These groups are Word of Mouth Productions, from the Boston area, Everyday Theatre in Washington, D.C., and Workers' Stage from New York City.

Word of Mouth Productions (WOMP) is an all-woman "political theatre collective" that is "attempting to reach a working-class audience, primarily women." They write, "We are indebted to all the women workers who have come before us—whose stories have rarely been told—and to their strength, ability to survive and courage to challenge their conditions."[21] Although there are a good number of feminist theatres in the United States today, relatively few are aimed primarily at working-class women or deal with specifically working-class concerns. Word of Mouth Productions is a leader in this regard. Others also concerned with working-class women include At the Foot of the Mountain (Minneapolis), Spiderwoman Theater (New York City), and Wallflower Order (Boston), a modern-dance troupe.

Susan Eisenberg founded Word of Mouth Productions in 1978 with a one-woman show, *Calamity Jane! Tales of a Preacher's Daughter Who Ran Away From Home First Chance She Got*. Eisenberg, who at the time was a five-year veteran of the left-wing and feminist theatres of Boston, used the solo piece "as a means of building an ensemble that would function as a political theatre collective." Through *Calamity Jane* and a series of workshops, she built Word of Mouth into a four-woman collective that in the fall of 1979 opened *Why Don't You Find a Rich Guy and Marry Him?*, which they describe as "a musical play about the lives and history of working women." They toured *Rich Guy* throughout the Boston area and to New York City for a year. In 1981, with the collective's membership up to five, they began work on their third major production, *We're All Gonna Die Sometime Anyway*, a play about occupational health and safety.

All of the members of Word of Mouth work in other jobs, and among them they are active members in the International Brotherhood of Electrical Workers, the United Steel Workers, the Massachusetts Teachers Association, and City

Life/Vida Urbana, a Boston-based socialist organization. Their roots in the working-class organizations of the area are reflected in the groups that have sponsored their performances which include "striking school bus drivers; workers at City Hospital organizing around daycare; a New Hampshire College program for older women returning to school; a program for teenage mothers; . . . [and] the Dorchester Women's Committee, a working-class community group that sponsors an annual International Women's Day event." The fact that its members must work outside the theatre is seen by Word of Mouth as having a positive affect on its ability to reach the audience it is aiming at, since they are free to make political, rather than financial, choices about their performances.

Whereas Word of Mouth sees its primary focus as working women, the Everyday Theatre of Washington, D.C., plays to working-class tenants. Like Word of Mouth, the nine members of the Everyday Theatre are directly involved in the struggles of their constituency as activists in the tenants'-rights movement in the D.C. area. Their first show, *The Arcade*, grew out of a workshop led by artistic director Susie Solf in 1979. Like Modern Times Theatre's *The Eight Million, The Arcade* was the story of a group of tenants caught up in the gentrification process. They performed the show free at benefits for tenant groups throughout Washington for a year. In that year, as might be expected, the Everyday Theatre established a strong base among the city's tenant groups. Since then they have created and toured two other full-length plays related to tenant struggles: *Rent Strike*, which was "based on real life stories" from the hard-hit Columbia Heights section of D.C., and *Ghost Story*, a history play about the "urban renewal" of southwest Washington in the 1950s. Both shows were based on interviews and discussions with the people actually involved. The Everyday Theatre has, by its own account, been very successful in reaching their intended audience with the consequence that "each performance is also a community education project." In addition to their tenant shows, the Everyday Theatre has also produced two Brecht plays and *The Arrest*, an original work written by theatre member Nicki Burton. They are currently working on a piece about crime and its effects on working and poor people.

Workers' Stage of New York City doesn't restrict itself to a particular segment of the working class but is very specific about the type of situation it chooses to work in. For the most part, they perform for workers engaged in collective action to improve their lives, defining such "struggle situations" as "strikes, contract negotiations, organizing drives, etc." They feel that "such situations provide the most fertile environment for interacting with the audiences' lives and connecting specific experiences to broader political concepts." Although Workers' Stage emphasizes that it will perform "for any organization based in the working-class and engaged in struggle to improve the lives of its members," the vast majority of its work has been for trade unions. In general, its contacts with the unions have been initiated at the rank-and-file and "hands on" organizer level.

Emerging from a political play-reading group in the early months of 1980,[22]

Workers' Stage began by holding a series of workshops in which they experimented with "finding dramatic images to illustrate and explain basic political and economic concepts such as: class struggle, surplus value, real wages, relative impoverishment, stagflation and the nature of the state." Within a few months, they had their first chance to perform for an audience. They write:

Through a labor organizer contact, our first play was for a shop of garment workers who were on strike and organizing into the I.L.G.W.U. We performed a series of three skits on the street for the picket line. The skits were based on real incidents and people (characters) that we learned of in discussion with the workers themselves. The skits were performed at important points in the strike about two weeks apart.

These performances in the garment center established two major precedents for Workers' Stage. First was the practice of creating plays from the direct experiences, grievances, and demands of their audience. All of their work begins with extensive discussions with the organizers and rank and filers involved in the particular struggle, and each skit is specific to the audience it is performed for. The second precedent was the close cooperation among the union organizer, the strike committee, and the theatre. They write that they "strive to perform for situations in which political organizers with roots in the specific audience are involved. The organizers can then utilize the play to draw broader political conclusions and refer back to the play in future struggles." The fact that in its three years of existence it has been asked back to perform a second or third time by three separate unions speaks to the success of this ongoing relationship with the organizers and other activists.

Since its first performances in the garment center, Workers' Stage has performed for a wide variety of workers throughout the New York City metropolitan area, creating shows ranging from ten to forty minutes for, among others, the Columbia University Local of District 65; the Staff Association of the National Council of Churches; the Committee for Abortion Rights and Against Sterilization Abuse; the Fur, Leather and Machine Workers Union; the United Auto Workers in conjunction with an organizing drive in Union City, New Jersey; and the Chinese Workers and Staff Association, a group based in New York's Chinatown that has played a pivotal role in the organization of New York's Chinese restaurant workers into an independent union.

Workers' Stage has reached its audience almost exclusively through word of mouth among labor activists in the New York area. Growing from four people in 1980 to a core group of seven, Workers' Stage has shown a remarkable stability of membership. Its four founders are still active, and no one who has joined the core group has ever left, despite the fact that financially the group can barely meet expenses and all of its members must work outside of the theatre. When it began in 1980, Workers' Stage had to perform free to prove in practice the value of their work to the labor movement; today they receive honoraria of up to $250 per show. Although this is still providing little more than enough to mount the next show, it does indicate the beginning of a recognition on the part of trade unions and other workers' organizations of the value that theatre can provide for its members involved in struggle.

In reading the letters Workers' Stage has received from the unions it has performed for, one is struck by the references to the theatre's value as an organizing tool and morale booster. The organizing committee of the Columbia Local of District 65, for example, which was organizing clerical workers at Columbia University, wrote to Workers' Stage concerning a skit the theatre performed eight times at various points on campus: "It was hilarious, and proved a very effective organizing tool. It reached a remarkable number of Columbia workers and served as a springboard for union supporters to talk over the issues with other workers who saw the play. Even those who didn't see the show were not unaffected, as it was the talk of the Support Staff for at least a week."[23]

Word of Mouth Productions, the Everyday Theatre, and Workers' Stage— the newest of the existing theatres for working-class audiences—have important things in common. They are poor, specific in determining their intended audience, and integrated by work, community, and organizational ties to that audience; and they all emphasize the *organizing* function of their theatre. Within their limited goals, they have been remarkably successful in reaching and motivating their working-class spectators.

HISTORY IV: SUMMARY

Aside from the San Francisco Mime Troupe and the New York Street Theatre Caravan, all of America's existing theatres for working-class audiences have emerged in the 1970s and the early years of the 1980s. There never was an explosion of such groups. Instead, they have appeared in a relatively steady trickle over the last thirteen years until they now number at least thirty-two nationwide.

Broadly speaking, there are significant differences between theatres founded in the first half of the 1970s and those founded after that. The older troupes developed within the antiwar and countercultural movements. What differentiated them from the scores of other politically or aesthetically radical troupes of the time were their attempts to create and perform plays for working people. The theatres founded since the middle of the decade have developed in the context of a diminished left whose center of gravity was shifting from the campuses to the working class. Generally, these younger groups were founded with the intent of performing for and about a working-class audience and have had relatively rapid success in reaching this group.

A few of the groups (San Francisco Mime Troupe, Little Flags Theatre Collective, and Modern Times Theatre) began by performing primarily for left-wing audiences which, in addition to radical workers, has included a large proportion of students, intellectuals, and professionals. Most of the other groups have located their theatre work more directly within the working-class rank and file. All three groups have made progress in broadening the working-class base of their audiences. In this regard, it should be noted that the distinction between a left and a working-class audience is not always clear-cut, particularly in the last five years as former campus radicals have become integrated into the working-class population. The audience for almost all of the troupes discussed contains some degree of crossover. The only exceptions are the Dakota Theatre Caravan and the Roadside Theater which perform where there is virtually no left-wing community.

The channels used by the troupes to reach the working class have varied. In the early seventies, the major channel was the community center. Mass Transit, El Teatro de la Esperanza, the Irish Rebel Theatre and the Charlestown Working Theatre, all founded before 1975, used community centers in working-class neighborhoods in their early years. The latter two now function as community theatres. Community centers have also been a major place of performance for groups that toured nationally. Tenant unions, too, became an important channel for several troupes including the Mass Transit Street Theatre, the Everday Theatre, and, to a lesser extent, the Modern Times Theatre. The trend in the last five years has been toward the major mass organizations of the working class: the trade unions. Unions, of course, have provided audiences for working-class theatres for over a hundred years. In the sixties and early seventies, however, any relationship between theatres and unions tended to be short-lived and unique. The New York Street Theatre Caravan did its first performances for a union in 1970. The Labor Theatre played a pioneer role in this regard by building a financial and audience base with the unions. Since the mid-seventies, most of the theatres have been performing with increasing frequency for union audiences. Among the troupes that now cite the unions as a major part of their audience are Mass Transit, Little Flags, the New York Street Theatre Caravan, the Iron Clad Agreement, and, of course, the Labor Theatre and Workers' Stage, both of whom perform primarily for union members.

A final useful distinction is geographical: between those troupes that function on a national or regional level and those that work within a more limited area. The San Francisco Mime Troupe, the New York Street Theatre Caravan, El Teatro de la Esperanza, and the Iron Clad Agreement tour extensively. The Little Flags Theatre Collective also has national touring aspirations but so far has toured primarily in its home region. The Roadside Theatre and the Dakota Theatre Caravan tour continually, but they are primarily concerned with their respective regions. Most of the other groups perform within a metropolitan area.

In discussing the groups' histories, I have only been able to refer in passing to their politics, finances, internal organization, creative processes, and aesthetics. To examine these effectively, I must now move from historical description to comparative analysis.

POLITICS

Aside from the nature of the audience they perform for, the theatres discussed here have another important factor in common: strong political convictions. In fact, these political convictions inform and, in large part, motivate their work and draw these theatre companies to the working class. Three political-artistic assumptions run through the responses of the fourteen theatres who answered the questionnaire: (1) the American working class is bereft of a culture that gives them a positive image of themselves or that reflects their history, needs, and aspirations; (2) the working class should have more economic and political power in our country; and (3) culture in general, and live theatre in particular, can play an important role in the process of empowering the working class.

The New York Street Theatre Caravan writes that its "commitment has always been to bring theatre of the highest quality to those not included in the country's mainstream: the poor and dispossessed, and the working people." Obviously, the Caravan and the other theatres don't intend to bring just any theatre to the "poor and dispossessed." Their production histories prove this. The few theatres, such as the Charlestown Working Theatre and the Irish Rebel Theatre, that have drawn from the established dramatic repertory have produced scripts by playwrights who sided with the working class in the political struggles of their own countries—playwrights like O'Casey and Brecht. However, the vast majority of the contemporary theatres for working-class audiences have created new plays for and about the contemporary American working class. They view their work not so much as the "bringing" of culture to the working class but more as a collaborative process of creation with their audience. Workers' Stage writes, "We want to work with and for people with limited access to 'culture.' By this we mean limited both in creating culture and in experiencing culture that reflects them 'realistically,' that is, their *real* interests and experience." Most of the troupes see the theatre thus created not merely as an entertainment, or even as education in the static sense of providing the audience with information, but as a dynamic interaction between troupe and audience that is both a cultural and political experience. The Everyday Theatre writes:

People are confused about what they can do. Many feel helpless and resign themselves to fate, not knowing that there are realistic actions they can take to have greater control over the situation. Everyday Theatre seeks to counter the feelings of insignificance and helplessness by dramatizing the problem and affirming that their feelings *are* important and should be dealt with. . . . What runs through all our plays is our desire to help people empower themselves.[24]

This desire to create theatre that will help the audience "empower" themselves runs explicitly or implicitly through the responses of most of the theatres. For some, this empowering process is indirect. It is viewed in terms of providing ideas or information that will enable the working-class audience to better understand and act in its own interests. The Iron Clad Agreement views itself as "a platform for ideas, in which many pieces of evidence are presented to an audience in an historical context and in an entertaining format." The Irish Rebel Theatre writes, "Our goal is to produce original work which will reflect the Irish experience in political/cultural terms."

For many of the troupes, however, the empowering function of their work is more direct. They view empowerment as a process of organization, and they believe, or at least hope, that their theatre work can play a role in helping to organize their audience. The view that theatre can and should play an organizing function vis-à-vis its audience is perhaps most forcefully expressed by Lynn Pyle of Mass Transit:

We feel a unity around the fact that [empowerment] needs to happen through organization, that it doesn't happen through individuals changing themselves. It takes working together and figuring out how to work together. That is central at this point: for us to develop the ability to organize ourselves and work together. I think that's what our focus is at this point. We see culture as a way of giving support to those kinds of changes.

While there appears to be widespread consensus among the groups on the need to create a positive working-class culture and on the contribution such a culture can make in empowering and organizing the working class, the groups are far less unified or specific about the "kinds of changes" needed and about what the working class is being organized *for*. Since socialist theory in general and Marxism in particular maintain that working-class power is essential for the economic, social, and cultural advance of humankind, it might be expected that socialist and Marxist theory has had a significant impact on most contemporary theatres for working-class audiences. Yet only two groups explicitly identify themselves as socialist. Workers' Stage writes that its members share "a Socialist perspective and Marxist analysis," while the San Francisco Mime Troupe describes itself as "independent socialist" in political orientation. A third troupe, the Modern Times Theatre, while not referring to its political perspective as a group, does describe its membership as being made up of "some left-wing social democrats, some anarchists, always anti-capitalist." The founders of two other groups identified themselves as socialists in the questionnaire or in the course of an interview but made a point of emphasizing that their political perspective was not necessarily shared by other members of the troupe and that it was not a basis for unity for the theatre. Another two troupes, while declining to label their ideological perspective, described their political unity in a way that might easily be interpreted as socialist. Mass Transit writes, "We're an organization that believes that things have to change in some very significant ways. Decisions made in this country are based on property . . . and we think they shouldn't be. And that means the system has to be changed because the system that we have, in effect, works on that principle." The Little Flags Theatre Collective states, quite concisely, "The political notion that is shared by all of the theatre [is] 'Workers deserve to control that which they produce.' That's about as far as our politics go."

That's quite a bit farther than many of the other troupes go, however. The Charlestown Working Theatre sidesteps the question, describing its politics as doing "shows about the people in Charlestown, by and for the people of Charlestown." The Roadside Theater sums up its political perspective as "a belief in democracy." The Iron Clad Agreement labels itself "populist," a term that has been open to highly divergent interpretations in the twentieth century. The Irish Rebel Theatre describes itself as "left-rationalist," and the Everyday Theatre uses the term "radical." Three of the troupes choose to describe their politics in terms of a series of specific issues or ideals rather than an overall ideology. The New York Street Theatre Caravan writes, "We prefer to have our stand identified by what our pieces say. For instance, our skits reveal that we are pro-labor and anti-nuclear, that we are feminist and anti-racist. That we connect the rise in crime to unemployment. Our play *Molly Maguire* connected us with the rebellion of the Northern Irish against the British." They then go on to describe the political content of a number of their other major works. Along the same lines, Word of Mouth Productions writes, "We are committed to ending oppression based on class, race, sex, age, and sexual preference." The Dakota Theatre Caravan, in a strikingly similar formulation, explains its politics as follows, "We all agree, and all who join must agree, that the company will be non-ageist, -sexist, -racist, -elitist in personal relationships, professional work, work in the play, and in relationships with all people encountered during touring."

Whatever the differences in the political self-definitions offered by the troupes, the questionnaire and the interviews indicated a high level of political sophistication among virtually all of the theatres and the belief that their theatrical work is political as well as artistic activity. Implicitly or explicitly, most made it clear that they would agree with Mass Transit's statement that "everyone in the group sees the theatre as their political work." Further, the vast majority of troupes—nine out of fourteen (with one, Little Flags, refusing to respond)— report that at least some of their members are involved in other working-class organizations as well (trade unions, tenant unions, community centers, and political organizations of various sorts). Given the deep political convictions and the concern with empowering and organizing the working class expressed by most of the groups, such involvement is not surprising.

Of the four troupes whose members appear not to be involved in other working-class organizations, three (the New York Street Theatre Caravan, the San Francisco Mime Troupe, and the Dakota Theatre Caravan) tour extensively, a factor that may mediate against other commitments. The fourth exception is the Modern Times Theatre. Among the nine troupes who report other organizational involvement for their members, the levels of involvement vary considerably, from 100 percent to 10 percent. The vast majority of these extra-theatre political commitments are in single- or multi-issue reform organizations (i.e., trade unions, tenant unions, liberation-support groups). All are concerned with the creation of a distinctly working-class culture. Only three of the theatres report that members are involved in socialist political organizations.

Consequently, it is difficult to generalize about the politics of contemporary theatres for working-class audiences. All are concerned with the creation of a distinctly working-class culture. Most view the creation of this culture as a means of empowering the working class, and to many this empowerment involves the self-organization of the class. Inherent in these views is the assumption that America's working people should have more economic and political power within the body-politic, "more control over their own lives," to lift a phrase from the Everyday Theatre. Closely connected to this assumption is the conviction that America's workers (and others who are oppressed because of their race, sex, age, or sexual preference) can only achieve more power through an extension of democracy on both the economic and political levels and that this extension of democracy can only be achieved through the self-organization of the oppressed. The theatres' commitment to political organization is reflected by the fact that the majority of them have members actively involved in other working-class organizations.

These views put the theatres on the left of the contemporary American political spectrum. However, within this broad framework, politics range from the Roadside Theater's general "belief in democracy" to the specific "socialist perspective and Marxist analysis" of the Workers' Stage. This range of views among the theatres is representative of the American left as a whole. The political self-definition of El Teatro de la Esperanza perhaps comes the closest to an all-encompassing definition of the politics of these theatres. El Teatro writes, "As artists our politics are to take professional theatre to those audiences that do not have access to the art. . . . As political people, our work is to end exploitation in our world." It is likely that most of the theatres discussed would accept this as a general definition of their work and views.

What is most significant about these theatres at this point in American cultural history is not their specific political views (which clearly vary) but their choice of audience and their relationship to it. This is what they have in common and what differentiates them from other contemporary theatres (politically leftist or otherwise). As Maxine Klein of the Little Flags Theatre Collective put it, the groups' political views provide "a certain bias, a certain support" for the work of the theatres, "but the really important thing is a respect we have for workers and workers' history, and workers' possibilities." It is this respect that is the most profound political and cultural assumption of the theatres under consideration.

FINANCES

The finances of the theatres have been touched on, in some cases, in the history section. However, an overview of financing patterns has not yet been provided. How to make ends meet takes on a special significance for the theatres under consideration since they are clearly functioning outside the cultural mainstream and in many cases presenting shows with controversial political content. Locating the sources of financial support for the troupes will indicate both the willingness of the cultural funding establishment over the last thirteen years to support nonconventional theatrical projects and perhaps of more significance the willingness and the ability of the targeted audience, the working class and its mass organizations, to support their own cultural institutions.

Financially, the theatres can be divided between those that derive most of their support from grants (government and private) and those that survive on support from their audiences (admission, performance fees, and honoraria from sponsoring organizations). The majority fit into the latter category, although it is a slim majority. Of the groups responding, five are financed primarily from grants, seven are financed primarily by their audience, and one, the Roadside Theater, seems about evenly divided between both sources. It should be noted that these generalizations are derived from responses to a question in the questionnaire, not from any detailed study of the theatres' financial records. Further, placement in one category or the other is based on overall funding patterns. All but three of the troupes have received some grant money at some point in their histories. Only those groups for whom grants have consistently provided a financial base are included in the first category.

There are obvious political implications in whether a troupe's survival is dependent on state or corporate subsidy or working-class audience support. However, at this point in their development, no direct correlation can be drawn between a troupe's political self-definition and its financial base. There is too much divergence in the theatres' geographical locations, their production histories, and the status and connections their founders have had in the arts establishment to draw any simple parallels. For example, the Dakota Theatre Caravan is the first and only theatre to express an interest in touring the rural areas of South Dakota. It is therefore not surprising that it has obtained considerable support from the South Dakota Arts Council and the Affiliated State Arts Agencies of the Upper Midwest. Nor is it surprising that three of the troupes that have received consistent support from the National Endowment for the Arts (the New York Street Theatre Caravan, the Little Flags Theatre Collective, and the Iron Clad Agreement) were each founded by individuals who already had a degree of local status and some connections within the arts establishment. Location, history, and connections appear to have had a considerable influence on the availability of grants.

Political ideology and the content of plays has, of course, had a bearing on funding patterns. It is worth observing, for example, that the two troupes that have publicly declared themselves socialist—Workers' Stage and the San Francisco Mime Troupe—have received very little grant support. Workers' Stage has received none, deriving literally all of its very modest operating funds from the unions it performs for. For most of its history, the San Francisco Mime Troupe was equally bereft of grant support. In recent years, it has begun to receive some city and state grants for its free summer performances in the parks, though such funding only accounts for about 25 percent of the Mime Troupe's budget; the majority of its financing, which supports a full-time professional theatre company year-round, comes from its audiences. Aside from these few observations, no correlation emerges in relation to the troupes' political self-definitions and their funding sources.

All of the theatres seem to share the goal of finding primary support in their working-class audiences. Most agree that this is a long-term goal and that funds sufficient to support full-time professional theatre work will not be forthcoming from working-class sources. In this regard, it should be pointed out that, with the exceptions of the San Francisco Mime Troupe and Modern Times Theatre, all of the theatres that have achieved full-time year-round professional status—the Iron Clad Agreement, El Teatro de la Esperanza, the New York Street Theatre Caravan, the Little Flags Theatre Collective, and the Dakota Theatre Caravan (which discontinued year-round work in 1981)—have done so with substantial grant support. The Everyday Theatre, which remains part-time, has received most of its funds from the District of Columbia Community Humanities Council. Conversely, most troupes that rely primarily on their audiences for financial backing have been forced to remain part-time, "amateur" endeavors. These theatres include Mass Transit (which has survived for thirteen years without substantial grant support), Charlestown Working Theatre, the Irish Rebel Theatre, Word of Mouth Productions, and Workers' Stage. The Roadside Theater is an exceptional case. It is a full-time year-round theatre, which realizes half of its annual budget from performance fees and the rest from outside grants and from Appalshop, the independent working-class-based cultural institution which also produces films, records, and so forth.

This lack of financial support from their target audience poses the most serious obstacle to the survival of these theatres and the development of others like them. Although the Mass Transit Street Theatre has proven that with intense dedication it is possible to survive with little or no financial support for a long period of time, their longevity under these conditions is exceptional. Even granting the possibility of such long-term survival, the part-time nature of the work is bound to act as a retardant to the artistic development of the troupe. Without the ability to work full-time at their theatre, it is unlikely that these troupes will be able to achieve their full artistic potential. Troupes that have achieved full-time status with the help of grants also face a dubious future. Given the drastic federal cutbacks in funds for the social services and the arts, these theatres may find their funding substantially diminished or eliminated. If this happens, will they be able, based on their current reputations and popularity, to make up the funding losses with audience admission or support from workers' organizations such as the trade unions? If such support is not forthcoming and they are forced to go part-time, will they be able to survive?

It is clear that the long-term survival of these troupes depends, to a large extent, on whether the labor movement begins to grow again and, probably more important, on whether the working class develops its own independent political movement. Without these developments, it is not likely that a stable and sufficient financial base within the working class can be generated for the theatres. It is not, however, a one-way street. The theatres themselves can play a significant role in helping to develop a working-class audience and a working-class political movement. By working as they have, they can prove in practice the benefits of developing a working-class theatre and help to inspire and inform the self-organization of the working class.

INTERNAL ORGANIZATION AND CREATIVE PROCESS

The belief in democracy expressed by the theatres finds articulation not only in choice of audience, content of scripts, and the political involvement of their members, but also in the internal organization of their administrative and creative tasks. Common to most of the theatres (with a few significant exceptions) is the practice of democracy in relation to the theatre's work. This democratic self-organization is most often expressed by the theatres as a commitment to the collective process, which for most of the troupes means that all members participate, on one level or another, in all aspects of the theatre's work, both administrative and artistic. An assumption at work for most of the theatres is that this collective process will have a positive effect on the artistic development of their members and on the finished production. Ideologically, this commitment to the practice of democracy in the traditionally hierarchical and autocratic field of theatre can be understood as a manifestation of the troupes' "practicing what they preach." Historically, this practice can be viewed as a legacy of the New Left through which most of these theatre workers passed in the late sixties and early seventies.

Among the fourteen groups who responded to the questionnaire, four basic forms of internal organiation can be ascertained. The largest number of theatres (five) make all administrative and creative decisions democratically and maintain no permanent division of labor—that is, all members function as actors, directors, writers, administrators at different times or at the same time. The second largest number (four), while making all fundamental administrative and creative decisions democratically, maintain a permanent division of labor at least in regard to artistic tasks. The third group (composed of three troupes) use a relatively traditional hierarchical internal structure, not fundamentally different from other nonprofit theatres functioning in the United States today. Finally, the two groups that function as community theatres are organized much like other community or club theatres across the country.

Among the first group, those who made all administrative and creative decisions democratically and maintain no permanent division of labor, Workers' Stage practices the most informal and perhaps the most direct form of democracy. Not only are all administrative and creative decisions made democratically, but all members are expected to participate on an equal basis in all the creative tasks necessary in the creation of a theatre piece. They write:

Throughout the entire process of creating a play, all members of Workers' Stage write, act, direct, and re-write. All artistic and political decisions are made collectively. The creative process begins when a group [of workers] invites Workers' Stage to perform.

. . . Workers' Stage then holds a meeting for discussion with the group of workers. The numbers involved have ranged from eight to thirty. Based on this first meeting, Workers' Stage attempts to define the political and theatrical content appropriate to the situation and to create a scenario based on the incidents, grievances and characters provided by the workers. If Workers' Stage has more questions or the [workers'] group desires further discussion, we will arrange additional meetings. Once an overall approach to plot, character, and political content has been agreed upon, scenes are created collectively through improvisation. When we are satisfied with the form and content of a script as improvised, an individual is given responsibility to script it. In this way, the play is gradually created.

Although the other theatres in this category also lack a permanent, ongoing division of labor within the troupe, they, unlike Workers' Stage, do divide creative tasks for each particular production. Thus Word of Mouth writes, "For each production, there is a primary writer, a director and a technical director. We try to have one person clearly responsible for a task or area of work that must be done." Similarly, the Roadside Theatre reports that for each production they divide themselves "into areas of major responsibility with a project director" while still making all "major decisions by group." Mass Transit, which has gone through many changes in its internal organization during the thirteen years of its history, now functions with a rotating steering committee which provides leadership and helps divide responsibility for each project.

Like the other theatres in this category, El Teatro de la Esperanza maintains no permanent division of labor (except for a tour coordinator) and makes all decisions democratically. What differentiates them is the formality and complexity of their internal organization and creative process. All tasks, both creative and administrative, are performed by committees. At present, El Teatro de la Esperanza is divided into six standing committees: child care, finance, programming, tour, artistic, and administrative. All members of the theatre must belong to one or more of the committees (although they did not make it clear if, or how often, individuals are rotated among the various committees). It is the function of the committees to initiate and carry through tasks in their various areas of responsibility. However, no committee can make a policy decision on its own. El Teatro writes, "We used majority rule. . . . The committee will present a proposal, we debate as a whole and vote or table it for further discussion."

The six committees mentioned are relatively permanent and together are responsible for the long-term functioning of the group. In addition, a production committee is organized for each new production. Within the production committee, El Teatro de la Esperanza's creative process takes place. This process, developed through more than a decade of experience, reflects their commitment to collectivity and the complexities of creating full-length plays without a director or playwright:

We begin with a group meeting to discuss possible topics for a new play. Each member usually brings in a topic of interest to themselves and presents it at this meeting. A topic is then assigned to each member and they go out and research it. A time limit of about two weeks is given. Each member then "teaches" their topic to the entire group. They present it and it is debated and questioned. At the end of this presentation, the topics are narrowed down to about four. These are assigned and further intensive research is done. Then they are presented to the troupe. The final topic is then selected and the entire group does research on the same topic. The next step is to form a Production Committee which is made of three coordinators, Artistic, Political, and Playwright. These three individuals now are responsible for formulating a political thesis for the piece. What do we want to say with this play? It is written down. It will form the base from which to debate all aspects of the play. (Now these people are entrusted to come up with a story or vehicle to present this thesis). Improvisations are done to try to find a story line. The style of the piece is also being developed at the same time. At the end of these improvs, a story is written. The next set of improvs are structured to try to develop scenes and acts for this story. Most of the structured improvs come from the committee, even though throughout the process anyone can add or try things. The Committee then scenarios the play based on each scene and act. The next step is to assign playwrights and directors for each scene and to devise a schedule of 1) improvisations for that scene; 2) playwrighting schedule for each scene. [Now] each scene goes through an improvisation, which is tape recorded. The director assigned to that scene is responsible for structuring that improv and will direct the scene until it is fitted into the play. The same time that the directors and playwrights are assigned, the Casting is done. Not bad considering that we don't have a play yet. The cast is selected by everyone. People state their preference and the group is the judge of whether or not they can pull off that role or sometimes we put someone in a role to challenge and help them grow. The advantage of casting at this point for us is that the playwrights can write for a specific actor and the actor actually creates the character instead of him being asked to assume one. After the improvs, the playwright goes into writing with the tape. He is given a deadline and must return with the scene scripted. The scene is read by the actors to the entire group and is critiqued. The playwright retreats again with his usually massacred script and returns with a second re-write. I might add that the playwright cannot defend his script. They must just listen and clarify points that are misread or not understood by the group. Finally, the third Re-write occurs and the script is usually accepted and [only] requires some minor changes that will be done in rehearsal. If the script is rejected for some reason at this point, it is re-assigned to another playwright, with the thinking that the original one is too subjective to continue on the piece. Now all this while, we have not been working on just one scene. All the play is undergoing this process. So one day we may reach Act 1, Scene 1, and then improv Act II, Scene 2 and then read the second Re-Write of Act 1, Scene 6 and so on. When a scene is approved, then it moves into the staging phase. The director and actors then take the script and go off. The whole time the committee keeps all the schedules straight. The Artistic helps structure improvs for those directors who need help, the Political keeps the course of the play intact, and the Playwright lends a hand when a playwright needs help. Finally the entire play is finished and the Playwright Coordinator takes it and does a continuity write. Since different people have written different things, it does not usually mesh right. Language is different, style is different and even characters are not consistent. He also writes the transitions between each scene and act. The Artistic Coordinator does the same with the direction of the play. The style of the play must come under one line of thinking and with different directors, this usually is not the case. The set is usually built by one person with the help of others and is designed by necessity more than concept. We need a table for this scene and bench for that, a wall here, etc.

Music is usually selected by the Artistic Coordinator also. Costumes usually evolve and are not designed.

This creative process is similar in many important ways to that of Workers' Stage where all members "write, act, direct and re-write." Because El Teatro has more members, creates longer and more complex plays, and works full-time, it has developed a far more sophisticated and formal creative process. Significantly, the plays thus collectively created by El Teatro de la Esperanza are, as dramatic literature, among the best produced by contemporary theatres for working-class audiences and, on the levels of craft and intellectual and emotional depth, rival many new plays done commercially in the United States today.

What distinguishes the second group of theatres from the first is not a weakening of their commitment to internal democracy but rather a permanent division of labor within that democracy. The specifics of this division of labor vary except for the tasks of playwright and director. The San Francisco Mime Troupe's description of its creative process (which they emphasize varies somewhat with each production) is typical of the theatres in this group:

At the start of every season we hold discussion of possible topics; when someone comes up with a good topic, the next step is for someone . . . to come up with a good idea for a play; the writer . . . takes it from there. Rehearsals always start before a script is finished, and a lot of rewriting is generally done in the course of production. I guess you could call the process one of close collaboration between the writer, the director, and the actors.

This "close collaboration," meaning an equal voice in all major creative and administrative decisions, is characteristic of all the theatres in this group. Modern Times describes its version of this collaboration:

We sit round and talk for months about what we want to do a play about. Personal experiences (love lives, having a baby, being broke, fighting with a landlord) are all valid subjects and of great concern to us. We assume that what occupies our minds is not trivial or irrelevant. We are also involved in more external, though not necessarily more political matters, racism, sexism, capitalism, Reagonomics, etc. We try to begin with characters and a story—Steve Friedman is our resident playwright—he talks to everyone, listens, then sits in a room and thinks for a few more months. He writes for specific actors and with the theatre's realities (budgets, touring plans, etc.) in mind. When we rehearse, although we have a director, Denny Partridge, we try to work out the details of the play closely with the actors—all of whom are theatre members, not employees. We continue to work in depth on a play throughout its run.

The Dakota Theatre Caravan describes a similar process, although, like Workers' Stage, they place a good deal of emphasis on direct interviews and research with people they want to do the show for as an initial step. They then decide on the play's objective and its characters and work out a detailed scenario collectively. It is only at this point that the playwright takes over. Doug Paterson, the principal writer for the Caravan's plays, relates:

I as playwright then write the material into dialogue, giving it language, detailed character and incident, consistency of style, and (hopefully) imaginative surprises. The play then goes immediately back to the company and we begin immediately to stage it, with Scott as director. The play can then be adjusted in any way the company sees fit. The best way to see this overall process is that of an hourglass. Much information and material focusing down to the group, then to the playwright, then back to the group and then back to the audience.

The final troupe in this category, the Everyday Theatre, uses an improvisational creative process similar to that used by the theatres that have no permanent division of labor. The major difference is that the improvisation is done under a single, permanent playwright, Nicki Burton. Burton provides an "outline of action" at the beginning of the rehearsal process, and, she explains, "when we start improvising, I come home and write up a lot of what we've done. Having it written enables us to keep jumping higher from level to level." The complete script is not written out until after the production.

It should be noted that in all four of these theatres, the resident playwright is also an actor. The directors of the Dakota Theatre Caravan and the Everyday Theatre act as well. With the San Francisco Mime Troupe, the director sometimes acts. Denny Partridge of Modern Times only directs. But no matter how many "hats" the playwrights and directors may wear, their primary function within the creative process remains writing or directing. They practice these crafts, however, within a democratic framework that allows for a close and flexible collaborative process not often found on the American stage.

This commitment to internal democratic organization is not found in the three theatres in the third category (the Iron Clad Agreement, the New York Street Theatre Caravan, and the Little Flags Theatre Collective). Although administrative organization varies among the three groups, in the creative sphere their organization is based on a division of labor within a generally hierarchical power structure.

The organizational structure of the Iron Clad Agreement resembles, on the surface, that of other nonprofit regional theatres, although in practice its division of labor is more informal and overlapping than in other professional regional theatres. It is headed by producer-director Julia Swoyer who originates most of the theatre's general ideas and raises the money. There is a board of directors and advisory board which meets once a year and whose function is primarily legal and financial. Actors have sometimes been auditioned in New York City, and directors, designers, writers, and composers are hired "on a professional-fee basis" for various productions. Within this general framework, the Iron Clad Agreement maintains a core of actors that it works with over a long period of time to "retain our style and identity." In addition, since the theatre does only original material commissioned specifically for it, they have developed a rehearsal process that allows actors to have input into the finished product, and actors have sometimes written plays. Swoyer writes, "everyone works together, often trying dozens of ideas in order to find the one which best communicates the thought, the action, the concept." Finally, everyone in the company, "has a specific share in making all aspects of touring work."

Until the fall of 1979, the actors of the New York Street Theatre Caravan shared administrative tasks among themselves. Since then, they have had a full-time administrator. However, "there is still a company member attached to nearly every administrative function, providing the expertise and experience of five or ten years handling that particular job." In the creative sphere, power has resided with a single artistic director, Marketta Kimbrell, since the early 1970s. Although the company participates in and maintains final control over administrative decisions, all major artistic decisions are made by Kimbrell who writes (based on company improvisation under her direction) and directs all shows. The Caravan describes its decision-making process as "one man/woman, one vote (lots of discussion). With the exception of artistic decisions, where artistic director has final say."

One-person rule is even more pronounced in the Little Flags Theatre Collective where founder Maxine Klein functions as playwright, director, and tour director. When asked about the group's internal decision-making process, Klein replied, "I decide.... Whatever I say goes." She went on to articulate views strikingly different from those of most of the other theatres under discussion. Maintaining that "art is not a collective experience . . . most collectives I know are just an endless mish-mash," Klein controls the creative process of Little Flags. "I'm a very tough director; everything is tightly controlled artistically.... If you sneeze, the director controls . . . ; nobody can do anything I don't have a stamp on." In reference to the impact on the actors, Klein said, "I don't care how you feel. It has to be done. I couldn't care less." When asked to justify the "collective" in the theatre's name, Klein rationalized its use by saying that the pay is roughly equal: "We don't operate hierarchically in that I get more of this or more of that."

The last two groups under discussion, the Charlestown Working Theatre and the Irish Rebel Theatre are both community theatres in the sense that they base themselves in a particular geographic or ethnic community and draw actors and audience from that community. Internally, they are organized like other community theatres around the country. The Charlestown Working Theatre has a full-time managing director, Peggy Ings, but the play selection is done by a playreading committee drawn from the community. Occasionally, outsiders are brought in to direct a play, but for the most part, directing, acting, technical, and other work are done on a voluntary basis by community members. The Irish Rebel Theatre is a club theatre: those who wish to work with it must join and pay dues. These members come from the "Irish immigrant [and] blue-collar American Irish" community that the theatre serves. Within this context, the

Irish Rebel Theatre functions democratically: "Those who do the work, make the decisions. Major policy questions, selection of plays, directors and casting are decided by a democratic committee of dues-paying performers and tech staff." In addition, the Irish Rebel Theatre has a policy of work rotation to avoid the development of cliques or stars and to provide all members with experience in all aspects of theatre production. They write, "This production's star is the next production's house manager."

While the range of internal organizational forms among the theatres that responded to the questionnaire is wide, generalizations can be drawn about the majority of the troupes. Ten of the fourteen (if the Irish Rebel Theatre is included) practice a democratic decision-making process in all administrative and creative areas. Many of the troupes are also committed to breaking down the traditional division of labor and hierarchy of power within the theatre. While only two groups (Workers' Stage and El Teatro de la Esperanza) attempt to involve all members in all aspects of every production, many others rotate jobs with each production. Even among theatres that have a permanent division of labor, there is a tendency for individuals to do more than one task, usually acting, in addition to their area of specialization.

Improvisation plays an important role in the creative process of the vast majority of the troupes. This appears related to their attempts to create democratically, as well as to the dearth of existing scripts with appropriate content. In troupes with resident playwrights, the process of improvisation tends to be an important contribution to the playwright's work, both before and after the play is formally scripted. Even in the New York Street Theatre Caravan, where all creative power is concentrated in one individual, improvisation with the actors is the process by which the artistic director "writes" the plays.

In general, the organization of contemporary theatres for working-class audiences, both administratively and creatively, reflects their politics—their commitment to democracy and egalitarianism. This internal organization and creative process, some of the troupes maintain, has an important influence on their finished product and on the impact that product has on their audience. According to Mass Transit Street Theatre:

One of the things we've found is that aside from what our play might be saying, the response of the audience always is very strong to what they perceive in us as a group. . . . A comment that we hear very often is "You all seem to be very close and to work together so well." . . . They respond as much to the group as they do to the play.

PERFORMANCE STYLE AND AESTHETIC FRAMEWORK

The following self-descriptions that the troupes gave of their performance styles and aesthetic frameworks should be taken as an indication of their performance goals, not necessarily as an objective description of actual productions.

The Charlestown Working Theatre did not respond to the question of performance style and aesthetics, so they are not included in this discussion.

As is obvious from the preceding section on internal organizations and creative processes, virtually all of the theatres who responded place great emphasis on ensemble performance. Even those theatres where creative control is in an individual's hands feel that their productions do not reflect a star approach. The New York Street Theatre Caravan, for example, writes: "The company's performance style, as a result of the form of our training, is very much as an ensemble," and the Iron Clad Agreement describes its work as "an ensemble presentational style."

In addition to a commitment to ensemble production work, the contemporary theatres for working-class audiences have a good number of other aesthetic assumptions in common. By far, the most pervasive influence is the theoretical and practical work of Bertolt Brecht. Six of the thirteen theatres that responded to this question cite Brecht either by name, by using the term "epic theatre" to describe their work, or by describing aesthetic approaches clearly derived from Brecht. The Everyday Theatre, which takes its name from a poem by Brecht, describes its aesthetic as "very similar" to Brecht: "The idea that you should always be showing something . . . We don't try to present a grand illusion, but [make it clear] that we are showing a story." Workers' Stage writes that its actors share a background in "Brechtian and epic theatre techniques" and that they are "interested in theatre that recognizes itself—there is no illusion that performance is not just that." El Teatro de la Esperanza reports, "Our style is based heavily on Brechtian elements. Even though we can not say that we have achieved a true Brechtian style . . . The use of signs, quotes from actors as demonstrators, multiple characters by one actor, using female for male roles and vice versa are all elements of our style." Mass Transit states, "It's always clear in our plays [that] this is a play." In their work, they often alternate a "realistic" scene with a song or a dance to create an estrangement effect and allow the audience to "be clear, to see and understand what's happening." The other two theatres that cite Brecht as an influence are the San Francisco Mime Troupe and the Modern Times Theatre.

Even some of the theatres that do not refer to Brecht in any of these ways use production elements or performance techniques that, if not derived from, are at least parallel to Brecht. The Dakota Theatre Caravan, for example, which labels its performance style as " 'filled' realism," describes the following production elements: "We use almost no set . . . and play numerous characters per show (anywhere from 1 to 12 per actor), and are visible all the time (when not on stage, sitting and watching the action—watching simply, not with labored vision, but focused)." The Iron Clad Agreement uses "few performers to create all the characters and machines, using only their bodies, voices and a few simple props. We do not transform our venue into a theatre, rather we use it as a backdrop." The Roadside Theater refers to its performers as "actor/storytellers," and the Irish Rebel Theatre writes that its realism is "informed by traditional storytelling."

Among the theatres that responded, two can be described as being anti-Brechtian. The aesthetic of the New York Street Theatre Caravan is derived from Konstantin Stanislawski through Lee Strasberg (with whom Kimbrell studied) and further informed by Jerzy Grotowski and other psychologically-based acting techniques. The result is an acting style that the Caravan calls "warm, emotional, poetic," adding that "the thoughts occurring in the plays are not told, but felt." Maxine Klein of Little Flags is explicit in her opposition not only to Brechtian aesthetics but to a presentational approach in general. She states that their group's "performance style [is] founded on dead center of reality because you're dealing with working people . . . not hoched-up presentational shit, they [working people] can't relate to that."

After Brecht, the most frequently cited influence is Charlie Chaplin; three of the thirteen groups mentioned him by name. Maxine Klein of Little Flags maintains, "I direct like Charlie Chaplin." Modern Times Theatre, which named itself after one of Chaplin's films, says, "Our major aesthetic models are Brecht and Chaplin." The Everyday Theatre, in discussing influences on its work, writes, "Chaplin [has] a lot to offer." In addition, the San Francisco Mime Troupe, while not mentioning Chaplin specifically, credits "silent-film slapstick" as a major influence on their work. This congruence of Brecht and Chaplin as influences is not surprising since Brecht himself cited Chaplin as an epic actor.[25] Other individuals cited were Grotowski and Joseph Chaikin (both by Word of Mouth Productions) and Richard Schechner (by the Everyday Theatre). On the whole, however, the work of the so-called avant garde seems to have little influence on the theatres for working-class audiences, with only Word of Mouth Productions citing it as a major influence.

Of more importance seems to be the influence of folklore (traditional music, song, stories, performance rituals). This influence is most obvious with the Roadside Theater which sets as one of its major goals the preservation and creative expansion of "the Appalachian region's unique aesthetic, language, and imagery." Both their content and style are drawn from Appalachian folklore. "The Roadside Theater's style is drawn from the region's musical, church, and storytelling traditions, and its original scripts are strongly influenced by the area's oral history and heritage of traditional tales." Even the context of their performances resembles the informal gatherings at which folktales and songs are often performed. They continue, "The audience is usually fifty to one hundred next door neighbors. The mood is comfortable and intimate. All of Roadside Theater's actor/storytellers and musicians were born and reared in the region, and without use of costumes, props or sets they tell and act their stories a few feet from the audience." While not as thoroughly committed to an aesthetic that is based on traditional folklore, the Irish Rebel Theatre often makes use of traditional Irish music and writes that its aesthetic is "informed by traditional story telling.'' The New York Street Theatre Caravan also draws heavily from folklore both for content, as in the case of *Hard Times Blues* (based on the ''Bremmen Town Musicians''), and for its performance style and music. All the members of the Caravan play various folk instruments and study the ''dance and vocal styles and the musical styles of many cultures.'' El Teatro de la Esperanza links its performance style to that developed by El Teatro Campesino, which in turn, draws on traditional Mexican forms. They write, ''We use a lot of the Acto techniques which have been classified as a cross between commedia dell'arte and Cantinflas [Mexican comic actor].''

The influence of Cantinflas on El Teatro de la Esperanza points to another influence on these theatres: the popular entertainment forms of the past. This is most pronounced with the San Francisco Mime Troupe, which, in addition to the influence of Brecht, has experimented with commedia dell'arte, the minstrel show, nineteenth-century melodrama, puppet shows, vaudeville, thrillers, silent film, and circus techniques (most of its members are accomplished jugglers),[26] and refers to its present style as ''musical-comic political cartoon.'' The Mass Transit Theatre has also made use of nineteenth-century melodrama, and at least one Workers' Stage show has involved the use of puppets.

Finally, although not cited directly, at least two of the theatres seem to have been influenced by the theatrical experiments of Augusto Boal. The essence of Boal's work among working-class audiences in Peru was to stop the performance at climactic points and encourage the audience to become directly involved in resolving problems or questions posed by the play.[27] This is precisely what Mass Transit did with developmental skits that it used in creating its occupational health play. They report,

[The] Skit would go up to the point where the conflict was clear, then [we] would stop the skit and ask people what: 1) the worst fear about the outcome would be; 2) their most far-out fantasy, most terrific thing that could happen; and 3) the reality, what the most progressive next step could realistically be . . . [The] Actors would [then] go out of the room and quickly come up with three endings to the story, come back and act them out.

Word of Mouth Productions experimented along similar lines in their play, *Why Don't You Find a Rich Guy and Marry Him?*:

Midway through the show, performers enter the audience and ask people to share their childhood work fantasies; [and] just as the dream [scene] ends, the audience participates in a sexual harassment survey; [and] the two patrons who appear at the close of the play in the restaurant are pre-selected audience members.

The majority of the contemporary theatres for working-class audiences, whether or not they cite Brechtian aesthetic assumptions, are clearly within the realm of presentational theatre. Most, for both practical and aesthetic reasons, work with minimal sets in which, to quote Workers' Stage, ''the actors basically create the environments with a few broad and significant props.'' Costumes, when they are used, tend to be, as the New York Caravan says, ''suggestive'' rather than literal. In addition, an overwhelming number—ten of the thirteen respondents—report that music is an important element of their productions.

Only three of the groups label themselves ''realistic,'' and all three do so only with qualification. The Dakota Theatre Caravan writes, ''Our performance style is basically realistic within a highly theatrical milieu. . . . However, this realism is a filled realism, with considerable energy in those characters (most of them) which can support energy.'' The Little Flags Theatre Collective, after describing its aesthetic as being in the ''dead center of reality,'' adds, ''But it's big because we're dealing panoramically and we're dealing with large people. We try to be as big as the characters we write about and it's musical; everyone of our plays is musical.'' As already mentioned, the Irish Rebel Theatre describes its aesthetic as ''realism'' but ''informed by traditional story telling.'' In this context, the realism referred to is clearly not ''fourth wall'' illusionism (except perhaps for the Irish Rebel Theatre) nor verisimilitude in set and costume, nor the ''cause and effect'' structures of the traditional realistic drama. The various qualifications given indicate that the troupes are referring to a psychological and subjective approach to the creation and performance of *character*, in contrast to a Brechtian approach in which the actor's performance includes a political attitude toward his character. Given this definition, the New York Street Theatre Caravan must be added to the list of realistic troupes, although their Stanislawski-trained actors ''die and live again, and everyone plays at least three parts,'' demonstrating that psychological acting and presentational theatre are not incompatible.

The contemporary theatres for working-class audiences, though seldom in direct contact with each other, display a remarkable similarity in regard to their aesthetic frameworks and performance styles. All strive for ensemble perform- ance, and almost all of them to one extent or another do so within a presentational performance style. While six of the thirteen cite Brecht as a major influence, and four use a psychological approach to acting, virtually all of them use minimal sets, suggestive costumes, and music as an important production element. Three of the thirteen describe their work as basically comic, and at least two rely on the direct participation of the audience in the course of the play. In bringing theatre back to the working class, none is attempting to compete with the movies and TV in regard to conventional realism. They are building on elements that are unique to theatre and that are theatre's strong points vis-à-vis the other dramatic forms. Today's theatre for working-class audiences is a theatre that recognizes itself as theatre.

CONCLUSION

The isolated and independent development that has characterized the growth of contemporary theatres for working-class audiences in the United States has begun to change in the last few years. Collaboration and networking among the groups have increased, and regional and national institutions have emerged that include theatres for working-class audiences.

The earliest attempt by troupes to work together—New York's Shared Season begun in 1979—has already been discussed. Even earlier, in 1977, an annual People's Theatre Festival was begun in the San Francisco Bay area in which the various alternative, political, and working-class theatres of northern California held workshops and performed for each other. Initially organized by two individuals, Bob Martin and Susan Hoffman, these festivals engendered interaction that gave birth to the People's Theatre Coalition, a year-round organization that works to increase cooperation among the area's theatres and to develop resources and sponsor projects beyond the scope of any individual troupe.[28] Its latest and perhaps most significant project was the establishment in 1983 of the People's School of Dramatic Arts, the only left-oriented theatre school in the United States today. Drawing its faculty from constituent groups including the San Francisco Mime Troupe, the school's aim is "raising the artistic standards of popular theatre" through "professional skills development" with an "emphasis on popular and indigenous performance values."[29] If the school survives, it has the potential to play an important role in developing and spreading the performance styles and values developed by many alternative theatres, including working-class troupes. Although there is no equivalent institution in southern California, that region's two most significant theatres for working-class audiences, El Teatro de la Esperanza (Santa Barbara) and the Provisional Theatre (Los Angeles), have stepped up their interaction and work together in the 1980s. This work has included a collaborative piece, *The Tecolote Visions*, which members of both troupes wrote and performed together in 1982.[30]

In the southeastern United States, the Regional Organization of Theatres-South, popularly known as "Alternative ROOTS," based in Atlanta, has over the last few years played a role similar to the San Francisco People's Theatre Coalition for the South's alternative, political, and working-class theatres.

On the national level, two institutions play a significant role in relation to America's theatres for working-class audiences. The first is Alliance for Cultural Democracy, formerly Neighborhood Arts Programs' National Organizing Committee (NAPNOC), and the other is the magazine, *Theatrework*. The Alliance for Cultural Democracy, which is based in Baltimore, was founded in 1975 as "a national organization of neighborhood artists and community cultural programs." Membership is open to individuals and groups, and today Cultural Democracy includes "muralists, theatre people, writers, video people, craftspeople, musicians and organizers." The unifying factor among all its members is a commitment to "cultural democracy" and "to make our work useful to our communities."[31] The overlap in constituencies and values between Cultural Democracy and the contemporary theatres for working-class audiences is obvious, and many of the theatres discussed here are members. Cultural Democracy's monthly newsletter solicits and publishes news of theatrical activity as well as occasional articles on theatre history and theory. The annual Cultural

Democracy membership meetings provide an opportunity for the theatre workers to meet each other and other community-based artists. In addition, Cultural Democracy acts as a general clearinghouse for information on the activities of its members.[32]

Cherry Creek is a theatre company in the small Minnesota town of St. Peter. In addition to its performance work in its community, Cherry Creek has played an important catalytic function on the national level. In 1981 they organized The Gathering, held in their hometown, which was the first national conference for alternative theatre held in almost ten years. A number of the theatres for working-class audiences, including the New York Street Theatre Caravan, the Dakota Theatre Caravan, and Word of Mouth Productions, attended and performed at the conference. The Gathering thus served as the first national showcase for the work of contemporary theatres for working-class audiences and as a way for these theatres to observe and discuss each other's work and to influence and be influenced by the more broadly defined alternative theatres in attendance.

Of even more significance has been Cherry Creek's editing and publication of *Theatrework* magazine. *Theatrework*, founded in 1980, has, through a national subscription circulation, become the unofficial journal of America's alternative, political, and working-class theatres. Published six times a year, *Theatrework* not only provides reports and analysis on the work of alternative theatres around the country, but has become a forum for the discussion of politics, aesthetics, and theatre history within the alternative theatre movement. Members of theatres for working-class audiences have had an important and influential voice in these discussions, and their work has been covered with regularity in the magazine.

The theatres for working-class audiences have been welcomed on their own terms in the two regional coalitions, the Alliance for Cultural Democracy, and in the pages of *Theatrework*. While the working-class theatres neither determine nor dominate the direction of these institutions, they have often provided leadership in organizational and theoretical matters, and their influence on the other alternative theatres is significant. They have been active, and will obviously continue to be, in debates between those in the alternative theatre movement for whom formal experimentation takes precedence and those for whom consideration of politics and the nature of the audience are more important.[33]

Equally significant, these regional and national institutions have provided the theatres for working-class audiences with the opportunity to learn of each other, view each other's work, and get to know each other personally. While this networking is still far from complete (many of the theatres discussed are not members of any of these regional or national institutions), it nonetheless represents a significant increase over such activity in the 1970s.

The exchange of experience and the artistic and political cross-fertilization that goes on in these contexts can only have a positive effect on the morale and work of the troupes involved. Finally, the theatres' involvement in regional and national organizations can help bring about the awareness of themselves as a movement and provides an institutional framework that has the potential to allow for the survival and perpetuation of their work and values, regardless of the history of any particular group.

Theatre for working-class audiences has survived as a small but significant stream in the American theatre for over a decade. They have survived and increased their numbers despite financial hardship, despite little or no support from the arts establishment, despite being ignored by their fellow artists in the mainstream theatre, despite lack of acknowledgment from academia or the critics, and despite a lack of any of the gratifications afforded the artist in the commercial theatre. What has kept them going is the audience. Over and over again in their responses, the theatres talked about the enthusiasm, the joy, the intellectual and emotional excitement displayed by their audiences when they experienced their lives, their problems, and their concerns and aspirations in theatrical form. The theatres have continued to build a base in the working class because their work has begun to excite America's working people. Doug Paterson of the Dakota Theatre Caravan writes of America's workers, "They are a people who deserve respect, who deserve to have their histories explored and told, and who deserve celebration of their lives."[34] This is what America's theatres for working-class audiences have done and will continue to do as most of them enter their second decade.

NOTES

1. The New York Street Theatre Caravan and the San Francisco Mime Troupe tour extensively throughout the United States. The Little Flags Theatre Collective (Boston) tours throughout the East and Southeast. El Teatro de la Esperanza (Santa Barbara) tours extensively in the Southwest and has appeared in the Midwest and New York City. The Iron Clad Agreement (formerly of Pittsburgh, now of New York City) has toured as far south as South Carolina, as well as in England. The New York Street Theatre Caravan and the Mime Troupe also tour Western Europe regularly. El Teatro de la Esperanza tours Mexico regularly and in addition has performed in Sweden, Yugoslavia, and Poland. The San Francisco Mime Troupe and Teatro 4 have performed in Cuba, and the Caravan is the only North American theatre to have appeared in Nicaragua since the revolution of 1979. These and all other specific facts about the troupes are drawn from answers to a questionnaire that the author sent to the various groups or from interviews and discussions with members of the troupes. (For the full text of the questionnaire and a list of the thirty-two theatres, see appendix A and appendix B.) If the source is other than the questionnaire or an interview, it will be noted.

2. All quotes, unless otherwise cited, are from responses to the questionnaire or from interviews conducted by the author or by Bruce McConachie.

3. From an undated New York Street Theatre Caravan promotional leaflet.

4. From an unsigned Workers' Stage grant application, 1981.

5. Robert Scheer, "Introduction," *The San Francisco Mime Troupe: The First Ten Years*, by R. G. Davis (Palo Alto, 1975), p. 11.

6. For contemporaneous accounts of these theatres see *Guerrilla Street Theatre*, ed. Henry Lesnick (New York, 1973); Karen Malpede Taylor, *People's Theatre in Amerika*

(New York, 1972); and John Weisman, *Guerrilla Theatre: Scenarios for Revolution* (New York, 1973).

7. By 1970 Luis Valdez was writing, "Not a teatro composed of actos or agit-prop but a teatro of ritual, of music, of beauty and spiritual sensitivity. A teatro of legends and myths," in "Notes on Chicano Theater," *Actos* (San Juan Bautista, California, 1971), p. 3.

8. Louis R. Torres, "Hope Abroad," *Nuestro, The Magazine for Latinos*, 3 (August 1979), 50.

9. Jorge Huerta, "El Teatro de la Esperanza: Keeping in Touch with the People," *The Drama Review*, 21 (March 1977), 45.

10. Quoted by W. Perri, "Appalshop—Already a Mountain Tradition," *In These Times*, 6 (October 20, 1982), 20.

11. Ibid.

12. Quoted in a "Memo to Friends of Little Flags," (December 5, 1977).

13. Letter from Jon Weissman for the Steering Committee of the Massachusetts Organization to Repeal the Taft-Hartley Act to the Little Flags Theatre Collective, October 18, 1979.

14. From an undated leaflet advertising a performance of the Iron Clad Agreement's *Father K*.

15. From a press release by the Iron Clad Agreement, dated September 2, 1981.

16. Ibid.

17. Quoted in undated Modern Times Theatre promotional flyer.

18. Nancy Langer, quoted in Morris Edelson, "Theater Troupes Share Politics, Same Roof," *In These Times*, 5 (January 21–22, 1981), 20.

19. Among the unions listed in the program of their production of *Night Shift* as making possible their 1977 season were eleven locals and two joint boards of the International Ladies Garment Workers Union; two locals and three joint boards of the Amalgamated Clothing and Textile Workers Union; Local 1 of the Pocketbook and Novelty Workers Union; two locals of the Amalgamated Meat Cutters; Local 3 of the Bakery and Confectionary Workers Union; Local 840 of the Teamsters; Local 25 of the United Auto Workers; Local 1 of the Department Store Workers; American Federation of State, County and Municipal Workers Union; and Joint Board of Fur and Leatherworkers; Furriers' Joint Council.

20. Edelson, p. 20.

21. From undated program for Word of Mouth's production, *Why Don't You Find a Rich Guy and Marry Him?*

22. Workers' Stage ceased functioning as an ongoing theatre group in the summer of 1983.

23. Letter to Workers' Stage from the organizing committee of the Columbia Local, District 65, UAW, November 4, 1981.

24. Compiled from an undated piece of promotional literature entitled "Purpose" and an unpublished interview with Nicki Barton of the Everyday Theatre conducted by Bruce McConachie, Summer 1982.

25. Bertolt Brecht, "The Question of Criteria for Judging Acting," in *Brecht on Theatre: The Development of an Aesthetic*, ed. John Willet (New York, 1964), p. 56.

26. For a discussion of the San Francisco Mime Troupe in relation to popular entertainment forms of the past, see Theodore Shank, "Political Theatre as Popular Entertainment: San Francisco Mime Troupe," *The Drama Review*, 18 (March 1974), 110–17.

27. Augusto Boal, *Theatre of the Oppressed* (New York, 1979).

28. Don Adams and Arlene Goldband, "Vital Signs: People's Theatre Festival and American Writers' Congress," *NAPNOC Notes*, No. 16 (October 1981), p. 1.

29. "People's School of Dramatic Arts to Open January 24, 1983," *Theatrework*, 3 (January–February 1983), 4.

30. Susanna Halpert, *"The Tecolote Visions*—The Dynamics of a Collaboration," *Theatrework*, 3 (January–February 1983), 23–28.

31. This and previous NAPNOC/Cultural Democracy quotes from an undated promotional brochure entitled "Join NAPNOC and Help Build Cultural Democracy."

32. Arlene Goldband, former NAPNOC Co-director, was an important source for names and addresses of theatres contacted in this study.

33. For an account of a debate of these issues at the 1981 People's Theatre Festival in San Francisco, see Adams and Goldband, "Vital Signs," p. 3.

34. Doug Paterson, "Some Theoretical Questions of People's Theatre," *Theatrework*, 3 (January–February 1983), 9.

Appendix A

Theatre Questionnaire

1. Please provide a brief history of your theatre. (No more than one, single-spaced typed page.)

2. How would you define the politics of your theatre?

3. How would you characterize your group's performance style? Its general aesthetic framework?

4. How many members in your group? How many actors?

5. Do you work with a relatively permanent group of actors or does the cast change for each show? What is your rate of turnover?

6. How many members of your theatre earn a living from your theatre?

7. How do the others earn a living? (Be specific).

8. How many of your members belong to a trade union, political organization, or political party? If it does not violate the security standards of your theatre or the individuals involved, please specify the organization they belong to.

9. What is the nature of the division of labor in your theatre?

10. What decision-making process does your theatre utilize?

11. What percentage of your plays do you create yourself?

12. In plays your theatre creates, what process of creation do you use? (Be as specific as possible.)

13. Do you consider scripts created/written outside your group?

14. How is your theatre financed?
    ——— Government grants
    ——— Private grants
    ——— Contributions from trade unions or political parties
    ——— Individual contributions
    ——— Audience admission
    ——— Other (please specify)

15. Does your theatre have a permanent performance space? If so is it:
    ——— Community Center
    ——— Trade Union Hall
    ——— Church
    ——— Other (please specify)

16. What percentage of your productions are mounted in your home space? How much of it is toured?

17. When you tour, how far do you travel? What type of places do you play on tour?

18. What audience are you attempting to reach?

19. What audience are you actually reaching?

20. How many productions did you mount last year?

Contemporary Theatres for Working-Class Audiences in the United States that Had Been in Existence for at Least Two Years in 1983

At the Foot of the Mountain
3144 10th Avenue South
Minneapolis, Minnesota 55407

Baltimore Voices
c/o Baltimore Theatre Project
45 West Preston Street
Baltimore, Maryland 21201

The Bar Nothing Ranch
934 Eighteenth Avenue
Seattle, Washington 98122

Bay Area Labor Theatre
c/o KPFA
2207 Shattuck Avenue
Berkeley, California 94704

*Charlestown Working Theatre
442 Bunker Hill Street
Charlestown, Massachusetts 02129

The Cherry Creek Theater
406 South 3 Street
St. Peter, Minnesota 56082

Common Ground Theatre Ensemble
218 North Division
Ann Arbor, Michigan 48104

*Dakota Theatre Caravan
909 North 48th Avenue, Apt. 6
Omaha, Nebraska 68132

El Teatro Campesino
Box 1278
San Juan Bautista, California 95045

*El Teatro de la Esperanza
P.O. Box 1508
Santa Barbara, California 93102

*Everyday Theatre
3437 Mt. Pleasant Street, N.W.
Washington, D.C. 20010

The Folksbiene
c/o Workmen's Circle
123 East 55 Street
New York, New York 10022

Fourth Wall Repertory Company
79 East 4 Street
New York, New York 10022

Heart of the Beast Puppet and Mask Theatre
1628 East Lake Street
Minneapolis, Minnesota 55407

*Irish Rebel Theatre
553 West 51 Street
New York, New York 10019

*The Iron Clad Agreement
12 Wakeman Road
Fairfield, Connecticut 06430

The Labor Theater
100 East 17 Street
New York, New York

*Little Flags Theatre Collective
Boston Center for the Arts
539 Tremont Street
Boston, Massachusetts 02116

*Mass Transit Street Theatre
P.O. Box 347
Bronx, New York 10468

*Modern Times Theatre
250 West 65th Street
New York, New York 10023

*The New York Street Theatre Caravan
87-05 Chelsea Street
Jamaica, New York 11432

Pickle Family Circus
400 Missouri Street
San Francisco, California 94107

Provisional Theatre
1816 1/2 North Vermont Avenue
Los Angeles, California 90027

*Roadside Theater
c/o Appalshop, Inc.
Box 743
Whitesburg, Kentucky 41858

*San Francisco Mime Troupe
855 Treat Avenue
San Francisco, California 94110

Talespinners
c/o Feedback Productions
Building C
Fort Mason
San Francisco, California 94123

Teatro 4
175 East 104 Street
New York, New York 10029

Teatro Latino de San Francisco
Mission Cultural Center
2868 Mission Street
San Francisco, California 94110

A Traveling Jewish Theatre
P.O. Box 421985
San Francisco, California 94142-1985

United Mime Workers
P.O. Box 2088
Station A
Champaign, Illinois 61820

*Word of Mouth Productions
24 Kinsboro Park
Jamaica Plain, Massachusetts 02130

*Workers' Stage

(*Indicates that theatre responded to author's questionnaire or was interviewed by author or Bruce McConachie.)

Selected Bibliography

Bruce A. McConachie

This bibliography includes all major secondary sources relating to American theatre for working-class audiences between 1830 and 1980 listed in the notes following each chapter. Also included are a few books and articles not mentioned in the preceding chapters but deemed useful to the investigator interested in further exploration. Indeed, the shortness of this bibliographical essay testifies to the paucity of research done by scholars in this largely uncharted territory of critical-historical investigation.

The bibliography is divided into seven sections, roughly corresponding to the primary chapter divisions: (1) general historical and theoretical, (2) nineteenth-century native-American, (3) ethnic-American theatres, (4) early twentieth-century, (5) the decade of the 1930s, (6) post-1940 theatres, and (7) theatres for working-class audiences in other countries. Within each section, secondary sources in theatrical history per se have been separated, whenever possible, from general working-class histories. Because the latter are more numerous and accessible to researchers, only major books and journals, but not articles, are included. Other divisions within sections have been made as appropriate.

Of course there remain numerous primary sources listed in the end notes but excluded in this bibliography. We did not wish to give the illusion that our few essays had exhausted the mountains of primary material relating to the history of theatre for workers in the United States. At the most, researchers here and elsewhere have dug into a tenth of the plays, newspaper articles, scrapbooks, possible interviews, and related materials awaiting future scholarship. This bibliography, then, is intended to provide an overview of the tentative work accomplished thus far and to invite researchers to continue mining operations.

GENERAL HISTORICAL AND THEORETICAL

No general history of theatre for working-class audiences in the United States exists. Two surveys of significant stretches of the modern period, however, may be found in Harry Goldman and Mel Gordon, "Workers' Theatre in America: A Survey, 1913–1978," *Journal of American Culture*, 1 (Spring 1978) and May Wells Jones, "A History of the Political Theatre in the United States from 1930–1970," (Diss., Tulane University, 1971).

General histories of working-class life and popular entertainment include Richard Boyer and Herbert Morais, *Labors' Untold Story* (New York, 1935); Philip S. Foner, *History of the Labor Movement in the United States*, 4 vols. (New York, 1974); Irving Howe, *World of Our Fathers* (New York, 1976); Russel Nye, *The Unembarassed Muse: The Popular Arts in America* (New York, 1970); *The Peoples of Philadelphia: A History of Ethnic Groups and Lower-Class Life*, ed. Allen F. Davis and Mark H. Hall (Philadelphia, 1973); *Proletarian Literature in the United States*, ed. Granville Michs (New York, 1935); Joseph G. Rayback, *A History of American Labor* (New York, 1966); Robert Sklar, *Movie-Made America: A Cultural History of American Movies* (New York, 1975); Sam Bass Warner, *The Private City: Philadelphia in Three Periods of its Growth* (Philadelphia, 1968); *Working-Class America*, ed. Daniel Walkowitz and Michael Frisch (Urbana-Champaign, 1983).

In addition, the following journals feature occasional articles on American working-class culture: *American Quarterly; Journal of American Culture; Journal of American History; Journal of Popular Culture; Journal of Social History; Labor History.*

These writers combine historical accounts of theatres for working-class audiences with theoretical insight: Eric Bentley, *The Life of the Drama* (New York, 1964) and *The Theatre of Commitment* (New York, 1967); Oscar G. Brockett, *Perspectives on Contemporary Theatre*, (Baton Rouge, 1971); Morgan Y. Himelstein, "Theory and Performance in the Depression Theatre," *Modern Drama*, 14 (February 1972); Douglas McDermott, "Propaganda and Art: Dramatic Theory and the American Depression," *Modern Drama*, 11 (May 1968); George Phillopson, "Workers' Theatre: Forms and Techniques," *Modern Drama*, 22 (December 1977); Sam Smiley, *The Drama of Attack: Didactic Plays of the American Depression* (Columbia, 1972) and "Thought As Plot In Didactic Drama" in *Studies in Theatre and Drama: Essays in Honor of Hubert C. Heffner*, ed. O. G. Brockett (The Hague, 1972).

Several of our contributors have drawn on Marxist traditions of social-aesthetic theory to shape their essays. These theortical works include Fredric Jameson, *The Political Unconscious: Narrative As a Socially Symbolic Act* (Ithaca, New York, 1981) and "Reification and Utopia in Mass Culture," *Social Text*, (Winter 1979); Gareth Stedman Jones, "Class Expression versus Social Control? A Critique of Recent Trends in the Social History of Leisure," *History Workshop*, 4 (Autumn 1977) and "Working-Class Culture and Working-Class Politics in London 1870–1900; Notes of the Remaking of a Working Class," *Journal of Social History*, 7 (Summer 1974); Herbert Marcuse, *The Aesthetic Dimension: Towards a Critique of Marxist Aesthetics* (Boston, 1978); *Counterrevolution and Revolt* (Boston, 1972) and *An Essay on Liberation* (Boston, 1972); John McGrath, "The Theory and Practice of Political Theatre," *Theatre Quarterly*, 9 (Autumn 1979), *Radical Perspectives on the Arts*, ed. Lee Baxandall (Harmondsworth, England, 1972); E. P. Thompson, "Patrician Society, Plebeian Culture," *Journal of Social History*, 7 (Summer 1974); and Janet Wolff, *The Social Production of Art* (New York, 1981).

Other of our essayists draw on theoretical works informed by fusions of structuralism and sociology. These theorists are Philip Abrams, *Historical Sociology* (Ithaca, New York, 1982); Elizabeth Burns, *Theatricality: A Study of Convention in the Theatre and in Social Life* (New York, 1972); Peter L. Berger and Thomas Luckmann, *The Social Construction of Reality: A Treatise in the Sociology of*

Knowledge, 2nd ed. (Garden City, New York, 1966); John G. Cawelti, *Adventure, Mystery and Romance: Formula Stories as Art and Popular Culture*, (Chicago, 1976); several contributors to *The New Theatre: Performance Documentation* (New York, 1974); Jeffrey L. Sammons, *Literary Sociology and Popular Criticism* (Bloomington, Indiana, 1977); and Hayden V. White, "Structuralism and Popular Culture," *Journal of Popular Culture*, 7 (1974).

The formulations of Kenneth Burke, who unites significant strands of Marxism and structuralism, have provided theoretical foundations for some contributions. Books by and about Burke include *A Grammar of Motives* (New York, 1945); "From Lexicon Rhetoricae," in *Terms of Order*, ed. Stanley Edgar Hyman (Bloomington, Indiana, 1964); *The Philosophy of Literary Form* (New York, 1957); Frank Lentricchia, *Criticism and Social Change* (Chicago, 1983); and William Rueckert, *Kenneth Burke and the Drama of Human Relations* (Berkeley, 1982).

Finally, two works on propaganda figure in theoretical discussions in the preceding pages: Jacques Ellul, *Propaganda: The Formation of Men's Attitudes*, trans. Konrad Kellen and Jean Lerner (New York, 1966); and George H. Szanto, *Theatre and Propaganda* (Austin, 1978).

NINETEENTH-CENTURY NATIVE-AMERICAN

Melodrama was the dominant form of theatre for working-class audiences throughout the period. Useful commentary on melodramatic theatre may be found in Peter Brooks, *The Melodramatic Imagination: Balzac, Henry James, Melodrama and the Mode of Excess* (New Haven, Connecticut and London, 1976); Alan S. Downer, "Players and the Painted Stage: 19th-century Acting, *PMLA*, 61 (June 1946); David Grimsted, *Melodrama Unveiled: American Theater and Culture, 1800– 1850* (Chicago, 1968); Bruce Alan McConachie, "Economic Values in Popular American Melodramas" (Diss., University of Wisconsin, 1977); Donald C. Mullin, "Methods and Manners of Traditional Acting," *Educational Theatre Journal*, 27 (March 1975); Frank Rahill, *The World of Melodrama* (University Park, Pennsylvania, 1967); Wylie Sypher, "Aesthetic of Revolution: The Marxist Melodrama," *Kenyon Review*, 10 (Summer 1948).

Theatre histories of the period featuring or referring to working-class audiences include Barnard Hewitt, *Theatre U.S.A., 1668–1957* (New York, 1959); Mary C. Henderson, *The City and the Theatre: New York Playhouses from Bowling Green to Times Square* (Clifton, New Jersey, 1973); Claudia Johnson, "Burlesques of Shakespeare: The Democratic American's 'Light Artillery,' " *Theatre Survey*, 21 (May 1980); James A. Lowrie, "A History of the Pittsburgh Stage, 1861–1891," (Diss., University of Pittsburgh, 1943); Richard Moody, *The Astor Place Riot* (Bloomington, Indiana, 1958); George C. D. Odell, *Annals of the New York Stage*, 15 vols. (New York, 1927–1949); Theodore Shank, "The Bowery Theatre, 1826– 1836," (Diss., Stanford University, 1956); Robert C. Toll, *Blacking Up: The Minstrel Show in Nineteenth-Century America* (New York, 1974).

There are several books on American working-class history and culture during the nineteenth century. The major ones used by our contributors are Paul Boyer, *Urban Masses and Moral Order, 1820–1920* (Cambridge, 1978); Asa Briggs, *Mass Entertainments: The Origins of a Modern Industry* (Adelaide, 1960); David Brody, *Steelworkers in America: The Non-Union Era* (Cambridge, 1960); Herbert

G. Gutman, *Work, Culture and Society in Industrializing America* (New York, 1976); Susan E. Hirsch, *Roots of the American Working Class: The Industrialization of the Crafts in Newark, 1800–1860* (Philadelphia, 1978); Edward Pessen, *Most Uncommon Jacksonians: The Radical Leaders of the Early Labor Movement* (Albany, 1967); Howard B. Rock, *Artisans of the New Republic: The Tradesmen of New York City in the Age of Jefferson* (New York, 1979); Norman Ware, *The Industrial Worker, 1840–1860: The Reaction of American Industrial Society to the Advance of the Industrial Revolution* (Cambridge, 1924); Sam Bass Warner, *Streetcar Suburbs: The Process of Growth in Boston, 1870–1900* (Cambridge, 1962).

Further, these works deal more specifically with nineteenth-century working-class life in Pennsylvania: Francis G. Couvares, "Work, Leisure and Reform in Pittsburgh: The Transformation of an Urban Culture, 1860–1920," (Diss., University of Michigan, 1980); Henry O. Evans, *Iron Pioneer: Henry W. Oliver, 1850–1905* (New York, 1942); Michael Feldberg, *The Philadelphia Riots of 1844: A Study of Ethnic Conflict*, Contributions in American History, No. 43 (Westport, Connecticut, 1975); George T. Fleming, *History of Pittsburgh and Environs* (Pittsburgh, 1922); Joel A. Tarr, *Transportation and Innovation and Changing Spatial Patterns: Pittsburgh, 1850–1910* (Washington, D.C., 1972); Edwin Wolf, *Philadelphia: Portrait of an American City* (Harrisburg, 1975).

ETHNIC-AMERICAN THEATRES

Ethnic Theatre in the United States, ed. Maxime S. Seller (Westport, Connecticut, 1983) features historical essays and bibliographies on the theatres of many ethnic minorities, most of which, of course, were predominantly working-class in the first and second generations. Odell's *Annals*, previously cited, provide extensive information on ethnic theatres in New York City up to the mid-1890s.

There are several general histories of immigrant life in the United States, including Thomas J. Archdeacon, *Becoming American: An Ethnic History* (New York, 1983); Robert Ernst, *Immigrant Life in New York City, 1825–1863* (Port Washington, New Jersey, 1949); Nathan Glazer and Daniel Patrick Moynihan, *Beyond the Melting Pot* (Cambridge, 1970); Hutchins Hapgood, *The Spirit of the Ghetto* (1902; rpt., New York, 1966); John Higham, *Strangers in the Land* (rpt., New York, 1973); Frances Jerome Woods, *Cultural Values of American Ethnic Groups* (New York, 1956).

Works having to do with German-American theatre and society embrace August Otto-Walster, *Leben und Werk* (Berlin, 1966); Fritz A. Leachs, *The Early German Theatre in New York, 1840–1872* (New York, 1928); Carol Poore, "German-American Socialist Literature in the Late Nineteenth Century," (Diss., University of Wisconsin, 1979); LaVern J. Rippley, *The German Americans* (Boston, 1976); Rudolf Rocker, *Johann Most* (Berlin, 1924); Don Heinrich Tolzmann, *German-Americana: A Bibliography* (Metuchen, New Jersey, 1975).

The following books and articles comprise some of the secondary sources on Italian-American theatre and culture: Laurence Estavan, "The Italian Theatre in San Francisco," *San Francisco Theatre Research*, NS 21 (San Francisco, Works Projects Administration, 1939); Richard Gambino, *Blood of My Blood: The Plight of the Italian American* (New York, 1974); Deanna Paoli Gamina, "Connazionali,

Stentorello and Farfariello: Italian Variety Theatre in San Francisco,'' *California Historical Quarterly*, 54 (Spring 1975); Hutchins Hapgood, ''The Foreign Stage in New York, III: The Italian Theatre,'' *Bookman*, 11 (August 1900); Joseph Lopreato, *Italian-Americans* (New York, 1970); Eliot Lord, et al., *The Italian in America* (New York, 1950); Lawrence Frank Pisani, *The Italians in America: A Social Study and History* (New York, 1957); two books by Andrew F. Rolle, *The Immigrant Upraised: Italian Adventures and Colonists in An Expanding America* (Norman, Oklahoma, 1968) and *The Italian-Americans: Troubled Roots* (New York, 1980); and Joseph Tigani, ''Italian-American Pens,'' *Italian Heritage* (May 1971).

The Yiddish theatre is the best-documented of all ethnic theatres in America. Apart from many books in Yiddish on the subject, major secondary sources in English include Isaac Goldberg, *The Drama of Transition* (Cincinatti, 1922); Jerome Lawrence, *Actor: The Life and Times of Paul Muni* (New York, 1974); David Lifson, *The Yiddish Theatre in America* (New York, 1975); Lulla Rosenfeld, *Bright Star of Exile: Jacob Adler and the Yiddish Theatre* (New York, 1977); and Nahma Sandrow, *Vagabond Stars* (New York, 1977).

EARLY TWENTIETH-CENTURY

Books on pageantry include Esther Willard Bates, *Pageants and Pageantry* (Boston, 1912); Ralph Davol, *A Handbook of American Pageantry* (Tauton, Massachusetts, 1914); and several books by Percy MacKaye, informal pageant-master of America, *The Civic Theater in Relation to the Redemption of Leisure* (New York, 1912); *Community Drama: Its Method of Neighborliness* (Boston, 1917); *The New Citizenship: A Civic Ritual Devised for Places of Public Meeting in America* (New York, 1915).

Some secondary material on working-class life and culture may be found in Loren Baritz, *The Servants of Power: A History of the Use of Social Science in American Industry* (Middletown, Connecticut, 1960); Joseph Robert Conlin, *Bread and Roses Too: Studies of the Wobblies* (Westport, Connecticut, 1969); Meloyn Dubofsky, *We Shall Be All: A History of the Industrial Workers of the World* (Chicago, 1969); Joyce L. Kornbluh, *Rebel Voices: An IWW Anthology* (Ann Arbor, 1964); John Howard Lawson, ''Introduction,'' to *Ten Days That Shook the World*, by John Reed (1919; rpt., New York, 1967); Robert S. Smith, *Mill on the Dan: A History of Dan River Mills, 1882–1950* (Durham, North Carolina, 1960); Frederick W. Taylor, *The Principles of Scientific Management* (New York, 1916).

THE 1930s

More has been written about theatre for working-class audiences during this decade than for any other. Our contributors have found these sources helpful: Ben Blake, *The Awakening of the American Theatre* (New York, 1935); Evelyn Quita Craig, *Black Drama of the Federal Theatre Era* (Amherst, 1980); Hallie Flanagan, *Arena* (New York, 1940); Daniel Friedman, ''The Prolet-Buehne: America's First Agit-Prop Theatre'' (Diss., University of Wisconsin, 1979); Harry Goldman, ''When Social Significance Came to Broadway: Pins and Needles in Production,'' *Theatre*

Quarterly, 7 (Winter 1978); Malcolm Goldstein, *The Political Stage: American Drama and the Great Depression* (New York, 1974); Morgan Y. Himelstein, *Drama Was a Weapon: The Left-Wing Theatre in New York, 1929–1941* (New Brunswick, New Jersey, 1963); Norris Houghton, *Advance From Broadway* (New York, 1941); Malcolm Page, "The Early Years of Unity," *Theatre Quarterly*, 1 (October–December 1971); and Jay Williams, *Stage Left* (New York, 1974).

In addition, Douglas McDermott has written extensively on workers' theatres in the 1930s. These works include "Agitprop: Production Practice in the Workers' Theatre, 1932–42," *Theatre Survey*, 7 (November 1966); "The Living Newspaper as a Dramatic Form," (Diss., University of Iowa, 1963); "The Living Newspaper as a Dramatic Form," *Modern Drama*, 7 (May 1965); "New Theatre Schools, 1932–42," *The Speech Teacher*, 14 (November 1965); "The Odyssey of John Bonn: A Note on German Theatre in America," *The German Quarterly*, 73 (May 1965); and the previously mentioned, "Propaganda and Art: Dramatic Theory and the American Depression," *Modern Drama*, 11 (May 1968).

SINCE 1940

General coverage of aspects of theatre for working-class audiences in the 1960s, 1970s, and early 1980s may be found in Don Adams and Arlene Goldband, "Vital Signs: People's Theatre Festival and American Writers' Congress," *NAPNOC Notes* (October 1981); Free Southern Theater, *The Free Southern Theatre, ed. Thomas C. Dent, et al.* (Indianapolis, 1969); *Guerilla Street Theatre*, ed. Henry Lesnick (New York, 1973); Loften Mitchell, *Voices of Black Theatre (Clifton, New Jersey, 1975); Doug Paterson, "Some Theoretical Questions of People's Theatres," Theatrework*, 3 (January–February 1983). Arthur Sainer, *Radical Theatre Notebook* (New York, 1975); Karen Malpede Taylor, *People's Theatre in Amerika* (New York, 1972); and John Weisman, *Guerilla Theatre: Scenarios for Revolution* (New York, 1973).

Many books and articles have been written on the San Francisco Mime Troupe, including Ruby Cohn, "Joan Holden and the San Francisco Mime Troupe," *The Drama Review*, 24 (June 1980); R. G. Davis, *The San Francisco Mime Troupe: The First Ten Years* (Palo Alto, 1975); Joan Holden, "Collective Playmaking: The Why and the How," *Theatre Quarterly*, 5 (June–August 1975); Theodore Shank, "Political Theatre as Popular Entertainment: San Francisco Mime Troupe," *The Drama Review*, 18 (March 1974) and "The San Francisco Mime Troupe's Production of False Promises," *Theatre Quarterly*, 7 (Autumn 1977); Richard Toscan and Kathryn Ripley, "The San Francisco Mime Troupe: Commedia to Collective Creation," *Theatre Quarterly*, 5 (June–August 1975).

Several scholars and commentators have written about El Teatro Campesino, El Teatro de la Esperanza, and other Chicano troupes: Beth Bagsby, "El Teatro Campesino, Interviews with Luis Valdez," *The Drama Review*, 11 (Summer 1967); Susan Bassnett-McGuire, "El Teatro Campesino: From Actos to Mitos," *Theatre Quarterly*, 9 (Summer 1979); R. G. Davis and Betty Diamond, *"Zoot Suit on the Road,"* *Theatre Quarterly*, 9 (Summer 1979); Susanna Halpert, *"The Tecolote Visions*: The Dynamics of a Collaboration," *Theatrework* 3 (January–February 1983); John Harrop and Jorge Huerta, "The Agitprop Pilgrimage of Louis Valdez and El Teatro Campesino," *Theatre Quarterly*, 5 (March–May 1975); Jorge Huerta, "El

Teatro de la Esperanza: Keeping in Touch with the People,'' *The Drama Review*, 21 (March 1977); Nicholas Kanellos, "Chicano Theatre: A Popular Culture Battleground," *Journal of Popular Culture*, 13 (Spring 1980); Francoise Kourilsky, "Approaching Quetzalcoatl: The Evolution of El Teatro Campesino," *Performance*, 2 (Fall 1973); Carlos Morton, "The Teatro Campesino," *The Drama Review*, 18 (December 1974); Theodore Shank, "A Return to Mayan and Aztec Roots," *The Drama Review*, 18 (December 1974); Louis R. Torres, "Hope Abroad," *Nuestro, The Magazine for Latinos* (August 1979); Luis Valdez, "History of the Teatro Campesino," *La Raza*, 1 (Summer 1971).

THEATRES FOR WORKING-CLASS AUDIENCES IN OTHER COUNTRIES

Workers in many nations, especially western ones, have attended and continue to patronize theatres that dramatize their political and social needs and aspirations. Some of the scholarship dealing with these theatres, listed by country, include France: David Bradby, "The October Group and Theatre under the Front Populaire," in *Performance and Politics in Popular Drama*, ed. David Bradby, et al. (London, 1980); Frederick Brown, *Theater and Revolution: The Culture of the French Stage* (New York, 1980); Marvin Carlson, *The Theatre of the French Revolution* (Ithaca, New York, 1966); Michael Hays, *The Public Performance: Essays in the History of French and German Theatre, 1871–1900* (Ann Arbor, Michigan, 1981); Francoise Kourilsky and Lenora Champagne, "Political Theatre in France Since 1968," *The Drama Review*, 19 (June 1975); Vera Lee, *Quest for a Public: French Popular Theatre Since 1945 (Cambridge, 1970); Susan Spitzer, "Prévert's Political Theatre: Two Versions of La Bataille de Fontenoy,"* Theatre Research International, 3 (October 1977). Two articles feature the work of Le Theatre du Soliel: Christopher D. Kirkland, "The Golden Age, First Draft," *The Drama Review*, 19 (June 1975) and Arian Mnouchkine, "L'Age d'Or, The Long Journey from 1793 to 1975," *Theatre Quarterly*, 5 (June–August 1975).

Germany: Denis Calandra, "Rote Rübe: Terror," *The Drama Review*, 19 (June 1975); Cecil W. Davies, "Working-Class Theatre in the Weimer Republic, 1919–1933," *Theatre Quarterly*, 10 (Summer 1980); Horst Denkler, *Restauration und Revolution: Polit. Tendenzen in Deutschen Drama zwischen Wiener Kongress und Marzrevolution* (Munich, 1973); *Deutschesarbeitertheater, 1918–1933, Eine Dokumentation* ed. Ludwig Hoffman and Daniel Hoffman-Oswald (Berlin, 1961); Henning Eichberg et al., *Massenspiele N.S.—Thingspiel Arbeiterweihespiel und Olympisches Zeremoniell* (Stuttgart, 1977); Friedrich Knilli and Ursula Münchow, *Frühes Sozialistisches Arbeitertheater, 1947–1918* (Munich, 1970); Robert Eben Sackett, *Popular Entertainment, Class and Politics in Munich, 1900–1923* (Cambridge, 1982); Gerald Stieg and Bernd Witte, *Abrib einer Geschichte der dentschen Arbeiterliteratur* (Stuttgart, 1973); V. and Peter von Rüden, *Socialdemokratisches Arbeitertheater (1848–1914)* (Frankfort, 1973); Zentralinstitut fur Literaturgeschichte der Akademie der Wissenschaften der DDR, *Texta sgaben zur frühen socialistischen Literatur in Deutschland*, ed., Ursula Münchow (Berlin, 1964); Bruce Zortman, "The Theatre of Ideology in Nazi Germany," (Diss., University of California–Los Angeles, 1969).

Works on Piscator and Brecht found useful by our contributors include C. D. Innes, *Irwin Piscator's Political Theatre* (Cambridge, 1972); James K. Lyon, *Bertolt Brecht in America (Princeton, 1980); and John Willett, The Theatre of Bertolt Brecht*, 2nd ed. (New York, 1960) and *The Theatre of Irwin Piscator: Half a Century of Politics in the Theatre* (London, 1978).

Great Britain: Douglas Allen, "Glasgow Workers' Theatre Group and the Methodology of Theatre Studies," *Theatre Quarterly*, 4 (Winter 1980); Peter Ansorge, *Disrupting the Spectacle: Five Years of Experimental and Fringe Theatre in Britain* (London, 1975); David Edgar, "Ten Years of Political Theatre, 1968–1978," *Theatre Quarterly*, 8 (Winter 1979); Ronald Hayman, *British Theatre Since 1955, A Reassessment* (London, 1979); John Hill, "Towards a Scottish People's Theatre: The Rise and Fall of Glasgow Unity," *Theatre Quarterly*, 7 (Autumn 1977); Leonard Abraham Jones, "The Workers' Theatre Movement in the Twenties," *Zeitschrift fur Anglstik und Amerikanistik*, 14 (1966); and essays by several contributors in *Performance and Politics in Popular Drama*, ed. David Bradby et al. (London, 1980).

Italy: Two works by Suzanne Cowan on Dario Fo are *Dario Fo*, Theatre Checklist, No. 17 (London, 1978) and "The Throw-Away Theatre of Dario Fo," *The Drama Review*, 19 (June 1975).

Soviet Union: František Deak, "Russian Mass Spectacles," *The Drama Review*, 19 (June 1975); Nikolai Gorchakov, *The Theatre in Soviet Russia*, trans. Edgar Lehrman (New York, 1957); Llewellyn Hedgbeth, "Meyerhold's 'D.E.,' " *The Drama Review*, 19 (June 1975); Marc Slonim, *Russian Theatre: From the Empire to the Soviets* (Cleveland, 1961); *Soviet Theatres, 1917–1941*, ed. Martha Bradshaw (Ann Arbor, 1954); and Abram Tertz, *On Socialist Realism*, trans. Dennis George (New York, 1969).

Other countries: Augusto Boal, *Theatre of the Oppressed*, trans. Charles A. and Maria-Odillia Leal McBride (New York, 1979); David Goodman, "Japanese Political Theatre," *The Drama Review*, 19 (June 1975); Roger Howard, "Agitation and Anaesthesia: Aspects of Chinese Theatre Today," *Theatre Research International*, 2 (October 1976); James McCarthy, "The Republican Theatre During the Spanish Civil War: Rafael Alberti's *Numancia*," *Theatre Research International*, 5 (Autumn 1980); and James Peacock, *Rites of Modernization: Symbolic and Social Aspects of Indonesian Proletarian Drama* (Chicago, 1968).

Index

Contributors

Francis G. Couvares
Department of History
Amherst College

Daniel Friedman
Otto Rene Castillo Center for
    Working Class Culture
New York, New York

Mel Gordon
School of Performing Arts
New York University

Bruce A. McConachie
Graduate Program in American
    Studies
College of William and Mary

Douglas McDermott
Department of Drama
California State College,
    Stanislaus

Linda Nochlin
Department of Art History
Graduate School and University
    Center
City University of New York

John O'Conner
Department of English
George Mason University

Carol Poore
Department of German
Brown University

Theodore J. Shank
Department of Dramatic Arts
University of California, Davis

A. Richard Sogliuzzo
"All Things Considered"
Public Broadcasting System

Paul Sporn
Department of English
Wayne State University

Hiroko Tsuchiya
Flushing, New York

ABOUT THE EDITORS

BRUCE A. McCONACHIE is Associate Professor of Theatre and Speech at the College of William and Mary, and he directs the college's graduate program in American Studies. He has published articles in *Theatre Journal, Theatre Survey,* and *Southern Theatre*.

DANIEL FRIEDMAN is Artistic Director of the Castillo Theatre Company, which is associated with the Otto Rene Castillo Center for Working Class Culture. He is an Adjunct Assistant Professor of English at York College, C.U.N.Y., and is Cultural Editor of *National Alliance* newsweekly. He is the author of twelve plays, the latest of which, *The Learning Play of Levi Yitzhok, Son of Sara, of Berditchev* was produced by the Gene Frankel Theatre Workshop.